Behaviour for Learning

Behaviour for Learning offers teachers a clear conceptual framework for making sense of the many behaviour management strategies on offer, allowing them to make a critical assessment of the appropriateness and effectiveness of particular strategies in the classroom.

Teachers need to be asking themselves the question 'How can I improve a child's learning?', rather than 'How can I get them to behave?'. The authors present a unique focus on the relationships that underpin learning, placing an emphasis on the development of 'learning behaviours', and endorsing Ofsted's view that it is essential to evaluate the efficacy of behaviour management against progress in learning.

Essentially, this book will help teachers:

- decide what strategy is best for individuals in their classroom;
- be aware of the evidence/theoretical base that underpins that strategy use;
- be able to evaluate the effectiveness of that strategy.

Located within an emerging body of research focused on improving holistic outcomes for individuals and increased partnership working, this book seeks to synthesise the practical with the theoretical.

Authoritative and timely, *Behaviour for Learning* is compelling reading for all training and practising teachers, CPD coordinators and other professionals working with challenging pupils.

Simon Ellis is a Senior Lecturer in the Faculty of Education at Canterbury Christ Church University. He has previously worked as a Key Stage 3 National Strategy Behaviour and Attendance Consultant and a local authority Behaviour Support Service Manager.

Janet Tod is a Professor of Education and Head of Educational Research at Canterbury Christ Church University. She is a qualified speech therapist and a British Psychological Society (BPS) chartered educational and clinical psychologist.

Behaviour for Learning

Proactive approaches to behaviour management

Simon Ellis and Janet Tod

Routledge
Taylor & Francis Group

LONDON AND NEW YORK

First published 2009
by Routledge
2 Park Square, Milton Park, Abingdon, Oxon OX14 4RN

Simultaneously published in the USA and Canada
by Routledge
711 Third Avenue, New York, NY 10017 (8th Floor)

Routledge is an imprint of the Taylor & Francis Group, an informa business

© 2009 Simon Ellis and Janet Tod

Typeset in Bembo by Pindar NZ, Auckland, New Zealand
Printed and bound in Great Britain by TJ International Ltd, Padstow, Cornwall

British Library Cataloguing in Publication Data
A catalogue record for this book is available from the British Library

Library of Congress Cataloguing-in-Publication Data
Ellis, Simon.
Behaviour for Learning: proactive approaches to behaviour management / Simon Ellis and Janet Tod.
  p. cm.
  1. Classroom management. 2. Behaviour modification. 3. Behaviour disorders
in children—Treatment. 4. Problem children—Education. I. Tod, Janet. II. Title.
  LB3013.E485 2009
  370.15'28—dc22   2008041119

ISBN 10: 0-415-49167-3 (hbk)
ISBN 10: 1-84312-466-1 (pbk)

ISBN 13: 978-0-415-49167-9 (hbk)
ISBN 13: 978-1-84312-466-5 (pbk)

Contents

Figures

Tables

Acknowledgements

This book is based on work that developed from a research project commissioned by the then Teacher Training Agency (TTA), now the Training and Development Agency for Schools (TDA), and managed at Canterbury Christ Church University. The original research project (Powell and Tod 2004) was conducted following the procedures developed for systematic review by the Evidence for Policy and Practice Information and Co-ordinating Centre (EPPI-Centre), http://eppi.ioe.ac.uk/cms/.

The authors would like to express thanks to those involved in the original EPPI review and also to colleagues and students who have contributed to our thinking.

The views represented in this book are those of the authors and are not intended to represent the views or policies of any particular body.

Introduction

This book expands upon a conceptual framework that emerged from a systematic literature review (Powell and Tod 2004) funded by the Teacher Training Agency (TTA). The framework has evolved over four years, having been tried and tested with teachers, trainees and tutors.

We acknowledge there is already a plethora of books, guidance and support material available to trainees, teachers and tutors in relation to pupil behaviour. This text does not seek to replace these but we consider it to be different in several ways:

It builds on teachers' existing expertise

Teaching as a profession promotes learning, normally in group contexts and conditions. The conceptual framework builds on this area of expertise as a route to improving behaviour in the classroom. As such the key theme of this book is the explicit linking of learning and behaviour, via the term 'learning behaviour'. The use of this term will hopefully serve to reduce perceptions that 'promoting learning' and 'managing behaviour' are separate issues for teachers (McNally, *et al.* 2005). Teachers and schools already have experience in using a range of existing behaviour management techniques. This book does not seek to replace such approaches but in Chapters 8, 9 and 10 examines ways in which such management techniques may be enhanced via the behaviour for learning conceptual framework.

It provides a way of evaluating the efficacy of behaviour management strategies

Through the use of the term 'learning behaviour', pupil-progress in *learning* provides a relevant indicator against which to measure the efficacy of school-based *behaviour* management strategies.

It promotes the development of learning relationships

A core feature of the behaviour for learning conceptual framework is that it places emphasis on the relationships that underpin learning and behaviour in school contexts. It endorses the view that learning and behaviour are influenced by the quality of relationships that characterise classroom interactions. These relationships are changing, interdependent and reciprocal, and as such do not lend themselves to any one quick-fix set of strategies.

However teachers and others can prepare for – and pupils can contribute positively to – these relationships.

Within classroom contexts the three core relationships identified from the research that underpins this book are:

- relationship with others;
- relationship with self;
- relationship with the curriculum.

It explicitly recognises and utilises the interdependence of the cognitive, social and emotional aspects of learning and behaviour

These three relationships reflect the social, emotional and cognitive factors that influence pupil behaviour and learning. Although in school contexts the relationship with the curriculum is seen as a priority and teachers are able to draw upon extensive curriculum guidance in this area, it is clear that for some pupils improving their relationship with the curriculum will require attention to their relationship with self and/or their relationship with others.

It adopts a proactive approach to behaviour management

The behaviour for learning approach does not seek to pathologise individual pupil behaviour or place blame on teachers. This book adopts a proactive approach to behaviour management, placing an emphasis on supporting teachers to identify and develop the learning behaviours that are relevant to *all* pupils.

It recognises diversity, delay and difference within individuals in group contexts

This book accepts that teaching necessitates 'responding to the complex needs of individual learners and therefore involves making multiple decisions in non-routine situations' (Haggarty 2002). It places emphasis on the fact that contexts and conditions of the classroom designed for groups will be experienced differently by individuals. In asking teachers to consider how their behaviour management strategies are experienced by individuals, it is anticipated that teachers will become more confident in supporting pupils with diverse needs, including those with special educational needs (SEN).

The book is realistic in its aims

The book is honest in accepting that it does not seek to provide a solution to the range of behaviour problems that trainees and teachers encounter or fear. This is an unrealistic pursuit given that individual pupils interpret, experience, and make sense of classroom events from their own personal perspective. However, the behaviour for learning conceptual framework enables teachers to make informed choices from the existing and ever-emerging plethora of behaviour management strategies and approaches.

Ways of using this book

This book explores and explains a relatively new and emergent conceptual framework designed to support teachers in addressing behavioural concerns in school contexts. As such it necessarily combines exploratory content related to underpinning concepts alongside sections that relate familiar existing practices to these concepts.

As with many educational texts it is more likely that many readers will home in on particular chapters, dependent on their time, need and experience. Readers will note from Chapter 3 that there are three broad levels of use of the behaviour for learning conceptual framework. These are:

- day-to-day;
- core;
- extended.

Day-to-day use

At whole-school and class levels, teachers need to provide contexts and conditions that promote the development of learning behaviours through a focus on learning and teaching. Readers who seek to improve their understanding at this level of practice will be best directed towards Chapter 3, followed by Chapters 8, 9 and 10. This will provide a working understanding of the behaviour for learning conceptual framework and its relationship to more conventional behaviour management approaches. It would also be beneficial, particularly for trainees, to have an idea of the origins of practice in relation to behaviour management. Chapters 1 and 2 provide this historical context.

Core use

At the core of this book is the concern for groups and individuals for whom the day-to-day behaviour management strategies do not suffice. We believe that a *core* behaviour for learning stance would be particularly useful and suggest once again that Chapter 3 is pivotal. Chapters 4, 5, 6 and 7 then explore the framework in more depth, allowing readers to secure greater understanding of the relational aspects of learning as well as the interdependence of the cognitive, social and emotional components of learning and behaviour.

Extended use

For those individuals who experience significant delay, difficulty or difference in the development of their learning behaviour, there may be a need to go beyond 'day-to-day' and 'core' use of the conceptual framework. Chapters 11 and 12 consider *Dealing with more challenging behaviour* and *Reframing special educational needs (SEN)* so as to support schools and teachers in the extended use of the behaviour for learning conceptual framework.

The final chapter of the book endorses a developmental view of behaviour and covers *Transitions*, in recognition of the differing expectations and conditions that pupils experience as they progress through school.

Our own thinking with regard to the behaviour for learning conceptual framework has developed through our face-to-face teaching in contexts that allow for discussion and critical debate. This book represents a further stage in development in that we have had to communicate to practicing teachers and tutors through the more limited medium of the written text. In producing a book format we would hope that this text will provide the necessary content and impetus for active engagement with fellow trainees, school colleagues, mentors and tutors. Such engagement will allow readers to activate this book and apply it to their own practice-based concerns and professional development.

The chapters

Chapter 1 adopts a historical perspective, starting with the 1944 Education Act. The rationale behind this chapter is that behaviour and learning do not occur in a vacuum. An understanding of past developments, priorities and political, social and economic agendas is necessary in order to make sense of the current educational challenges in relation to learning and behaviour. There is a social and political context that has shaped perceptions of what acceptable behaviour is, what school based learning is, the type of learning that is valued, the desirable curriculum content, and the role of educational settings in developing this learning and behaviour in children and young people.

Chapter 2 looks specifically at policy and guidance since 1989 related to behaviour and discipline in schools. It reveals a considerable degree of consistency over the years regarding the overall principles of good practice in relation to pupil behaviour. Policy and guidance has typically attempted to balance a concern for both discipline and control with a need for pastoral support and nurture. Despite reassurances (e.g. Ofsted 2005a) that the great majority of children and young people enjoy learning, work hard and behave well, behaviour in schools has continued to remain a concern with regard to its negative impact on pupils' learning, the recruitment and retention of teachers and the needs of society.

Chapter 3 argues that the traditional separation of learning and behaviour is not only conceptually flawed but is ultimately unhelpful to those who seek to improve behaviour in school and raise achievement in school contexts. The chapter examines the limitations of an exclusive focus on behaviour management. Central to this chapter is the introduction of the behaviour for learning conceptual framework. The key terminology within the framework is explored and a case study is provided that illustrates how a behaviour for learning stance could change the approach to tackling behaviour issues and would change approaches to the evaluation of the efficacy of the behaviour strategy employed by the teacher.

Chapter 4 focuses exclusively on 'learning behaviours'. This is a relatively new term that is used to represent the fusion of learning and behaviour that is a central theme of this book. The chapter seeks to maintain a view that promoting positive behaviours is more effective than seeking to stop negative behaviours. In order to support teachers to identify particular behaviours, this chapter draws on relevant literature as a source for descriptors and definitions. This critical review of learning behaviours allows readers access to the meaning and the utility of the term in school contexts.

Chapter 5 sets the scene for working within a framework that roots classroom practice within the building and maintenance of positive relationships. Teachers are familiar with the term and have experience of relationships. This chapter builds on this knowledge to explicitly place relationships within the behaviour for learning conceptual framework and notes the dynamic interactions and interdependence that make up the activity and purpose of the classroom.

The chapter steers readers towards an understanding of how a focus on relationships may not necessarily change what they are doing in the classroom but will change their thinking and in so doing will allow them to develop increasing confidence in their choice and evaluation of strategies.

Chapter 6 focuses specifically on the 'relationship with the curriculum'. In so doing it explores what it means to have a relationship with something that is inanimate but nonetheless mirrors what we experience in human relationships. If, for example, we experience success and enjoyment, this usually leads to positive approaches to relationships; whereas failure is more likely to lead to relationships characterised by a cycle of negativity, such as a will to disrupt or harm the relationship. This chapter draws on literature to consider what it might mean in practice to have a positive relationship with the curriculum. It directs attention towards factors that should then influence choice of strategies that will support the building and maintenance of a positive relationship with the curriculum.

Chapter 7 focuses on the pupil's relationship with self and others. Pupils cannot easily escape working within the public gaze of the classroom and will almost inevitably make assessments of their position relative to their peers and of themselves as individuals. Pupils need to both work with others, and also concentrate on their own, if they are to build an effective relationship with the curriculum. As such they need to develop learning behaviours that reflect responsiveness, responsibility and resilience. The chapter looks at how pupils make sense of their classroom experiences and highlights the importance of relationship with self as an enduring and potentially powerful influence on their relationship with others and relationship with the curriculum

Chapter 8 looks specifically at whole-school behaviour policies. It examines some of the key elements of behaviour policies to evaluate their potential compatibility with the principles of the behaviour for learning conceptual framework.

Chapter 9 focuses on the contexts and conditions for developing learning behaviour within the classroom. It considers the nature of the pupil-teacher relationship, general group management and aspects of the physical environment.

Chapter 10 focuses on what are commonly known as 'positive correction' techniques. It is recognised within this chapter that there will be occasions when teachers need to correct or re-direct. A number of familiar positive correction strategies are outlined and discussed in the context of their potential to address the behaviour whilst also protecting the three relationships at the core of the behaviour for learning framework.

Chapter 11 deals with more challenging behaviour. It considers procedures for exiting a pupil from the classroom in a manner that minimises the risk of compromising one or more of the behaviour for learning relationships. The chapter also looks at behaviour that is motivated by anger. The nature and dynamics of anger are explored. The assault cycle (Breakwell 1997) is presented as a means by which a pupil's behaviour in an angry incident can be understood. Each stage of the assault cycle is discussed in the context of the implications for the teacher's priorities.

Chapter 12 is concerned with those individual learners who may experience particular difficulties, delay or difference in developing the relationships that underpin their learning in school contexts. These learners are likely to include, but are not necessarily restricted to, those who are described as having special educational needs (SEN). Using the examples of dyslexia, Asperger syndrome and social, emotional and behavioural difficulties, the chapter reframes special educational needs in terms of the behaviour for learning conceptual framework. The chapter seeks to look at provision in terms of supporting the development of meaningful relationships from the perspective of the individual and in so doing supports teachers in making informed choices from the plethora of available strategies.

Chapter 13 covers transitions. The focus is on four specific transitions: Foundation Stage to Year 1, Year 2 to Year 3, primary to secondary school, and Key Stage 3 to Key Stage 4. These transitions are considered from the perspective of identifying risks to the three behaviour for learning relationships and the practices that can help to reduce these.

We hope you enjoy reading this book and experience a positive impact on your thinking, learning and teaching and above all on the experience and behaviour of individuals in your class.

Chapter 1

Learning from history

As you enter your classroom you may wonder about the relevance to your practice of starting with an overview of educational history. The answer is that behaviour and learning do not occur in a vacuum. As a teacher you will be working within a context that reflects some inheritances from history alongside relatively new practices emerging from ongoing innovation and change. Understanding of past developments and priorities, and political, social and economic agendas, is necessary in order to make sense of the current educational challenges in relation to learning and behaviour.

Each successive educational change leaves its mark and potentially exerts an influence on future thinking and practice. Even after the more significant changes, residual elements of the previous era continue to influence practice or remain in practitioners' consciousness. This leads to tensions, inconsistencies and contradictions that teachers need to resolve at the level of classroom practice. This point is illustrated by Newby (2005) in his observation that:

> Today's curriculum is disjointed. At primary school, we struggle to reconcile a post-Plowden, child-centred, progressive curriculum and a National Curriculum emphasising (some would say, 'fixating upon') literacy and numeracy. In the secondary school, we teach young people an amalgamation of the subjects of a content-based curriculum (which remains in many ways that of the grammar school opened up to the comprehensive) and an instrumental, vocational curriculum focused on the world of work.
>
> (Newby 2005: 297)

Starting from the 1944 Education Act we seek, through this chapter, to provide an understanding of the sources of some of these tensions, inconsistencies and contradictions, as well as exploring how the current policy context has developed and the challenges this presents.

The 1944 Education Act

The 1944 Education Act (the 'Butler Act') implemented the tripartite system of secondary schools (grammar, secondary modern and technical high schools), with the principle of free and compulsory schooling for all primary and secondary aged children. The three types of secondary school were designed to cater for different types of ability which could, it was believed, be distinguished through the administration of the '11 plus' test (Allen and Ainley 2007). In addition, the Act raised the school leaving age to 15. Previously, since the 1918 Fisher Act, education had only been compulsory up until 14 years old.

The Butler Act was part of the general social and economic reconstruction and modern-isation of society after the Second World War that also saw, for example, the establishment of the National Health Service (NHS). The Act had to satisfy the interests of a range of different interested parties (Allen and Ainley 2007), including the political parties that had made up the wartime coalition government, the churches, teachers, fee-paying schools, industry and trades unions.

Education for the majority therefore was very much functional and utilitarian, providing sufficient skills in reading, writing and arithmetic, together with some practical life skills. Though individual teachers and their schools may have had higher aspirations for their pupils, based on a desire to instill a love of learning and a belief in learning's intrinsic value, government *requirements* of education immediately post war were distinctly limited, focused on producing a functionally literate and numerate workforce. In terms of pedagogy, rote learning to establish functional – as opposed to conceptual – understanding was largely sufficient.

In terms of the legacy of the tripartite secondary system set up post war, a division was confirmed between academic and vocational routes. Arguably, though this tension has been recognised, it has never truly been resolved. Despite subsequent attempts to raise the status of the vocational routes by providing more meaningful qualifications, parity of esteem between the academic and vocational routes has yet to be achieved. Vocational education has often failed to command the confidence of employers, the higher education sector and the general public (Ofsted 2005b). At the time of writing changes are being introduced through the 14–19 Diploma. The aim is to offer pupils more choice in relation to academic and/or vocational routes. The diplomas combine theoretical and practical learning, including functional English, Maths and Information and Communication Technology (ICT) in order to equip young people with the skills, knowledge and understanding they need for further or higher education and long-term employability.

The comprehensive school

The comprehensive movement emerged based on a desire to establish a more egalitarian system of secondary education. During the 1950s, through the work of Floud, *et al.* (1956) and others, evidence mounted that the 1944 Education Act was not promoting equality of educational opportunity for children from working-class backgrounds to either enter grammar schools or receive a balanced and well-resourced curriculum in the secondary modern schools (Tomlinson 2005). Alongside the concern – particularly among some Labour politicians – regarding these inequalities, there was also recognition by the Conservative government of the early 1960s that in an expanding economy, all young people, not just the grammar school minority, needed to be educated to a much higher level. Blue-collar manual workers needed to be educated for more demanding employment and white-collar and service work was expanding (Allen and Ainley 2007). There was therefore broad political consensus that comprehensive schools should be established (Tomlinson 2005). However the Labour government, returning to power in 1964, took the decision not to legislate but, through Circular 10/65, to request Local Authorities to submit plans for reform (Allen and Ainley 2007). As with many educational changes, local interpretation was a factor and the move towards comprehensives was by no means universal and their development was therefore gradual, uneven and *ad hoc*. A number of Local Authorities still retain grammar schools and operate selection tests to decide on admission.

A sally into the secret garden

Whilst the period immediately post war saw major educational change, neither Labour nor Conservative governments intervened significantly in relation to curriculum and pedagogy. The 1944 Education Act offered no directive in relation to the curriculum other than the compulsory inclusion of religious education and a daily act of worship (Kelly 2004). Education debates were devoted largely to bricks and mortar and to the organisation of the system – a point noted by Conservative Minister of Education, David Eccles in 1960 (Chitty 1990). Eccles spoke of 'the secret garden of the curriculum' (quoted by Chitty 1990: 5), and declared a desire to open that garden up to greater public scrutiny (Kelly 2004). Eccles was keen to reassure with the clear statement that, 'Of course, Parliament would never attempt to dictate the curriculum' (quoted in Chitty 1990: 5), whilst also proposing that 'From time to time, we could, with advantage, express views on what is taught in schools and in training colleges' (quoted by Chitty 1990: 5) and expressing an intention to 'make the Ministry's own voice heard rather more often, more positively, and no doubt, sometimes more controversially' (quoted in Chitty 1990: 5).

This was the first suggestion of a venture by central government into what previously had been considered forbidden territory (Chitty 1990).

The Plowden Report

The 1967 Plowden Report describes its remit in terms of informing the Minister for Education how far the intentions of Sir Henry Hadow and his committee, set out in three reports between 1926 and 1933, had been carried out and how well they had stood the test of time (CACE 1967). Though, as described earlier, the government had fairly modest requirements of education immediately post war, the three Hadow Reports, looking at *The Education of the Adolescent* (1926), *The Primary School* (1931) and *Infant and Nursery Schools* (1933), had been visionary and aspirational. They wrestled with issues regarding an appropriate curriculum for each of these phases and flagged up enduring issues such as, in the 1926 report, the need for a balance between offering 'the fullest possible scope to individuality, while keeping steadily in view the claims and needs of the society in which every individual citizen must live' (Hadow 1926, cited in Dent 1942: 146–7).

The Plowden Report was unequivocal in its message that 'At the heart of the educational process lies the child' (CACE 1967: 7). It promoted a focus on the individual and emphasised the differences between children rather than the commonalities, stating: 'Individual differences between children of the same age are so great that any class, however homogeneous it seems, must always be treated as a body of children needing individual and different attention' (CACE 1967: 25).

The child-centred philosophy at the heart of the Plowden Report emphasised the individualism of each pupil. This had implications for both the curriculum and methods of grouping children as, based on this principle, a common curriculum delivered via a stereotypical traditional teaching model of rows of children receiving the same chalk-and-talk input from the teacher, could hardly be considered effective.

The challenge, of course, was that, whilst acceptance of a child-centred philosophy inevitably leads to an approach based on the individual needs of the child, teachers needed to find ways of making this both manageable and effective when teaching classes of 30–35, which was the limit the Plowden Report recommended a primary teacher could satisfactorily work with. It was mainly only primary schools that were able to adopt the child-centred philosophy advocated by Hadow and endorsed by Plowden. Secondary schools were constrained by examination boards and associated syllabuses and retained a strong commitment to a subject-based curriculum.

Plowden welcomed the intention of government to end selective education and was also highly critical of the widespread process of streaming according to ability that had been common practice in primary schools, claiming it could be 'wounding to children' (CACE 1967: 292).

Reflective Exercise 1.1

The Plowden Report made a number of comments and recommendations regarding the primary curriculum, including:

> There is little place for the type of scheme which sets down exactly what ground should be covered and what skill should be acquired by each class in the school.
>
> (CACE 1967: 198)

> When a class of seven-year-olds notice the birds that come to the bird table outside the classroom window, they may decide, after discussion with their teacher, to make their own aviary. They will set to with a will, and paint birds in flight, make models of them in clay or *papier mache*, write stories and poems about them and look up reference books to find out more.
>
> (CACE 1967: 199)

> Some topic, such as "transport" is chosen, ideally by the children, but frequently by the teacher. The topic cuts across the boundaries of subjects and is treated as its nature requires without reference to subjects as such.
>
> (CACE 1967: 198–9)

- What problems might this degree of flexibility create in terms of providing a broad and balanced curriculum?
- What might be the benefits of the flexible approach advocated by Plowden?
- What could be the effects on pupil behaviour of an increased emphasis on this type of pupil directed learning?

The Plowden Report drew on Piaget's theory of child-development for much of its theoretical underpinning. Piaget suggested that there were four sequential stages in intellectual development: sensori-motor, intuitive thought, concrete operations, and formal operations. For teachers therefore, a knowledge of child-development was important as, following Piaget's theory, there were implications for what and how a child was taught depending on their stage of development.

During the 1970s and 1980s there was a gradual lessening in the acceptance of Piaget's view of cognitive development (Halsey and Sylva 1987). Alexander *et al.* (1992) suggested that Piagetian theories about developmental ages and stages led to chronologically fixed notions of 'readiness which depressed expectations and discouraged teacher intervention' (Alexander *et al.* 1992: 18). Because Piagetian theory was so central to the Plowden Report, criticisms of this impacted on its credibility. However, leaving aside the specifics, the general principle that children develop at different rates and that there are issues of 'readiness' that teachers must take into account when planning both content and teaching methods, is an enduring issue.

Storming the secret garden

If David Eccles' comments had represented, as he described it, 'a sally into the secret garden of the curriculum' (Chitty 1990: 5), what followed in subsequent decades was more like an all-out assault.

The mid-seventies saw what was to be the start of increased central government involvement in education. In 1976 the Labour Prime Minister James Callaghan gave a speech at Ruskin College setting out his views on education and encouraging public debate, involving parents, teachers, learned and professional bodies, and representatives of higher education and industry, on the purpose and priorities of schools. Callaghan raised significant concerns about progressive education, stating that: 'There is the unease felt by parents and teachers about the new informal methods of teaching which seem to produce excellent results when they are in well-qualified hands but are much more dubious in their effects when they are not' (Callaghan 1976, cited in Morley and Rassool 1999: 25).

He also conveyed concerns from industry: 'I am concerned on my journeys to find complaints from industry that new recruits from the schools sometimes do not have the basic tools to do the job that is required … there is concern about the standards of numeracy of school leavers' (Callaghan 1976, cited in Morley and Rassool 1999: 25).

Contained in these lines was a clear indication that in the government's mind, a major role for schools was to prepare pupils to be part of the nation's workforce. Powerful trade unions, strikes and the three-day week had characterised the early seventies, and by the end of the decade Britain was experiencing the 'Winter of Discontent', and the Conservative Party was campaigning successfully with the slogan 'Labour isn't Working', referring to the figure of 1.1 million unemployed. Whether one subscribes to the functional vision of education as preparing future adult citizens implied in Callaghan's comments, or to a broader view of what this preparatory role might be, it undoubtedly has a shaping role. Tomlinson (2005), referring to the changes in the 1970s, comments: 'Education was to return to its role as an allocator of occupations, a defender of traditional academic values, teaching respect for authority, discipline, morality and "Englishness" and preparing a workforce for the new conditions of flexible, insecure labour markets' (Tomlinson 2005: 26).

If indeed education has the capacity to exert such influence, it is little wonder that Callaghan, speaking at Ruskin College in the middle of a decade of considerable turmoil involving both social and economic change, was keen for greater government involvement.

Though Callaghan's government had started the move towards greater central government control of education, it was Margaret Thatcher's Conservative government that took it forward apace. Whilst in the period from 1944 to 1979 there were only three Education Acts (Finch 1984), during the twenty-five year period from 1980 to 2005 some 34 Education Acts were passed, together with hundreds of accompanying circulars, regulations and statutory instruments (Tomlinson 2005).

Significantly in 1981 the Department of Education and Science (DES) stated: 'The school curriculum is at the heart of education' (DES 1981) which was in contrast to the view expressed in the Plowden Report which had placed the child in this position. Though arguably this is not a simple either/or distinction, the choice of wording is indicative of a rejection of Plowden and an endorsement of a new philosophy.

Reflective Exercise 1.2

The Plowden Report stated: 'At the heart of the educational process lies the child' (CACE 1967: 7).
   The DES stated: 'The school curriculum is at the heart of education' (DES 1981).

- How might each of these distinctly different views influence your teaching in terms of your practice and priorities?
- How might the adoption of one or other approach influence pupil behaviour?
- To what extent do you think it is possible to balance these two perspectives in your practice?

During the 1980s central government and the DES increased centralised control over the curriculum, with teacher input and influence scaled down (Tomlinson 2005). A series of official documents (DES 1980, DES 1981, HMI 1981) supported the principle of a common curriculum, though with some notable differences in the form this might take (Tomlinson 2005).

The 1988 Education Reform Act introduced the National Curriculum, which comprised three core and seven foundation subjects. As Tomlinson (2005) observes, these were uncannily similar to the subjects laid down by the Board of Education in 1904. The principle of a national curriculum had received much professional and public support, but the model introduced attracted a number of criticisms; in particular of the subject-basis, which had ignored much of the curriculum thinking of the preceding twenty years and neglected important areas of learning such as political understanding, economic awareness, moral development, and many other cross-curricular themes (Lawton 1989).

The subject-based structure of the National Curriculum was a greater challenge for primary teachers than their secondary colleagues who had always operated a curriculum separated into distinct subject areas. However, it would be wrong to think of the introduction of the National Curriculum as a curtain closing on an age of cross-curricular topic work and heralding subject-based primary teaching. Most primary schools already organised the curriculum in terms of subjects and topic work (Alexander *et al.* 1992). It tended to be the foundation subjects, as the National Curriculum was to term them, and often Science, that were taught via topic work. The National Curriculum did not preclude topic-teaching but, in the words of Alexander, Rose and Woodhead (or 'the three wise men', as they were sometimes referred to):

> whatever the mode of (curriculum) organisation, pupils must be able to grasp the
> particular principles and procedures of each subject, and, what is equally important,

they must be able to progress from one level of knowledge, understanding and skill to another within the subject.

(Alexander *et al.* 1992: 22)

This type of expectation, together with the extensive areas for coverage in each subject, specified in a separate National Curriculum document for each subject, inevitably encouraged the introduction of far more subject-based teaching in primary schools. In 2003 however, *Excellence and Enjoyment* gave its approval to topic work, stating: 'There is no requirement for subjects to be taught discretely – they can be grouped, or taught through projects – if strong enough links are created between subjects, pupils' knowledge and skills can be used across the whole curriculum' (DfES 2003a:17).

Undoubtedly the National Curriculum published in 1999 is significantly different to the original 1988 version in its overall tone, the opportunities it allows for professional flexibility, the emphasis placed on learning across the curriculum and the endorsement of inclusion through the inclusion statement. The introduction of the *Foundation Stage Curriculum* (DfEE/QCA 2000) in 2000 was also significant in recognising that broad areas of learning, rather than a traditional subject-based structure, were more appropriate for the youngest children. The question however is whether despite these positive revisions in subsequent incarnations, the original National Curriculum has left a legacy that continues to promote a focus on group outcomes based on norms, benchmarks, average performance and normative data, in the name of standards-raising.

Perhaps more significant than any of the detail of the changes introduced by increased government involvement, was the effect of government involvement itself. Inevitably as education becomes increasingly politicised, the views of the electorate and other stakeholders become important and compete with professionals to prescribe the direction of education, and at times may over-ride the evidence base. Education has become a legitimate area over which the political parties are able to trade blows and attempt to convince the electorate of their commitment to tackle issues ranging from standards in literacy and numeracy to levels of classroom disruption. The latter is a frequent area of media debate and has been a significant trigger for at least two major government reports (DES 1989, DfES 2005a).

A maximum of five years in office inevitably means that policy needs to be devised and implemented quickly if a government is to deliver against its election promises. Consequently educational research and theory have typically been relegated to a perfunctory role, used mainly to justify an ideology or change in practice rather than a driving role in developing practice, constructing evidence bases and contributing to professional knowledge.

School improvement and the pursuit of excellence

Inextricably linked to developments in government involvement in schools and control over the curriculum was the growth of the 'school effectiveness/school improvement' movement. Within this brief consideration of educational history we have used the terms 'school effectiveness' and 'school improvement' interchangeably though we acknowledge that there are some authors (e.g. Chaplain 2003, Harris *et al.* 2004) who identify a number of differences. One of the seminal works in the 'school effectiveness/school improvement' field was Rutter *et al.*'s (1979) *Fifteen Thousand Hours*. This study of twelve secondary schools in inner London produced evidence to suggest that, despite serving broadly similar socially disadvantaged areas, there were marked differences in the behaviour and attainment of the pupils. These differences could not be explained by different intakes or levels of social disadvantage but were attributable to factors within the school. Rutter *et al.* (1979) summed up the implication succinctly, stating: 'This meant that pupils were more likely to show good behaviour and good scholastic attainments if they attend some schools than if they attend others' (Rutter *et al.* 1979: 178).

Pointing to the influence that schools could exert, Rutter *et al.* (1979) suggested:

> Factors as varied as the degree of academic emphasis, teacher actions in lessons, the availability of incentives and rewards, good conditions for pupils, and the extent to which children were able to take responsibility were all significantly associated with outcome differences between schools.
>
> (Rutter *et al.* 1979: 178)

Whilst Rutter *et al.*'s (1979) work set the scene for the growth in influence of the school effectiveness/school improvement movement on educational policy, like many aspects of education, balance is an important issue. Rutter *et al.*'s (1979) work and that of others looking at the influence of schools, provided a welcome antidote to previously held views and challenged low expectations based on pupils' social class; but this did not mean social and economic disadvantage exerted no influence on learning. The inevitable questions provoked by Rutter *et al.*'s (1979) findings were first, why if certain schools made a positive difference others failed to do so, and second, what should be done about them? Politicians were quick to recognise the implications. As Tomlinson observes: 'the realities of social class were obscured by governments which seized on school effectiveness research, which superficially supported the political message that "poverty is no excuse" for schools in deprived areas obtaining low examination results, to create a blame and shame culture' (Tomlinson 2005: 170).

Increased accountability was an emerging feature in most 'western' education systems at the time (Hopkins 2001), reflected in the publication of school league tables and the creation of Ofsted in 1992. Tomlinson (2005) sums up the prevailing beliefs:

> Governments from the 1980s believed that schools could be manipulated as technical systems (Lingard *et al.* 1998) to make a difference to performance, with individuals being responsible for their own levels of performance, and schools, whatever their history or clientele, being held responsible for failure to meet targets.
>
> (Tomlinson 2005: 170)

League tables were one of the most controversial aspects of the accountability culture. These appeared in 1992. They used raw outcomes data based on the number of pupils reaching nationally prescribed, age-related targets, and arguably demonstrated more about social class composition than educational performance in the area (Tomlinson 2005). For some schools receiving, for example, predominantly motivated pupils, who had attended quality pre-school provision and came from stable, financially secure, supportive homes, adequate teaching would be sufficient to attain the national, age-related expectations. Other schools, because of relatively low levels of attainment on entry, might in contrast have to provide exceptional teaching to secure meaningful progress, but still struggle to even get close to the national expectations with a significant number of their pupils. Not surprisingly the schools topping the league tables were private schools, remaining grammar schools and other selective schools (Tomlinson 2005). To address this issue, value added data has been used in the Achievement and Attainment Tables (formerly known as Performance Tables) since 2002. Value added is a measure of the progress pupils make between different stages of education in comparison to pupils with similar prior attainment. A recent change has been the introduction of contextual value added measures in recognition that there are many other factors that are related to the progress that pupils make in a school, such as levels of deprivation or special educational needs. Contextual value added data aims to take account of these factors when measuring the effectiveness of a school or the progress made by individual pupils.

The use of value added and contextual value added data is a positive development for the morale of teachers and other members of the wider school workforce as it recognises the efforts made to secure progress. For special schools in particular, value added data allows them to demonstrate pupil progress even though many of their pupils are unlikely to reach national, age-related targets. However there is also a less positive interpretation. The filtering out of a range of factors to allow a direct comparison of different schools' performance could be criticised for diminishing the significance of and sanitising racism, sexism, poverty and disabling practices (Gillborn and Youdell 2000). These factors are effectively reduced to 'noise' – as 'outside' background (Gillborn and Youdell 2000) – that can be isolated statistically and 'stripped away so that the researcher can concentrate on the important domain of school factors' (Angus 1993: 341).

High stakes testing

Systems of national testing are now an established part of the educational landscape. Since their introduction following the arrival of the first National Curriculum they have come to be used for a wide variety of purposes across many different levels – national, local, institutional and individual (House of Commons Children, Schools and Families Committee 2008). Within the field of school improvement they have come to represent the essential tools for measuring school performance.

Significantly the House of Commons Children, Schools and Families Committee, reporting in 2008, has concluded that 'the use of national test results for the purpose of school accountability has resulted in some schools emphasising the maximisation of test results at the expense of a more rounded education for their pupils' (House of Commons 2008: 3). The report continues:

> A variety of classroom practices aimed at improving test results has distorted the education of some children, which may leave them unprepared for higher education and employment. We find that 'teaching to the test' and narrowing of the taught curriculum are widespread phenomena in schools, resulting in a disproportionate focus on the 'core' subjects of English, Mathematics and Science and, in particular, on those aspects of these subjects which are likely to be tested in an examination.
> (House of Commons Children, Schools and Families Committee 2008: 3)

A narrowing of the curriculum was not the only problem associated with national testing. In relation to the General Certificate of Secondary Education (GCSE), Gillborn and Youdell identified what they termed the 'A–C economy' (Gillborn and Youdell 2000: 12), referring to the fact that those pupils who could, with additional support, achieve within the A–C grade band were a valuable commodity in school improvement terms. This phenomenon does not just apply to GCSEs. At every point of national testing there is potentially a group of pupils who with additional support can reach the all-important national expectations. It is easy to see how this could influence allocation of support within a school concerned to improve its performance in terms of comparison with national expectations.

The case of national testing is a powerful example of how a national policy change can have unintended effects when locally interpreted in terms of both teachers' practice and pupils' experience. The recent criticism from the House of Commons Children, Schools and Families Committee also demonstrates how even an established part of the educational landscape that has influenced the practice and priorities in schools for almost two decades can begin to fall from favour.

New Labour

Tony Blair's Labour government, elected in 1997, openly embraced and pursued with a passion the standards-raising agenda. *Excellence in Schools* promised that there would be 'unrelenting pressure on schools and teachers for improvement' (DfEE 1997a: 3) and talked in terms of 'zero tolerance' of underperformance by schools.

Reflective Exercise 1.3

How might a policy of 'unrelenting pressure on schools and teachers for improvement' (DfEE 1997a: 3) and 'zero tolerance' of underperformance by schools influence:

- your attitude towards pupils who misbehave in your lessons?
- your purpose when managing behaviour?
- your views about what should happen to pupils who persistently disrupt?

Though Labour pursued a similar policy line on education to the previous Conservative government (Demaine 1999), there were also emerging social democratic elements within policy (Muschamp *et al.* 1999). This was illustrated through the new government's concern for social exclusion (e.g. DfEE 1999a), its commitment to a policy of inclusion (e.g. DfEE 1997b) and support for life-long learning (Phillips 2001).

The introduction of the National Curriculum under the previous Conservative administration had established central government involvement in defining *what* should be taught; it was not long before the New Labour government exerted an influence over *how* to teach. A Literacy Task Force was set up to raise primary literacy standards and a Numeracy Task Force to do the same for standards in mathematics. These groups influenced the development of the Literacy and Numeracy strategies (DfEE 1998a, DfEE 1999b) within the primary sector (Tomlinson 2005). The Literacy Strategy (DfEE 1998a), which emerged first, was highly prescriptive setting both the time to be spent on Literacy (the 'Literacy Hour') and how this time was to be divided.

Reflective Exercise 1.4

When the Literacy Hour (DfEE 1998a) was first introduced into primary schools it was highly prescriptive. The 20 minutes guided group and independent work claimed to have two complementary purposes:

- to enable the teacher to teach at least one group per day, differentiated by ability, for a sustained period through 'guided' reading and writing;
- to enable other pupils to work independently – individually, in pairs or in groups – without recourse to the teacher.

During this time the teacher was required to work at Key Stage 1 with at least two ability groups and at Key Stage 2 with at least one ability group each day.

Inevitably the practice introduced behaviour management problems when some pupils were unable to work independently for sufficient periods of time while the teacher was with another group.

- Do you view the ability to work independently as a behaviour management issue or a learning issue?
- How might your view influence the approach you adopt to the issue?
- How might the ability-grouping described impact on pupils' views of themselves as learners or their relationships with their peers?

In 2003, in what could be viewed as an enactment at policy level of the old behavioural adage 'don't smile until Christmas', *Excellence and Enjoyment* was softer in tone than preceding documents and acknowledged that primary education was in a strong position with improving results and good comparisons internationally and stated: 'We want schools to continue to focus on raising standards while not being afraid to combine that with making learning fun' (DfES 2003a: 4). It reassured teachers that, '[they] have much more freedom than they often realise to design the timetable and decide what and how they teach' (DfES 2003a: 4).

Teachers could be forgiven a wry smile over the second of these quotes. It appears to attribute the belief within the profession that there was limited freedom to *teachers'* misunderstanding, rather than to the influence of a period since 1989 of unprecedented government prescription in relation to the curriculum.

Whilst the language of standards-raising was still evident in *Excellence and Enjoyment*, the language used to talk about schools was far more positive; emphasising what was going well and representing a marked contrast to the prescriptive, more confrontational style (Tomlinson 2005) of the first section of *Excellence in Schools*. Through *Excellence and Enjoyment* the Literacy and Numeracy Strategies evolved into the Primary National Strategy, which has subsequently produced copious, largely high-quality materials to support classroom practice.

The Key Stage 3 (KS3) National Strategy was launched in 2000 as a pilot involving 205 secondary schools in 17 volunteer Local Education Authorities (LEAs). It was launched nationally in Summer 2001 (Ofsted 2003a). The KS3 National Strategy aimed to raise standards by strengthening teaching and learning across the curriculum for all 11–14 year olds.

One interpretation of the National Strategies was of a continuation of the erosion of teachers' professional autonomy that had begun in the mid-seventies and gathered pace through the eighties and nineties. A more positive reading however is that the focus on issues of pedagogy encouraged by the National Strategies was recognition that teaching was a professional occupation with its own technical language and practices. Teaching could no longer be considered, if ever it was, as simply involving an older and wiser adult with a body of subject knowledge who transferred this to a younger, less wise group of pupils.

Special educational needs

At the start of the twentieth century, doctors could diagnose four levels of special 'conditions': 'idiot', 'imbecile', 'feeble-minded' and 'moral-defective' (Kellett 2004). In 1898 the Departmental Committee on Defective and Epileptic Children investigated whether the educational system could be adapted for any of these children. It concluded that 'imbeciles' were best placed in an asylum and the 'feeble-minded' and 'moral defectives' could attend special schools, but 'idiots' were deemed ineducable and excluded from the education system altogether (Kellet 2004). School boards appointed medical officers to decide a child's condition and educational placement. The 1921 Education Act required that the numbers of 'feeble-minded' and 'backward' children within each local authority were recorded so that separate education could be provided.

The significance of these developments in terms of the legacy left was the strong link between the diagnosis of a category and the allocation of a type of education. The need to categorise in order to allocate provision was the impetus that led to the development and rapid adoption of the intelligence test as a diagnostic tool to determine degrees of special educational need (Kellett 2004). This was not simply an English phenomenon. In France Alfred Binet was asked by the Parisian board of education to develop a test that would allow educationally subnormal children to be identified, so that these children could then be placed in special classes to assist their learning. Binet's test allowed the authorities to reduce the child's intelligence to a number, or Intelligence Quotient (IQ) as Binet termed it (Gould 1996). In this country it was Cyril Burt who developed this area of work. Burt was appointed by London as the first educational psychologist after educational psychology services were introduced in 1913 (Attfield *et al.* 2004). Burt's work on intelligence was hugely influential on educational policy from the 1920s until the 1970s. However much of his work was discredited in the mid-1970s, shortly after his death, amid claims (e.g. Hearnshaw 1979, Gillie 1976, Kamin 1974) that he had fabricated data.

The response to those who would later be encompassed by the term 'special educational needs' (SEN) was one of segregation if, based on the measures used at the time, the individual's development varied sufficiently from that of the general population of same-aged peers. Whilst the tendency may be to accept this process as reflecting the prevailing view of the time of how best to care for the more vulnerable members of society and thus ultimately underpinned by benign intentions, there was a more disturbing side. The Eugenics movement, which had emerged in the second half of the nineteenth century, was growing in influence. Members of the British Eugenics Society were small in number but powerful, including influential figures such as George Bernard Shaw, Marie Stopes, D.H. Lawrence, Winston Churchill and Cyril Burt (Mason 2005). Based on a distortion of Darwin's theories of evolution and natural selection, the Eugenicist belief was that the quality of the human race could be improved by selective breeding, sterilisation and segregation (Barnes 1992). Mason (2005) has argued powerfully that whilst it would be viewed as entirely unacceptable now to state the sorts of views expressed by members of the Eugenicist movement, many of today's practices, upheld by a wide range of professionals, have their origins in the Eugenicist laws, values and beliefs of the early twentieth century.

The 1944 Education Act

The 1944 Education Act (the 'Butler Act') established a wider range of categories of need:

- partially sighted
- blind
- partially deaf
- deaf
- delicate
- epileptic
- diabetic
- physically handicapped
- educationally sub-normal [ESN]
- speech defect
- maladjusted.

(Tomlinson 1982)

In marked contrast to the policy of inclusion pursued now, the Ministry of Education stated: 'Anyone who has known children in any of the categories will agree that the varieties of education offered in ordinary primary and secondary schools do not meet their needs' (Ministry of Education 1946, quoted in Tomlinson 1982: 50). Children considered uneducable were passed on to the health service and were designated 'severely subnormal' (Barnes 1992).

Whilst the terminology was somewhat less stigmatising than that which had preceded it, the focus was largely on individual deficit and heavily rooted in diagnosis and labelling. The introduction of more categories served to perpetuate a medical model of need where children were diagnosed, principally by medical authorities, and then assigned to a particular category with which particular institutions and curriculum forms were associated. Intelligence testing and medical examination were thus seen as crucial to the workings of special education (Jones 2003).

The Warnock Report

It was not until the 1970 Education (Handicapped Children) Act that the category of 'ineducable' was abolished and all children were brought into the framework of education irrespective of their disability or degree of learning difficulty. The establishment of an absolute right to a full education for all children inevitably led to new interest in special education. The *Report by the Committee of Enquiry into the Education of Handicapped Children and Young People* (Warnock 1978), better known as the Warnock Report, was the biggest ever study of special education in England, Scotland and Wales, putting the issue of the integration of disabled children into ordinary schools on to the national agenda for the first time. The report introduced the term 'special educational needs' and a focus on appropriate provision rather than on a 'condition' and treatment, and said that the stigmatising terms such as 'educationally sub-normal' should be replaced by 'children with learning difficulties'.

A key proposal was the integration of children into mainstream schools wherever possible. Three levels were described in the report:

*   *locational integration*, where provision for children with special educational needs was to be made on the same site as their mainstream peers;
*   *social integration*, where children shared social spaces, in the playground or in extra-curricular activities;
*   *functional integration*, where children with special needs and mainstream children were to be educated together, pursuing the same set of curriculum goals and activities.

Though the Warnock Report, and the subsequent 1981 Act which incorporated its principles, firmly established integration as policy, there was no expectation or obligation for this to be in the form of functional integration, which arguably is the most advanced level and relates most closely to concepts of inclusion. In other words, the child simply being in mainstream school alongside other pupils was seen as sufficient.

The principles of integration established by Warnock (1978) and the Education Act 1981 continued to inform practice through the 1980s and led to the development of Local Education Authority (LEA) policies on integration (Gibson and Blandford 2005). In summary then, policy was that children with special educational needs should be integrated in mainstream schools where possible, with specialist provision for those whose needs were such that integration was impractical.

Inclusion

Whilst the UK was continuing to enact the principles of integration from the Warnock Report and the 1981 Education Act, through the *Code of Practice on the Identification and Assessment of Special Educational Needs* (DfE 1994a), interest in the concept of inclusion was developing internationally and in 1994 the Salamanca Statement was issued. This was a catalyst for much educational policy within the UK from the mid-nineties that attempted to develop more inclusive practices in schools. Unlike integration which implies a threshold to be crossed before the pupil is deemed suitable to be admitted, based on a concept of educational or social 'readiness' for placement in the mainstream school (Blamires 1999), 'inclusion' recognises the individual child's right to be included. It carries the expectation that schools need to be prepared to change aspects of curriculum, assessment, pedagogy and groupings of pupils to facilitate this.

The New Labour government's commitment to inclusion was expressed through *Excellence for all Children* (DfEE 1997b). The document couched the government's endorsement of the principles of the Salamanca statement in the context of a school improvement agenda. Following in the wake of *Excellence in Schools* (DfEE 1997a), *Excellence for all Children* (DfEE 1997b) set out the government's proposals for children with special educational needs. Excellence for such children was to be achieved through the development of more inclusive practice in mainstream schools. Armstrong sums up this shift in thinking, suggesting

> The 'enlightenment' of educational policy was grounded in the school-effectiveness and school improvement movements. The language of individual pupil needs was

ostensibly rejected and replaced by a policy focused upon failing schools and the actions required to transform institutional failure into success and by this means into individual achievement.

(Armstrong 2005: 137)

In many ways *Excellence for all Children* (DfEE 1997b) represented a melding of the inclusion and standards-raising agendas. Central to the philosophy of inclusion is the need for schools to develop their practices in order to become more inclusive. Booth and Ainscow (2002) have argued that inclusion is a process rather than a state, reinforcing the idea that inclusion is an ongoing process of improvement. The school improvement agenda would therefore seem to be an ally in this aim, being similarly rooted in the notion of schools continually improving their practice. However, as we shall consider in the next section, policies for school improvement, inclusion and special educational needs may not sit entirely comfortably together.

The challenge of three agendas

Educational policies in relation to SEN, inclusion, and school improvement have pragmatically tended to develop in parallel, rather than as coherent synergised directives that serve to inform planning and practice in schools (Ellis *et al.* 2008). As we have already outlined, the heritage and end-goals of each of these three agendas are different. This is a potential source of tension at the level of the classroom experience of pupils and their teachers.

Standards-raising and inclusion

The notion of school improvement per se is not problematic in relation to inclusion. As Florian and Rouse (2001) suggest:

Effective schools and school improvement literature raises important issues for those who are struggling to create more inclusive schools because it suggests ways in which schools themselves, through the development of their own policies and practice, might become more effective at meeting the learning needs of *all* children.

(Florian and Rouse 2001: 154)

The potential conflict is that school improvement has tended to be judged in terms of higher National Curriculum test scores or GCSE results. Often the focus is on attainment in the areas of literacy and numeracy. Arguably there are many other areas in which a school can demonstrate its improvement and effectiveness but it is these two that tend to dominate. A key reason may be measurability. For example, it is very easy to show that 73 per cent of pupils gained Level 5 in Science in Year 9 last year compared to 80 per cent in the current year, whereas improvements in emotional health and well-being would be more difficult to measure. School improvement has often therefore become synonymous with standards-raising, defined in terms of improvements in core subjects and frequently just literacy and numeracy. Standards-raising is predominantly concerned with reaching or exceeding age-related success criteria. The Secondary National Strategy for example aimed for 85 per cent of 14 year olds to achieve at least Level 5 in English, Mathematics and ICT, with 80 per cent achieving Level 5 in Science, by 2007. Such targets establish a focus for schools on groups of pupils. There are those that will achieve these standards, those that could achieve them with targeted intervention, and those who, despite making progress from their own baselines, are not likely to contribute to the total percentage of pupils in the school reaching national expectations. This creates a normalisation agenda: there is a 'normal' level in learning that we expect the majority of pupils will reach at a certain age. There is then an inherent tension between a standards–raising agenda that is seen to attach great value and significance to reaching or exceeding a 'norm', and a philosophy of inclusion that regards diversity and difference as normal (Mittler 2000).

As Parsons (1999a) suggests, if school improvement is narrowly conceived as National Curriculum test scores and GCSE results it will always conflict with inclusion. The inclusion agenda requires schools to develop to embrace diversity. The purpose of improvements in practice therefore is not to raise standards in terms of percentage of pupils reaching national targets, but to increase the learning and participation of *all* pupils. While these purposes are not mutually exclusive the inclusion agenda is underpinned by a different priority and end goal. The focus is on meaningful progress for the individual from their own baseline, coupled with a recognition that such progress may be in other areas besides the academic.

Special educational needs and inclusion

It may at first seem strange to suggest that inclusion and special educational needs represent separate agendas given that policy makers, practitioners and parents commonly use the term inclusion to describe educational provision for children and young people with SEN in mainstream schools (Pirrie *et al.* 2005). However the roots of the distinction lie in the history of special education already outlined in this chapter. The medical model of disability, difficulty and difference has exerted a pervasive influence over many years. This model attributes difficulties in learning to deficiencies or impairments within the pupil. Current guidance (e.g. DfES 2001) in relation to special educational needs still continues to place a strong emphasis on identifying individual difference and implementing additional and/ or different provision to respond to this.

Through placing the emphasis on diagnosis and labelling, originally exclusively by psychologists and doctors, the medical model also served to create a belief in specialist assessment and specialist pedagogy. After all, as schools for such pupils were entitled 'special', it logically suggested something *special* went on there that was significantly different to what went on in 'non-special' schools. Thomas and Loxley (2007) make the point regarding the effects on teachers' practice of the rise of special education through the twentieth century:

> Unfortunately, special education has been so successful at continually devising more glossy and more elaborate forms of assessment and pedagogy that teachers have begun to lose confidence in their own ability to assess and teach all children in their charge. Children who are difficult to teach have become by default 'special' children. Teachers have really begun to believe that they are not skilled enough to deal with 'special' children – children who are finding their work 'difficult'.
>
> (Thomas and Loxley 2007: 27)

Inclusion is underpinned by a social model of disability. In contrast to the medical model, the social model of disability is concerned with the barriers that may exist in the nature of the setting or arise through the interaction between pupils and their contexts. This essential difference between social and medical models is captured in the Union of the Physically

Impaired Against Segregation (UPIAS) description of disability as: 'The disadvantage or restriction of ability caused by a contemporary social organisation which takes little or no account of people who have physical impairments and thus excludes them from participation in the mainstream of social activities' (UPIAS 1976: 14).

Much of the guidance issued since *Excellence for all Children* (DfEE 1997b) has emphasised a move away from a focus on individual categories of need associated with the medical model towards improving the quality of teaching, in order to improve the learning of all children, including those with special educational needs and other vulnerable groups. National Strategy documents have for example made reference to notions of 'quality first inclusive teaching' (e.g. DfES 2002, 2005b) and the 'dyslexia-friendly classroom' (DfES 2002).

For the classroom teacher there is a need to balance two expectations:

- the duty expressed within the *Code of Practice* (DfES 2001) to 'provide interventions that are additional to or different from those provided as part of the school's usual differentiated curriculum offer and strategies' (DfES 2001: 52);
- a policy of inclusion that is based on *extending* the usual differentiated curriculum offer and strategies so that increasingly much of what was once additional and different becomes part of quality first inclusive teaching.

The *Code of Practice* definition of special educational needs begins to look increasingly dated in the context of inclusion, as shown in Table 1.1.

Table 1.1 Possible tensions between the definition of SEN and a philosophy of inclusion

Code of Practice definition (DfES 2001: 6)	Potential tension with a philosophy of inclusion
'Children have a learning difficulty if they ... have a significantly greater difficulty in learning than the majority of children of the same age'.	• There is an inherent contradiction between the need to make comparison against the 'norm' and a philosophy of inclusion that regards diversity and difference as normal (Mittler 2000). • Inclusive teaching may mean the pupil does not have a greater difficulty in learning because what they are required to learn is planned so that it is appropriate and accessible for them.
'Children have a learning difficulty if they ... have a disability which prevents or hinders them from making use of educational facilities of a kind generally provided for children of the same age in schools within the area of the local education authority'.	• The implication of these statements is that there is a range of 'normal' provision available that the pupil needs to fit in with. However, a philosophy of inclusion is based on changing what is generally available by reforming the organisation and the curriculum of schools and the education system as a whole to meet a wider range of needs.
'Special educational provision means ... educational provision which is additional to, or otherwise different from, the educational provision made generally for children of their age in schools maintained by the LEA, other than special schools, in the area'.	• Requiring additional or different provision becomes a measure of what the school is *not* yet providing as part of quality first inclusive teaching rather than a measure of an individual's level of need. • As schools become more inclusive what was once 'additional' or 'different' may become the *standard* provision. The pupil would therefore not be in need of *special* educational provision.

At the heart of the problem may be that the definition of special educational needs in its comparison to the norm and reference to provision generally made available for children of the same age bears a striking resemblance to the definition of 'feeble-minded' used at the start of the twentieth century. This defines such children as suffering from, 'such an incomplete cerebral development that they are behind other children, at the same age and station in life, in mind and conduct, and do not profit by their environment and by education to the same extent as average children' (Hollander 1916: 46).

As we have illustrated in this chapter, this definition was from a completely different policy context and yet it captures the key components of our current definition of special educational needs, which we continue to seek to apply in a policy context of inclusion. It is little wonder that Ofsted reports of the inconsistency with which pupils are defined as having SEN, stating:

> Some schools use the term to cover all who are low-attaining, or simply below average, on entry, whether or not the cause is a learning difficulty. Clearly, if pupils are not achieving their potential this is a concern, regardless of whether the school has identified them as having SEN. However, looseness in the use of the SEN designation does not help to focus on the action needed to resolve problems and, in the worst cases, it can distract schools' attention from doing what is necessary to improve the provision they make for all low or below average attainers.
>
> (Ofsted 2004a: 10)

It remains to be seen whether *Every Child Matters* (Treasury Office 2003, DfES 2004a) will support schools in both balancing and deriving synergies from the SEN, inclusion and standards-raising agendas in pursuit of five common, holistic outcomes.

Every Child Matters: putting the child back at the heart of education?

In 2000, the death of Victoria Climbié, an eight-year-old child, led to a public enquiry into the failure of children's services to provide appropriate support and protection. The Green Paper *Every Child Matters* (Treasury Office 2003) was the response to the findings of this enquiry. A Children's Act was passed in 2004 requiring schools, health and social services to work more closely together. Though the origins of *Every Child Matters* were in child protection, subsequent policy and guidance has a far wider influence, seeking to improve the well-being of children and young people from birth to age 19. While the tragic case of Victoria Climbié provided a strong moral imperative, *Every Child Matters* can be seen as a continuation of a range of socially progressive legislation introduced since 1997, designed to promote a more inclusive educational system and to reduce social exclusion among vulnerable groups (Rouse and McLaughlin 2007).

The *Every Child Matters* policy is built around five central outcomes – 'be healthy', 'stay safe', 'enjoy and achieve', 'make a positive contribution', and 'achieve economic well-being'.

Every Child Matters: Change for Children (DfES 2004a) expanded on each of these outcomes (Table 1.2).

These represent *holistic* outcomes; they relate to the whole child not just academic achievement. It is difficult to take issue with any of these outcomes, particularly when

Table 1.2 Every Child Matters outcomes

ECM outcome	What the outcome means
Be healthy	Physically healthy Mentally and emotionally healthy Sexually healthy Healthy lifestyles Choose not to take illegal drugs *Parents, carers and families promote healthy choices*
Stay safe	Safe from maltreatment, neglect violence and sexual exploitation Safe from accidental injury and death Safe from bullying and discrimination Safe from crime and anti-social behaviour in and out of school Have security, stability and are cared for *Parents, carers and families provide safe homes and stability*
Enjoy and achieve	Ready for school Attend and enjoy school Achieve stretching national educational standards at primary school Achieve personal and social development and enjoy recreation Achieve stretching national educational standards at secondary school *Parents, carers and families support learning*
Make a positive contribution	Engage in decision-making and support the community and environment Engage in law-abiding and positive behaviour in and out of school Develop positive relationships and choose not to bully and discriminate Develop self-confidence and successfully deal with significant life changes and challenges Develop enterprising behaviour *Parents, carers and families promote positive behaviour*
Achieve economic wellbeing	Engage in further education, employment or training on leaving school Ready for employment Live in decent homes and sustainable communities Access to transport and material goods Live in households free from low income *Parents, carers and families are supported to be economically active*

© Crown copyright [2004] Department for Education and Skills (from DfES 2004a: 9).

expanded in this way. They are unashamedly needs-centred with the fundamental purpose of meeting the needs of children and young people (Kirk and Broadhead 2007). However we should be aware that though expressed largely in terms of outcomes for individuals, the five ECM outcomes also represent society's needs. This dual purpose was reflected in a comment in a summary of *Every Child Matters*: 'We all stand to share the benefits of an economy and society with less educational failure, higher skills, less crime, and better health. We all share a duty to do everything we can to ensure every child has the chance to fulfil their potential' (DfES 2003b: 6–7).

Kirk and Broadhead (2007) point to a range of drivers for the *Every Child Matters* agenda:

> Failure to make proper provision to combat exclusion increased the likelihood that subsequent forms of social and personal breakdown would make even heavier demands on the public purse. Sound investment in tackling the roots of exclusion was not only a way of creating a more just and cohesive society, one in which life chances were less unequal, but also represented a wiser use of community resources.
>
> (Kirk and Broadhead 2007: 4)

For teachers and their schools therefore, *Every Child Matters* represented an expanded set of responsibilities within a wider agenda for change that seeks to address concerns relating to social cohesion and issues of societal fragmentation. This wider set of outcomes, alongside associated extended schools, workforce reform and multi-agency working, make it a requirement that teachers will have to find the time and ways to work with a variety of professionals, agencies, volunteers and others. The use of additional expertise and resources to *compensate* for educational disadvantage, disability and difference is not new. The significant shift now is towards *collaborative* working between education, health and social services, which serves to recognise that individual children develop and respond holistically. While the evidence base for this has yet to be established, this integration of expertise and resources has potential to improve children's outcomes and experiences.

The five *Every Child Matters* outcomes now represent the cornerstone of services for children and young people. They have been incorporated into the professional standards for teachers and form part of the framework for Ofsted inspections of schools, children's centres and local authority provision for children (Kirk and Broadhead 2007). After an era where the dominant focus had been on narrowly defined academic standards, *Every Child Matters* (DfES 2004a) conveyed upon teachers both a responsibility and permission to look at their practice and priorities in relation to a range of holistic outcomes. Inevitably the standards-raising agenda is still present. The extended description of *Enjoy And Achieve* refers to children achieving stretching national educational standards in primary and secondary schools. The significant shift in emphasis however is that *achieve* is paired with *enjoy* and that this outcome is just one of five that schools, services and Local Authorities are seeking to secure for pupils. The subsequent document *Every Child Matters: Next Steps* set out a clear role for schools:

> Schools are critical to ensuring every child has the opportunity to fulfil their potential. Our ambitions have to be bolder than merely protecting children from falling through the net: we must have high ambitions for all children. Raising standards in schools and inclusion must go hand in hand. In particular, schools have a critical role in raising the educational achievement of children in care and other groups that have consistently underachieved, for example some ethnic minority groups.
>
> (DfES 2004a: 38)

This illustrates the government rationale for translating public and political concern over a child protection issue into a change of policy for all. This trajectory from a concern over an issue affecting some children into initiatives that affect all children has also been a characteristic of some other government policy-making.

Personalised learning

Every Child Matters: Next Steps (DfES 2004a) also made mention of 'personalised learning', stating:

> Our reforms support the efforts to raise standards by personalising learning to suit the individual aspirations, circumstances and talents of each child. Instead of a deficit model that provides consistent but uniform services for most children, and only provides tailored support when children have more complex needs identified by the child protection process, our aim is to ensure that every child gets personalised learning, care and support.
>
> (DfES 2004a: 38)

Personalised learning is part of a wider agenda of personalisation. Personalisation involves putting users at the heart of public services and enabling them to have a say in their design and delivery. In essence this requires services to be responsive to the needs and wishes of their users rather than adopting a one-size-fits-all approach to delivery. *Every Child Matters: Next Steps* (DfES 2004a) presents a vision of personalised and high quality, integrated universal services, which give easy access to effective and targeted specialist services. For schools the concept of personalised learning has become increasingly significant in policy. This is based on the principle of tailoring education to individual need, interest and aptitude in order to fulfil every child and young person's potential (DfES 2004b). This requires the school to be responsive to individuals rather than adopting a stance of expecting pupils always to fit in with existing practices. Therefore although pupils will continue to be taught as groups or classes there is an expectation that the teacher will have a heightened awareness of how individuals achieve best and be prepared to make changes to practice based on this.

The five outcomes from *Every Child Matters* and the emphasis placed on personalised learning would suggest that the child has regained their rightful place at the heart of the educational process. Many teachers have never seen the child as residing anywhere else.

Summary

When we think about pupil learning and behaviour, we need to do so with a recognition that it occurs in a social, political and cultural context that has defined what acceptable behaviour is, what school-based learning is, the type of learning that is valued, the desirable curriculum content and the role of educational settings in developing this learning and behaviour in children and young people.

The politicising of education from the late seventies has led to education frequently being framed as a problem to be *solved*, dominated by the language of 'failure', 'crisis' and 'decline' (Jones 2003). Based on this perspective a 'top down' approach from government is only to be expected and, as this chapter has shown, there has been no shortage of this. Educational changes at policy level naturally affect the teacher's priorities in the classroom and may on occasions have direct implications for classroom management. However as concerns expressed about national testing (House of Commons Children, Schools and Families Committee 2008) have demonstrated these effects may be different to those intended by policy makers.

The period of history considered in this chapter has seen a significant shift in priorities. Our predecessors teaching in the period following the 1944 Education Act were part of an educational system with a largely functional role, based on preparing the majority for a fairly predictable, stable range of jobs at a time of full employment. Pupils with special educational needs, including those falling within the maladjusted category, who we might now refer to as experiencing social, emotional and behavioural difficulties, were mainly placed in segregated provision. In contrast to the modest post war aspirations, educational policy now requires teachers to fulfil a significant role in developing transferable skills that enable their pupils to become life-long learners, capable of adapting in response to fast-paced technological change. In addition to the more traditional roles and responsibilities relating to transmitting society's values and passing on a body of knowledge (both factual and cultural) to future generations, schools have accrued many others. These are more recent in origin and include embracing diversity, reducing social exclusion and building social cohesion. Teachers are now explicitly expected to secure a range of holistic outcomes, focused on the whole child's well-being, and not solely academic learning.

Education is likely to face more challenges as the traditional role of the classroom teacher is reconfigured and reconceptualised in response to a fast-changing world. Looking ahead to the curriculum in 2020, Newby (2005) predicts:

> More important than familiarity with particular bodies of knowledge will be intellectual approaches; ways of knowing. Ability to synthesise and analyse will be crucial. The curriculum must be designed in order to animate these, rather than to stress the accumulation, retention and recapitulation of information in exams. The power to interpret, to be critical and to be able to navigate will be highly-prized attributes in the well-educated person of the twenty-first century, so our curriculum will have to position young minds to know how to think in ways like these.
>
> (Newby 2005: 299)

For the twenty-first-century teacher it is necessary to accept that as part of one's role there will be ongoing innovations from a range of sources and that these will require a creative and critical response. This is potentially less stressful and more empowering than believing that there is a status quo to be maintained in the face of externally imposed change. Nevertheless, there are some enduring features of the teacher's role: we continue to educate pupils in group settings and our purpose is to promote learning. It is these two themes that underpin this book. It invites the reader to examine the learning they promote and how they can effectively promote this learning in group settings.

Chapter 2

Policy and guidance on pupil behaviour

Introduction

Pupil behaviour in schools is frequently presented as a concern, even though the consistent message is that the great majority of children and young people enjoy learning, work hard and behave well (Ofsted 2005a). Behaviour in schools has been the subject of government policy and numerous reports and guidance documents.

This chapter seeks to examine some of these key documents from the Elton Report (DES 1989) onwards. The evolution of policy and guidance on behaviour in the two decades since the Elton Report needs to be understood within the context of the previous chapter, which looked at how educational policy, shaped by a range of drivers, has influenced beliefs about the roles and responsibilities of schools and teachers and the nature, purpose and content of school-based learning.

The Elton Report

The Elton Report emerged in the wake of media interest in an apparent decline in standards of behaviour in schools (DES 1989) and perceived increases in violent incidents. This moral panic regarding a breakdown in the social fabric due to the behaviour of youth is a regular occurrence. Pearson (1983) has commented on this issue:

> History is not usually written backwards, of course, although the logic of this history of respectable fears – repeatedly accusing the here-and-now present of succumbing to an unprecedented deluge of crime and immorality, while gazing back fondly to the recently and dearly departed past – has insisted that we follow it step by step, leafing back through the pages of history in search of the still unlocated 'golden age'. A golden age, it is so often said, where, by its emphasis on 'traditional' discipline and the unswerving distinction between right and wrong, the British way of life kept the hooligan wolf from the door.
>
> (Pearson 1983: 207)

There are sensible debates to be had about changing patterns of behaviour in schools but a simple assumption that it is worse is unhelpful. Changes in pupil behaviour have to be seen within the changing social, cultural and educational context in which they occur. The Elton Report (DES 1989) was an enduring, comprehensive response to the media interest of the time. It was a wide-ranging enquiry regarding discipline in schools and used information from schools to form its views and make recommendations.

The timing of the publication of these findings was significant and somewhat unfortunate as it coincided with the introduction of the first National Curriculum. In addition, at a strategic level Local Authorities, governing bodies and head teachers were also dealing with the introduction of Local Management of Schools (LMS) in 1990, which brought with it significant implications for budget management responsibilities.

The Elton Report's status as an advisory document together with the educational reform that was currently underway did little to make it a high priority for action. Though the introduction of a National Curriculum represented a particularly major change in the education system, it is not uncommon for reports, policy and guidance on behaviour to be issued against a background of other priorities for schools.

Drawing on research by Rutter *et al.* (1979), referred to in more detail in the previous chapter, and similar work by Mortimore *et al.* (1988) looking at primary schools, the Elton Report reinforced the message that schools can make a difference, stating:

> Our conversations with teachers left us convinced that some schools have a more positive atmosphere than others. It was in these positive schools that we tended to see the work and behaviour that impressed us most. We found that we could not explain these different school atmospheres by saying that the pupils came from different home backgrounds. Almost all the schools we visited were in what many teachers would describe as difficult urban areas. We had to conclude that these differences had something to do with what went on in the schools themselves.
>
> (DES 1989: 88)

Nevertheless, the Elton Report did not discount entirely the effects of home background, commenting:

> Some schools are much more effective than others in promoting good work and behaviour. This does not mean that schools can eliminate the effects of social differences between pupils. A child from a disadvantaged background is still likely on average to do less well than a child from an advantaged home when they attend the same school. But if the disadvantaged child attends an effective school he may well do better than a more advantaged child attending an ineffective school.
>
> (DES 1989: 88)

Despite this caveat, the key message from the Elton Report is that when a pupil exhibits problematic behaviour it is not solely the result of factors within the child or their home background; the school exerts a powerful influence – for good or ill. The report went on to clarify these influences, stating:

> Research evidence suggests that pupils' behaviour can be influenced by all the major features and processes of a school. These include the quality of its leadership, classroom management, behaviour policy, curriculum, pastoral care, buildings and physical environment, organisation and timetable and relationships with parents.
>
> (DES 1989: 89–90)

The concept of whole-school approaches to secure behavioural change has been an enduring theme. The first set of training materials (DfES 2003c) introduced by the Key

Stage 3 National Strategy Behaviour and Attendance materials in 2003 were very much a handbook for auditing and addressing the whole-school elements identified by the Elton Report. Recent reports on behaviour (e.g. DfES 2005a, Ofsted 2005a) have also reiterated the significant influence of whole-school factors.

Responding to the types of concerns that had led to the setting up of the Elton enquiry, the report made three important points about behaviour in schools generally, commenting that:

- bad behaviour is a not new problem, nor is it confined to England and Wales (DES 1989: 65);
- reducing misbehaviour is a realistic aim, eliminating it completely is not (DES 1989: 65);
- persistent, low level disruptive behaviour is the type of behaviour that concerns teachers most, due largely to its frequent, wearing nature.

Through these statements the Elton Report (DES 1989) challenged the view promulgated by the media and others that there was a significant recent deterioration of behaviour in schools in England and Wales, encouraged realism in recognising that some misbehaviour was inevitable, and put into perspective the type of behaviour with which teachers regularly had to deal. The Elton Report (DES 1989) also offered a perspective on the perception that a tougher, more punitive approach was necessary, commenting:

> The general conclusion which seems most relevant to our work is that some schools appear to have more punitive regimes than others, and that punitive regimes seem to be associated with worse rather than better standards of behaviour.
>
> (DES 1989: 99)

The Elton Report advocated what it termed a healthy balance between punishments and rewards.

Like the majority of schools at the time and now, the Elton Report did not adopt a purely behavioural approach. It coupled a belief in the power of rewards and sanctions with an acknowledgement of the central influence of the teacher–pupil relationship, the pastoral role of teachers, the importance of personal and social education, and the need for involvement of parents.

Significantly the Elton Report itself did not use the term 'behaviour management' and instead referred to 'classroom management'. 'Group management skills' were viewed as a component of 'classroom management'. 'Classroom management' represented a wider concept than 'behaviour management' and included the teacher's knowledge of the subject being taught and the ability to plan and deliver a lesson, which flowed smoothly and held pupils' attention (DES 1989). Group management skills, the Elton Report suggested, included: 'the ability to relate to young people, to encourage them in good behaviour and learning, and to deal calmly but firmly with inappropriate or disruptive behaviour' (DES 1989: 67).

Furthermore, the idea these skills were a natural gift and could not be taught was firmly refuted. The Elton Report stated: 'The central problem of disruption could be significantly reduced by helping teachers to become more effective classroom managers' (DES 1989: 12).

The commonly applied term 'behaviour management' can be considered as a conflating of these ideas, pulling together the notion that there is a set of skills relating to group management that a teacher can be taught, and a need to deal calmly but firmly with inappropriate or disruptive behaviour. It could be argued that this conflation lost some of the more subtle elements of the Elton Report's depiction of 'group management' as a sub-set of skills within the broader concept of 'classroom management', which had served to maintain a stronger link between behaviour and learning and emphasised the importance of relationships.

Though overall a helpful document, the Elton Report may inadvertently have reinforced a separation of behaviour management from learning through its emphasis on classroom management and in particular group management skills.

The practical nature of much of the content of the Elton Report was exemplified by the inclusion of messages emerging from literature regarding good practice. The Report advised that teachers should:

- Know their pupils as individuals. This means knowing their names, their personalities and interests and who their friends are.
- Plan and organise both the classroom and the lesson to keep pupils interested and minimise the opportunities for disruption. This requires attention to such basics as furniture layout, grouping of pupils, matching work to pupils' abilities, pacing lessons well, being enthusiastic and using humour to create a positive classroom atmosphere.
- Be flexible in order to take advantage of unexpected events rather than being thrown off balance by them.
- Continually observe or 'scan' the behaviour of the class.
- Be aware of, and control their own behaviour, including stance and tone of voice.
- Model the standards of courtesy that they expect from pupils.
- Emphasise the positive, including praise for good behaviour as well as good work.
- Make the rules for classroom behaviour clear to pupils from the first lesson and explain why they are necessary.
- Make sparing and consistent use of reprimands. This means being firm rather than aggressive, targeting the right pupil, criticising the behaviour and not the person, using private rather than public reprimands whenever possible, being fair and consistent, and avoiding sarcasm and idle threats.
- Make sparing and consistent use of punishments. This includes avoiding whole-group punishment, which pupils see as unfair. It also means avoiding punishments that humiliate pupils by, for example, making them look ridiculous. This breeds resentment.
- Analyse their own classroom management performance and learn from it. This is the most important message of all (DES 1989: 71–2).

Reflective Exercise 2.1

Consider the advice from the Elton Report given in the eleven bullet points above.

- To what extent do you adhere to these principles in your practice?
- To what extent do these principles represent sound advice for twenty-first-century classrooms?

Many of the elements of good practice identified by the Elton Report (DES 1989) have subsequently been expanded upon in numerous classroom management texts (e.g. Rogers 2002, Hook and Vass 2002, Robertson 1996) and are enduring features of accepted good practice. Despite its less than ideal timing in terms of competing educational priorities for schools, the Elton Report identified numerous issues that have remained relevant and have been explored and reiterated in national policy and guidance documents and numerous texts on behaviour since. While the National Curriculum had set out what to teach, in a rather more low-key manner the Elton Report had set out how to manage behaviour in schools.

Pupils with Problems

The Elton Report was followed with a set of circulars issued in 1994. It was entitled *Pupils with Problems*, but known informally as the 'six pack'. It is worth noting that the formal title, which seems to locate the problem entirely within the pupil, gives an indication of prevailing beliefs regarding the causes of difficulties experienced by pupils in relation to learning and behaviour.

Pupils with Problems contained the following circulars:

- *Pupil Behaviour and Discipline* (8/94);
- *Education of Children with Emotional and Behavioural Difficulties* (9/94);
- *Exclusions from School* (10/94);
- *The Education by LEAs of Children otherwise than at School* (11/94);
- *The Education of Sick Children* (12/94);
- *The Education of Children being Looked After by Local Authorities* (13/94).

In the context of this book, the two significant circulars were Circular 8/94 *Pupil Behaviour and Discipline* (DfE 1994b) and Circular 9/94 *The Education of Children with Emotional and Behavioural Difficulties* (DfE 1994c).

Circular 8/94 Pupil Behaviour and Discipline

Circular 8/94 emphasised the themes from the Elton Report relating to the ethos of the school and the core values and principles underpinning practice, and stressed the importance of a whole-school approach to behaviour and discipline. The specific aims of Circular 8/94 were to:

- help schools to manage behaviour effectively;
- encourage a whole-school approach to behaviour and discipline;
- help schools to promote respect for others amongst young people;
- promote firm action against all forms of bullying;
- reduce the levels of truancy from school;
- reduce the poor behaviour that can lead to pupils being excluded, either temporarily or permanently.

Importantly, the Circular framed pupil behaviour and discipline in a context beyond simply maintaining order, recognising that schools play:

[a] vital part in promoting spiritual, cultural, social, mental and physical development of young people. The ethos of the school should include a clear vision of values which matter within the school and in the community around it. These values included: respect for others, for property and the environment; honesty; trust and fairness; tolerance and compassion; and the virtues of self respect and self discipline.

(DfE 1994b: 6)

This statement is an acknowledgement that there are behaviours that teachers should be attempting to promote. Therefore the focus is not just on managing or stopping undesirable behaviour but on promoting positive behaviours.

The Circular offered particular advice regarding good practice in classrooms in the most successful schools, noting that:

- procedures are clearly understood regarding pupil discussion, participation in lessons, movement in class, the way in which work is handed in, and what pupils should do when tasks are completed;
- explanations are clear;
- work requirements of pupils are clearly set out, and progress is monitored carefully;
- clear instructions are given so that activities run smoothly;
- misbehaviour is handled quickly and calmly so that the pace of a lesson is not lost and further disruption is minimised;
- teachers have developed good listening skills, and react appropriately to pupils' responses;
- work set is appropriate to pupils' abilities;
- clear goals are set for each work activity and all pupils understand them before an activity begins;
- lessons start and end on time;
- classrooms are suited to a particular activity as far as possible;
- seating arrangements are suitable. These will often be dictated by the activity, but particular attention should be paid to the location of the more troublesome pupils and those easily distracted;
- external interruptions are minimised wherever possible;
- necessary materials for a given activity are available.

(DfE 1994b: 14)

Through the Circular, the DfE reiterated key messages from the Elton Report (DES 1989) regarding the importance of a whole-school behaviour policy, based on clear values and principles, that reflected the role of the school in ensuring that children grow into responsible adults, thus benefiting society as a whole (Blandford 1998). Guidance was also provided at the classroom level on the role and influence of the teacher.

Whilst within the text appropriate messages were given regarding the importance of the curriculum and the quality of teaching, ultimately its existence as a distinct Circular entitled *Behaviour and Discipline* and its stated aims gave a stronger unintentional message that behaviour and discipline were distinct from learning.

Circular 9/94 The Education of Children with Emotional and Behavioural Difficulties

Circular 9/94, *The Education of Children with Emotional and Behavioural Difficulties* (DfE 1994c), differed from 8/94 in that it focused on a specific group of pupils. It attempted to define a category of pupils who exhibited behaviour that was beyond sporadic naughtiness or moodiness but not sufficiently severe to be classed as mental illness (DfE 1994c).

The problematic aspect of attempting to define 'emotional and behavioural difficulties' (EBD) was that although the term related the difficulty to the individual pupil, there was still a strong contextual element that determined both the degree to which the problems manifested themselves and whether these problems warranted categorising the pupil as having EBD. The DfE suggested that 'Perceptions of whether a child's behaviour constitutes an emotional and behavioural difficulty are likely to differ according to the context in which it occurs as well as the individual teacher's management skills, tolerance levels, temperament and expectations' (DfE 1994c: 9).

This raised the issue of the relative nature of EBD; in one school, with one teacher, a pupil might be considered to have EBD whereas in another school with another teacher the difficulties may be less pronounced or even non-existent. The DfE (1994c) continued:

> Schools vary widely in the extent to which they successfully help children overcome their difficulties and the extent to which they either create, minimise or exacerbate the levels of disruption or distress associated with emotional and behavioural difficulties … [The school] may, through appropriate action, be able to keep the difficulty within manageable limits or even prevent it developing in the first place.
>
> (DfE 1994c: 8)

In these comments the DfE (1994c) seemed to be struggling to form an understanding of the degree to which emotional and behavioural difficulties are socially constructed, on the one hand using language that located the need firmly within the pupil (i.e. *their* difficulties) but at the same time presenting a message that in some cases schools themselves were the determining factor in whether a pupil had an emotional and behavioural difficulty or not.

It is also not beyond the realms of possibility that a prescribed, fast-paced National Curriculum with age-related testing and a culture of increased accountability of schools and teachers, was in part responsible for reconstructing those pupils who negatively impact on these priorities as pupils with emotional and behavioural difficulties. The rise in exclusion figures though the early nineties to a 1996/97 peak of just over 12 000 has been traced in parallel with the increasing pressures placed on teachers and the decreasing opportunities for curriculum flexibility (Hacker and Rowe 1997, Rustique-Forrester 2000).

Thomas (2005) suggests there has been insufficient discussion of the provenance, status, robustness, legitimacy or meaning of the term EBD, and argues that there has been a 'clinicalising' of unacceptable behaviour that transforms an institutional need for order into a pupil's emotional need. Many of the behaviours and characteristics that are typically associated with emotional and behavioural difficulties rarely have any manifest or covert association with the pupil's emotional makeup, but concern 'the school's need to regulate time (punishing tardiness and truancy), activity (punishing lack of effort or overactivity), speech (punishing chatter or insolence), and the body (punishing hairstyles, clothes, the use of make-up or the tidiness of the individual)' (Thomas 2005: 66).

The relationship between EBD and the school's need for institutional order is supported by Cornwall's (2004) observation that much of the language used to describe pupils with EBD is based on the effect they have in the classroom, the effect they have on others, and the effect they have on the traditional school system of managing learning. This is reflected in phrases such as 'disruptive', 'disturbing' and 'presenting challenging behaviours'. In contrast, with other forms of SEN the nature of the difficulty that the child is experiencing tends to be recognised and categorised in relation to their learning needs or relative attainment.

In trying to define who might exhibit EBD Circular 9/94 produced an extensive list of behaviours that might be exhibited by a pupil who had an emotional and behavioural difficulty. It stated:

> Their behaviour may be evident at the personal level (for example through low self-image, anxiety, depression or withdrawal; or through resentment, vindictiveness or defiance); at the verbal level (for example the child may be silent or may threaten, or interrupt, argue or swear a great deal); at the non-verbal level (for example through clinginess, or truancy, failure to observe rules, disruptiveness, aggression or violence); or at the work skills level (for example through an inability or unwillingness to work without direct supervision, to concentrate, to complete tasks or to follow instructions).
>
> (DfE 1994c: 7–8)

The DfE (1994c) acknowledges earlier in the document that it could be argued every child has an emotional and behavioural difficulty of some kind at some point in their development. The extensive nature of this list would seem to support rather than refute that argument, though DfE (1994c) qualifies it with the statement that 'Whether or not a child has emotional or behavioural difficulties will depend on the nature, frequency, persistence, severity or abnormality and cumulative effect of the behaviour, in context, compared to normal expectations of a child of the age concerned' (DfE 1994c: 8).

Emotional and behavioural difficulties is therefore a relative concept as its meaning varies between observers and across time and place (Fogell and Long 1997).

Reflective Exercise 2.2

- How might the categorisation as 'EBD' affect the teacher's expectations of the pupil?
- How might the categorisation as 'EBD' affect the teacher's perceptions of their responsibilities in relation to the pupil with this label?
- How might the categorisation as 'EBD' affect the teacher's confidence and perceptions of competence in relation to the pupil with this label?

EBD is a concept that may serve to confuse and possibly disempower teachers. In defining this group, the DfE (1994c) both endowed EBD with the status of a diagnosis and created the impression firstly that there might be different learning priorities for these pupils and secondly that specialist teaching was necessary to achieve these. In a sense therefore the teacher, when a pupil is identified as having emotional and behavioural difficulties, may find that the teaching and learning agenda with which they are familiar is supplanted by a less familiar agenda based on the traditions of special education, psychology, social work and counselling.

Whilst Circular 9/94 (DfE 1994c) used the term emotional and behavioural difficulties, the revised *Code of Practice* (DfES 2001) uses the term 'behaviour, emotional and social development' (BESD), though 'development' is often replaced by 'difficulty' in common usage. Ofsted (e.g. 2004a, 2005a) uses 'emotional, behavioural and social difficulties' (EBSD). Davis and Florian (2004) found that within educational literature 'social, emotional and behavioural difficulties' (SEBD) appears to be the preferred term. We will use the latter phrase within this book, unless referring to a source that uses one of the other terms, as it appropriately places greater emphasis on the social and emotional elements that influence presenting behaviour.

National strategies for behaviour and attendance

In 2003, after the subject strands were in place, the Key Stage 3 National Strategy Behaviour and Attendance strand was introduced. Through the Primary National Strategy, behaviour and attendance materials were piloted in 25 Local Education Authorities.

The development of a separate strand for behaviour and attendance within the Key Stage 3 National Strategy rather than its integration within the subject strands potentially created the impression of a separation of behaviour from learning and teaching. However, within individual Local Authorities the appointment, organisation and deployment of Key Stage 3 behaviour and attendance consultants served to either minimise or emphasise this separation. The introduction of the new behaviour and attendance strand also coincided with an emphasis on the promotion of the Key Stage 3 National Strategy as being six strands but one strategy. This notion was beneficial in ensuring that the behaviour and attendance materials maintained some connection with the teaching and learning priorities of the rest of the KS3 National Strategy documents.

The *Key Messages* leaflet introducing the strand to LEA officers succinctly summed up its *raison d'être*:

- raising standards is heavily dependent on staff recruitment and retention;
- recruitment and retention is influenced by standards of behaviour;
- support and training for improving standards of behaviour in schools is in great demand by both staff and pupils;
- standards of behaviour are unsatisfactory in 1 in 12 secondary schools;
- levels of unauthorised absence remain unchanged, with a clear link between poor attendance and poor attainment;
- pupils frequently report that disruptive behaviour prevents higher attainment in class;
- school managers are too frequently preoccupied with dealing with poor behaviour and are unable to focus on longer-term school improvement issues;
- pupils who are most at risk of poor behaviour and irregular attendance need to be supported to engage in all aspects of school life.

(DfES 2003d: 4)

It is interesting to reflect on how few of the bullet points relate to the learning of the individual concerned and how many relate to the needs of others. Behaviour is presented as impeding core business and the implied underlying view is that if this distraction could be dealt with then the focus could return to core business once again. However, whilst the brevity of these bullet points may have implied that behaviour was a distracting separate element, the content of KS3 National Strategy materials for behaviour and attendance made a strong and welcome link with teaching and learning and emphasised the strengthening of pedagogy and practice as the route to improving behaviour and attendance.

Social and emotional aspects of learning

A significant feature of both the Primary and Secondary National Strategy materials has been a focus on the development of pupils' 'social, emotional and behavioural skills' (SEBS). The social and emotional aspects of learning (SEAL) materials (DfES 2005c) launched through the Primary National Strategy offer a whole-curriculum framework for explicitly promoting social, emotional and behavioural skills, with built-in progression for each year group within a school. The guidance (DfES 2005c) acknowledges there is overlap between SEAL and the activities schools have typically undertaken as part of PSHE and Citizenship. SEAL is framed in terms of supplementing rather than replacing 'the effective work many schools and settings are already doing to develop, social, emotional and behavioural skills' (DfES 2005c: 11). Within the guidance (DfES 2005c) the SEAL resource materials are 'offered either as a set of additional activities and resources to support what is already going on in school, or as a stand-alone framework into which similar work can be slotted' (DfES 2005c: 11).

The resource materials are intended to facilitate a systematic and spiral approach to learning. The argument for the spiral curriculum approach presented by DfES (2005c) is that most social, emotional and behavioural skills are developmental and change over time. These skills cannot therefore be taught as a one-off. There is a need to revisit and develop the concepts, understanding and skills over time, building on what has been learned previously (DfES 2005c).

The government's endorsement of the *explicit teaching* of social, emotional and behavioural skills is based largely upon DfES-funded research conducted by Weare and Gray (2003). Referring to an array of programmes examined as part of their research, they state:

> There is clear evidence on the principles that underlie these programmes, for example teaching behaviours and skills explicitly and in participative and empowering ways, using a step by step approach, generalising to real life and making use of using co-operative group work and peer education as well as whole class approaches. It is recommended that the DfES encourages the use of explicit programmes and provides curriculum guidance that outlines these key principles. Ideally this would include some recommended materials, examples of lesson plans and schemes of work, and ideas for curriculum development.
>
> (Weare and Gray 2003: 7)

DfES (2005c) defined the social and emotional aspects of learning as:

- self awareness
- managing feelings
- motivation
- empathy
- social skills.

These reflect those identified by Goleman (1998) in his work on emotional intelligence, with the exception that within the DfES (2005c) list 'managing feelings' replaces 'self regulation'. Goleman's (1995) book *Emotional Intelligence: Why it Can Matter More Than IQ* popularised emotional intelligence, but Salovey and Mayer (1990) had proposed the first formal definition and model of the construct in 1990 (Petrides *et al.* 2004). Origins of emotional intelligence can be traced back to Thorndike's (1920) social intelligence and Gardner's (1983) intrapersonal and interpersonal intelligences (Petrides *et al.* 2004).

The use of the term 'social and emotional aspects of learning' (SEAL) seeks to address some of the disadvantages associated with the term 'emotional intelligence' noted by Weare and Gray (2003), which include:

•   the term 'intelligence' tends to focus the attention on measurement rather than on teaching and learning;
•   the term 'intelligence' tends to suggest a capacity that is innate and fixed, not teachable;
•   in the strict sense 'emotional and social intelligence' could be value-neutral, for example it is theoretically possible to be highly emotionally intelligent in the sense of having 'the capacity to perceive, integrate, understand and manage emotions' but still do undesirable things (Weare and Gray 2003: 16).

The model (see Figure 2.1) advocated for using the SEAL materials is based on the 'waves' model that features in other DfES guidance materials (e.g. DfES 2002, 2005b).

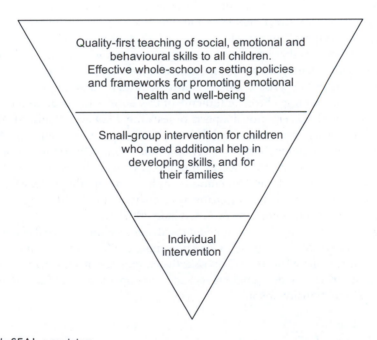

Quality-first teaching of social, emotional and behavioural skills to all children. Effective whole-school or setting policies and frameworks for promoting emotional health and well-being

Small-group intervention for children who need additional help in developing skills, and for their families

Individual intervention

Figure 2.1 SEAL provision.
© Crown copyright [2005] Department for Education and Skills (from DfES 2005c).

The approach is underpinned by the premise that all pupils require the teaching of social, emotional and behavioural skills. In addition, there are some pupils for whom small-group or individual interventions are necessary.

Within the Primary Strategy SEAL has been a dominant element since the original behaviour and attendance pilot materials, whereas it was not until 2007 that secondary SEAL materials were launched through the Secondary National Strategy (formerly Key Stage 3 National Strategy). However, the fourth set of Core Day training materials (DfES 2004c) within the KS3 National Strategy Behaviour and Attendance strand, had previously emphasised the importance of whole-school approaches to the development of pupils' emotional health and well-being.

Whilst the Primary SEAL materials arrived as a comprehensive package of resource materials structured around seven repeating themes to be covered each academic year, Secondary SEAL has been introduced in a different manner. Whilst the materials that have been produced for Year 7 are designed to build on the approaches and themes of Primary SEAL, the guidance booklet (DfES 2007a) simply encourages schools to consider how these can be extended into Years 8 and 9.

In terms of development of central government thinking, the emphasis placed on emotional health and well-being (e.g. DoH/DfES 2004) and the social and emotional aspects of learning, was indicative of an adoption of a more psychological perspective on behaviour. The emphasis therefore was not simply on controlling misbehaviour but on *teaching* social, emotional and behavioural skills. The recognition that learning involves not only cognitive but also social and emotional aspects reflected the holistic priorities of *Every Child Matters*, and in particular its focus on emotional health and well-being. Such a policy direction is not without its critics. Ecclestone and Hayes (2008) have argued that too much emphasis has been placed on 'therapeutic education', which they define as any activity focusing 'on perceived emotional problems and which aims to make educational content and learning processes more "emotionally engaging"' (Ecclestone and Hayes 2008: x). Their perception and concern is that emotional competence, emotional literacy and well-being are increasingly being seen as the most important outcomes of education.

We broadly welcome SEAL's explicit acknowledgment that there are social and emotional aspects of learning. The central theme of this book is the need to retain a focus on the cognitive, social and emotional aspects of learning. However, whilst SEAL carries considerable face validity and is supported by compelling, optimistic arguments regarding potential benefits for individuals and society, it would seem important at this stage to retain an appropriately critical stance. We are mindful of Craig's observation that 'Formally teaching children from 3–18 about their emotions or how to calm themselves, for example, has never been done before in the systematic, year-on-year way SEAL suggests. We have no idea whether this will be beneficial or not' (Craig 2007: 3).

Like Craig (2007) we would be concerned if the direct teaching of social and emotional skills led to these aspects of young people's lives becoming the focus of checklists of learning outcomes, assessments and evaluations. This risks the emergence of a normative rather than developmental approach, encouraging targets and 'catch up' groups for those deemed not to be sufficiently emotionally literate.

Reflective Exercise 2.3

Ecclestone and Hayes (2008) have been critical of schools' engagement with activities that they consider to represent 'therapeutic education'. The SEAL initiative is one such activity. Consider the following quotes:

- 'Social and emotional skills are the skills of making positive relationships with other people, of understanding and managing ourselves and our own emotions, thoughts and behaviours. If people have these skills they can then respond to the emotions and behaviour of others, in ways that are in the best long-term interest of themselves and others' (DfES 2007a: 4).
- 'Feelings, emotions and relationships are the core of our personal lives. They are an intimate part of us. The Centre believes that any initiative which suggests that government departments, schools and teachers should micromanage young people's feelings is Orwellian and a good enough reason on its own to say we have to drop this idea altogether' (Craig 2007: 5).
- 'The ultimate aim of much emotional literacy work is to help produce more socially-minded citizens, who see the benefit of participating in social and community processes, increased levels of social capital (a feeling of belonging to a community), a more flexible, resilient and effective workforce, and a reduction in violence and crime. Ultimately emotional literacy should also make communities better places to live, with higher levels of tolerance, understanding, care, compassion and citizenship' (Weare 2004: 15–16).
- 'An overload of emotional awareness can lead to paralysing introspection, self-centredness, and/or dwelling on or getting stuck in a difficult mood rather than trying to deal with it' (Weare 2004: 32).
- 'Children are learning from an early age that life, with all its trivial and serious tribulations, mundane and difficult low moments, "sucks", and requires an array of "therapeutic support workers" in the form of peer-buddies, theatre educators, teachers trained in various therapeutic approaches, life coaches and mentors, or specialist counsellors. Therapeutic education elevates everyday feelings of uncertainty, vulnerability, discomfort or lack of confidence and depicts them as "treatable"' (Ecclestone and Hayes 2008: 155).

1 Which of these perspectives do you align yourself with?
2 Do you find that more than one of these quotes resonates with your own perspective?

Additionally, we believe that schools and policy-makers need to keep a watchful eye on the effect that accustoming children and young people to talking about and openly sharing emotions has on those who live in families and communities where such a culture does not exist. Whilst concerns about cultural mismatches do not suffice in themselves to curtail the use of the SEAL programme, thought needs to given to how any mismatch is experienced and interpreted by the child or young person.

The Steer Report

The Steer Report, *Learning Behaviour: The Report of the Practitioners' Group on School Behaviour and Discipline* (DfES 2005a), sought to review the current situation in schools and make recommendations for the way forward. As was the case with the Elton Report (DES 1989), media interest in behaviour in schools was one of the influences. The practitioners' group had a remit to report on:

*   how effective practice in promoting positive behaviour and preventing misbehaviour can be embedded in all schools, drawing on the approaches currently used by successful schools, including specific consideration of:
    *   how we can build up effective collaboration between schools;
    *   whether teachers need further support through initial teacher training or professional development in managing behaviour;
    *   whether there is merit in a national code of behaviour setting out the responsibilities of schools, pupils and parents in promoting good behaviour;

*   whether there are any further developments in policy or new powers for head teachers which would help in enforcing school discipline, including specific consideration of the process for exclusion appeal panels;
*   how parents can be more effectively engaged in supporting schools in promoting good behaviour and respect.

(DfES 2005a: 8)

In responding to this remit the practitioners' group came up with some 147 recommendations. The findings of the Steer Report were incorporated into the subsequent white paper *Higher Standards, Better Schools For All* (DfES 2005d). In section 2 entitled *Principles And Practice: What Works in Schools?* the Steer Report outlined ten aspects of school practice that, when effective, contribute to the quality of pupil behaviour. These were:

*   a consistent approach to behaviour management, teaching and learning;
*   school leadership;
*   classroom management, learning and teaching;
*   rewards and sanctions;
*   behaviour strategies and the teaching of good behaviour;
*   staff development and support;
*   pupil support systems;
*   liaison with parents and other agencies;
*   managing pupil transitions;
*   organisation and facilities.

Each of these areas is also identifiable in the Elton Report, produced 16 years earlier. This is not to criticise the Steer Report, which acknowledged that the overall principles of good practice are already well established, but to recognise that there is little new to discover about the management of pupil behaviour as the key principles have been known for a long time. Bulleted lists included earlier in this chapter drawn from the Elton Report (DES 1989) and *Pupil Behaviour and Discipline* (8/94) form a useful, enduring summary of the essential components for effective classroom management. The Steer Report succeeds in updating the language of these key principles and arguably makes the link between behaviour and teaching and learning more prominent than earlier documents, reflecting the work of the National Strategies in recent years on broadening and strengthening pedagogy.

Education and Inspections Act 2006

The Education and Inspections Act 2006 introduced, for the first time, a statutory power for teachers and certain other school staff to discipline pupils. This addressed concerns raised in the Elton Report (DES 1989) and subsequently in the Steer Report (DfES 2005a) about teachers' legal authority continuing to be based on the principle of *in loco parentis*. The *in loco parentis* principle gave teachers the same authority over their pupils as parents have over their children. As the Elton Report (DES 1989) noted, many of the legal judgements that supported it were very old – predating the introduction of compulsory education and including one judgement from as far back as 1865 (DfES 2005a). *In loco parentis* originally embodied the nineteenth-century common-law principle that a teacher's authority was delegated by a parent so far as it was necessary for the welfare of the child. The case law was brought more up-to-date in the 1950s and early 1960s (NUT 2003).

School discipline and pupil behaviour policies (DfES 2007b)

The provisions of the Education and Inspections Act (2006) were set out in the guidance document *School Discipline and Pupil Behaviour Policies* (DfES 2007b). This covered the statutory power to discipline introduced in the Act as well as including a range of other guidance that aimed to help schools understand their overall legal powers and duties as regards establishing a school behaviour policy and disciplining pupils. It provided general advice on good practice regarding rules, rewards and sanctions, as well as more specific advice on certain key sanctions such as the use of detentions and the confiscation of pupils' property.

Rights and responsibilities

A significant development in the 2007 guidance was the emphasis placed on 'rights and responsibilities'. In itself this was not new. For example, writers such as Hook and Vass (2002) and Rogers (1990, 2002) have referred to rights and responsibilities in their work. However the inclusion of this terminology in an official guidance document on school behaviour and discipline policies demonstrated a clear belief that, 'Effective approaches to discipline are characterised by a healthy balance between the rights and responsibilities of staff and pupils based on mutual respect' (DfES 2007b: 63).

Individual differences

The Elton Report (DES 1989) and Circular 8/94 (DfE 1994b) were produced prior to the government's commitment in policy to inclusion (DfEE 1997b). Reflecting this development, the DfES (2007b) guidance reiterated the enduring messages regarding whole-school policies and consistent use of rewards and sanctions, but also included a section on taking account of individual needs. This section focused primarily on pupils with special educational needs or disabilities, but also referred to other groups defined by Ofsted (2000) as 'at risk' within the education system, including:

*   minority ethnic and faith groups, travellers, asylum seekers and refugees;
*   pupils who need support to learn English as an additional language (EAL);
*   children looked after by the local authority;
*   sick children;
*   young carers;
*   children from families under stress;
*   pregnant schoolgirls and teenage mothers;
*   any other pupils at risk of disaffection and exclusion.

(DfES 2007b)

Reflective Exercise 2.4

One of the school responsibilities listed in the *School discipline and pupil behaviour policies* (DfES 2007b) is 'to apply sanctions fairly, consistently, proportionately and reasonably – taking account of SEN, disability and the needs of vulnerable children, and offering support as appropriate' (DfES 2007b: 64).

*   What tensions and difficulties might there be in achieving consistency (with its implication of a uniformity of response) with a requirement to take into account individual differences?

Effectively the guidance (DfES 2007b) required schools to differentiate in its responses to behaviour. This poses a particular challenge to any schools that operate policies based on a standard disciplinary response to certain offences.

Summary

Policy and guidance across the two decades from 1989 reflect a concern over the extent to which behaviour impacts negatively on pupils' learning, recruitment and retention of teachers and the needs of society. This enduring emphasis is cushioned by an optimistic belief in whole-school approaches and more recently in the development of pupils' social, emotional and behavioural skills through the SEAL materials (DfES 2005c, 2007a).

Policy and guidance has sought to support schools in securing behaviour that allows individuals to learn in group settings. Significantly there has been considerable consistency over the years regarding the overall principles of good practice in relation to pupil behaviour. It is probably reasonable to assume therefore that there is little new to discover at the level of general principles. Policy and guidance has typically reflected a concern for both discipline and control and pastoral support and nurture. At the level of school and class interpretation and implementation, the balance between these can become skewed to meet the demands of the situation.

An emerging issue has been a change in pupil population due, in part, to a commitment to inclusion at the level of national policy that has been interpreted and enacted at local authority and school levels. In enacting whole-school policies, consistency, whilst still being considered necessary, is not, in itself, sufficient to address the individual needs of an increasingly diverse population of pupils. Schools need to take account of pupils' individual needs and circumstances when developing, applying and evaluating the school's behaviour policy (DfES 2007b).

The focus on the individual within *Every Child Matters* has emphasised the need for schools to look at the relative efficacy of policies that seek to develop appropriate behaviour within individuals and those existing polices that seek to secure and sustain appropriate behaviour from groups. Behaviour policies designed for groups characteristically rely on external controls such as rewards and sanctions and assume that pupils are able to behave appropriately but might choose not to do so. Policies designed to improve the behaviour of individuals are more concerned with developing the internal control of pupils and assume that some pupils have yet to develop appropriate social and emotional behaviours. Increasing concern about individuals who do not respond to existing whole-school behaviour policies has been paralleled by initiatives for schools to explicitly teach social, emotional and behavioural skills. Schools are now charged with developing practice that promotes social responsibility and resilience for pupils as individuals. This priority co-exists with a requirement to maintain policies that seek to establish a level of conformity, compliance and control that is perceived necessary for learning in group settings.

Chapter 3

Reframing behaviour management

Introduction

The term 'behaviour management' is an established part of school discourse, appearing no fewer than nineteen times in the Steer Report (DfES 2005a) and five times in the DfES (2007b) guidance on *School Discipline and Pupil Behaviour Policies*. It is also likely that many readers will have read books about behaviour management and attended courses to learn about it. The phrase has a respectable, quasi-professional tone and its provenance is rarely explored. This chapter invites the reader to focus on the *outcomes* of behaviour management and introduces the behaviour for learning conceptual framework as a way of achieving this. It reframes behaviour management in terms of promoting learning behaviour.

The separation of learning and behaviour

A popular text on behaviour management begins: 'Behaviour management: if you get it right, your life is easy, you're free to do what you're meant to do, which is of course to teach!' (Cowley 2003: xiii).

The quote is explicit in its message that behaviour management and the promotion of learning are distinct elements of the teacher's role. If the teacher can do the first, then they will be free to do the second. The management of behaviour is portrayed as a necessary activity in order to allow the teacher to teach and the pupils to learn. In other words it is a functional, house-keeping activity. The implication of an emphasis on behaviour management is that there is a discrete set of skills that can be learned by the teacher. This identification of a set of skills that can be learned is not in itself a problem. The problematic element is when these skills are seen as distinct from the teacher's role in promoting learning. If we look at the phrase 'behaviour management', it neatly encapsulates both the purpose and success indicator of any strategy undertaken:

- The purpose is to manage behaviour.
- The indicator of success is that behaviour is managed.

This is illustrated by the Scenario 3.1.

Scenario 3.1

You are ready to start your lesson and the class is too noisy. You adopt a strategy of writing on the board: 'Whole class detention – 1 minute.' As the noise persists you keep adding minutes. Eventually some pupils notice and start to 'shush' the others (Cowley 2003). By the time you have written '8 minutes' on the board you have established quiet. At lunchtime you keep the class in for 8 minutes.

In behaviour management terms you have been successful: the behaviour has been managed and compliance has been achieved. The emphasis is firmly on extinguishing or reducing those unwanted behaviours that impede the smooth running of the classroom with its pre-set learning agenda. There is little attention paid to the behaviour that is desirable to enable pupils to learn best in the classroom – all the attention is on *stopping* the undesirable behaviour. There is also little regard for the potential damage to the teacher–pupil relationships of such strategy, or to peer relationships if the peer-group pressure this approach seeks to enlist takes the form of social isolation or verbal and physical aggression towards those considered to be to blame for the whole class' fate. We return to the theme of problems associated with whole-group punishments in more depth in Chapter 8.

Thinking about the outcomes of behaviour management

Reflective Exercise 3.1

Answer these questions in relation to *learning*:

*   What indicators of progress do you look for?
*   What methods do you use to assess progress?

Answer these questions in relation to *behaviour*:

*   What indicators of progress do you look for?
*   What methods do you use to assess progress?

You may find from this reflective exercise that progress in learning is measured in a variety of ways ranging from informal observation through to national tests. Indicators may have been in the form of *increases* and *mastery*. However when thinking about progress in behaviour you may have found a blurring of the distinction between *methods* and *indicators* and identified things such as reductions in referrals to senior members of staff, receiving less sanctions, causing less disruption, being able to remain in class and perceptions of changes in attitude. Overall you may have found that when thinking about behaviour the emphasis was generally on *reduction* or *cessation*.

It is useful to reflect on how we view mistakes in learning compared to mistakes in behaviour. Porter (2007) makes the distinction:

Academic errors	*Behavioural errors*
Errors are accidental	Errors are deliberate
Errors are inevitable	Errors should not happen
Errors signal the need for teaching	Errors should be punished
Students with learning difficulties need modified teaching	Students with behavioural difficulties need punishment

(Porter 2007: 18)

Not only are we inclined to see errors as inevitable in learning, we may even see them as essential. Indeed Ofsted commented in guidance to inspectors on making judgements based on samples of work: 'Pupils' work that is always marked right is almost certainly too easy' (Ofsted 2003b: 78).

We rarely apply a similar line of thinking in relation to behaviour. The interpretation of behavioural errors shifts the focus away from a teaching and learning agenda to one that emphasises the ascription of motive (i.e. 'deliberate'), dealing with aberrations, limiting and sanctioning.

Why is the separation of learning and behaviour a problem?

Some readers at this point may have accepted the academic argument that there is a separation between learning and behaviour, but may be questioning whether in practice this presents any problem. The problem lies in the priorities this separation creates and the implications of these priorities for the selection and evaluation of strategies and approaches. This issue is explored in Reflective Exercise 3.2.

Reflective Exercise 3.2

Think about the quote from the start of this chapter:

> Behaviour management: if you get it right, your life is easy, you're free to do what you're meant to do, which is of course to teach! (Cowley 2003: xiii).

Now consider this scenario:
The teacher has already noticed Lauren, a Year 6 pupil, turn round a number of times to talk to some pupils sitting behind her. She does it again and she, and those she is talking to, giggle loudly.
    Three different teachers respond to this situation:

Teacher A: 'Lauren, facing this way, thanks.'

Reflective Exercise 3.2 (continued)

Lauren dutifully faces the front and does not turn round again for the duration of the lesson.

Teacher B: 'Lauren, facing this way, thanks.'

Lauren briefly glances in the teacher's direction when she hears her name but continues turning round and talking. This pattern continues for the remainder of the lesson.

Teacher C: 'Lauren, stand up. (Lauren stands up) Would you like to tell the rest of the class what it is that's so interesting? (Lauren is silent) Come on, I'm sure it was fascinating. We're all waiting to hear.'

Lauren sits down sheepishly and remains quiet for the rest of the lesson. The rest of the class are noticeably quieter too.

Which of these teachers *got it right?*

If we are just interested in stopping behaviour then both A and C *got it right*. Hopefully however you feel at least a little uncomfortable with C, as, although it works at the level of stopping behaviour, in terms of the teacher's relationship with Lauren it has probably been detrimental. It has also modeled to Lauren and any observers that in a power relationship it is acceptable for the dominant party to embarrass the other in front of their peers. Teacher A used an appropriate strategy that we would fully endorse. The teacher *got it right*. Let's look now at Teacher B. It is the same strategy. Did they still *get it right*? If the definition of *getting it right* is that the teacher is free to teach, then presumably they did not as the behaviour still continued.

Two problems begin to emerge. Firstly, the limited evaluation criterion of stopping the behaviour makes the teacher a hostage to fortune because it is impossible to plan and predict every child's response in every situation. With no better criteria by which to judge the efficacy of the chosen strategy, Teacher B is in this position. Lauren did not comply, therefore was the strategy flawed? Would it be better to try Teacher C's approach next time? If we link judgements about the efficacy of a strategy simply to pupil compliance we inevitably embark on a futile, never-ending journey to find the perfect strategy because no strategy, whatever its good practice credentials, will be effective with every pupil. Secondly, as professionals, teachers cannot be satisfied with an *end justifies the means* outlook. They need to be able to select strategies based on ethicality and compatibility with the both the school's stated core values and principles and a wider national policy agenda that claims to be interested in pupils' emotional health and well-being.

The priority is not the acquisition of more strategies or climbing on board the next educational bandwagon, but rather developing the means by which to select effectively from the plethora already available and to make informed professional decisions about the contribution any new approach or package could potentially make to the development of behaviours necessary for learning.

'Be independent, use your initiative and take risks – but only when I say'

As Chapter 1 explored, teachers have been provided with a role in securing a range of holistic outcomes through *Every Child Matters* (Treasury Office 2003, DfES 2004a) and the development of transferable skills through the curriculum as well as retaining the more traditional role of transmission of subject knowledge.

This expanded remit introduces tensions and incongruities. Many teachers would for example endorse the importance of promoting collaborative learning. Corrie (2002) compared this priority with what she termed cooperative behaviour (Table 3.1).

Table 3.1 Collaborative learning and cooperative behaviours

Collaborative learning	Cooperative (with teacher) behaviour
• Interact with peers/adults to construct knowledge, often in small groups.	• Complete the teacher's set tasks by working independently.
• Interact with others by posing questions, negotiating meanings, problem solving, constructing creative solutions.	• Speak when the teacher gives permission. • Answer the teacher's questions, following the class rules for doing so.
• Use materials and equipment with others in creative ways.	• Follow teacher's instructions quickly, quietly and with little deviation expected.
• Are risk takers, who pursue their interests, and build on their strengths and competencies with others.	• Follow the rules and routines of the classroom.

(Based on Corrie, 2002: 33 (Fig. 2.2)).

Corrie (2002) sought to illustrate the potential for these two sets of behaviours to result in incongruent messages being received by certain pupils. The behaviours Corrie includes in the term 'cooperative' are essentially about *compliance*. There are some inherent contradictions when we manage for basic compliance and seek strategies to achieve this in isolation from our loftier priorities in relation to learning, involving the promotion of qualities such as independence, risk-taking, resourcefulness, resilience and persistence.

In classrooms we generally expect children in their role as a member of the group to be *responsive* to teacher instruction, whereas as individuals we want them to develop self-regulation and personal responsibility. When managing the group teachers need also to have due regard for the messages this gives to individuals. The previous example of the use of group detention (Scenario 3.1) clearly illustrates that those pupils who had taken personal responsibility to remain quiet were similarly punished as those who had not. In this scenario the individual's demonstration of personal responsibility was neither recognised, nor rewarded, which may also have a negative effect on their respect and regard for the teacher. The compliance of the group is afforded greater status than any individual's response and any sense of personal agency is reduced as it is not within any *individual's* power to change the outcome.

In areas of learning teachers continue to develop their expertise and government guidance, particularly through National Strategy materials, has supported them in this pursuit. The profession has moved over the years from a traditional transmission–based model of teaching where the teacher transmitted the knowledge they held, and allowed pupils to practice and refine their knowledge and skill (Corrie 2002), often through a very limited range of pedagogic approaches. Yet where behaviour is concerned, little of this sophistication is displayed. Rewards and sanctions are still the mainstay and the evaluation of the efficacy of any approach rarely extends beyond short-term, pragmatic consideration of whether it stops the behaviour. Walker *et al.* (1995) suggests that interventions for pupils with behavioural difficulties are rarely evidence-based. Rarely do teachers adopt strategies in relation to behaviour on the basis of evaluated effectiveness, instead basing strategy choice either on ideology, common sense, or school-based experience (Olsen and Cooper 2001). Whole-school policies provide a degree of coherence and consistency for the majority of pupils and ensure that teachers make decisions about the strategies they employ within an agreed framework. However, for those pupils who do not respond to such approaches, the picture that emerges is one in which a 'trial and error' use of existing behaviour management strategies is the dominant practice; rather than the development of approaches based on appropriate assessment, a coherent framework and a supporting knowledge base (Powell and Tod 2004).

At the heart of our concerns surrounding the management of behaviour in schools is the separation of behaviour and learning within the teacher's thinking and practice. This would seem to leave teachers in a position where they are able to achieve increasing confidence and competence in their main area of expertise (i.e. that of promoting learning) but continue to seek security in the area of behaviour management through a search for more and more strategies.

An alternative perspective

As outlined in the introduction to this book, the behaviour for learning conceptual framework emerged from an EPPI review conducted by Powell and Tod (2004). Powell and Tod's (2004) synthesis of material within the EPPI review led them to suggest that a linking of learning and behaviour, via the term 'learning behaviour', may reduce perceptions that 'promoting learning' and 'managing behaviour' are separate issues for teachers (McNally *et al.* 2005).

The behaviour for learning approach is underpinned by a conceptual framework depicted in Figure 3.1. In this diagram 'learning behaviour' is placed at the centre of the triangle in recognition that the 'promotion of learning behaviour' provides a shared aim and a purpose for the ever-widening group of people with responsibility for providing appropriate learning experiences for children and young people.

The triangle surrounding the term 'learning behaviour' symbolises that the development of this learning behaviour is influenced by social, emotional and cognitive factors – this triangle is referred to as the 'triangle of influence'.

This allows learning behaviour to be explored and addressed through the influences of the curriculum or task (cognitive), the feelings and interpretations of the learner (emotional) and the social context in which the learner is placed (social).

The arrows that surround the triangle represent the dynamic nature of learning and reflect the reciprocal influence that these emotional, social and cognitive factors have on the development of learning behaviour. The use of the terms 'engagement', 'access' and 'participation' in the diagram illustrate the processes that underpin learning and support inclusion in group settings. These processes are fostered by the development of a set of relationships, which provide the focus for assessment, intervention, and positive change. The circle surrounding the triangle of influence, entitled 'School Ethos', and the terms that lie outside this circle, are acknowledgement that the development of learning behaviours takes place in a context which itself exerts an influence.

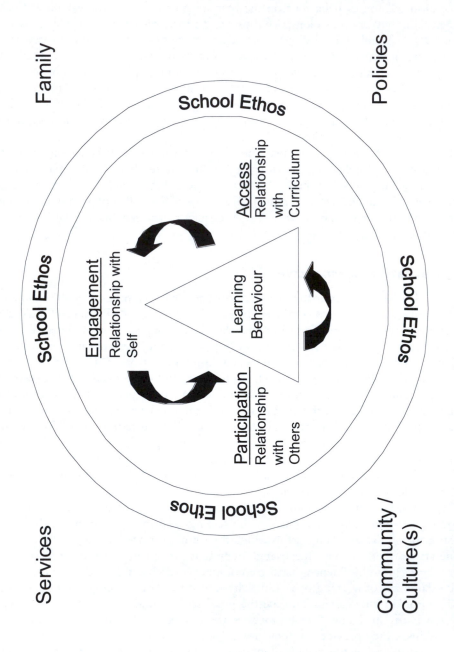

Figure 3./ The behaviour for learning conceptual framework.
Adapted from Powell and Tod 2004.

The overall purpose of the behaviour for learning conceptual framework is to encourage teachers to focus on what learning behaviour they need to develop in order to replace or reduce the problematic behaviour the pupil currently exhibits. The framework's acknowledgement that behaviours have a cognitive, social and emotional component provides a means by which teachers can select the most appropriate strategies and evaluate their efficacy.

What is 'learning behaviour'?

The use of the term 'learning behaviour' within the EPPI review contained a deliberate double meaning dependent on the emphasis placed on the two words. The first meaning, applying *learning* as verb, in the same way as we might talk about learning French or learning the piano, captured the idea that it is necessary for pupils to learn behaviour. In other words, we should not assume that pupils will enter the school or move to a new phase of their school careers with a specific set of behaviours already learned, but should recognise the role of teachers in seeking to create opportunities to develop these. The second meaning used the word *learning* as a descriptive term referring to a particular type of behaviour, in the same way as we might, for example, refer to a behaviour as *disruptive* or *off task*.

When using the behaviour for learning framework a focus is maintained on these two elements:

- that it is necessary for teachers to think consciously about how they create opportunities to develop learning behaviour;
- that there are particular behaviours necessary for learning.

Reflective Exercise 3.3

Think about what you have learned since the subtitle *What is 'learning behaviour'?* You have probably learned something from this and are now in a position where you could tell another person about the dual meaning of the phrase learning behaviour.

(a) What skills did you use to learn something from this text?
(b) Are there different or additional skills that you would have used if instead of reading it somebody was explaining this to you?
(c) Are there different or additional skills that you would have used if, instead of reading it, somebody was explaining this to you whilst you were in the company of others?
(d) What additional or different skills might be necessary if you were discussing with others what you had learned from the text?
(e) If you were unclear about the meaning of part of the text what skills would you draw on if you were reading it alone? Are these different to the skills you would use in the situations described in (b), (c) or (d)?

Reflective Exercise 3.3 allows you to consider many of the important elements that define learning behaviour. There are behaviours as a learner that you need to be able to perform in order to learn, and there are some differences between those required to learn individually and those required to learn within groups. As a well-developed learner, in your reflection you may have neglected certain elements because they have largely become automated: you learned them at a young age and you no longer have to give them any conscious thought. In situations (c) and (d), for example, a range of social skills are involved that as adult learners we take for granted. It is for this reason that the EPPI review retained a strong focus on learning in group settings, acknowledging that even when pupils are required to learn individually they typically do it in the company of others, and this requires certain behaviours that may be different to those employed if learning alone.

Within the reflective exercise the focus was on *skills*, but when thinking about learning behaviours this is only half of the picture. For example, what made you pick up this book in the first place and how did you keep yourself motivated to continue – even through any difficult bits or in the face of other competing demands? This introduces the notion that learning behaviour involves both skills and *dispositions* (Carr and Claxton 2002). This is discussed in more detail in Chapter 4.

The three relationships that underpin the promotion of learning behaviour

Classrooms are places characterised by individual teachers seeking to 'manage' groups of diverse individuals. Within this context, interactions, influences and outcomes are complex. The behaviour for learning framework seeks to unpick this complexity in order to allow teachers to make sense of and address problematic behaviour whilst maintaining a focus on learning.

When thinking about your own learning at school the factors that influenced your behaviour in class probably included:

- how interested and capable you were in the subject;
- how well you got on with your teacher and peers in your class;
- how you were feeling emotionally.

This reflects, in a simple way, that if we want to improve a pupil's learning behaviour, we could systematically seek to address one or more of these areas. For this reason the behaviour for learning framework focuses on three key relationships identified by Powell and Tod (2004). These are:

- relationship with curriculum;
- relationship with others;
- relationship with self.

The behaviour for learning conceptual framework uses the term 'relationship' deliberately to capture a sense of the reciprocity and interdependence we generally accept as present and necessary in positive social relationships. Emphasis is placed on the teacher consciously selecting strategies and approaches based on what these will do to the quality of the relationships.

The four functions of the behaviour for learning conceptual framework

The learning behaviour model has the potential to fulfil four main functions:

- *The selection function*

    - What is the *purpose* of this strategy I've read about, observed or been told about in relation to the development of *learning* behaviour?
    - Does this strategy maintain, enhance or risk undermining one or more of the three behaviour for learning relationships?

- *The assessment function*

    - What learning behaviours is it desirable to develop?
    - What are the pupil's strengths and weaknesses in the areas of 'relationship with self', 'relationship with others' or 'relationship with the curriculum'?
    - What is it feasible to do in the classroom context?

- *The planning function*

    - What learning behaviour do I need to promote?
    - Can this learning behaviour best be developed by strategies targeting 'relationship with self', 'relationship with others' or 'relationship with the curriculum'?
    - What can I feasibly do in the classroom context?
    - What additional support (if any) do I need? (e.g. teaching assistant, multi-agency involvement, increased parental involvement, etc.).

- *The evaluative function*

    - Did my strategy or intervention contribute to the promotion of learning behaviour(s) in the individual?
    - Did it contribute to the promotion of the learning behaviour(s) of the rest of the class?
    - Did it impact positively, or at least not compromise, the individual pupil's 'relationship with self', 'relationship with others' or 'relationship with the curriculum'?
    - Did it impact positively, or at least not compromise, the other pupils' 'relationship with self', 'relationship with others' or 'relationship with the curriculum'?
    - Was my intervention focused on the appropriate relationship(s)?

The model therefore has a number of linked applications. The 'selection' function is of particular significance in recognising that there is a plethora of information in existence already that relates to the field of behaviour management.

How might a behaviour for learning approach influence your practice?

Day-to-day practice

Within this categorisation of teacher activity we include the approaches the teacher uses to respond to misbehaviour and those used to acknowledge the required behaviour.

Traditionally the focus of strategies in both of these areas has been to secure a level of behaviour that maintains the level of order and discipline considered necessary by the teacher for learning to take place. In adopting the behaviour for learning approach the teacher is required to consider in the selection of strategies and approaches:

1 the effect on the development of learning behaviour;
2 the effect on the three relationships within the conceptual framework.

In both cases the effect of the strategy employed should not be negative. The teacher should be either able to identify a neutral or, ideally, positive effect. Because the behaviour for learning approach seeks to link learning and behaviour these two considerations are not just restricted to behaviour management strategies but to any practice within school, including curricular approaches, assessment procedures, SEN interventions and pastoral systems.

Longer-term planning

Some pupils present ongoing difficulties within the classroom. The behaviour for learning conceptual framework allows the teacher to plan proactively to develop the necessary learning behaviours in individuals. It is in this area of teacher activity that the versatility of the conceptual framework is revealed. We can define two broad levels of use: *core* and *extended*.

Core

The core use of the model makes use of a clear, sequential process:

- What is the learning behaviour(s) that I need to promote?
- In order to promote this, will it be most effective to work in the area of 'relationship with self', 'relationship with others' or 'relationship with the curriculum', or a combination?
- What strategies, interventions and approaches can I use to work in the selected area(s)?
- Can I do this on my own or do I need help?
- Is there a relationship area that I feel more confident/competent to work in initially?
- How will I know if I'm being successful in promoting this learning behaviour(s)?

Because the purpose is to promote learning behaviour, progress is always judged against this. The answer to the last question will always therefore be the same; the teacher is always looking for signs that the learning behaviour(s) is developing.

Extended use

For most pupils it will suffice to follow the sequence of activities outlined above. For a few pupils, who may have developed a *repertoire*, *range* and *frequency* of adaptive learning behaviours that cluster around particular relationships, we may need to focus on the *learning relationship* itself rather than on any one underlying learning behaviour. The sequence of decisions becomes:

- What is the relationship that I need to promote for learning in a group setting?

- Is it better for the individual pupil if I focus directly on the target relationship or seek to develop it via one of the other two?
- Is there a relationship area that I feel more confident/competent to work in initially?
- Which cluster of learning behaviours (or specific significant learning behaviour) do I need to promote in order to have a pervasive, positive effect on the relationship?
- What strategies, interventions and approaches can I use to promote the targeted relationship?
- What knowledge, skills and understanding does the pupil bring to this relationship?
- What knowledge, skills and understanding can I contribute to this relationship?
- Do I need any additional advice, guidance and support from within my school or from multi-agency partners?
- How will I know if I'm being successful in promoting the target relationship?

It is important to recognise the differences between the extended use of the behaviour for learning conceptual framework and its 'everyday' and 'core' applications. If applying the behaviour for learning conceptual framework in its 'everyday' and 'core' form, the teacher is attempting to promote positive learning behaviours *through* the three relationships. As previously stated, therefore, the success indicator will be the development of this learning behaviour. When applying the framework in its 'extended' form the teacher is seeking to promote positive relationships in one or more of the three areas as the route to improving a cluster of learning behaviours. The success indicators are improvements in the target relationship. Because we are dealing with a *relationship*, improvement would be assessed with reference to all participating members – the pupil, the teacher and peers. Therefore, when thinking about success indicators for improvement in the target relationship, we would look not just for changes in pupil's learning behaviours but also changes in what teachers and peers bring to the relationship.

Behaviour management: necessary but not sufficient?

We are not suggesting that teachers do not need a toolkit of strategies at their disposal to use within the classroom. We concur with the Professional Standards (TDA 2007) that require teachers to have a knowledge and understanding of a range of strategies to manage behaviour and know how to use and adapt them, as well as an ability to 'establish a clear framework for classroom discipline to manage learners' behaviour constructively and promote their self-control and independence' (TDA 2007: 12). Our view is that this is necessary, but not sufficient. This is illustrated through the following case study.

Case Study 3.1

A Year 9 teacher is taking a middle-ability English group. They are studying Shakespeare's *Much Ado About Nothing*. The first activity is based on a worksheet that requires pupils individually to use a dictionary to look up a set of words from a passage from the play and copy down the meanings. Once all the word have been found, the pupils then have to complete a cloze procedure, writing the words in the correct

(continued)

Case Study 3.1 (continued)

space in the passage. Most pupils get on with this. There are number of pupils who wander around the room for no obvious task-related purpose. Others talk about non-task related matters. A few call remarks across to others. The teacher circulates, stopping to help various pupils or address the more overt behaviours.

After about 20 minutes the teacher attempts to take some feedback from the group. Only one or two put their hands up and they are asked to answer. Most of the others are not listening. The situation is not helped by the table arrangement which has the pupils grouped in fours, leading to a significant number facing away from the teacher.

The teacher's professional integrity means that whilst she recognises that providing the pupils with structured activities like the cloze procedure can maintain behaviour at a reasonably acceptable level, pupils are missing out on so much that the subject has to offer. For this reason, she has valiantly, but with a little trepidation, planned a role-play exercise as the next activity.

Knowledge of some behaviour management strategies would undoubtedly be useful in this situation. An injection of some Bill Rogers (e.g. 2002) strategies into this teacher's repertoire would provide a way of directing the wanderers to their seats and of dealing with the extraneous chatter and calling out. A class reward scheme to which individuals contribute may provide the teacher with a tool with which to motivate pupils to behave. A more decisive use of the school's system of warnings, leading to sanctions, may help curb some of the excesses of some members of the group. Use of different questioning techniques may lead to pupils perceiving there to be a greater risk of being asked and consequently to greater attentiveness when the teacher attempts to take feedback.

We would want teachers to be thinking about these aspects of their practice, but we would also want them to have a clear reason as to *why* they are applying these techniques, which extends beyond simply freeing the teacher to teach. In the scenario, the teacher's trepidation was based on a realistic prediction, based on an assessment of pupils' performance in more structured activities such as the cloze procedure, that the role-play would be difficult. A behaviour management focus may encourage the pursuit of a robust enough set of techniques to *control* behaviour during the role-play. In contrast, a behaviour for learning focus places attention on the original assessment, looking at the learning behaviours exhibited in the structured activities in comparison to those necessary to take part in the planned role-play. The teacher needs to ask questions in relation to the learning behaviour:

- What can they do now unaided?
- What can they do now with support?
- What do they need to learn to do next?
- How can I, through my subject teaching, develop this learning behaviour?

This sort of thinking is regularly applied in relation to learning, but less so in relation to behaviour. Within this thinking process, behaviour management is relegated to its rightful place as a description of a particular set of techniques *integrated within* the extensive range of techniques teachers use to promote learning.

Our concern is that, for some teachers, the emphasis in educational discourse on behaviour management has led to the mistaken belief that a bigger toolkit of strategies or a new framework in the form of the latest package on the market will allow them to anticipate and prepare for the entire range of pupil responses they will experience in the classroom. In many ways the Elton Report's (DES 1989) term, 'group management', was rather better in capturing the notion that when pupils are learning together this needs to be managed. Conceivably, as well as directing and correcting, this could encompass questioning techniques used, the drawing out of more reticent pupils and the containing of the more dominant, and the offering of well-timed encouragement if group motivation flags. The teacher's role in relation to pupils could be likened to that of a conductor and an orchestra.

We believe that even in situations where it is necessary to stop or limit behaviour, this can be done with a focus on learning behaviour. There will be occasions when pupils talk out of turn, distract or interfere with others, fail to comply with instructions, answer back and engage in other behaviours identified by the Elton Report (DES 1989) as low-level disruption. Teachers undoubtedly need to be familiar with and skilled at using a range of strategies to address these issues as part of their repertoire to facilitate learning in group settings.

The strength of the behaviour for learning conceptual framework is that it does not seek to prescribe a range of strategies to respond to such behaviours, rather it encourages teachers to harness the plethora of strategies currently available, but always keeping a critical eye on the two consistent questions:

- Does the strategy have the potential to promote, or at least not undermine the promotion of learning behaviour?
- Does the strategy have the potential to promote, or at least not undermine the three relationships that underpin the development of learning behaviour?

Even in an immediate management situation, the teacher should aspire through their verbal and non-verbal communication to ensure that they do not do anything that undermines the three relationships or promote what we might term a 'negative' learning behaviour. Strategies, for example, that are intended to cause fear or embarrassment, though superficially working at the level of the class being quiet, may promote alienation, resentment, reticence, an unwillingness to take risks in learning and a preoccupation with remaining unnoticed by the teacher. A key feature of much of advice in texts such as Hook and Vass (2002) and Rogers (1997, 2002) is a focus on language that maintains the relationship with others, both in terms of the teacher's relationship with the child even at the point of correction and the child's relationship with their peers. The language encouraged is respectful and focused upon the behaviour that infringes the clear and fair rules rather than upon the character of the individual pupil. As well as minimising the risk of damage to the relationship between the pupil and the teacher, it also relates to the pupil's relationship with self. If we use verbal 'put downs' or use language that labels the individual rather than the behaviour we risk impacting negatively on this.

We have considered what we might term 'positive correction' so far but the other element of behaviour management is 'positive reinforcement'. In this area too, we need to consider how we are promoting learning behaviour or the three relationships that underpin its development. If for example a reward system places an emphasis on competition between pupils by rewarding only the child who gains most gold stars over a period of time, it may motivate individuals but do little to promote the learning behaviour of collaboration as it transforms peers into rivals. How and when we praise and reward is an important consideration in the promotion of learning behaviour.

Table 3.2 Key differences between positive behaviour management and behaviour for learning

Positive behaviour management	Behaviour for learning
'Positive behaviour management' is a generic term for a range of strategies and approaches that are delivered in a particular way. Positive behaviour management is well known and used in many schools.	Behaviour for learning is based on a conceptual framework developed from an EPPI review (Powell and Tod 2004) and as such is relatively new.
In practice positive behaviour management strategies discussed in this book – *if* applied in the spirit and manner intended by their authors – are likely to be compatible with behaviour for learning principles.	Behaviour for learning encourages the use of a range of existing positive behaviour management strategies but requires that they are evaluated against the extent to which they promote learning behaviour.
Positive behaviour management does not *necessarily* demand a concern with anything other than achieving compliance – albeit through positive means.	Whilst accepting that compliance may be necessary, behaviour for learning explicitly demands the systematic evaluation against the development of learning behaviour.
Positive behaviour management often evaluates in terms of reduction or absence of behaviour (e.g. less calling out).	Behaviour for learning always evaluates in terms of an increase or presence of behaviour.
Positive behaviour management has regard for, but is not based upon, recognition of the social, emotional and cognitive aspects of learning.	The promotion of learning behaviour depends on the maintenance and development of three key *relationships* reflecting the social, emotional and cognitive aspects involved in learning.
Positive behaviour management places emphasis on preserving positive interactions with pupils through strategy and language use.	Behaviour for learning places emphasis on the need to balance the three key relationships and to avoid promoting any one of these to the detriment of another.
Positive behaviour management places value on a repertoire of good practice strategies.	Behaviour for learning endorses the need for a toolkit of strategies but explicitly acknowledges that no one set of strategies will 'work' for all pupils. Individuals inevitably experience and interpret the strategy in different ways – whatever its good practice credentials. A teacher using the behaviour for learning approach is constantly alert to this.

Is the behaviour for learning approach just another version of 'positive behaviour management'?

'Positive behaviour management' is a generic phrase used to describe a range of strategies and approaches that are delivered in a particular way. Typically the teacher frames any corrections positively and places emphasis on recognising and acknowledging 'good' behaviour. Though the central purpose is usually the management of behaviour there is also likely to be an accompanying intention to achieve this without damage to the teacher–pupil relationship or to the pupil's emotional well being. From this description it should be clear that there is a relationship between 'positive behaviour management' and the behaviour for learning approach, but they are not the same. It is perhaps easiest to understand this relationship if we think about positive behaviour management strategies as *one* of a range of tools available to support the teacher in promoting learning behaviour.

Table 3.2 highlights the distinctions between the types of positive behaviour management approaches (e.g. Hook and Vass 2002, Rogers 2002) that many readers will already be familiar with and behaviour for learning.

In highlighting these distinctions there is no intention to criticise or devalue either the term 'positive behaviour management' or the practices that ensue from this perspective. Quite to the contrary, we fully endorse this approach. It is important however for readers to understand the distinctions between positive behaviour management and behaviour for learning if they are to appreciate the conceptual framework within this book as more than re-branding.

The conceptual framework that is central to the behaviour for learning approach allows teachers to explore and understand the determinants of learning behaviour and make sense of, and evaluate, the efficacy of the plethora of strategies available.

We are not advocating that the phrase 'behaviour management' is abandoned, indeed we will use it on occasions within this book. Instead we are encouraging readers to think more about the extent to which their management of behaviour is integrated into their promotion of learning.

Whilst we hope readers do increasingly think and talk in terms of learning behaviour and behaviour for learning, we would encourage more than a superficial re-branding. It requires a conceptual shift rather than just the replacement of any reference to behaviour management or managing behaviour in policy or teacher language with the term behaviour for learning.

Planning for the individual using the behaviour for learning conceptual framework

The following case study (Table 3.3) provides an example of the line of thinking about the promotion of learning within the context of behaviour management. This thinking takes us from an initial focus on reducing disruptive behaviour to one which seeks to promote more positive learning behaviours. Emphasis is placed on the behaviour for learning relationships as experienced by the pupil. This allows us to identify and select strategies to personalise a response, based on an awareness of the individual's level of social, emotional and cognitive development.

Table 3.3 Case study with a behaviour for learning commentary

Pen Picture: Steven, Year 6 (age 11)	Behaviour for learning commentary
Steven regularly distracts others. This often takes the form of irritating pieces of behaviour such as poking others, taking equipment without asking, and trying to talk to other pupils when they are engaged in an activity and clearly don't want to be interrupted. He can also disrupt teacher inputs to the class by calling out. The comments that he calls out are usually related to the subject but their frequency is disruptive and irritating to others. Some of the other pupils have taken to saying 'Shut up, Steven' in these and other situations when his behaviour becomes irritating. Steven often takes this as an affront and will either answer the pupil back aggressively or complain loudly, e.g. 'S/he told me to shut up.' As well as distracting others, he is easily distracted and may play with objects such as rubbers or sharpeners or other small items.	• Frequency is an issue and is impacting negatively on his relationship with others. • Is he choosing not to behave or does he not have the necessary behaviour in his repertoire? • What is the purpose of the behaviour for him?
Verbally Steven is very able – in fact some staff say he has 'the gift of the gab' in reference to the long winded excuses he uses to try to talk himself out of the frequent trouble he gets into. On a one-to-one basis some staff describe him as 'charming'.	• He does seem to be able to form relationships with some others. • Do I need to know more about who and under what conditions?
He seldom appears totally absorbed in a lesson and doesn't appear to have a favourite subject. He shows some interest in practical Science activities, but finds it difficult to work with others as he tries to dominate.	• This could point to a relationship with the curriculum issue.
When he does receive praise for a good piece of work it seems that he deliberately then spoils it, either by throwing it away, scribbling on it or rubbing and crossing out large chunks of what he has done. He shows a similar reaction when praised for behaviour – it is as though he wants to reject any positive recognition.	• The rejection of praise could point to a relationship with self issue.
He is good at recalling facts verbally but is slow to produce written work. The reasons for this seem to be because he distracts himself and others, as when made to complete work on his own at break time he can do it quickly and to a reasonable standard.	• Verbal recall of facts is a useful learning behaviour. • He can do the work alone – this could be a relationship with peers issue.
Organisationally he is chaotic – regularly losing things, not having the right equipment to hand and forgetting/ignoring the standard conventions for setting out work. His parents report that he is much the same at home – very *laissez-faire* in his attitude, not really taking care of his possessions or taking any responsibility for organising himself.	• Learning behaviour is not evident in the area of personal organisation. • The problem doesn't only occur in one context – so it suggests he lacks the skills. • Are we sure about the will?

Table 3.3 (continued)

Pen Picture: Steven, Year 6 (age 11)	Behaviour for learning commentary
Steven is good at P.E. and most games, which attracts some admiration from his peers. However he is not a 'team player', so although his prowess impresses others they soon become irritated with him.	• His relationship with one particular curriculum area is good, but his relationship with other pupils is an issue.
Socially it is difficult to make a judgement about his popularity amongst his peers. He is able to get others to join in conversations, often at inappropriate times but he doesn't seem to have any close friends and often appears isolated at break times. He appears to like the idea of having one or two best friends but these friendships rarely last as he cannot accept that his 'best' friends might also want to associate with others or pursue other interests. This has led to some major 'fall-outs', including physical altercations. The most notable occasion was last term when he was excluded for three days after giving another pupil a black eye.	• This presents as a relationship with others issue, but we would need to be aware that this could also indicate an underlying relationship with self issue. • The learning behaviours needed to mix with others AND protect self emotionally are not evident.

From the thinking and analysis we can progress to synthesis. The analysis appears to indicate that:

- He has some relevant learning behaviours:

  - good verbal memory
  - good grasp of language
  - ability to defend his position verbally and avoid punishment
  - listening (the comments he calls out are usually subject-related)
  - initiates social interaction.

- He does not have sufficiently well-developed learning behaviours in the area of:

  - personal organisation
  - peer relationships, though he is marginally better with adults
  - collaborative working
  - self-regulation
  - empathy
  - ignoring distractions
  - responding to criticism from peers
  - accepting praise.

- He has skills that are only evident in some contexts:

  - relating to adults
  - completion of work when alone.

Let's assume that from this analysis we decide that personal organisation is the issue that we want to prioritise. Without the analysis we might simply move into a system of rewards for bringing the right equipment and some form of consequence when it is forgotten. The analysis and synthesis leads us to a more personalised, sophisticated response that is planned in relation to social, emotional and cognitive relationships.

The key issue emerging is that aged 11, and with secondary transfer looming, Steven is using insufficient planning in many aspects of his life. The area of difficulty does not just relate to what we might term *cognitive* planning; there are issues to address in relation to *emotional* and *social* planning. The overall aim is to provide him with a range of strategies for planning at which he can succeed. He can then experience the benefits of this and in so doing increase his motivation to take responsibility for his own planning. Based on the analysis and synthesis we could implement the following strategies in the three areas.

Cognitive planning (relates to 'relationship with curriculum')

- The use of vegetable racks labelled with days of the week at home in which he can place the items he needs for the next day – this could be developed into a written planner in preparation for secondary transfer.
- Opportunities to state to an adult the equipment he needs for the task in advance, with a view to promoting 'out loud' self-talk at first and moving towards silent self-talk.
- Provide a personal timetable, which could be visual, to allow self-monitoring.
- Use of rule-reminders by teachers in response to calling out.
- A personal reminder of rules for asking for help or making a contribution could be attached to his desk.
- Provide opportunities to work with peers on a curriculum-based task that makes limited social and emotional demands, e.g. a collaborative Science activity with teacher-defined roles for each member of the group.

Emotional planning (relates to 'relationship with self')

- *Planning and rehearsing his response to criticism*
  Rehearsal can be depersonalised initially through the use of role-play, puppets and stories. The purpose of this strategy is designed to develop a disposition that allows for criticism to be an accepted, though not always pleasant, part of human interaction. We cannot seek to avoid it forever but what matters is our response to it.
- *Planning and rehearsing his response to praise*
  Rehearsal can be depersonalised initially through the use of role-play, puppets and stories.
- *Planning for reward and failure*
  The traditional reward system is unlikely to be effective as Steven already appears to have a fear of failure. For him a reward based on total success may simply represent another potential source of failure. Therefore in looking at the vegetable rack strategy to target personal organisation, our emphasis would not be on rewarding him for bringing the right equipment, but for telling us when the system has worked and when it didn't. In this way we are giving him the message that there is information in failure that can positively inform future learning.

Social planning (relates to 'relationship with others')

- Use role play as a means to rehearse social situations that require communication with others. The purpose is to develop and practice the *skills* involved in communication in a safe social context.
- Use comic strip conversations (Gray 1994) to aid understanding of social situations. Typically this involves drawings of stick people to depict a particular social situation. In Steven's case this might be when a friend wants to play a game with someone else. Taking this example, stick people would be drawn to represent Steven and the friend. Speech bubbles and thought bubbles would then be used to distinguish between what the friend actually says and what Steven *believes* they might be thinking. Steven's own responses in this social situation can also be explored. In his speech bubble there might be a verbally aggressive phrase, but in his thought bubble there might be phrases that indicate that he feels rejected or vulnerable.

Although these strategies are designed with Steven in mind, the planning involving visual timetables, rule reminders and planners would be appropriate for the whole group. Additionally, given the emotional and social overlap in strategies, aspects of the SEAL programme (DfES 2005c) may prove useful. The difference for Steven is in the way his response is assessed through the development of appropriate learning behaviours. He may also require a more individualised approach involving discussion as to the purpose behind the strategies and the contribution expected from him.

Summary

The behaviour for learning conceptual framework outlined in this chapter is intended to encourage teachers and trainees to focus on the purpose and *outcomes* of behaviour management. As such it encourages a shift in thinking away from a concern with stopping unwanted behaviour towards the promotion of effective learning behaviours.

The framework acknowledges the complexity inherent within definitions of learning and its associated cognitive, affective and social behaviours. The framework has sought to address this complexity through identifying and addressing the three core relationships relevant to the development of learning behaviours in school settings. Each relationship impacts on the other and the use of an apparently simple visual model, in some ways, belies the complexity and dynamism of those relationships. Learning is clearly not fragmented, as described by the conceptual framework, but the application of this model is intended to strengthen the development of learning behaviours in school settings.

This chapter has been designed to provide the reader with a basic grounding in the behaviour for learning approach. The key elements of the conceptual framework within this chapter are explored in more detail in the next four chapters.

Chapter 4

Learning behaviours

Introduction

As described in the previous chapter, this book is based on a conceptual framework (Powell and Tod 2004) that links learning and behaviour, via the term 'learning behaviour'. The use of this term is deliberate in that it seeks to promote the view that 'promoting learning' and 'managing behaviour' should not be seen as separate issues for teachers. This is important given that teachers as a profession normally regard the promotion of learning as their core aim. How 'behaviour' fits with that aim is of crucial importance, with some viewing the *control* of behaviour as a necessary prerequisite for school learning to occur, while others view the curriculum and classroom as a medium through which children and young people develop social skills and individual responsibility needed for life-long learning.

The terms 'learning behaviour' and 'behaviour for learning' have now slipped almost effortlessly into educational discourse. For example the Steer Report (DfES 2005a) incorporated the term 'learning behaviour' into its title, Key Stage 3 National Strategy training materials (DfES 2003c) identified a set of 'behaviours for learning' and the TDA sponsored an initial teacher education professional resource network (IPRN) entitled *Behaviour4Learning*. The phrase 'learning behaviour' itself is not new and has been used previously by writers such as Day and Libertini (1992), Norwich (1994) and Norwich and Rovoli (1993). It is important to note therefore that the juxtaposition of the terms 'learning' and 'behaviour' does not necessarily imply some agreed meaning or carry the same implications for practice. For example, Elkin (2006) reports on a particular school's approach to behaviour management that bears the title *Behaviour for Learning* but has no link with the conceptual framework that underpins this book.

This chapter is concerned with both the concept and development of learning behaviour as used in the behaviour for learning conceptual framework described in Chapter 3. This allows learning behaviour to be explored and addressed through the influences of the curriculum or task (cognitive), the feelings and interpretations of the learner (emotional), and the social context in which the learner is placed (social). The next section explores what we understand by the term 'learning behaviour'.

What are learning behaviours?

The EPPI review (Powell and Tod 2004) identified a set of learning behaviours drawn from the TTA QTS standards (2002) that could help teachers identify a set of purposes and/or activities relevant to all pupils and curriculum areas.

These were:

- engagement
- collaboration
- participation
- communication
- motivation
- independent activity
- responsiveness
- self-regard
- self-esteem
- responsibility.

The purpose of this list was to provide examples that illustrated three underpinning principles behind the model, rather than to attempt to prescribe or establish a definitive set of learning behaviours. These principles are:

- Learning behaviour(s) transcends curriculum areas, age and stages of development and arguably should be of life-long relevance to the learner. As such their identification and development focus on the needs of the individual which may be different to those prescribed by policy makers.
- The learning behaviour is the focus for development and should be used to evaluate the effectiveness of ongoing teaching and interventions.
- Learning behaviours recognise the social, emotional and cognitive components of development and are underpinned by a set of relationships – the relationship with self, the relationship with others, and the relationship with the curriculum and/or task.

Although it makes sense for teachers to synthesise their thinking and practice in relation to promoting learning and managing behaviour, we have found that there is a problem when we ask teachers what learning behaviours they would like to promote. Reflective Exercise 4.1 provides the opportunity to attempt to identify some learning behaviours.

Reflective Exercise 4.1

You have a pupil in your class who exhibits the following behaviours:	What learning behaviour do you want to promote?
He is very vocal and disruptive in class which frequently leads to him being sent out.	
He is regularly involved in playground incidents for which he blames other pupils.	
He presents as moody and unpredictable.	

(continued)

Reflective Exercise 4.1 (continued)

You have a pupil in your class who exhibits the following behaviours:	*What learning behaviour do you want to promote?*
He reacts negatively to praise.	
He rips up his work and throws it away.	
He makes negative self-reference statements – frequently starts by saying 'I can't do this'.	
He seeks frequent, non-specific support and reassurance.	
He avoids failure and is very sensitive to any perceived criticism.	

In thinking about your response to Reflective Exercise 4.1, it is interesting to note how long it took. It does seem to be much easier for teachers to identify behaviours that they do not want than those they want to promote. Behaviour management has encouraged a language that is focused towards defining and reducing unwanted behaviours. Teachers therefore may have had limited practice and experience in thinking about what learning behaviours are needed across contexts to improve learning and behaviour in the group setting of the classroom. In this chapter we aim to identify some descriptors from the literature so that readers have a resource from which they can select the most appropriate learning behaviours to promote. Would Reflective Exercise 4.1 have been easier if you knew the pupil? If so, why do you think this is?

The learning behaviours identified from a range of sources in this chapter lack the precision of the measurable competencies that often characterise assessment in educational contexts. This is understandable if learning behaviours are viewed as *unique* individual responses to the experiences and opportunities provided in the *group* settings of the school and classroom. For example if we have a pupil in the class who we feel has 'low self-esteem' we may seek to improve this situation. Although we can identify self-esteem as a focus for effort we may not be able to explicitly state what learning behaviour we expect to see, simply because how an individual demonstrates self-esteem will depend on the context and their individual characteristics. For this reason we do not seek to pre-define learning behaviours in any rigid way, but we do need to identify and share with the pupil the aspects of their learning they need to develop in order that they can build positive relationships with the curriculum, with self and with others. Once learning behaviour(s) appropriate for the individual have been identified and communicated they provide the indicator(s) against which strategy use will be evaluated. The deliberate lack of prescription leaves open the option for teachers to consider, and select from, the range of choices that are available within the literature and policy that is concerned with learning and behaviour in school contexts.

Examples of learning behaviour from government documentation and guidance

The QCA (2001) document *Supporting School Improvement: Emotional and Behavioural Development* emerged from a piece of QCA-commissioned research carried out by the University of Birmingham School of Education Assessment Research Unit. The project was aimed at developing criteria that schools might use for measuring pupils' emotional and behavioural development. Drawing on a range of existing criteria used throughout Local Authorities in England, the criteria developed by the Birmingham team addressed three distinct aspects of behaviour:

- learning behaviour
- conduct behaviour
- emotional behaviour.

The QCA (2001) guidance outlined five criteria (Table 4.1) for each aspect supported by descriptors and a record sheet.

Table 4.1 Criteria for measuring emotional and behavioural development (QCA 2001)

Learning behaviour	Conduct behaviour	Emotional behaviour
1 Is attentive and has an interest in schoolwork	1 Behaves respectfully towards staff	1 Has empathy
2 Has good learning organisation	2 Shows respect to other pupils	2 Is socially aware
3 Is an effective communicator	3 Only interrupts and seeks attention appropriately	3 Is happy
4 Works efficiently in a group	4 Is physically peaceable	4 Is confident
5 Seeks help where necessary	5 Respects property	5 Is emotionally stable and shows good self-control

The QCA (2001) expanded on each of the three areas:

Learning behaviour
- *Is attentive and has an interest in schoolwork* e.g. is not easily distracted, completes work, keeps on task and concentrates, has good motivation, shows interest, enjoys schoolwork.
- *Good learning organisation* e.g. works systematically, at a reasonable pace, knows when to move on to the next activity or stage, can make choices, is organised.
- *Is an effective communicator* e.g. speech is coherent, thinks before answering.
- *Works efficiently in a group* e.g. takes part in discussions, contributes readily to group tasks, listens well in groups, and works collaboratively.
- *Seeks help where necessary* e.g. can work independently until there is a problem that cannot be solved without the teacher's intervention.

Conduct behaviour
- *Behaves respectfully towards staff* e.g. respects staff and answers them politely, does not interrupt or deliberately annoy, does not show verbal aggression.

- *Shows respect to other pupils* e.g. interacts with other pupils politely and thoughtfully, does not tease, call names, swear, use psychological intimidation.
- *Only interrupts and seeks attention appropriately* e.g. behaves in ways warranted by the classroom activity, does not disrupt unnecessarily, or distract or interfere with others, does not pass notes, talk when others are talking, does not seek unwarranted attention.
- *Is physically peaceable* e.g. is not physically aggressive, avoids fights, is pleasant to other pupils, is not cruel or spiteful, does not strike out in temper.
- *Respects property* e.g. values and looks after property, does not damage or destroy property, does not steal.

Emotional behaviour
- *Has empathy* e.g. is tolerant of others, shows understanding and sympathy, is considerate.
- *Is socially aware* e.g. interacts appropriately with others, is not a loner or isolated, reads social situations well.
- *Is happy* e.g. has fun when appropriate, smiles, laughs, is cheerful, is not tearful or depressed.
- *Is confident* e.g. is not anxious, has high self-esteem, is relaxed, does not fear failure, is not shy, is not afraid of new things, is robust.
- *Is emotionally stable and shows self-control* e.g. moods remain relatively stable, does not have frequent mood swings, is patient, is not easily flustered, is not touchy.

(QCA 2001: 10–11)

This allocation of behaviour into three areas is interesting in that it resonates with the behaviour for learning conceptual framework that seeks to address the development of social, cognitive and emotional learning behaviours. If we scrutinise the QCA lists closely it is apparent that they include both *skills* (e.g. 'good learning organisation') and *dispositions* (e.g. 'is confident'). This is an important distinction and one that we explore later in this chapter.

Within the Key Stage 3 National Strategy Behaviour and Attendance Core Day 1 (DfES 2003c) materials suggest a range of 'behaviours for learning'. These are shown in Table 4.2.

Table 4.2 Suggested behaviours for learning

Positive interaction staff/pupil	Listening to each other Responding to requests Speaking politely Asking questions Showing concern and understanding Following instructions and requests
Sensible use of resources	Bringing correct material to class Sharing equipment Looking after own/others property Keeping desk/classroom tidy
Appropriate use of language	Speaking politely Using proper names Waiting turn to speak

Table 4.2 (continued)

Appropriate use of language (continued)	Listening to ideas of others without negative comment Giving way in an argument Accepting ideas and suggestions of others and act upon them Tone of voice congruent with body language Appropriate tone of voice for task
Acceptance of new challenges	Setting appropriate goals Taking risks Trying new things Asking for help Using peer support Making mistakes and moving on Self-aware – knowing how and when to get help
Able to work independently	Correct equipment for tasks Good time-keeping Attention focused on task Ignoring distractions Persistent Monitoring own progress

© Crown copyright [2003] Department for Education and Skills (DfES 2003c).

Effective Lessons and Behaviour for Learning (DfES 2004d) also used the terms 'learning behaviour' and 'behaviour for learning', stating 'Specific learning behaviours need to be taught, reinforced and reviewed in the same way as any other skill we expect children to master' (DfES 2004d: 5).

However, the document did not dwell on what these learning behaviours might be, only providing an indication through some examples in a staff development activity. These were:

- sharing space;
- hands up;
- listening to each other;
- cooperating in a group;
- waiting turn.

(DfES 2004d: 10)

The staff–development activity itself drew teachers' attention to the need to consider the learning behaviours necessary at different stages of a lesson (Figure 4.1).

The document *Behaviour in the Classroom: a Course for Newly Qualified Teachers* (DfES 2004e) treats 'behaviour for learning' and 'learning behaviour' in a similar manner. Within these course materials facilitators are advised to use the following points to elaborate on the term 'learning behaviour':

- 'Learning behaviours' is a positive description. It tells the children what you do want them to do and why this will help them to learn rather than focusing on what you don't want.
- It puts value on behaving in ways which enable and maximise learning.

- Depending on the child, effective learning behaviours can range from high-level listening or collaborative learning skills to remaining on your seat for two minutes.
- The concept is one which is relevant to all children.

(DfES 2004e: 96)

Further indicators are given within the document of the types of learning behaviours it is desirable to promote. Positives examples including 'putting hand up to speak' and 'sticking with tasks even when they are difficult' are contrasted with 'shouting out' and 'giving up easily' (DfES 2004e: 96). This set of materials also reinforces the idea of identifying the learning behaviours necessary at different points in the lesson, using the identical exercise (see Figure 4.1) as *Effective Lessons and Behaviour for Learning* (DfES 2004d).

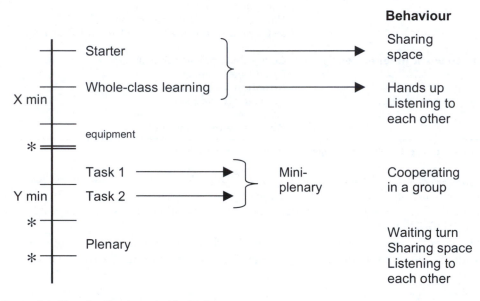

Figure 4.1 Planning for learning behaviour.
© Crown copyright [2004] Department for Education and Skills (DfES 2004d: 99).

In addition to the examples of government documents outlined that have explicitly used the terminology of 'behaviour for learning' and 'learning behaviour', a number of others have referred to skills and dispositions that it is thought desirable to develop in individuals in order to improve more holistic outcomes from learning across a range of contexts. These descriptors have not been referred to as learning behaviours but suggest directions and purposes that could support teachers to identify which particular learning behaviours they need to promote. The DoH/DfES (2004) noted, for example, in their guidance intended to raise pupil attainment, promote social inclusion and reduce health inequalities, that the following behaviours contribute to the development of health and well-being:

- being an effective and successful learner;
- making and sustaining friendships;
- dealing with and resolving conflict effectively and fairly;
- being able to solve problems with others and alone;

- managing strong feelings such as frustration, anger and anxiety;
- recovering from setbacks and persisting in the face of difficulties;
- working and playing cooperatively;
- competing fairly and losing with dignity and respect for competitors;
- recognising and standing up for your rights and the rights of others;
- understanding and valuing the differences between people and respecting the right of others to have beliefs and values different from your own.

(DoH/DfES 2004: 7)

In contrast to these more social and emotionally relevant behaviours, the DfES (2005e), in thinking about learning for 14–19-year-olds, produced a list that seems very much linked to cognitive activity and traditional 'attainment', albeit within the context of developments for a curriculum that includes an applied vocational focus. The key thinking and learning skills identified in the DfES White Paper *14–19 Education and Skills* (DfES 2005e) can be readily framed as learning behaviours. These are:

- enquiry: can ask relevant questions, can plan and test conclusions;
- creative thinking: can suggest hypotheses and imaginatively challenging ideas;
- information processing: can locate and classify information;
- reasoning: can explain opinions, actions and decisions, and can use deduction;
- evaluation: can assess evidence, judging against criteria and values.

(based on DfES 2005e: 41)

This list of what are termed 'thinking skills' has also previously been included in the National Curriculum Handbooks (DfEE/QCA 1999a, 1999b).

'Personal skills' advocated within *14–19 Education and Skills* (DfES 2005e) may also provide teachers with sources for the development of learning behaviour. They include:

- communication: can communicate through personal presentation for a range of audiences;
- diligence, reliability and capability to improve: is willing to learn and shows organisation and initiative;
- working with others: can negotiate, demonstrates leadership and has an awareness of others' needs;
- moral and ethical awareness: can distinguish between right and wrong, and is prepared to take responsibility within family and community and for achieving their own potential.

(based on DfES 2005e: 41)

Within the *Training and Development Guidance for Teachers of Diplomas*, it is stated that:

as they (students) progress through their learning pathway they will develop a broad range of skills that they need for life, learning and work. These skills include personal, learning and thinking skills (PLTS) and functional skills, move (*sic*) beyond applied or technical competence. They include their ability to solve problems, to communicate effectively and to work productively with others.

(TDA LLUK 2007: 15)

An emphasis is placed within this programme on personalised learning, the principles of which include:

- the systematic and explicit development of learning skills and strategies across the curriculum;
- its role in enabling learners to take responsibility for their own learning;
- its value in equipping learners to transfer their learning to different contexts;
- meeting individual learner needs and ensuring an inclusive provision.

(TDA LLUK 2007: 3)

The benefits are described as:

- acknowledging and valuing the learner voice;
- enabling learners to maximise their potential regardless of abilities or background;
- promoting learner engagement and achievement;
- increasing learner confidence and self-esteem and their ability to make a positive contribution in all they do.

(TDA LLUK 2007: 6)

The guidance acknowledges that teachers and tutors delivering this programme will promote the development of a range of learning behaviours that support teaching and learning within and between the classroom, workshop and workplace.

Issues relating to learning behaviours that come from government guidance

As can be seen, learning behaviours have particular purposes within government documents to support particular initiatives such as addressing mental health issues, improving education for work, and addressing issues of citizenship and social cohesion. In so doing they are somewhat aspirational and although promoted in educational contexts, may not be easily achievable for certain pupils – including some of those whom policy-makers most hoped to positively influence.

The lists from QCA (2001) and DfES (2003c) are to be commended for their focus on *required* rather than *unwanted* behaviours. They are expressed in terms of the behaviours that we *do* want pupils to demonstrate rather than dwelling on behaviours that we want to stop. Interestingly, however, QCA (2001) did note that teachers were more confident in rating pupils' performance against criteria when descriptions of undesirable behaviours were also provided. The question these behaviours raise however is whether the focus is upon behaviours necessary for the learner or the school. Thomas (2005) paraphrasing Miller (1993) comments:

A moment's thought discloses that the things which children habitually do wrong at school … concern the school's need to regulate time (punishing tardiness and truancy), activity (punishing lack of effort or overactivity), speech (punishing chatter or insolence) and the body (punishing hairstyles, clothes, use of make-up or tidiness of the individual).

(Thomas 2005: 66)

Whilst the use of the term 'punishment' is somewhat emotive out of Thomas' original context which was drawing, via Miller (1993), on the writings of French philosopher Michel Foucault, the central message is that schools as large organisations need ways of keeping order. We would not want to disagree with this point: institutions that require the collecting together of groups of 20 or 30 in classes, and perhaps hundreds in assemblies, dining halls and playgrounds, need to be able to regulate space and control activity (Thomas 2005). The need though, when thinking about defining learning behaviours, is to balance what are predominantly the behaviours necessary for the smooth running of the organisation and the behaviours necessary for learning that are intrinsically valuable to the learner. If we look for example at *Sensible Use of Resources* from the Key Stage 3 *National Strategy Document* (DfES 2003c) we could ask ourselves whether bringing correct materials to class, sharing equipment, looking after one's own/others' property and keeping the desk/classroom tidy, are essential behaviours for learning or a reflection of a school's organisational needs. We would ultimately need to question the extent to which these behaviours do adhere to the principle of transcending curriculum areas, age and stages of development, and have life-long relevance to the learner.

Balance though is the crucial element in this consideration. Because a learning behaviour appears to reflect a school's organisational need does not mean it does not have value to the individual. To pursue the example of bringing the correct equipment to class, this does not have value in itself or ensure that learning will happen, but arguably it is an element of *responsibility* in terms of the individual pupil getting themselves organised rather than relying on others. Therefore if the teacher decides to teach the pupil what equipment they need to have out, provides a checklist as a reminder and then rewards them when they have this equipment it could be argued that this is promoting *responsibility* or possibly *independence*. This raises the important issue of purpose. Having the right equipment out should not be seen as the end goal and valuable in itself; the purpose is the promotion of *responsibility* or *independence*. Evidence of developing *responsibility* or *independence* then becomes the evaluation criteria, not simply whether the pupil has the right equipment out, though this may be an indicator.

Other sources of learning behaviour

The EPPI review (Powell and Tod 2004) did not attempt to be prescriptive about the learning behaviours and allowed the possibility that there could be additional or different learning behaviours to those on the illustrative list provided within the review. Pre-dating the EPPI review (Powell and Tod 2004) and the other references to learning behaviours and behaviour for learning noted so far (e.g. DfES 2003c, 2004d, 2004e and QCA 2001), White and Mitchell (1994) termed the following 'learning behaviours':

- pupil rarely makes contributions of own ideas to lessons;
- pupil expects to be told what to do – not prepared to try and work it out;
- pupil accepts what they hear or read without question;
- pupil repeats the same mistakes time and time again;
- pupil fails to make links with other lessons;
- pupil tells the teacher when they do not understand;
- pupil asks the teacher why they went wrong;
- pupil refers to previous work before asking the teacher for help;

- pupil thinks through their ideas before offering an opinion – and is able to justify what they have said;
- pupil looks for link with other subjects.

(White and Mitchell 1994)

An interesting feature of White and Mitchell's (1994) list is that it introduces the possibility of what we might term 'negative' learning behaviours. Teachers therefore need to be aware that through both their teaching methods and behaviour management strategies they could be promoting unhelpful or unwanted learning behaviours. A salient point too is that, looked at in terms of the success criteria of securing compliance, the first five bullet points on the list are not problematic. Rarely contributing in lessons, for example does not present a behaviour management problem. It is only when it is evaluated in terms of learning that this behaviour presents as a significant issue to be addressed.

When attempting to define learning behaviour, the DfES (2003c), QCA (2001) and White and Mitchell (1994) sets are more obvious starting points because they reflect the terminology of the EPPI review (Powell and Tod 2004). However there may be other sources of 'learning behaviours' that are not defined as such through their title. An example would be Guy Claxton's *Building Learning Power* (2002), which emphasises the importance of the development of 'reciprocity', 'reflectiveness', 'resilience' and 'resourcefulness'. Claxton (2002) provides a useful language for talking about learning. His extensive work in this area has given teachers and their schools ways in which 'learning power' can be developed. His list below (Table 4.3) provides a useful and often insightful view that has resonance with teachers' experiences.

Table 4.3 Attributes that underpin 'learning power'

Resilience	being ready, willing and able to lock on to learning
Absorption	flow – the pleasure of being rapt in learning
Managing distractions	recognising and reducing interruptions
Noticing	really sensing what is out here
Perseverance	stickability, tolerating the feelings of learning
Resourcefulness	being ready, willing and able to learn in different ways
Questioning	getting below the surface, playing with situations
Making links	seeking coherence, relevance and meaning
Imagining	using the mind's eye as a learning theatre
Reasoning	thinking rigorously and methodologically
Capitalising	making good use of resources
Reflectiveness	being ready, willing and able to become more strategic about learning
Planning	working learning out in advance
Revising	monitoring and adapting along the way
Distilling	drawing out from experience
Meta-learning	understanding learning, and yourself as a learner.
Reciprocity	being ready, willing and able to learn alone and with others
Interdependence	balancing self-reliance and sociability
Collaboration	the skills of learning with others
Empathy and Listening	getting inside others' minds
Imitation	picking up others' habits and values

(Taken from Claxton 2002, reproduced by permission of TLO Ltd.)

It can be seen from Table 4.3 above that there is an opportunity to replace an emphasis on behaviour management that may emanate from 'off task' behaviour or a pupil's comment of 'It's boring Miss', with a focus on developing 'tolerance of the feeling of learning' (Claxton 2002: 17). It does take self-control and responsibility to stick at something that is perceived as hard and/or boring and individual learners need to be prepared for this particularly as they progress through their schooling.

Learning is frequently problematic and involves setbacks, mistakes and experience of failure. This may in some way be denied by the Primary National Strategy title *Excellence and Enjoyment* (DfES 2003a) and the linking of achieving with *enjoying* within the *Every Child Matters* (DfES 2004a) outcomes. This focus may build teachers up to fail if they cannot make learning enjoyable all of the time, particularly if some pupils expect this to be the case. That is not to say that we have to make it dull or purposely implement a 'no pain, no gain' approach but rather that we should seek to promote realistic learning behaviours in children, albeit through some intrinsically interesting learning activities and in a supportive context.

Such a view has implications for how we acknowledge effort and achievement through marking and grading systems, and create contexts and conditions that may make 'uncomfortable effort' more sustainable. We might for example consider such approaches as working in groups, submitting plans before assignments, rewarding progress throughout the task as well as the final outcome, and drawing on examples from literature of fictional and non-fictional characters who have persisted in spite of adversity and from everyday experience when effort has paid off. Pupils, as they go through the education system, will need to learn to sustain effort that is uncomfortable and which clashes with other competing social and personal agendas. No teacher, parent or carer underestimates the challenge of how to foster the kind of effort that is needed for exam preparation and assignment completion. What is apparent however is that such behaviour does not just appear once a pupil has reached 16 years and is reminded 'if you do not improve your attitude to work you will not pass your exams'. It needs to be developed over time and with support. It is influenced by the individual's beliefs about the place of effort in success and the differing values placed by their peers on 'being clever' and 'trying hard' – as if the two were somehow mutually exclusive. Clearly influences of home, community and culture also influence disposition towards tolerating the uncomfortableness of sustained effort. Recognition that this is the case and that some pupils will need support to 'tolerate the feelings of learning' does however provide a more productive stance associated with the development of responsibility and self-discipline (Duckworth and Seligman 2006) than one that sees lack of effort as purely a behaviour management issue.

Assessing progress in the development of learning behaviours in school contexts

Educational assessment of behaviour, particularly in the field of special educational needs has tended to place emphasis on SMART (specific, manageable, achievable, relevant and timed) (Lloyd and Berthelot 1992) targets, and teachers are very familiar with the competency model that underpins the National Curriculum and the TDA Professional Standards (TDA 2007). We are accustomed therefore to embrace the readily measurable and shun that which is seemingly amorphous or less well defined. In the case of learning behaviours, we would adopt a view expressed by Muncey and McGinty (1998), who noted that we need 'to measure what is valuable rather than merely value what is easily measurable' (Muncey and

McGinty 1998: 173). Few would argue that the learning behaviours from the EPPI review (Powell and Tod 2004) are valuable, but a possible criticism is that they are very difficult to measure. They are not always readily observable behaviours in the same way as behaviours such as 'waiting your turn to speak' or 'bringing the correct equipment to a lesson' are.

If we are to work successfully with the concept of learning behaviours it is necessary to address the need for measurability without reducing them to a checklist of behaviours to be achieved by certain ages. The problem of measuring learning dispositions has been more fully addressed by Carr and Claxton (2002). We have found that mapping the behaviours that you might want to promote in an individual around a more generic learning behaviour such as, say, 'collaboration' or 'responsibility', is useful for identifying and measuring progress. Such planning allows for personalisation and acknowledges that individuals vary in the way they demonstrate their development and progress towards any particular learning behaviour. An example of such planning is given in Figure 4.2.

In looking at Figure 4.2 it can be seen that it only describes a few of the many behaviours that could be identified as contributing to the successful completion of a collaborative task. These behaviours involve a subtle interplay of relationship with curriculum, relationship with others and relationship with self. Conceivably, for example, a pupil approaching a collaborative activity may feel motivated about working with other peers but also motivated to avoid compromising his/her relationship with self. Therefore if we have a pupil who displays a difficulty working in a group, targeting their social skills may not suffice. It is likely that we will also need to look at the cognitive (e.g. task requirements) and emotional (e.g. pupil's perception of self) components that are contributing to the difficulties experienced in working with others.

The diagram illustrates a range of behaviours that may be specific to the individual or apply to others in the class. Unlike generic learning behaviours that transcend curriculum areas, age and stages of development these 'sub' learning behaviours may be different depending on the age and stage of development of the learner and the curriculum area being taught.

Should learning behaviours be measured against a notional norm or against the individual's development?

In considering the identification of generic learning behaviours and their underlying components, consideration needs to be given to the question of whether such behaviours should be 'normatively referenced' or developmental. Inevitably teachers, as professionals, will know the level to which particular learning behaviours will typically have developed within the pupils that they teach. Equally they will be aware of pupils who have not developed to this level and those who have developed beyond that expected for their age. Assessments within school-based settings tend to be norm-referenced and teachers have expectations about how pupils should behave when they reach certain ages – particularly at stages of transition. Work by Bate and Moss (1997) has suggested that the older pupils are, the less teachers think they need to, or ought to have to, teach behavioural skills. Secondary teachers in the survey considered that 84 per cent of behavioural skills would have been established at either infant or junior level.

Given that learning behaviours reflect social, emotional and cognitive development, it is likely that pupils will exhibit uneven patterns of development depending on their prior learning experiences. For example a gifted and talented pupil might display relatively more advanced cognitive learning behaviours than those that relate to their social and or emotional

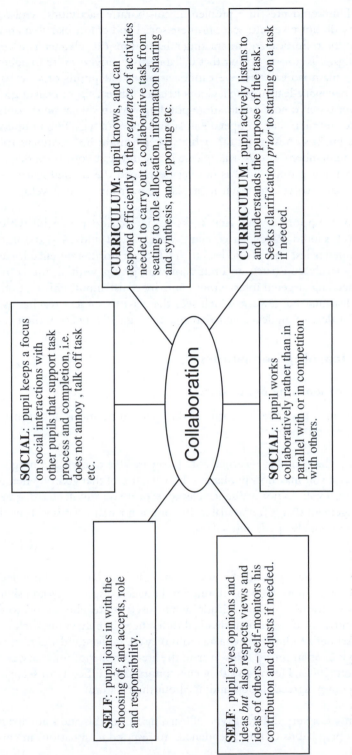

Figure 4.2 Identifying learning behaviours.

Collaboration

CURRICULUM: pupil knows, and can respond efficiently to the *sequence* of activities needed to carry out a collaborative task from seating to role allocation, information sharing and synthesis, and reporting etc.

CURRICULUM: pupil actively listens to and understands the purpose of the task. Seeks clarification *prior* to starting on a task if needed.

SOCIAL: pupil keeps a focus on social interactions with other pupils that support task process and completion, i.e. does not annoy , talk off task etc.

SOCIAL: pupil works collaboratively rather than in parallel with or in competition with others.

SELF: pupil joins in with the choosing of, and accepts, role and responsibility.

SELF: pupil gives opinions and ideas *but* also respects views and ideas of others – self-monitors his contribution and adjusts if needed.

development. This could present a problem if collaborative activities, whilst matched to cognitive ability, do not take into account these social and emotional elements.

In looking at the reciprocal and interacting relationships that characterise 'collaboration' in school settings, it is not surprising that collaborative activities often trigger disruptive behaviour. The main issue is that we cannot assume that pupils of a certain age have developed the necessary learning behaviours needed for learning in small group settings. We can however observe how pupils are responding, identify what behaviours we would like to promote and then seek to operate an appropriate strategy. For a pupil who knows how to behave but has chosen not to, such a strategy might be a standard rule reminder such as 'David, remember our class rule, please listen and wait your turn, thanks'. Whereas, in the case of a pupil/group who has not yet developed the desired learning behaviour, it may be necessary to seek to teach it or plan opportunities to develop it via subject teaching.

We would not support a view that seeks to define and prescribe which learning behaviours pupils should achieve at certain ages (e.g. 7, 11 and 14 years) in the form of prescribed competencies. This would lead to yet another norm-referenced, age-related set of targets that socially constructs an underachieving group, with all the connotations of such a group needing targeted interventions and 'specialist' input. This is at odds with the behaviour for learning framework which sees the class or subject teacher as having the responsibility for developing learning behaviour through all aspects of their teaching.

Promoting learning behaviours

The make-up of learning behaviours

Learning behaviours may take the form of skills and dispositions. Claxton (2006) summarises the distinction stating:

> Put crudely, when you have learned a skill, you are able to do something you couldn't do before. But you may not spontaneously make use of that ability when it is relevant in the future, if you do not realise its relevance; or if you still need a degree of support or encouragement that is not available. In common parlance, it is not much use being *able* if you are not also *ready* and *willing*.
>
> (Claxton 2006: 6)

In this section we move beyond this useful, though, as Claxton acknowledges, crude, definition to consider more fully the distinction between dispositions and skills.

Words such as 'disposition' or 'attitude' when used by teachers tend to function as explanatory constructs to describe individual differences in behaviour, such as 'He's got a bad attitude to school'. Although as explanations they are understood and rarely questioned, their definition is often imprecise. However, in the literature definitions vary, as explored by Carr and Caxton (2002). Definitions they cite confirm the difficulty of securing a precise definition but convey agreed understanding about their nature:

> Dispositions are a very different type of learning from skills and knowledge. They can be thought of as habits of mind, tendencies to respond to situations in certain ways.
>
> (Katz 1988: 30)

Dispositions ... are the proclivities that lead us in one direction rather than another, within the freedom of action that we have.

(Perkins 1995: 275)

In his research Claxton (1999) noted that 'learning power' consisted of two inter-related facets: capabilities and dispositions. Capabilities are the skills, strategies and abilities which learning require or, as Claxton (1999) puts it, the 'toolkit' of learning. These capabilities are necessary but not sufficient to be a good learner. As we know from looking at the differences in classroom behaviour pupils have to be disposed to learn. That is, they need to be ready and willing to take learning opportunities, as well as able. Katz (1993) pointed out that just as there is a big difference between being able to read and having the disposition to be a reader, and being able to listen and being disposed to listen, so is the case with learning more generally.

A disposition may be thought to be more entrenched within the individual's make-up and characteristics as a consequence of their ongoing response to, and attempts to 'make sense' of, their own personal life experiences. Capability is thought to be more easily influenced through appropriate teaching. It is important and indeed encouraging that the capability and disposition components of learning behaviours interact. This gives opportunities for each of these components to influence the other positively and for teachers to decide between strategies.

The challenge for teachers is to promote positive or 'good' learning behaviours. To do this they need to know more about them. One construct thought to be influential in the development of learning dispositions is relationship with self. Terms associated with this relationship include self-concept, self-esteem, self-efficacy and self-confidence. For example, if a pupil is interrupting others in the class we would need to know whether they have not yet developed the *skills* to ignore distractions and/or relate appropriately in a class setting, or whether the behaviour has the purpose for them of keeping faith with their own thinking about themselves, which might be 'I don't think I can do this work so I will distract others and neither the teacher nor peers will find out that I cannot do it.' For this reason we need to find out more about the relative contribution of 'skill' and 'will' in the incident so that we can identify the best strategies to use and decide upon how we will evaluate the efficacy of that strategy use.

Within the context of the behaviour for learning conceptual framework teachers are encouraged to ask themselves:

* Does the learning behaviour I have chosen to develop primarily focus on a skill or disposition?
* What evaluation criteria will I use in evaluating the efficacy of this strategy?

In some cases there may be additional concerns relating to the interdependence of dispositions and capabilities. For example, a teacher may seek to improve a pupil's capability in phonics through intensive practice but in so doing adversely affect the pupil's disposition towards reading for pleasure. The teacher therefore needs to be alert to the possibility that the promotion of one (e.g. capability) may compromise or have a negative impact upon the other (e.g. disposition).

It is now interesting to see in an era where context and conditions play a bigger role in assessing children's learning that 'look, listen and note' is an advocated approach to assessment within the Early Years Foundation Stage (DfES 2007c). This represents a very immediate type of formative assessment and is an approach that is likely to have utility across all age ranges in the assessment and promotion of learning behaviour.

Which learning behaviours should I choose?

The lists of possible learning behaviours so far presented (e.g. Powell and Tod 2004, DfES 2003c, QCA 2001, Claxton 2002, White and Mitchell 1994) are for illustrative purposes only, used to explore what we might mean by a 'learning behaviour'. It is not therefore a case of deciding whether our preference is for Claxton's list or the QCA interpretation or any of the others. Rather the priority, the significant shift in thinking, is defining a behaviour that you want to promote. This in itself however is only part of the process. The message that it is important to focus on the behaviour you *do* want is not a new one in the field of behaviour management. We might therefore want the pupil to, for example, remain in their seat, put their hand up rather than calling out, or use language appropriate to the classroom. Though it is a desired behaviour that is defined, the focus is still on achieving 'compliance behaviour' rather than developing 'learning behaviour'. The link therefore is not always made with learning. Ofsted (2004a) identified the problem that while schools were able to point to improvements in behaviour of pupils identified with social, emotional and behavioural difficulties (SEBD) in terms of, for example, the reduction of referrals to the Senior Leadership Team or in the use of sanctions, few schools analysed the progress such pupils made in their learning and were therefore unable to evaluate the impact of their provision.

The behaviour for learning model endorses the importance of focusing on behaviours that we want to promote, but encourages reflection on a *purpose* beyond simply stopping unwanted behaviour or promoting behaviours required by policy-makers, institutions and practitioners. This returns to the earlier point that the behaviours we seek to promote should transcend curriculum areas, age and stages of development, and arguably be of life-long relevance to the learner. These behaviours are not necessarily incompatible with the needs of policy makers, institutions or practitioners, indeed we would expect a considerable degree of correspondence. The difference is one of *purpose*, which has an influence on the selection of strategies and approaches and evaluation criteria.

Table 4.4 includes examples of real comments we have heard from secondary aged pupils during our classroom observations. Some, such as homophobic and other discriminatory comments, are likely to warrant a particular school response in line with its relevant policy. Our purpose in presenting them here is to consider the clues the use of these types of comment give the teacher about the possible learning behaviours to target. The teacher may then choose to promote these learning behaviours through relationship with the curriculum, relationship with others and relationship with self, depending on which area they feel will be most appropriate and in which they feel most confident.

Summary

Within this chapter we have deliberately provided readers with examples of learning behaviours, in the form of both skills and dispositions. We have also highlighted sources where desirable characteristics or behaviours have been documented but have not been described in terms of learning behaviours or may not meet our criteria for a learning

Table 4.4 Linking pupil comments to learning behaviour

Relationship area	What a pupil might say	Learning behaviour to work on?
Self	'Can't do it.'	Self-belief Self-efficacy Independence
	'I don't need GCSEs, I'm going to work for my dad.'	Planning and prediction Choices and consequences
	'I don't really understand this bit.'	Resourcefulness Perseverance/persistence
	'It wasn't just me doing it.'	Responsibility: ability to admit fault/accept consequences
	'I can't be bothered.'	Motivation Collaborative working
Others	'He's crap at this.'	Use of appropriate language Respect and empathy
	'He's gay. I'm not working with him.'	Acceptance and understanding of difference Self evaluation of personal prejudice
	'He doesn't care what I think so there's no point.'	Self-efficacy Resilience
	'I don't understand **any** of it.'	Metacognition Resourcefulness
	'We're doing it this way.'	Collaborative working/compromise
	'He's special (needs). Why is he in my group?'	Respect and empathy Self-evaluation of personal prejudice
Curriculum	'I hate maths because the teacher's rubbish.'	Express and justify opinions appropriately Respect and empathy Attribution style
	'I haven't done it before so I'm not doing it.'	Flexibility Openness to change Take risks in own learning
	'GCSEs are stupid. I don't need to know any of this.'	Responsibility Responsiveness to school systems Predict consequences

behaviour. They do however provide a resource from which teachers can develop a bank of learning behaviours that serve to promote improved relationships for learning for those individual pupils whose behaviour in class is of concern.

We have found, along with others in the field of behaviour management, that teachers, in spite of endorsing the need to promote positive behaviours, find it much easier to identify behaviours they want to reduce or 'manage' than the learning behaviours they need to promote. This chapter should help to promote a positive language with which to discuss pupil behaviour, both between professionals and in conversations with the child and his/her parents/carers.

For some readers, accustomed to SMART targets, the apparent lack of measurability may at first appear to be a barrier to the use of learning behaviours. Ultimately however, if we can define what 'generic' learning behaviour we wish to develop it is possible (see Figure 4.1) to break this down into more readily observable features. Working with the relatively new construct of 'learning behaviours' does require attention to how these will be monitored and assessed. This is crucial given that the development of learning behaviour(s) provides the criteria against which we assess the efficacy of our behaviour management strategies. It is important from the start of the process to have a clear, realistic idea of the observable features that will be looked for as confirmation that the desired learning behaviour is developing.

Once a learning behaviour has been identified it is possible to decide whether it will be most effective to promote this through a focus on relationship with self, relationship with others or relationship with the curriculum, or a combination. In Chapter 5 we will be exploring in depth what we understand by a relationship within the context of the behaviour for learning conceptual framework. In Chapters 6 and 7 we will look specifically at what we mean by relationship with curriculum, relationship with self and relationship with others.

Relationships for learning

Introduction

Within preceding chapters we have provided an initial introduction to the three relationships central to the behaviour for learning conceptual framework. This chapter is the first of a set of three that seeks to explore these relationships in more detail. Within these chapters we introduce the reader to a range of relevant literature and research in order to explore the nature of relationship with self, relationship with others and relationship with the curriculum and their role in enhancing learning behaviour in group settings.

That good teaching is rooted in relationships has become something of an accepted belief with considerable face validity. This chapter moves beyond unquestioning acceptance of the importance of relationships towards a critical understanding of their nature and influence.

The rationale behind the enumeration of three relationships

So far in the book we have outlined a conceptual framework that seeks to promote a closer link between behaviour management and learning. Its utility for teachers is through an explicit acknowledgement that their area of expertise and core activity is the promotion of learning behaviour. The behaviour for learning conceptual framework offers an approach for enhancing learning behaviour through an emphasis on building positive relationships in the following three areas:

- relationship with self;
- relationship with the curriculum;
- relationship with others.

The use of this conceptual framework does not deny the complexity of classroom interactions (Hayles 1991). It merely provides a workable model based on three relationships that allow teachers to plan for, and address, the social, emotional and cognitive aspects of learning that impact on pupil behaviour in the classroom.

Does the behaviour for learning conceptual framework prescribe a set of strategies?

The behaviour for learning approach does not seek to be prescriptive. We endorse Hammersley's point that, 'rather than taking the prescriptive role of providing specific solutions to particular problems, research is more likely to be concerned with explanations, with the production of theories that are continually modified to increase their explanatory power' (Hammersley 2001: 584).

The lack of prescription may be counter-intuitive in the context of an educational system that has increasingly relied upon nationally-given prescriptions of good practice. The implication of much policy and guidance is that if this 'good' practice is applied, it will automatically result in the changes intended. However, national policy and guidance is always locally interpreted and driven within the changing contexts and dynamics of the classroom. This is an important point for any teachers concerned with behaviour management, simply because there is a plethora of guidance on this subject from both national and local sources. Although much of this guidance is useful and necessary and can serve to secure coherence and consistency for schools and groups it can also foster a belief in teachers and trainees that the 'complete answer is out there.' Requests for 'more on behaviour' from trainees and teachers are likely to be based on this belief. Hammersley's (2001) view that the *implementation* of broad educational policies should be entrusted to the creative intelligence and initiative of teachers, reflects the reality of what happens in classrooms.

We are of the view that the search for solutions in relation to behaviour, underpinned by a belief-system based on security, certainty, prediction and control, needs to make way for one based on systematic problem-solving around strengthening the relationships that underpin learning. This conceptualisation entails a much greater degree of professional freedom for the teacher. However along with freedom comes increased responsibility and this brings with it a degree of professional challenge. Although many teachers may feel that there is too much external control and an over-emphasis on accountability based on how well their class/school achieves against pre-determined, age-linked 'outcomes', it does at least provide some security about direction and expectations.

If we move towards accepting that classrooms are sites of complexity within which pupils' individuality and adaptability are in competition with demands for standards, control and conformity, then teachers would have to take on board the responsibilities inherent within Radford's (2006) conclusions:

> Education becomes a much more open enterprise with the emphasis on a more flexible, tentative, imaginative and creative response to the multiple points at which alternative eventualities become possibilities. The evaluation of the school and classroom will be a more holistic and contextually sensitive process in which the evaluator is open to the intrinsic 'goods' that might be delivered within the system. Emphasis turns away from objectives or target-driven teaching towards a more process-orientated view. Standardisation gives way to diversity, from the tendency towards the mechanistic to one of organic fluidity.
>
> (Radford 2006: 189)

In this book we are suggesting that the intrinsic 'goods' referred to by Radford (2006), could be learning behaviours. These are concerned with cognitive, social and emotional development and transcend curriculum areas, and arguably should be of life-long relevance to individual learners. They may be different to those prescribed by policy makers, and interestingly it is unlikely that they can be predetermined given that they arise from unique *individual* responses to the experiences and opportunities of the *group* settings of the school and classroom.

How might you as teacher experience the three behaviour for learning relationships?

Although in this book the behaviour for learning conceptual framework is directed towards children and young people in educational settings, our understanding of the nature and influence of the three relationships can be enhanced by first reflecting upon how such a model relates to the teacher. Consider the following scenario:

Scenario 5.1

You have had a difficult day. Year 7B has constantly interrupted your teaching and you feel you have not got through the lesson content. You are worried that this may reflect badly on your progress when your tutor or school-based mentor is observing. Jason refused to do any work and publicly announced to the class 'It's boring, Miss.' You are worried that he is winning the 'battle' by reducing your authority and showing no respect to you as a teacher.

As the teacher you may have a number of responses to this. You might respond to this experience by saying to your colleagues, 'I have just had 7B ... they are impossible ... I've done my best with them but it is hopeless ... how are we supposed to raise standards with students like that?' However, on reflection you may start thinking about the relationships that underpin *your* learning in this context as a way of helping you to plan for your next session with Year 7B.

Table 5.1 Reflection on relationships and your learning behaviour

	What am I thinking?	How am I feeling?	What the class might be experiencing and learning
Relationship with self	I must not let the class see that I am worried; I must not fail – I want them to like and respect me.	A bit fearful, anxious at times; but more confident when things are going well.	Some hesitancy in delivery of lesson content; lack of clarity of expectation regarding outcomes to be achieved; signs of anxiety and vulnerability e.g. changes in pitch and tone, irritation, over-reaction to minor interruptions.
Relationship with others	I must keep the pupils on task – I mustn't lose control. I wish my mentor/ tutor could have seen things when they were going well.	Excited at putting my lesson plan into action with the class; but worried that it may go wrong and they will be noisy.	Your positive behaviour management statements; your emphasis on control; your concern with how other adults see you – with possibly less emphasis on student/pupil learning needs; your worry and vulnerability.

(continued)

Table 5.1 (continued)

	What am I thinking?	*How am I feeling?*	*What the class might be experiencing and learning*
Relationship with curriculum	I must 'get through' these topics during this lesson; I want them (the class) to be interested and enjoy the lesson.	Panicky because time is moving on and not all the objectives for the lesson have been met.	A well-prepared lesson with emphasis on what must be learned; lack of flexibility; hurrying up of responses and questions; irritation with diversions; requirement for conformity seems more important than whether students are interested and involved.

When thinking in this way you will be able to see how the three relationships that underpin your learning behaviour in the classroom are interlinked and how these are seen or experienced by individuals in your class. It follows that when you left the classroom saying, 'Class 7B are impossible', the class may have been thinking, on the basis of what they experienced, that 'Miss/Sir is not really interested in us unless we give her/him the answers s/he wants and let her/him get on with what s/he wants to teach us.'

In reality of course you *are* interested in your pupils' learning and many of the class members are interested in the subject you are teaching. There is a risk that these very positive features are being affected by your own relationships: with yourself, with your class and other staff, and with your subject.

Consider for example the message you give to individuals in your class when you start the lesson by asking them to write down the learning objectives. Are you doing this because it is deemed to be 'good practice' and because you are expected to do this by Ofsted and others, or are you seeking to build a reciprocal relationship with the pupil and giving them clear information about what you expect their contribution to be to this relationship? Interviewed in 2008, Sir Alan Steer makes this point by asking of adults 'how often (in your schooling) did anybody sit you down and say: "this is why we are doing this topic and this is what you have to do to be successful." And when you got your work back did anyone say: "if you'd done it this way you'd have got an A not a D"' (quoted Wilby 2008: 2).

Exploring the rationale behind the language of relationships used within the behaviour for learning conceptual framework

Table 5.1 sought to focus your attention on the impact that your own relationship with self, the curriculum and others has on pupil learning through the column 'what the class might be experiencing and learning'. Whatever else changes in your thinking and teaching as you progress through your training and career, impact on pupil learning is, after all, your main area of concern. By keeping a focus on the two-way aspect of the relationships you are building with your class, you will become more skilled at anticipating and evaluating what they are experiencing and learning from your behaviour.

Reflective Exercise 5.1

Think about two lessons you have taught recently, one of which you thought went well and one which you were not so happy with. In both cases think about:

- How your relationships with yourself, with others, and with the curriculum were 'experienced' by individuals in your class(s). What learning behaviours do you think were being fostered in your pupils?
- Which of the three relationships (with self, with others and with the curriculum) had the greatest influence, positive and negative, on *your* behaviour?
- Which of the three relationships do you feel it would be easiest to improve in order to achieve improved learning behaviour in your classroom?

You will notice that from Table 5.1 and your self-reflection, two key messages are apparent:

- learning relationships are *reciprocal*;
- they are influenced by context and can be *changed* and *improved*.

These points are of considerable importance and we can explore them by reflecting on the nature of a typical conversation between two people. When we engage in conversation we are aware of the two-way nature of the activity and consequently keep a focus on the *purpose* of our activity which is to 'communicate' with the other person. During the process of conversation we constantly monitor the other person's response to check their engagement and understanding and adjust our responses accordingly. As a teacher the underlying need to build a relationship and promote communication with individual pupils is paramount but in the context of the classroom the 'conversation' is typically from one person (i.e. the teacher) to a group. The close monitoring and instant adjustment that characterise one-to-one conversations and ongoing relationships is not possible and so it is important to keep in mind: 'What do I want the individual pupil to learn and what information can I use to monitor his/her response?'

This may appear obvious but under pressure and within constraints of time it is often more feasible to just prioritise the monitoring of: 'How well am I doing in terms of class-control and getting through what I planned to get through?'

There are of course also reciprocal influences involved within and between the relationships outlined in the behaviour for learning conceptual framework. In looking at the planning diagram (Figure 5.1), it can be seen that any intervention made to improve pupils' learning behaviour through an emphasis on *one* of the three areas (curriculum, self and others) is likely to have an effect on the other *two*. Thus if we choose to focus on the cognitive areas of development through an emphasis on adjustment to curriculum delivery and assessment and, as a consequence, the pupil achieves greater understanding of the lesson, then his/her relationship with self is likely to improve – at least for the short term. This could additionally lead to improved social behaviour with others in the classroom in the form of, for example, less 'messing about' and reduced irritation to peers and the teacher.

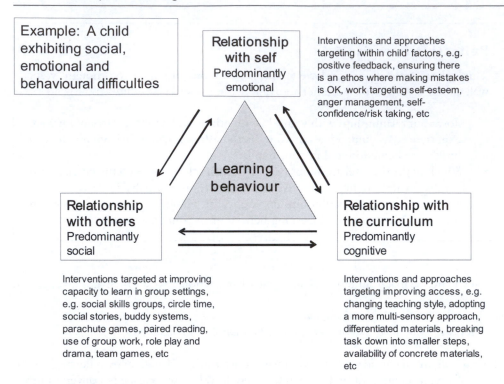

Example: A child exhibiting social, emotional and behavioural difficulties

Relationship with self
Predominantly emotional

Interventions and approaches targeting 'within child' factors, e.g. positive feedback, ensuring there is an ethos where making mistakes is OK, work targeting self-esteem, anger management, self-confidence/risk taking, etc

Learning behaviour

Relationship with others
Predominantly social

Relationship with the curriculum
Predominantly cognitive

Interventions targeted at improving capacity to learn in group settings, e.g. social skills groups, circle time, social stories, buddy systems, parachute games, paired reading, use of group work, role play and drama, team games, etc

Interventions and approaches targeting improving access, e.g. changing teaching style, adopting a more multi-sensory approach, differentiated materials, breaking task down into smaller steps, availability of concrete materials, etc

Figure 5.1 How commonly used classroom strategies link both learning and behaviour through the behaviour for learning conceptual framework.

The importance of the *interdependence* of the three relationships in the model is that:

1 It acknowledges that the promotion of effective learning behaviours in school contexts involves attention to the social, emotional and cognitive factors that influence relationships.
2 It affords teachers *flexibility* in allowing them to select a particular relationship to strengthen that best matches their current level of confidence and competence. As an example a beginning teacher may feel more comfortable concentrating on curriculum planning and delivery as a way of improving individual learning behaviour, whereas a more experienced teacher, who feels at ease with curriculum content and requirements and is familiar with the pupils in their class, is likely to feel confident in tackling some of the more challenging social and emotional relationships involved in classroom learning. Notions of *choice* and *feasibility* in selecting strategies for teaching allows for ongoing professional development and addresses the guilt that teachers may experience during an era in which prescriptions for 'good practice' through paper and electronic formats are in abundance (Ellis *et al.* 2008).
3 It reflects the dynamic and changing nature of pupil responses to teaching across contexts and conditions and acknowledges that: 'teaching necessitates responding to the complex needs of individual learners and therefore involves making multiple decisions in non-routine situations' (Haggarty 2002, drawing on the work of Darling-Hammond 2001).

Teaching conceived of in this way is viewed as an intellectually challenging task in which teachers continually examine and refine their practice.

What is the rationale for referring to a *relationship* with the curriculum, given its inanimate status?

In using the word 'relationship' alongside the word 'curriculum' there is a deliberate attempt within the behaviour for learning conceptual framework to move forward from the notion of *access to* the curriculum to that of *engagement with* the curriculum. While it is important to highlight issues of access to the curriculum when planning for teaching, particularly within the context of inclusion, most teachers know that access alone does not suffice to allow learning to take place. It may at first appear rather odd to think about a relationship with something inanimate such as the curriculum. However, the phrase *relationship with the curriculum* is intended to highlight that as well as being able to access the curriculum, learners need to *engage with* and *respond to* the curriculum and as such this parallels the processes that we regard as important in developing and sustaining any kind of relationship.

This view is endorsed by Beaty *et al.* (1997) who, through their interviews with Open University students, introduced the term 'learning orientation' based on the four main functions of higher education – academic, vocational, personal and social:

> learning orientation is defined by all those attitudes and aims which express the student's individual relationship with a course of study … It is the collection of purposes which form the personal context for the individual student's learning. The idea of an orientation assumes that students have an active relationship with their studying.
>
> (Beaty *et al.* 1997: 76)

Although the subjects under study by Beaty *et al.* (1997) were university students, there is substantial evidence from research studies (Carr and Claxton 2002) that in order to improve learning there is a need to address both learning environments and individual student orientation. We would go even further and suggest that it is the link between what the learning environment offers and what the learner is able and/or willing to 'take up' from those offers that is crucial. The link, which we refer to as a 'relationship', between the offer and the individual's willingness *and* ability, is reciprocal. Attempts to strengthen this link have typically involved either:

- changing the learning environment – this is often the subject of government guidance to schools; *or*
- changing the individual pupil's attitude to school through strategies often linked to personal, social and moral development both within and outside school contexts.

However, to pursue one or the other will not necessarily address the relationship between the two. Interestingly, if we look at the language used in the context of the school curriculum it does seem to sit within a more traditional transmission model. In this model the teacher initiates (or *delivers* the curriculum), already has a view on how the pupil should respond (*sets targets*) and then judges (*assesses*) that response accordingly.

If we apply a relationship model to the curriculum then we would still do many of the things in classrooms that are currently in operation, but we would be *thinking* differently. For example:

*   More attention would be given to the reciprocal nature of the process. We would be more aware of what the pupil brings to the process, accepting that this may or may not fit with what we had in mind. Whatever the behavioural manifestation, it is useful data about the ongoing nature of the relationship.
*   Strategy choice would be based on its likely impact on sustaining and improving the pupil's contribution to the relationship.
*   We would acknowledge that there are a few pupils who exhibit a *cluster* of learning behaviours that have pervasive effects on their behaviour in the classroom. For these pupils we would directly target one of the three relationships as the focus for action.

The rationale for the use of the term *relationship* reflects the dynamic and interdependent interaction between both the curriculum and the individual pupil and the emphasis that teachers place on both.

Is there an evidence-base to justify the practical application of the behaviour for learning conceptual framework?

The behaviour for learning conceptual framework emerged from evidence gathered through an EPPI systematic review (Powell and Tod 2004). In this book we are continuing to explore evidence that relates to the utility of the behaviour for learning conceptual framework in school contexts. As such we are introducing relatively new terms and ideas into educational discourse such as 'relationships with self', 'relationship with the curriculum' and 'relationship with others' as well as the term 'learning behaviour'. Although these terms have a common-sense feel to them, they do not appear as combined terms in the literature. We have therefore extrapolated evidence from the literature that relates to the relationships that are featured in the behaviour for learning conceptual framework. While underpinning research and theories may not be used *explicitly* by teachers to make decisions about strategy use (Clandini and Connelly 1995), reference to an evidence-base can, and should, lead to enhanced understanding and improved practice.

As we have previously noted, there remains a continued search for 'best practice'. This serves to condition teachers towards a belief that 'best practice' exists and that they *should* know what it is. While it is accepted that there are identifiable elements of *good* practice that it is beneficial for teachers to know, the notion that there is practice that is 'best' for all individuals (both teachers and pupils) and equally effective across a range of local contexts and within individual classrooms is not only questionable, but unlikely (Godfrey *et al.* 2007). Thus the purpose of looking at the evidence for the behaviour for learning conceptual framework is not to arrive at a set of strategies to be promoted by us as 'best practice'. In seeking to apply the behaviour for learning conceptual framework to practice we need to be aware of the strengths and limitations of the existing theory and evidence base. Many readers will be aware when looking at literature on improving school or individual outcomes that much of the empirical evidence is based on correlational evidence. This can be illustrated by looking at self-esteem and attainment. We might find that 'high self-esteem' and 'improved attainment' occur together and then assume that if we somehow raise the pupil's self-esteem that there will be a subsequent improvement in their attainment. Whilst of course we would continue to explore the relationship between these two variables that occur together it is important for researchers and policy makers not to assume a *causal* link. When either reviewing the existing evidence or researching one's own practice it is important to be aware that we are often reliant on correlational evidence and erroneously attribute a causal explanation.

The evidence-base relevant for relationships that underpins the development of learning behaviour is necessarily broad. Through linking the term 'behaviour' with 'learning' we have to identify relevant research from two broad fields. As Entwistle and Peterson note:

> what is the precise definition of 'learning' that would form a single educational target? The formal definition indicates a relatively stable change in behaviour or thinking, but that does not take account of the different processes that are used across a variety of tasks and situations or the personal, affective component which becomes attached to concepts such as learning.
>
> (Entwistle and Peterson 2004: 409)

A focus on relationships also broadens our search for an evidence-base into the wider fields of sociology and psychology. Potentially therefore research relevant to the implementation of the conceptual framework into educational settings is extensive. This breadth is a positive aspect, but it inevitably requires us to be selective. Therefore we need to acknowledge that in selecting the literature we are providing illustrative samples rather than a comprehensive evidence-base. We would encourage readers to engage critically with this text and read more widely from the full range of relevant literature.

Summary

This chapter has considered the usage and meaning of the term 'relationship' within the behaviour for learning conceptual framework. As we have indicated there is an evidence-base for the behaviour for learning conceptual framework provided through a systematic literature review (Powell and Tod 2004). Each of the components (i.e. 'self', 'others', 'curriculum', 'learning' and 'behaviour') that make up the behaviour for learning conceptual framework have an extensive evidence-base. However, the combining of these components, through such terms as 'learning behaviour' and 'relationship with curriculum', is a relatively new approach to behaviour management and as such has a developing evidence-base.

Within this chapter we have illustrated the view that the language of relationships can be helpful in reflecting the reciprocal and dynamic interactions that underpin teaching and learning in classrooms. If readers accept the premise within this chapter that teachers' intentions and actions are interpreted and experienced differently by individuals, it brings into question the utility of attempting to identify a definitive set of strategies for managing behaviour.

The following two chapters examine in more detail the concepts of relationship with the curriculum, relationship with self, and relationship with others.

Chapter 6

Relationship with the curriculum

Working definition

The dynamic interactions that make up the reciprocal activity between the learner and the curriculum.

This involves being able and willing to access, process and respond to the information available through the curriculum.

Introduction

In this chapter we will be looking at how we might further understand from the literature what it might mean in practice to have a positive relationship with the curriculum. In extrapolating relevant information we have focused on the following three questions to address whole-class, individual and teacher perspectives:

- How useful is 'on task' behaviour as a measure of the pupil's relationship with the curriculum?
- How can learning behaviours or a cluster of learning behaviours be used as an indicator of the pupil's relationship with the curriculum?
- How might teachers improve their pupils' relationship with the curriculum through their teaching?

How might we know whether a pupil has a positive or negative relationship with the curriculum?

'On' and 'off' task behaviour as an indicator of a relationship with the curriculum

In considering teachers' reasons for strengthening their pupils' relationship with the curriculum, the EPPI review of research (Powell and Tod 2004) noted that the majority of studies linked to behaviour in school contexts were concerned with pupils both *starting* and *staying on* task. This is understandable given that 'on task' is an observable behaviour that can be used by teachers to scan the response of the whole class. It clearly has some validity as a measure in that securing some form of 'joint attention to task' between the teacher and the pupil is frequently a necessary requirement for learning to take place.

Almost inevitably a focus on 'on task' behaviour generates a concern to identify and reduce 'off task' behaviour through behaviour management approaches. This has a number of limitations:

- There is an assumption that being off task is negatively correlated with learning. This may not necessarily be the case.
- The identification that a pupil is off task gives little indication of the reason, neither does it inform strategy selection.
- Constructing 'off task' behaviour as a behavioural difficulty denies the fact that most children, like most adults, will go off task from time to time and re-focus their attention if necessary.

Interestingly, as part of research into the efficacy of behavioural strategies, Wheldall and Merrett (1990) found that their sample of primary pupils spent about 70 per cent of their time on task. In secondary schools the figure was 80 per cent. The point we can draw from this is that in typical classes pupils are off task for 20–30 per cent of the time. The problem frequently is not so much the 'off task-ness', because, as Wheldall and Merrett's (1990) figures suggest, most pupils go off task, but the behaviours that certain individuals engage in whilst off task. Wheldall and Merrett (1990) successfully adopted a behavioural approach to increasing class on task behaviour through their 'rules, praise, ignore' technique. Behavioural approaches are often the first practical choice for teachers but fail to give due attention to the reasons for the off task behaviour. Table 6.1 looks more closely at the possible reasons for off task behaviour and the implications for strategy choice.

Table 6.1 Off task behaviour, possible explanations, theoretical underpinnings and strategy use

Frequent behaviour	Theory	Explanation/examples	Possible strategy
Off task	Behavioural	Child is getting more attention by being off task.	Reward on task behaviour.
Off task	Cognitive	Child thinks he is unable to do the task.	Encourage child to reappraise the task, identify what parts of the task he can do etc.
Off task	Affective	Child fears failure.	Circle time to build self-esteem – offer increased adult or peer support. Depersonalise failure.
Off task	Social/ environmental	'He has a brother who is just the same'.	Possibly nurture group and/ or work with parents.
Off task	Biological	Perhaps the child has ADHD?	Refer for multi-agency assessment; assess behaviour over range of contexts.
Off task	Developmental	Child not ready to work independently.	Allocate additional TA/ LSA support and set more suitable learning challenge.

As can be seen from the table there are many reasons why a particular pupil may be 'off task'. If the teacher thinks that the reason the pupil may be off task is that he/she is getting more attention from the teacher and/or peers then the teacher is likely to operate a strategy based on behaviourist principles that essentially ignores off task behaviour and rewards on task behaviour. However if the pupil is, for example, unable to work on their own independently then such a strategy would be unlikely to be effective in bringing about a change in behaviour. If this was the perceived reason then it would be more appropriate to draw on theories of child development.

The following scenario illustrates the potential difficulties that may arise if we ascribe the 'wrong' explanation to the off task behaviour and implement strategies based on this.

Scenario 6.1

Robin is off task in the classroom. This off task behaviour typically takes the form of interrupting the teacher with seemingly unnecessary or irrelevant questions and comments.

Teacher hypothesis: Robin is seeking attention.

Strategy selection: The teacher ignores Robin and gives him attention when he returns to the task.

- *Possible outcome:*
  Robin gradually spends longer on task and is able to attain – he learns more, he builds a good relationship with the subject and teacher and continues to make good progress. The class learns that being on task is recognised and rewarded and whole-class behaviour improves.

  Analysis:
  The teacher appears to have identified the appropriate explanation and chosen a compatible strategy. However, ongoing monitoring is necessary as Robin and the rest of class may have learned that asking questions or asking others is off task and not rewarded.

- *Alternative outcome:*
  Robin actually cannot do the task. Rewarding him for on task behaviour does not lead to a substantial increase in attention for him. His behaviour deteriorates. He develops a negative relationship with the subject, his teacher and possibly his peers. He may even begin to feel badly about his lack of progress.

  Analysis:
  The teacher appears to have identified an inaccurate explanation and based strategy selection on this. Robin cannot do the task. There may be at least two reasons for this. He may not have developed the skills needed to sustain his attention for a sufficient period; or he has focused his attention but he does not have the necessary knowledge, skills and understanding. He persists with off task behaviour because he has no alternative strategies to use. The class may learn that being persistently off task secures attention and prevents failure from being discovered.

Assessing possible reasons for the pupil's off task behaviour is clearly an important prerequisite to deciding which strategy or strategies to use. It is also important for the teacher to have an understanding of the link between theory and practice when making assessments and choices about strategy use in order to reduce reliance on a trial and error approach.

Although the reasons for off task behaviour may be varied, the reason for teachers managing behaviour is much clearer. Within the behaviour for learning conceptual framework the effective management of behaviour should be judged against a clear purpose, which is normally the extent to which it supports or enhances learning behaviour.

In returning to the question of whether on and off task behaviour tells us anything about the pupil's relationship with the curriculum, it needs to be remembered that we are promoting a view that this relationship is ongoing and dynamic. Monitoring on and off task behaviours provides snapshots in time of one aspect of that relationship. On task behaviour could indicate:

- The pupil is interested, motivated, involved and learning.
- The pupil has developed a range of strategies in the form of general 'busyness' that create the *impression* of being on task. However they are not engaged in the intended learning.
- The pupil is on task but is not actively engaging with the learning.
- The pupil is prepared to persist with the activity in order to secure an external reward (e.g. a good grade, approval). This does not necessarily lead to feeling positive about the subject and could lead to a negative relationship.

On task behaviour alone does not allow us readily to differentiate between these reasons. We would caution against using on and off task behaviour as a reliable *single* measure of the quality and efficacy of any relationship with the curriculum.

Pupil learning behaviours as an indicator of their relationship with the curriculum

In Chapter 4 we identified a range of learning behaviours that have been used in policy documents and in the literature. There is some consensus in the literature about the type of learning behaviours that are linked to the curriculum. These learning behaviours can be categorised under the three headings of 'accessing', 'processing' and 'responding' to the curriculum. Within each of these categories there are cognitive, social and emotional aspects of learning.

Readers should take note that the learning behaviours identified and listed in this section have been informed from existing literature in order to reflect what appear to be the current views on behaviours necessary for learning in school contexts. In using these descriptions from the literature for illustrative purposes we do not necessarily endorse them as either definitive or necessarily desirable. They are not intended to be prescriptive and may or may not meet the criteria for a learning behaviour outlined in Chapter 4. However, they provide a base from which readers can develop their own practice.

An approach to assessment of these learning behaviours is necessarily more demanding than simply using on and off task as an indicator of the relationship with the curriculum. As noted in Chapter 4, the assessment of learning behaviours does not readily fit with an emphasis on SMART (specific, measurable, achievable, relevant and timely) targets (Lloyd and Berthelot 1992) often required of teachers for reasons of accountability. If we accept that learning behaviours can be used to enhance both learning and behaviour then we need also to continue to develop ways of assessing the less readily measurable (see Carr and Claxton 2002).

In listing these behaviours it is possible to gain a view about what indicators are linked to having a positive relationship with the curriculum that we can feasibly assess and foster. It is important to note that there are social, emotional and cognitive aspects to relationship with the curriculum and this is reflected by the learning behaviours noted in the following section.

Access to curriculum

In the literature, access to the curriculum is characterised by learning behaviours that reflect a *disposition*, or personal willingness, to take part in the lesson and the organisational and planning *skills* needed to take in the necessary information within a group setting. These learning behaviours necessarily include social, emotional and cognitive aspects as illustrated by the following list:

Mainly *cognitive*:
- plans and works learning out in advance;
- brings necessary equipment to class;
- knows time frame involved in lesson and keeps to it;
- can focus attention primarily on the task;
- actively listens to teacher and monitors own understanding of instructions;
- aware of a variety of ways to learn and achieve and can make choices.

Supporting learning behaviours: mainly *social*:
- demonstrates the necessary social skills to relate and respond to the teacher and peers;
- can follow instructions and requests;
- willing and able to share equipment;
- willing and able to contribute to keeping own and shared equipment such that ongoing access for self and others is facilitated.

Supporting learning behaviours: mainly *emotional*:
- *willing* to relate and respond to teacher and peers;
- is able to plan and focus attention (i.e. is in appropriate mental state);
- has an interest in school and school work;
- is willing to look after their own and others' property;
- has an awareness of what s/he can do and where s/he needs help;
- has sufficient confidence to believe s/he can succeed – even if some help is needed;
- can manage fear of failure in order to access the task.

Processing the curriculum

In the literature processing the curriculum is characterised by learning behaviours that reflect the will and skills needed to actively process information, often with a pre-defined trajectory and/or purpose.

Mainly *cognitive*:
- actively seeks coherence, relevance and meaning (i.e. is an active not passive learner);
- actively looks for the links with other subjects or with previous similar activity;
- can process information independently until there is a problem that cannot be solved without the teacher's intervention;
- can identify when s/he needs help and can take appropriate action;
- asks why s/he went wrong;
- thinks through before offering an opinion and is able to justify what they have said;
- refers to previous work before asking the teacher for help;
- makes considered use of resources;
- not easily distracted from the task in hand.

Supporting learning behaviours: *social*:
- can time and ask questions appropriately;
- seeks and values advice and help from peers and teacher.

Supporting learning behaviours: *emotional*:
- will start task when told – does not start too quickly or put off starting;
- has some self-awareness of what s/he can and cannot do;
- can work independently unless a problem arises that cannot be solved without help.

Ongoing engagement with the curriculum

In the literature, ongoing engagement with the curriculum is characterised by learning behaviours that involve sustained engagement (self-regulation), persistence and motivation, along with the skills needed to select relevant and ignore irrelevant information required for successful task completion.

Learning behaviours: mainly *cognitive*:
- able to work systematically, at a reasonable pace, and knows when to move on to the next activity;
- can sustain concentration and refocus attention when needed;
- can recognise and either ignore or reduce interruptions;
- engages in active problem solving towards completion of task.

Supporting learning behaviours: mainly *social*:
Skills:
- knows class rules and systems;
- can listen to the teacher and others in class;
- knows when it is appropriate to speak;
- can alter pitch and tone and use non-verbal signals;
- allows others personal space and makes eye contact when seeking their attention;
- can organise communication in both individual and group settings.
Disposition:
- can act in a manner appropriate to the classroom situation;
- does not unnecessarily disrupt or interrupt other pupils who are working;
- understands how his/her behaviour affects others.

Supporting learning behaviours: mainly *emotional*:
- is able to monitor his/her own progress;
- persists on task – even if it requires extra effort;
- has the self-belief to carry on even if some difficulties are experienced;
- does not let progress of peers impact negatively on his/her work;
- knows how to attract attention appropriately from others in the classroom;
- seeks help from peers when appropriate;
- can accept and respond to discipline if fair;
- has regard for school equipment.

Responding to the curriculum

In the literature, responding to the curriculum is characterised by learning behaviours that involve being able to generate the required response to the lesson within the allotted time frame.

Learning behaviours: mainly *cognitive*:
- can plan and produce a response that is understandable to the recipient within the time frame.

Supporting behaviours: mainly *emotional*:
- is able to complete work without destroying it;
- can work at a reasonable pace in order to fit into time available (e.g. non- and slow starters and fast finishers);
- plans to achieve success;
- anxiety about failure does not prevent a response being generated.

Self-assessment

In the literature, self-assessment is characterised by learning behaviours that involve reflection, self-review and appraisal of work undertaken.

Learning behaviours: mainly *cognitive*:
- checks his/her work against teacher's and his/her own expectations.

Supporting behaviour: *social*:
- will work with peers to review learning.

Supporting learning behaviours: *emotional*:
- takes appropriate responsibility for own learning.

It is encouraging to note firstly that a plausible set of learning behaviours already exist in the literature and secondly that they are compatible with current thinking about the need to recognise the cognitive, social and emotional aspects of learning (e.g. DfES 2005c, 2007a). Engagement with the behaviour for learning conceptual framework does not therefore require teachers to invent any of the components but to build upon their current practice. Because the learning behaviours have come from educational literature they typically reflect what is required for learning in classrooms from the perspective of government, teachers and school managers. There is much less information on whether these learning behaviours are seen in the same way from the pupil's perspective and more importantly what the existence of such behaviours says about the relationship we want to develop between the pupil and the curriculum. The next section explores these issues.

Learning behaviours: purpose and priorities

As we explored in Chapter 5, the behaviour for learning conceptual framework is rooted in relationships, which by definition involve a reciprocal element. In addressing behavioural difficulties through these relationships we need to try to understand the perception of the individual pupil. This section of the chapter engages in critical reflection on the purposes and priorities conveyed by the learning behaviours identified previously and considers how these might be experienced by the pupil. This requires the teacher to understand the extent to which their purpose for the relationship, from their position of power, matches that of the pupil. This deeper understanding can provide an explanation as to why some pupils choose not to engage with that relationship and are subsequently described as having 'behaviour problems'.

From the previous synthesis of 'desirable' behaviours identified in the literature and policy documents, it can be seen that there is emphasis on the pupil having an initial disposition to get involved in the task and then having the cognitive *skills* to actively process information and produce a response. Learning behaviours linked to social aspects of learning were concerned with relating to the teacher so that tasks could be successfully completed whilst largely ignoring distractions from others. Aspects of the task that required self-regulation and control placed emphasis on having the necessary *disposition* towards school learning. The identification of these behaviours suggests that the relationship with the curriculum, as perceived by adults, is one that is dominated by the need to secure some conformity of response from individuals in a group setting so that subject learning can take place. In addition, the subject learning, and hence the desired response from the pupil, is largely prescribed by a nationally-given curriculum. The relationship is initiated by the teacher through the subject area and this allows him/her to influence the relationship with the curriculum through addressing cognitive, social and emotional aspects. The relationship is conducted in a group setting within the context of normatively referenced expectations, rules and regulations. The efficacy of the relationship is judged against whether it promotes or inhibits the attainment of individual pupils.

From the learning behaviours that fall into the 'cognitive' category it is evident that the teacher can make a positive impact by the way they plan the lesson, provide structure, give opportunities to process information in different ways, make links to familiar learning, give formative feedback on progress, use rewards, and make use of both material and human (peer and other adult) resources. The responsibility for developing most learning behaviours in the cognitive areas appears to be with the teacher. The teacher however has less direct control over emotional aspects of learning, such as self-regulation of learning (e.g. the persistence) and the internal self-appraisal of the purpose and value of any curriculum learning. These are areas of emerging importance across all phases of education, and particularly in relation to the *14–19 Curriculum* (TDA LLUK 2007).

In seeking to look at what we might expect to see if pupils have a good relationship with the curriculum, it can be seen that the literature endorses the occurrence of behaviours that reflect a pupil who is 'motivated' such that the relationship does not just involve the teacher as the active partner. In seeking to identify behaviours that reflect 'motivation', it can be seen that the learning behaviours identified are rooted within relationship with self and, as Harlen and Deakin Crick note in their 2002 review on motivation and assessment, embrace 'self efficacy, self regulation, interest, locus of control, self esteem, goal orientation and learning disposition' (Harlen and Deakin Crick 2002: 14).

Similarly, in their review of strategies to raise pupils' motivational efforts in Key Stage 4 Mathematics, Kyriacou and Goulding (2006) noted:

> When we say that a pupil is highly motivated towards Mathematics, this typically includes:
>
> i   *Positive attitudes towards mathematics:* The pupil finds mathematics interesting, enjoyable, important, do–able and relevant.
> ii *Positive beliefs about self-efficacy:* The pupil believes that making an effort will lead to success.
> iii *Positive intention:* The pupil has a desire to learn more and to do well in attainment tests.
> iv *Positive action:* The pupil displays effort and perseverance, and positively seeks out new challenges.
>
> (Kyriacou and Goulding 2006: 5)

However, although the learning behaviours linked to motivation are linked to the pupil's relationship with self, the *strategies* that foster this motivation involve securing positive relationships with the curriculum and with others as well as with self and as such reflect social, cognitive and emotional influences.

Implications for developing pupils' relationship with the curriculum

So far we have identified pupil learning behaviours that have been linked to the curriculum and have extrapolated something about the purpose and nature of that relationship from a school-based perspective. For the most part, there is an understanding and acceptance of this construction of the relationship with both the pupils and their teachers adapting accordingly. Teachers seek to make constant adjustments to their teaching, with no shortage of guidance from government, Local Authority advisors, consultants and others. Pupils, as they travel through their school life, acquire the dispositions and learn the skills that allow this relationship with the curriculum to be maintained, albeit with a range of differing outcomes.

In some cases the relationships break down both for the teacher and the pupil. The behaviour for learning conceptual framework seeks to address the learning behaviours that contribute to, and ensue from such breakdowns. Teachers typically find it difficult to include children with whom it is difficult to form relationships (Ellis *et al.* 2008), particularly those who exhibit social, emotional and behavioural difficulties, and this in turn has led to concerns about teacher stress and retention. Pupils' reaction to the breakdown of the relationship with the curriculum follows a pattern likely to be seen in any 'personal' relationship and includes:

- *Disruption and disturbance*: The pupil knows that the relationship with the curriculum is not good and reacts in order to note their protest or draw attention to the breakdown; the response is likely to range from repetition of minor disruptive behaviours through to more serious behaviours.
- *Disaffection*: The pupil no longer sees any purpose in keeping the relationship with the curriculum going. They feel that it has nothing to offer them and is irrelevant to their needs. They may or may not show behavioural difficulties; such a pupil is demotivated to learn but may be motivated to achieve minimum hassle.
- *Disengagement*: The pupil has lost connection with the relationship. They may see the point of keeping the relationship going but cannot find a way to get themselves involved or back into the relationship. Their reaction may be attributable to emotional factors or to the fact that they may not have developed the skills needed to repair and/or reconnect the relationship.

While traditionally for the teacher the relationship is judged largely against pupil *response* to teacher-led input and intention, the pupil is concerned with their personal *experience* and involvement in this relationship. In a study by West *et al.* (1997) looking at children aged 6–7 years' attitudes to the curriculum, the findings revealed that three key dimensions were conceptualised:

- interest v/s boredom
- level of difficulty
- success v/s failure.

In secondary age pupils, 11–16 years, Smith *et al.* (2005) examined research evidence concerning pupils' perception of influences on their motivation to learn in the classroom. The study reported that:

- Pupils recognise the positive contribution of effort.
- Some pupils perceive school work as boring and repetitive.
- Pupils appear to be more engaged with lessons that they perceive to be fun.
- Pupils appear less interested when classroom activity takes a formal passive form.
- Pupils express a preference for collaborative work.
- Authentic learning tasks are more likely to cognitively engage pupils.

What we can learn from these findings is that there are bound to be differing perceptions about the nature and purpose of the relationship with the curriculum from the teacher's and pupils' perspectives. If the relationship is going to work then these differences need to be recognised. If the relationship with the curriculum is not running smoothly we might usefully ask the following questions:

1 What is the purpose of the relationship?
   Is there a 'meeting of minds' as to the purpose of the relationship? If a teacher says 'if you don't work harder you will not get your GCSE's', this reflects *their* purpose. This may not link to the pupil's purpose for sustaining a relationship with curriculum at any given time, particularly when the end purpose that the teacher is prioritising is distant or there are competing priorities.

2   What is expected from the relationship?

The teacher may judge the relationship to be 'good' because the pupil achieves the learning objective. While success is also an important factor in the pupil's judgement, they may place priority on additional criteria such as enjoyment and involvement with peers.

3   What activities keep the relationship going?

A teacher, from their perspective, may intuitively identify a curriculum focus, such as 'catch-up' groups or increased practice in the subject area of concern. A pupil might regard this as the very worst response and it may trigger a complete breakdown of the relationship. From their perspective, strategies that involve a break from this focus, attention to social factors such as pupil-grouping or emotional factors that seek to reduce overall anxiety, might be more appropriate.

4   How will the relationship be assessed?

The teacher may seek to judge the relationship against time-framed, predetermined indicators, such as end of Key Stage assessments. The pupil may be judging the relationship more on a day-to-day basis against the extent to which it has been beneficial to them in a variety of ways such as personal success, peer involvement and avoidance of negative teacher attention.

A teacher cannot *make* a pupil relate to the curriculum in the way that suits the school's or government's purpose, any more than a pupil can ignore, throughout their schooling, the opportunities afforded by having a relationship with the curriculum. The pupil may seek 'fun' while the teacher needs 'to get through the work'. Unless there is a degree of compromise on behalf of the teacher, some pupils may express the mismatch within the relationship by exhibiting behavioural difficulties. This creates an even greater distance between what the teacher expects from the relationship and what the pupil is prepared to contribute and this could lead to a complete breakdown. The pupil may either exclude themselves from the relationship or be excluded from it.

Ultimately, if we are to support pupils in building a more positive *relationship* with the curriculum as a route to addressing behavioural issues then it is important that we seek to view this relationship from the pupil's perspective. As such we may need to prioritise notions of reciprocity, flexibility, feasibility, tolerance, responsiveness, resilience, involvement and commitment over notions of control and compliance.

Any search for the 'best' relationship with the curriculum in which variables will be controlled and outputs assured becomes in reality a focus towards 'the best it can be' for the individual concerned.

As we have noted in this section, promoting a positive relationship with the curriculum involves the teacher:

- Developing an awareness of the cognitive, social and emotional aspects of learning.
- Being aware of reciprocal and dynamic aspects of the relationship.
- Developing the capacity within pupils to think about and know more about their own learning strategies and techniques. This allows pupils to take some control for their learning and in so doing develop some personal resilience.

What can we learn about the relationship with the curriculum from research into strengthening teaching and learning?

When we think about young children involved in play we can have some idea about the nature of a 'positive relationship with the task'. We see it in their almost all-consuming approach towards play materials and opportunities. They appear very focused and self-directed. They are motivated to become actively engaged with the task and are not willing to be passive recipients of what is going on. They sometimes follow routines such as when in the 'play house' mimicking home activities, but they also put themselves personally into the situation and go beyond the constraints of the materials by using their imagination and creativity and by relating past and present experiences. They show willingness to communicate to others what they are doing and will often persist in order to achieve, or make their own discoveries. It is these learning behaviours that allow for the impressive development that we observe in children in their early years.

This description of a young child at play displays a number of important characteristics:

- the child initiates;
- the child has chosen to direct their attention to the activity;
- adult intervention is through shared and not directed attention;
- the child monitors their own pace and direction;
- the involvement of other children is often unintentional but valued;
- there is not necessarily a prescribed end-point;
- the reward is intrinsic to the activity;
- they use different and creative ways to explore the situation.

The challenge, when attempting to foster a positive relationship with the curriculum within a largely prescribed subject-based curriculum with prescribed age-related outcomes, is to continue to capture some of the elements of the relationship that we see in young children's play. As children get older, their relationship with the curriculum is likely to be judged against different criteria. For example, as noted in the preceding chapter, White and Mitchell (1994), in looking at secondary school behaviour, identified the learning behaviours desirable in classroom settings. These are used within Reflective Exercise 6.1.

Reflective Exercise 6.1

In considering the table below and from your understanding of the previous section, what does the learning behaviour tell us about the pupil's relationship with the curriculum? How might this inform your choice of strategy? A starting example has been provided.

(continued)

Reflective Exercise 6.1 (continued)

Learning behaviours (taken from White and Mitchell 1994)	What does this behaviour tell us about the pupil's relationship with the curriculum?	What are the implications for strategy choice?
Pupil expects to be told what to do – not prepared to try and work it out.	Pupil is adopting a passive approach to the relationship.	Teacher engineers an active approach e.g. by asking the pupil to identify parts of the task s/he can do.
Pupil refers to previous work before asking the teacher.		
Pupil tells the teacher when they do not understand.	Pupil is actively monitoring his/her relationship with the curriculum and takes responsibility for maintaining the relationship.	Teacher reinforces the pupil's attempt to sustain their relationship with the curriculum by responding warmly and informatively to queries rather than regarding questions as irritants.
Pupil rarely makes contributions of own ideas to lessons.		
Pupil looks for link with other subjects.		
Pupil repeats the same mistakes time and time again.		
Pupil asks teacher why they went wrong.		

What does Reflective Exercise 6.1 tell us about strengthening relationship with the curriculum for secondary age pupils?

In this example, White and Mitchell have identified the learning behaviours that they frequently observe and which they consider either promote or hinder learning in the classroom. By using observation to identify classroom learning behaviours and identifying those which promote learning (rather than simply concentrating on 'bad' or 'poor' behaviour), the teacher is able to identify a clear *purpose* for intervention against which their strategy use can be evaluated. The next step is to consider what the observed learning behaviour tells us about the pupil's relationship with the curriculum and which aspect of that relationship it would be most beneficial, or feasible to target. This then informs choice of strategy. In this example the behaviours identified for secondary age pupils were those that characterised the 'good' learner as an active, skilled participant who can monitor and self-regulate their learning.

Strengthening the relationship with the curriculum for primary age pupils

Powell *et al.* (2006) conducted research that sought to promote active pupil engagement in their relationship with literacy. Interestingly, in a summary description of Powell *et al.*'s (2006) research, DCSF (http://www.standards.dfes.gov.uk/research/themes/English/ sustainingpupil/ accessed 10/7/08) used the subtitle 'How can teachers keep pupils on task during literacy lessons?' Although Table 6.2 suggests that this was the starting point for the research the actual study was concerned with promoting not just 'on task' behaviour but active pupil engagement in that task. As such it endorses the view expressed earlier in this chapter about the need to look beyond 'on task' as a measure of the pupil's relationship with curriculum.

Table 6.2 Generic behaviours associated with 'on' and 'off' task (Powell *et al.* 2006)

Negative behaviours (resistance)	Positive behaviours
Interrupt teacher and peers	Willingness to persist
Distract others and refuse to comply to teacher requests	Choosing to work/read during leisure time

In this research an emphasis was placed on promoting the identified positive behaviours. Any relationship with the curriculum requires some commitment from the pupil and this study looked at children's motivational behaviour through their 'propensity to invest time and effort in learning to read' (Powell *et al.* 2006: 10). They assessed this through:

* children's use of reading strategies;
* children's persistence in solving problems and trying out new strategies;
* children's willingness and ability to use various volitional control strategies to see a task through to fruition.

These three learning behaviours were selected because they have been shown through research to be related to motivation and achievement in literacy. The study sought to look at how teaching styles and strategies in the classroom influenced these learning behaviours. Table 6.3 notes teacher strategies that were considered to either promote or inhibit pupil's positive relationship with the task.

Within Powell *et al.*'s (2006) research there was emphasis on the links between teaching approaches and responses from pupils. These approaches can broadly be grouped as 'passive' and 'active', as illustrated in the examples in Table 6.3.

Table 6.3 does not seek to suggest that all the 'passive' strategies are necessarily ineffective. A passive teaching strategy can be activated by the learner – if they have developed appropriate learning behaviours. For example listening to the teacher read, which may be considered a passive approach, could be a very useful strategy if the teacher is trying to get young pupils who may not be fluent readers to comprehend the story. However, both the teacher and the pupils need to *share* the purpose of the task (in this case comprehension) and the pupils will need to be directed towards *actively* listening and remembering. Strategy choice depends on what learning the teacher is seeking to promote and the state of readiness of the learner to share and engage with that purpose. If a teacher is seeking to impart new knowledge it may be that a didactic approach works well, providing

Table 6.3 Passive and active strategies that impact on pupil's learning behaviour

Passive	Active
Listening to teacher	Discussing ideas with partner
Adherence to procedures	Reading, writing, and manipulating, that required more strategic (versus mechanical) cognitive processes
Tasks that were either too difficult or too easy	Appropriately challenging tasks
'Defensive teaching' (i.e. teachers using instructional methods that they believed would lead to the least pupil resistance)	Responding to higher-level questions
Lack of pupil self-regulation	Peer collaboration
Explicit instruction that incorporated direct instructional techniques controlled by the teacher	Tasks that provided opportunities for pupils to use reading and writing for authentic purposes
Practice activities and worksheets, where the pupils were directed to use particular information (such as rhyming words) to arrive at a single, correct solution	Pupils to be actively involved in constructing meaning and metacognitions about literacy

the pupils have developed the required listening and engagement skills (note-taking, questioning, self-monitoring against learning objectives etc). It follows that an imbalance of passive and active strategies would serve to limit the development of effective learning behaviours.

Powell *et al.*'s (2006) study was informed from the work of Turner and Paris (1995) who suggested that there were six critical features of 'open' tasks that seemed to affect children's active engagement with literacy. They refer to these features as the 'six Cs':

• Choice: this allows children to select tasks that interest them or have personal relevance;
• Challenge: this enables scaffolding of children's learning. It gives children opportunities to demonstrate and build on what they know; it involves tasks that go beyond a single answer;
• Control: this enables children and teachers to share in the decision-making process, and supports children in taking ownership of their learning;
• Collaboration: this encourages social interaction. The aim is for children to learn from one another and support each other's efforts;
• Construct comprehension/meaning: this allows children to 'make sense' of what they are learning by using literacy to solve problems, to entertain, to inform. This also supports development of meta-cognitive abilities;
• Consequences: these influence children's motivation for literacy learning by providing either positive or negative feelings about achievement. Tasks involve those that require children to maintain a belief in their ability to be successful; closed tasks that have 'correct' responses or require single, narrow strategies for success are less motivating.

(Turner and Paris 1995, cited by Powell *et al.* 2006)

What does this research tell us about strengthening the relationship with the curriculum for primary age pupils?

The notion of looking at how best to promote learning behaviours that signify 'motivation', which in Powell *et al.*'s (2006) research is expressed as 'propensity to invest time and effort' (Powell *et al.* 2006: 10), is clearly crucial to the development of relationships for learning in school contexts. By seeking to develop this at primary level, it would be hoped that pupils come to recognise that such an investment reaps academic, personal and social dividends. Through placing an emphasis on what the pupil needs to experience from the relationship, in the form of Turner and Paris' (1995) 'six Cs', the teacher is able to deliver appropriate strategies and opportunities that serve to meet their purpose for deeper learning, engagement and improved attainment. This secures the *reciprocity* necessary within a positive relationship with the curriculum.

Powell *et al.*'s (2006) research focused on developing the active components of on task behaviour through teaching approaches that encourage pupil engagement. Having secured this, it is necessary within a successful relationship with the curriculum to ensure that such engagement serves to promote within pupils a deeper understanding of both subject content and their own learning.

Promoting deeper understanding of the subject and pupil involvement

A recent EPPI review (Kyriacou and Issitt 2008) concerning effective teacher–pupil dialogue in Mathematics looked at developing progression in understanding. The review distinguishes between teaching approaches for procedural fluency and those for conceptual understanding, stating

> for many years a distinction has been made in Mathematics education between teaching for 'procedural fluency' and teaching for 'conceptual understanding'. In procedural fluency the teacher generally demonstrates a technique to solve a particular problem and the pupils then use this technique to solve similar problems. Conceptual teaching largely takes the form of exploring with pupils their understanding of the principles underlying a problem and embedding the techniques for solving problems within this understanding.
>
> (Kyriacou and Issitt 2008: 1)

The significance of this piece of research for our exploration of relationship with the curriculum is that it builds on Powell *et al.*'s (2006) work that examined how best to improve pupils' cognitive engagement with the task. Kyriacou and Issitt's (2008) study is concerned with how to influence the direction and depth of such engagement through a focus on subject specific dialogue.

Kyriacou and Issitt's (2008) research looked at the role of effective teacher-initiated dialogue with pupils, and whether this can increase pupils' conceptual understanding of Mathematics. The study reported that dialogue in Maths lessons is dominated by an 'initiate' (teacher), 'response' (pupil) and 'feedback' (teacher) pattern (IRF) of pupil-teacher interaction.

The review identified eight possible characteristics of effective teacher-initiated dialogue aimed at improving conceptual understanding in Mathematics. These were:

- going beyond 'initiate, response, feedback' (IRF);
- focusing attention on Mathematics rather than 'getting the answer right';
- working collaboratively with pupils;
- transformative listening;
- scaffolding;
- enhancing pupils' self-knowledge about using dialogue as a learning experience;
- encouraging high-quality pupil dialogue;
- inclusive teaching.

Most of these terms will be familiar to teachers. Table 6.4 elaborates on a number of these that may be less familiar.

Table 6.4 Characteristics of effective teacher-initiated dialogue

Characteristic	*Description* (from Kyriacou and Issitt 2008)
Transformative listening	This relies on teachers listening to pupils' contributions in a manner that conveys that there is a genuine 'meeting of minds' and that the teacher is willing to change their own thinking in the light of what the pupil has said. Teachers may be able to do this through asking a question they do not know the answer to, responding to pupils' suggestions, asking for feedback from the whole class, or asking a pupil to explain their ideas to the class.
Encouraging high-quality pupil dialogue	There is a need for teachers to be accepting towards pupils' contributions, to encourage pupils to develop their contributions further and indeed, to allow the direction of a lesson to follow the pupils' contributions. Being accepting towards pupils' contributions may enhance the quality of the discourse, but may also create a tension for the teacher in wanting to direct pupils' attention towards mathematically acceptable strategies.
Inclusive teaching	Teachers can convey to *all* pupils regardless of ability that their contribution is equally valued and that all pupils in the class are engaged and have their answers taken seriously. 'Bright' pupils are more likely to engage in productive exchanges (characterised by their answers being taken more seriously by the teacher and being 'given the floor'). Inclusive teaching involves strategies to make sure less able pupils also feel able to contribute and have their ideas taken seriously, so that they do not develop a self-identity as non-participants.
Scaffolding	Scaffolding is when the teacher provides support (or scaffolds) to help the pupil's learning and this helps pupils build on prior knowledge. Different types of scaffolding can be used by teachers. For example the teacher may focus pupils' attention during a class discussion on key features and merits of particular strategies suggested by pupils for solving a challenging problem. Another example is to discuss with pupils a deliberate mistake in order to identify and clarify the nature of the mistake, thereby focusing pupil attention on the key features of investigating the particular problem at hand.

The information in Table 6.4 strongly suggests that a relationship with the curriculum has to be more than that conveyed by an IRF pattern of pupil–teacher interaction. The strategies cited sought to identify and meet the features of an effective relationship by offering pupils the opportunity to:

- experience reciprocity through connecting with the subject knowledge and the teacher's thinking;
- make mistakes and learn from them;
- have their contribution acknowledged and valued;
- be able to say what they could contribute and be supported to contribute further;
- become actively engaged and involved;
- have some control over their contribution to, and experience of, the relationship.

Many of the characteristics of effective teacher-initiated dialogue identified by Kyriacou and Issitt (2008) would generally be accepted as 'good teaching' and as such are nothing new. However by framing them within the context of developing learning behaviours through building a positive relationship with the curriculum there is additional justification for their use.

In looking at the role of active processing within a relationship with the curriculum, it is relevant to note the authors' conclusion that 'the strongest supporting evidence came from studies that focused on enhancing pupils' self-knowledge of how to use dialogue as a learning experience' (Kyriacou and Issitt 2008: 14). This illustrates that those teacher strategies that promote in pupils a greater understanding of themselves as learners are particularly powerful. This would be expected as such individual understanding allows pupils to have more control over their own learning. As such the pupil becomes a beneficiary by grasping learning opportunities and more resilient by becoming less vulnerable to changes in contexts and conditions.

The study reported that pupils need to appreciate how discussion and listening to teachers and other pupils makes a valuable contribution to their learning. Some pupils may have become accepting that classroom talking either involves listening to the teacher's questions and trying to respond with what they believe is an expected answer or engaging in social talk with peers possibly as a distraction from the task in hand. From this study on Maths dialogue it would appear that there is opportunity to improve the pupil's relationship with the curriculum by 'adopting an enquiry-based style of teaching' (Kyriacou and Issitt 2008: 12, drawing on Black 2006) that views dialogue as a tool for learning and uses whole-class discussions to create a communal space for developing understanding.

The teacher is likely to have superior knowledge of the curriculum and will, through assessment, have some knowledge of how much the pupil knows. The teacher also knows how they, as the adult, are thinking about the curriculum. The area where perhaps less is known is in relation to how the pupil is thinking about the curriculum. Kyriacou and Issitt's (2008) study shows how teacher dialogue with pupils about the curriculum can provide this necessary information. Essentially what Kyriacou and Issitt (2008) are implying is that the teacher has to broker the pupil's relationship with the curriculum through language.

Personal relationships do characteristically rely on this type of brokering through language. Language development and competence, both oral and written, play a significant role in brokering relationships with the curriculum. Teachers will be aware that for some of their pupils this may be a barrier, limiting the extent to which they can respond to some of the language-based strategies identified in the Kyriacou and Issitt's (2008) study into effective Maths teaching.

In a study relevant to this concern, which investigated effective teaching for low attaining groups, Dunne *et al.* (2007) identified the following approaches as beneficial:

- teachers addressed learning by considering both cognitive and affective strategies – a slower pace of delivery was used, increased scaffolding, peer support and more feedback and praise;
- differentiated materials were used *specifically* to address the (individual) needs of pupils;
- teachers gave pupils the opportunity to select and vary the level of challenge in their learning – this allowed for success but also served to reduce any stigma associated with the pupil being given 'easier work';
- practical and interactive approaches were used to motivate and reward;
- Assessment for Learning (AfL) and peer evaluation were used to balance challenge, opportunity for success and high expectation;
- many teachers went out of their way to cultivate positive relationships through use of praise, treating mistakes as part of learning, careful questioning techniques and paying attention to cultural sensitivities;
- teacher–pupil relationships were regarded as highly significant to low attaining learners – to achieve this teachers used a 'negotiated' approach;
- teachers needed to balance a more relaxed approach to teaching low attaining groups, adopted based on a desire to build positive teacher–pupil relations, with sufficient discipline to enable pupils to concentrate.

What we can learn from this study is that for some pupils the nature of the 'compromise' needed to broker the gap between teacher and pupil perspectives on the relationship with the curriculum may need to be different to that implied by Kyriacou and Issitt's (2008) work. In order to rebuild, develop, or strengthen that relationship, developing pupil *willingness* to engage may be a more important priority initially than developing subject based *skills*. Findings from Dunne *et al.* (2007) suggest that such a pursuit requires paying particular attention to the pupil's affective state. This can be achieved through the teacher initially moving nearer to the pupil's view of the relationship with curriculum. We know that pupils' liking of a school-based activity is linked to interest, fun, ease and success (West *et al.* 1997). Through their study Dunne *et al.* (2007) demonstrate that effective teaching for low-attaining secondary-aged pupils involved manipulating these factors (interest, fun, ease and success) in order to secure and sustain pupil *willingness* to engage. Significantly Dunne *et al.* (2007) also identified the importance of personal relationships with others as part of effective teaching.

Realities of relationships: how much should teachers compromise?

Dunne *et al.*'s (2007) study has highlighted that in order to encourage particular pupils to *re-engage* with learning, it is necessary to take note of their current perspective on the curriculum subject and school learning in general. In doing this we identify common ground and differences as we might in any personal relationship that is experiencing difficulties. If we want to re-build the relationship, we seek to compromise, as illustrated by Dunne *et al.*'s (2007) study. In making such a compromise the teacher may be adjusting the balance between having to get the pupils to learn in the context of a prescribed and assessed curriculum and incorporating the interest, fun, ease and success referred to by West *et al.* (1997). In thinking about this compromise it is probably true to say that:

- Having to do required aspects of the curriculum that are less enjoyable can often be brokered through good personal relationships. In other words, the motivation to tackle the task lies in the relationship with the teacher rather than the appeal of the task.
- In moving from a direct focus on the relationship with the curriculum towards a dominant focus on promoting a positive relationship with self and with others, teachers necessarily reposition themselves within the relationship. For some this may feel like a threat to their professional identity. This may be a particular issue for secondary teachers for whom subject specialism has traditionally represented 'a badge of professional identity' (Kirk and Broadhead 2007: 9).
- The extent of compromise needed is prescribed by the nature of the curriculum. For example, some pupils may cope with an inflexible results-oriented approach to the curriculum based on drilling in preparation for tests or examinations. However those pupils whose relationship with this form of curriculum breaks down may require a considerable degree of compromise to re-build their relationship. The teacher, influenced by the ethos of the school and used to teaching in this way, is likely to view the degree of compromise necessary as being significant.
- A curriculum that already incorporates elements of interest, fun, ease and success is likely to lead to fewer pupils requiring compromise and those that do requiring less. Arguably it is easier to incorporate these elements into certain key stages and subjects.
- Whilst we may see benefits in relationship with self and relationship with others, the efficacy of the compromise should be judged against the impact it has on the pupil's relationship with the curriculum.

Whilst shifting the balance of the relationship may be necessary, it does need to be undertaken with recognition of the need to develop longer-term *resilience* in the learner. Once the individual pupil leaves compulsory schooling, there is no assurance that within post-compulsory education, training or employment the kind of adjustments noted in Dunne *et al.*'s (2007) study will be made. It is paramount therefore that, from the start of their schooling and throughout their education, individuals develop resilience from their relationship with the curriculum.

School learning is not all 'fun' and does require effort, persistence and recovering from failure. Teachers can and need to make compromises to re-engage pupils and this often reaps necessary short-term benefits in relationships and learning. However, if the balance shifts too far the teacher could perceive their priority has solely become keeping the pupil happy or providing entertainment. Unless such a compromise is part of a longer term initiative that contributes to life-long learning, personal development and achievement of the pupil it is difficult to justify. Balance, as in all relationships, is needed and this rests in the hands of professional teachers and their managers.

Summary

In this section we have explored the nature and purpose of a relationship with the curriculum through a critical look at the traditional measure of 'time on task', learning behaviours that have been linked to having a 'positive' relationship with the curriculum, and studies that seek to improve this relationship.

Policy and prescription have moved from an emphasis on a largely one way relationship *for* securing subject attainment to one in which the more holistic social, emotional and cognitive outcomes reflected in *Every Child Matters* (DfES 2004a) are achieved *through* the relationship with curriculum.

There is growing evidence, some of which is highlighted in this chapter, to support a view that construing the pupil's contact with the curriculum as a *relationship* is timely, relevant and useful. It leads teachers to focus their thinking directly on how their teaching practices impact on individual pupils in their particular situations. Dunne *et al.* (2007) suggest 'this is partly about listening to pupils. It is also about looking for impacts on pupil progress and attainment, and about monitoring the quality, breadth and flexibility of provision' (Dunne *et al.* 2007: 6). An emphasis on developing the individual's role in the relationship supports 'the development of personalised learning by identifying teaching and learning strategies which actively engage and challenge learners, which develop their ability to focus on their learning skills and their capability to take ownership of their own progress' (Higgins *et al.* 2007: 1).

An understanding of the *reciprocal* changing nature of relationships between individuals and the curriculum helps teachers to understand not just what works in terms of specific teaching approaches in specific contexts but *why* different approaches are successful. This can

Table 6.5 Effective approaches to develop pupils' learning capabilities

Effective approach (Higgins et al. 2007)	Behaviour for learning comment
Structured tasks that focus on specific meta-cognitive strategies in the context of the lesson/subject.	Personal relationships break down because individuals do not know what they are required to do. Skills and strategies have to be learned and – in the case of the curriculum – taught.
Capacity in lessons for more explicit transactions between the learner and the teacher concerning the purpose of the activity.	The relationship needs to be explicitly and openly monitored so that both sides know the other's perspective. Personal relationships sometimes break down on the basis of one partner saying 'how am I expected to know what you wanted me to do?'
Small group interactions promoting the articulation of the use of strategies during teaching.	Pupils need safe places with peers to identify and practice strategies appropriate for their age group – and at times to learn about peers' successful strategies.
Mechanisms built into the task to promote the checking of mutual understanding of the goals by peers and with the teacher.	This allows the pupil a role in the relationship and opportunity to check what is wanted and what they can give, etc. E.g. 'Am I doing OK? … you could help by …'
Enhanced opportunities for the learner to receive diagnostic feedback linked directly to the task.	The pupil needs information on *how* to make things better and not just be told that what they had done was not good enough.

Table 6.6 Supportive conditions for effective approaches

Conditions	Behaviour for learning comment
The teacher needs to have a good understanding of learning, in terms of the subject and the context.	The teacher needs to understand where the tricky subject parts are for pupils and identify which of these can be learned through more 'fun' activities and collaborative work, and which have to be taught more formally.
There is also the need for the teacher to have access to concrete tools and strategies to guide the learner and enhance opportunities for feedback.	The teacher needs to know that for some pupils 'more of the same' will not suffice. Pupils may also need to develop their repertoire of strategies so that they do not persist with those that have proven unsuccessful. This can be achieved through development of metacognition, and the provision of opportunities to explicitly learn about effective strategies used by other pupils.
Both teachers and learners should have an orientation towards learning characterised by a willingness to engage in dialogue and negotiation regarding the intent and purpose of a particular teaching and learning episode.	In any personal relationship it is often not easy to guess what is expected by the other person. Open and clear negotiations about intent and purpose are essential to avoid misunderstanding and breakdown; the relationship is necessarily reciprocal and involves a willingness on both sides.
The focus should be on how to succeed in terms of the selection of appropriate strategies and making the right effort, rather than on ability.	Relationships for everyone require commitment and effort – it is not going to be lovely and fun all the time but both sides should see the benefits from actively pursuing the relationship. No one is born 'good at relationships' so there is a need for teachers to convey a view that values pupil progress in relation to being 'good at being in the relationship' rather than 'good at the product of that relationship.'

support teachers in making informed choices about what strategies are likely to be effective in their *own* context and move them away from a quest to find the definitive list of proven successful strategies that will work for their class. Teachers do need a toolkit of effective strategies in order to develop and promote the learning behaviours that characterise a positive relationship with the curriculum. However, whilst we have influence, we do not have control over the individual pupil's contribution and response to the relationship because they bring their own personal dispositions, attributes and attributions. We cannot therefore work within a framework that offers and prescribes 'best practice' although we can be mindful of some *principles* for building positive relationships with the curriculum and associated good practice. Higgins *et al.* (2007) identified a number of effective approaches which teachers can use to develop pupils' learning capabilities. We have paired these with behaviour for learning comments in Table 6.5.

Higgins *et al.* (2007) also identify a number of necessary conditions for the approaches in Table 6.5. These conditions, taken directly from Higgins *et al.*'s report (2007: 6, section 3:1), have been listed in Table 6.6 together with a behaviour for learning comment.

In exploring relationship with the curriculum through the studies cited above, and as noted in the previous chapter on learning behaviours, it can be seen that simply being *cognitively able* to learn in the classroom is not sufficient. The learner also has to be disposed to learn and to be ready and willing to take learning opportunities. The pupil may well have the ability to pay attention and listen but simply may not be *disposed* to do so and as a consequence may 'switch off' and/or disrupt others. The next chapter looks more closely at the individual's relationship with self and with others as a route to promoting a more positive relationship with the curriculum.

Relationship with self and relationship with others

Introduction

In the previous chapter we deliberately covered the topic of relationship with the curriculum in depth because of its relevance to school-based learning contexts. This relationship is the one with which the majority of teachers are likely to feel most competent and confident.

In this chapter we have given the two other relationships within the behaviour for learning conceptual framework less in-depth coverage because there is less of a need for reframing. The concept of a relationship with others is already likely to make perfect sense to most readers. In group settings, such as a classroom, pupils need to be able to get on with peers and adults. The concept of a relationship with self is also relatively easy to accept. We might hear people say, for example, 'He doesn't seem to like himself very much' regarding an individual who seems to be locked into a pattern of self-destructive behaviour, or 'She really loves herself!' regarding an individual who appears overly confident to the point of boastfulness. Self-esteem is a commonly used term and carries with it an acceptance that individuals actively make judgements about themselves based on their experiences and the perceptions of others.

The pupil's relationship with self and others is intrinsic to the behaviour for learning conceptual framework and our primary concern is the extent to which these relationships influence the relationship with the curriculum and how they help us to understand and address behaviour problems in school contexts.

Relationship with self

Working definition

To want to, and be able to, include him/herself in the learning opportunities and relationships on offer in the classroom and school context. This includes how the learner feels about themselves, their self-esteem, self-efficacy and their own *perceptions* of the relevance of school learning.

Relationship with self may seem to be the most daunting of the three behaviour for learning relationships for teachers as it relates to the 'emotional and motivational life of the mind' (Skinner 1976: 182) about which it is only possible to hypothesise and make tentative deductions.

This relationship has developed over time and is therefore likely to be resistant to change. Its development is subject to a number of influences – biological, psychological, familial and socio-cultural – which may be outside the teacher's sphere of influence. This relationship is strongly linked to emotion and affect which are known to be powerful determinants of behaviour.

The teacher cannot easily access or assess the pupil's relationship with self and has to interpret what it might be from pupil responses. The pupil may not have given thought to their own relationship with self or be conscious of its influence on their behaviour. The individual's particular relationship with self may not appear rational to others. A parent/carer or teacher might for example find themselves thinking 'he is doing really well; I have no idea why he does not believe in himself'.

It is important to note that within the behaviour for learning conceptual framework relationship with self is seen as supporting the development of the pupil's relationship with curriculum. It is an acknowledgement that there is an emotional *aspect* of learning, just as there are social and cognitive aspects. This emotional aspect is intrinsic to the relationship with the curriculum and, as such, contributes to the development of both positive and negative learning behaviours. Ecclestone and Hayes (2008) have questioned whether there has been an over-emphasis within the education system on what they term 'therapeutic education' and claim that this is 'turning children, young people and adults into anxious and self-occupied individuals' (Ecclestone and Hayes 2008: i). In referring to relationship with self and emotional aspects of learning we are aware that we are touching upon areas that Ecclestone and Hayes and others appear to find troublesome. Our stance is very clear: we do not seek to pathologise the normal human feelings that are experienced during learning in educational settings. As humans, we can and do at times feel:

- disappointed or cross when we fail;
- ill at ease when we compare our performance with some others;
- the discomfort of effort and persistence;
- resentful of the time 'work' takes away from more pleasant activities;
- angry toward those whose judgement of our work does not match our own;
- irritated and annoyed when working with some others;
- resentful if our 'work in progress' or our answers to questions are put up for peer group scrutiny;
- dissatisfied with our finished work;
- pressured if too much is asked of us;
- anxious about change;
- upset when friendships are not working.

All these feelings are part of learning and as 'life-long learners' we need to prepare pupils for this reality. Such feelings may become problematic if they become the *dominant* and *persistent* experience for the pupil. Our purpose in considering relationship with self is to improve pupil learning behaviour so that we can harness the pupil's potential for learning, develop their tolerance and resilience and most of all develop their autonomy. As the majority of children progress through home and school, they are able to compare the emotional 'downs' of learning with the emotional 'ups'. Arguably, successful learners do not learn without effort but, unlike those we might consider less successful learners, their effort more frequently results in a positive outcome. When they seek to 'make sense' of their learning experiences they are dealing with a different ratio of positive to negative feelings and are able to make a more balanced judgement such as: 'This is difficult for me but I've worked at this kind of problem before and succeeded eventually with effort, so I can do it again'.

This is the kind of thinking that leads to persistence and a style that teachers would want to develop in all their pupils. A pupil who has not experienced much success might think: 'I can't do this – others can do it easily, no one has told me how to do it –I don't want to do it anyway'.

This type of thinking makes this pupil vulnerable as they have not acknowledged effort as a variable in their own or others' learning. The pupil has chosen to attribute blame outside themselves, in this case to the teacher. Having made 'sense' to themselves in this way they are unlikely to take any responsibility for their own learning because they do not perceive that they have any control over it. We cannot escape from the fact that, however good our intentions for our teaching, individual pupils will seek to 'make sense' of their experiences from their personal perspectives. For a few pupils this may lead to emotionally influenced dispositions and behaviours that are either transient or entrenched and which significantly interfere with their academic learning and social behaviour in the classroom. This section of the chapter seeks to support teachers in providing experiences for such pupils that secure a better balance between the positive and negative feelings associated with their school learning. Teachers can make a positive contribution through their influence on pupils' dispositions towards learning and achievement.

Recognising difficulties linked to 'relationship with self'

In identifying difficulties linked to the pupil's relationship with self our main clues come from their presenting behaviour. Examples of behaviour that is influenced by relationship with self include:

- reluctance to try new things;
- being easily frustrated from lack of immediate success or understanding;
- attitudes that are hypercritical, negative, sarcastic and cynical;
- withdrawal, depression and unwillingness to communicate;
- blaming behaviour outside themselves;
- dependency on others to tell them what to do, what is good, what is acceptable;
- lying;
- non-compliance to authority.

The potential of these behaviours to impact negatively on relationship with the curriculum and relationship with others is immediately apparent.

The importance of emotions

If we look at how emotions affect the way individuals think we can see how they can explain some of the pupil behaviour we see in the classroom:

- Emotions can help or distract the pupil's focus of attention – for example if s/he feels confident s/he is likely to stay focused, if s/he feels unsure s/he may be distracted.
- Emotions can function cognitively if they embed beliefs – so a pupil who genuinely

believes s/he is not capable of being successful in a task will experience fear.
- Emotions can make things stand out by heightening our awareness and redirecting our attention.

(Department of Education and Training 2005)

Knowing how emotions impact on our cognitive processes, such as directing attention and influencing our thinking, allows us to use cognitive strategies to alter emotional states. The interdependence between cognition and emotion allows some flexibility in strategy selection. As an example, if a pupil arrives in the classroom in a heightened emotional state we could:

- Direct their attention towards a structured, predictable, pupil controllable curricular activity in which we know they can succeed. The source of their original emotionally charged state can be discussed at a later point when they are able to use their cognitive ability more effectively to reflect.
- If appropriate seek to reduce the intensity of emotional state through addressing the concern or cause and then direct their attention towards the curriculum.
- Acknowledge that they are in an emotional state and offer additional strategies if feasible such as time out, some enhanced personal space, or teaching assistant support.

Terminology and concepts associated with relationship with self

Relationship with self is more frequently referred to by terms such as 'self-esteem', 'self-concept' and 'self-efficacy'. We regard these terms as explanatory constructs and will discuss these in turn.

Understanding self-esteem theory

In his seminal work *The Antecedents of Self-Esteem*, Coopersmith (1967) defined self-esteem as

> the evaluation which an individual makes and customarily maintains with regard to himself: it expresses an attitude of approval or disapproval, and indicates the extent to which the individual believes himself to be capable, significant, successful, and worthy. In short, self-esteem is a *personal* judgment of worthiness that is expressed in the attitudes the individual holds towards himself. It is the subjective experience which the individual conveys to others by verbal reports and other overt, expressive behavior.
>
> (Coopersmith 1967: 5)

Whilst Coopersmith acknowledged that there were 'momentary, situational, limited shifts in self-evaluation' (1967: 5), he was clear that the definition he used in his research centred upon 'the relatively enduring estimate of general self-esteem rather than upon more specific and transitory changes in evaluation' (Coopersmith 1967: 5). He argued that the self-esteem of an individual remained relatively stable and enduring over several years and suggested that 'This appraisal can presumably be affected by specific incidents and environmental changes but apparently it reverts to its customary level when conditions resume their "normal" and typical course' (Coopersmith 1967: 5).

Coopersmith (1967) cites the earlier work of Aronson and Mills (1959) that showed that 'persons are generally unwilling to accept evidence that they are better or worse than they themselves have decided, and generally resolve any dissonance between the evidence and their judgment in favour of their customary judgment' (Coopersmith 1967: 5, citing Aronson and Mills 1959).

Drawing upon and developing the writings of Coopersmith (1967), Argyle (1967) and others, Lawrence's (2006) work on self-esteem has enjoyed considerable longevity with editions published in 1988, 1996 and 2006.

Lawrence (2006) defines self-esteem within the wider context of an individual's self-concept. Self-concept can be understood as an individual's awareness of his/her own self. Three areas underpin the development of self-concept: self-image, ideal self and self-esteem. Figure 7.1 illustrates the relationship between these three elements.

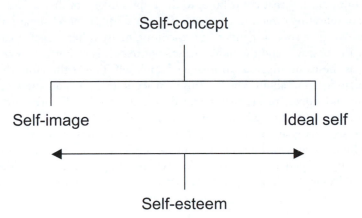

Figure 7.1 Understanding self-esteem (based on Lawrence 2006: 3). Reproduced by permission of the publisher (© SAGE 2006).

Self-image

Lawrence (2006) considers an individual's self-image to be the view they have of themselves. A key point for teachers to recognise is that it is a perception by the individual that has been formed and continues to be influenced by a range of feedback and experiences. For example in school, the pupil learns through a range of experiences whether they are the type of person who is popular with peers and whether they are the type of learner who succeeds in types of school-based learning. At home a different set of feedback and experiences will contribute to the development of self-image.

There is a cognitive dimension to the formation of self-image as the individuals reflect on and interpret their experiences (Lawrence 2006). For example, if I am a pupil who is reprimanded by a teacher there are a variety of ways I might interpret this, such as:

- I am a badly behaved or disruptive person.
- A just response to a behaviour I chose to exhibit on this occasion.
- An indication that the teacher is having a bad day. Sometimes adults have bad days.
- This teacher doesn't like me, but that's OK because I can't expect to like everyone or everyone to like me.

- I am not the kind of person that teachers like.
- Of little relevance because teacher disapproval or approval doesn't matter to me.
- Unfair on this occasion, but sometimes adults are like that.
- Unfair and a confirmation that I am a person who teachers treat unfairly.

However, it is impossible to separate this interpretation from the nature of feedback received. If for example the teacher frequently labels the pupil rather than the behaviour (e.g. 'you are unkind' rather than 'that was an unkind thing to do') it is more likely that over a period of time the behaviour will form part of the pupil's self-image (e.g. 'I am an unkind person'). Past experience will also affect the interpretation of events. If a pupil has been used to frequent criticism from parents/carers, perhaps based on developmentally unrealistic expectations in relation to behaviour, perceived criticism by the teacher may have a confirming quality that contributes to the pupil's image of themselves as naughty.

A further complicating dimension is that whilst some aspects of self-image are to a large extent incontrovertible such as gender or eye-colour, many other aspects may be viewed differently by the observer and the individual concerned. It is important to recognise that self-image is, as the name suggests, an image of one's self. This is therefore the reality for the individual; judgement about whether this is an accurate view is an assessment made by others. It is the individual's reality that we need to understand and work with.

In further considering discrepancies between the individual's self-image and how others see them it is also necessary to recognise that our own values as the observer and the context in which we are working make a difference. The child may view themselves as witty, entertaining and generally a bit of a joker, whereas, depending on how these qualities manifest themselves in the classroom, the teacher might view the same child as disrespectful or disruptive.

Ideal self

Lawrence (2006) proposes that not only does the individual develop an idea of self (self-image) but an ideal self. Ideal self can be thought of in terms of how an individual would like to be. Though there is a degree of free choice, it is feedback from a range of sources that is the major influence. Commonly cited examples are those that come from the media (celebrity status, looks, life-style) and from parents (academic achievement, sporting prowess) and from peers (popular, appearance, entertaining, daring). The child quickly learns that certain skills and behaviours are valued in certain contexts. This would seem to be confirmed by Coopersmith's (1967) findings that suggested that 'although individuals are theoretically free to select their values, the years spent in home, school, and peer-groups generally lead to acceptance of group standards and values' (Coopersmith 1967: 244). Lawrence (2006) suggests that increasingly as the child gets older peers exert an influence that can be more powerful than that of either teachers or parents.

Self-esteem

Self-esteem, as described by Lawrence (2006), is the individual's evaluation of the discrepancy between self-image and ideal self. Coopersmith (1967) too referred to self-judgement, involving 'a comparison of one's actual performance and capacities with one's standards and aspirations' (Coopersmith 1967: 245). Some discrepancy is inevitable and necessary in motivating individuals to change or develop their social, physical and academic skills. What we define as 'low self-esteem' results from the combined elements of the size of the discrepancy and the extent to which the discrepancy is a source of concern to the individual.

When considering self-esteem, Lawrence (2006) suggests it is important to distinguish between global and specific self-esteem. Global self-esteem is an individual's overall feeling of self-worth, but we may have feelings of worth or unworth in specific situations (Figure 7.2).

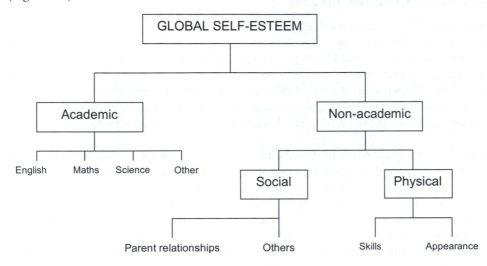

Figure 7.2 The self-esteem hierarchy (Lawrence 2006: 12). Reproduced by permission of the publisher (© SAGE 2006).

An individual may feel a sense of inadequacy in relation to some aspect of their life. Coopersmith (1967) considered it 'conceivable that an individual would regard himself as very worthy as a student, moderately worthy as a tennis player, and totally unworthy as a musician' (Coopersmith 1967: 6). Whether perceived unworthiness in relation to a particular activity influences global self-esteem is likely to be determined to a large extent by the value the individual and significant others attach to this activity and the extent to which it can be avoided. We can examine this through the example of a child experiencing difficulties in learning to read. Though as an activity this relates to academic self-esteem, because of the value attached to this skill by schools and society generally, the compulsory nature of schooling and the fact that the majority of peers are acquiring this skill more easily, the difficulty experienced is likely to impact on global self-esteem. Similarly, a skill such as playing football relates to a non-academic physical skill, but, if a child's circle of friends are all strong footballers, his/her parents have valued sporting prowess and his/her chosen role models are all footballers, perceived inadequacy in this area is likely to have a wider effect.

Implications for practice

The importance of feedback to individual learners has been referred to throughout the book. Through his research, Coopersmith (1967) showed that parents/carers, peers and teachers are all highly influential in shaping an individual's view of themselves through the feedback they provide (McNamara and Moreton 2001). Coopersmith (1967) also found that giving too little feedback can in itself be damaging as the pupil may assume this lack of feedback is because they or their endeavours are not worthy of attention. For the teacher and the school, in terms of its ethos, it is important to consciously manage the feedback that is being given both explicitly and implicitly.

Critiques of self-esteem theories

Coopersmith (1967) has been influential in the area of self-esteem through his identification of positive correlations between high self-esteem and confidence, activity levels, and both academic and social success. This has served as a rationale for much activity carried out in the name of raising self-esteem. However, more recently Emler (2002), in a review of the available research evidence, has cautioned against both an uncritical acceptance of low self-esteem as a risk factor for a broad range of psychological and behavioural problems and a tendency to view the raising of self-esteem as an all-purpose cure for a range of social problems.

From his exploration of the literature Emler (2002) concluded that it is difficult to answer with any confidence the critical question of whether self-esteem affects behaviour or not. Self-esteem is potentially linked to behaviour in complex ways. The simplest possibility is that self-esteem has its own direct effect on behaviour. In other words, an individual behaves in a particular way *because* they have low self-esteem. However, as Emler (2002) suggests, this simplest possibility is only one of many. Other possibilities might be that self-esteem is a consequence rather than the cause, or self-esteem and the behaviour are both influenced by something else (Emler 2002). Caution is always necessary with regard to studies of self-esteem due to the fact that self-esteem may be defined and assessed differently by different researchers and also that much of the data is correlational and as such does not necessarily justify a causal explanation. Emler (2002) identified from his review of the literature that there are two predominant definitions of self-esteem. These are:

- Self-esteem is primarily an emotional response: it is a generalised feeling about the self that is either more or less positive.
- Self-esteem is primarily the cumulative result of a set of judgements. These are judgements about one's adequacy across a range of dimensions – intellectual competence, social skills, appearance, physical co-ordination, and so on.

It is important to recognise these differing definitions as they do lead to alternative practical consequences for how self-esteem is measured and used in both research and practice.

O'Brien and Guiney (2001) are blunt in stating their claim 'self-esteem does not exist' (O'Brien and Guiney 2001: 132). This is not quite the damning indictment of Coopersmith (1967), Lawrence (2006) and others that it may first appear, but an attempt to clarify the status of the term 'self-esteem' as a descriptive and explanatory construct (O'Brien and Guiney 2001). They argue that 'self-esteem is a phrase and an explanatory construct that, although it feels intuitively right, promotes fixed rather than fluid and holistic thinking. Worse than this, because it is such a global term it can be a constant negative theme in a learner's career' (O'Brien and Guiney 2001: 140).

O'Brien and Guiney (2001) instead argue in favour of the concept of 'self-esteems'. This perspective recognises that the pupil's 'experience and emotions undulate according to their own perception of their ability in relation to achievement and attainment in different curriculum areas' (O'Brien and Guiney 2001: 140). This resonates with Coopersmith's (1967) view that it is possible for self-esteem to vary across different areas of experience and Lawrence's (2006) suggestion that 'In addition to this overall, or global, self-esteem we can have feelings of worth or unworthiness in specific situations' (Lawrence 2006: 11).

In summary, O'Brien and Guiney (2001) appear to be arguing that, in the case of most pupils, focusing on global low self-esteem is ultimately unhelpful as this locates the deficiency within the individual, albeit based upon recognising the role of environmental influences in contributing to this, and can lead to lowered expectations. Accepting O'Brien and Guiney's (2001) belief in multiple self-esteems encourages a view that the individual is responsive to different persons and contexts. This is a more optimistic proposition that encourages 'a more holistic view and one that matches the complexity of individuals and the processes of teaching and learning' (O'Brien and Guiney 2001: 142).

The challenges posed by Emler (2002) and O'Brien and Guiney (2001) regarding some of the commonly accepted ideas regarding self-esteem should not lead us to dismiss the work of Lawrence (2006) and Coopersmith (1967); rather they are a reminder that we should be cautious about using what, as O'Brien and Guiney (2001) suggest, is essentially an explanatory construct as both a diagnosis ('the pupil has low self-esteem') and a prescription for treatment ('the pupil's self-esteem needs raising').

Self-efficacy

Within considerations of relationship with self, self-efficacy is another key concept. It is perhaps not a term heard as frequently as self-esteem.

Self-efficacy can be defined as an individual's judgement of their ability to execute successfully a behaviour required to produce certain outcomes (Bandura 1986, Gibson and Dembo 1984). Giallo and Little (2003), writing about teachers rather than pupils, suggest that self-efficacy is a multi-dimensional construct involving both *efficacy expectations* and *outcome expectancy* (Gibson and Dembo 1984). Bandura (1977) defined outcome expectancy as a person's estimate that a given behaviour will lead to certain outcomes and efficacy expectation as the conviction that they can successfully execute the behaviour required to produce the outcomes. This has a number of implications as an individual may recognise and acknowledge that a course of action would produce certain outcomes, but have serious doubts about their ability to perform the action. Poulou and Norwich (2000) suggest that the individual's conviction in their own effectiveness is not only likely to affect how much effort they will expend and how long they will persist in the face of obstacles and aversive circumstances, but is also likely to affect whether they will even initiate a coping behaviour.

Self-efficacy is not primarily concerned with the skills that an individual has, but rather with the judgements the individual makes about their skills and their capacity to execute them which leads them to have certain *beliefs* about themselves. Self-efficacy beliefs are constructed from four fundamental sources of information: performance accomplishments, vicarious experience, verbal persuasion, and physiological states (Bandura 1977). Bandura (1977) suggested that performance accomplishments are the most influential source of efficacy information, as they provide the most authentic evidence of an individual's ability to successfully complete a task.

Porter (2007) describes self-efficacy as our sense of personal potency or ability to influence events in our lives. This sense of self-efficacy results from judgements about how potent we have felt in the past to influence events like the present task. This feeling may have become generalised to many activities, leading us in school to feel generally powerless/powerful to influence personal outcomes and experiences. An individual's self-efficacy may also relate to a specific area of activity such as a particular curriculum subject.

Attributions and locus of control

The concept of 'locus of control' (Rotter 1954) can be thought of as a continuum that stretches from, at one end, a belief that whatever happens to us is entirely within our control ('internal locus of control') to a belief at the other that whatever happens to us is entirely beyond our control ('external locus of control') (Lawrence 2006). To be located at either extreme poses problems for the individual. If we believe everything is entirely determined by us then every unfortunate, chance event is constructed as a personal failing. If we believe everything is entirely determined by others, then we become passive victims of circumstance with no personal agency. From this description, the links between self-efficacy and locus of control are immediately evident.

Attribution theory shares a number of common ideas with the concepts of locus of control and self-efficacy. When we experience an event in which we succeed or fail, we will generate explanations (or 'attributions') about the cause (Porter 2007). Some of these attributions will be internal, relating to the behaviour of the individual, others will be external factors such as luck, other people's behaviour or factors in the environment. People have causal explanations for their own behaviour (intrapersonal attributions) and for other people's behaviour (interpersonal attributions) (Chaplain 2003). These attributions may be faulty (Porter 2007). There are three main types of attribution error:

- a tendency – notably in Western society – to overemphasise personality, as opposed to situational attributes, as the cause of behaviour;
- a tendency in interpersonal situations for there to be a difference between how the person in the situation explains the causes, compared with how an observer sees things;
- a tendency to attribute successes to ourselves and failures to others.

(Based on Chaplain 2003)

Drawing on the work of Weiner (2000), Porter provides a useful analysis of the four properties our attributions have:

- Where we *locate* the cause of events – whether we believe them to be due to internal versus external forces.
- Whether we see these forces as *durable* (e.g. personal traits such as ability) or *temporary* events (e.g. lack of effort).
- Whether the causes are *pervasive* (e.g. inability at Maths) or *specific* (e.g. not understanding fractions).
- How *controllable* we believe events to be.

(Porter 2007: 80)

If a pupil attributes a difficulty experienced to internal, temporary, specific and controllable factors, then this encourages them to engage and persist. However, if the pupil blames external sources that are permanent, pervasive and uncontrollable, then this is likely to be problematic. Such attributions generate low self-efficacy, as a result of which the pupil may not attempt to manage their own actions because they feel powerless to affect what happens to them. Such attributions can lead to a lack of engagement and effort and to poor self-regulatory skills, with failure eventually becoming entrenched and habitual (Porter 2007). In its extreme form this pattern could be regarded as what Seligman (1975) termed 'learned helplessness'. Using the research method of subjecting dogs to unavoidable electric shocks and then placing them in an environment where avoidance or escape was possible, Seligman found that many of them did not learn how to avoid the shock. In contrast, dogs who had not been subjected to the unavoidable electric shocks who were then placed in a situation where they could avoid or escape the shock learned to do so quickly (Yeomans and Arnold 2006). Seligman (1975) argued that it was prior exposure to inescapable shock that interfered with the dogs' ability to learn. It was as though these dogs simply gave up and just accepted the shocks. Seligman (1975) used the term learned helplessness to describe the behaviour of this set of dogs. While we would not necessarily suggest that experiments on animals carry implications for human behaviour, Seligman's (1975) findings in relation to learned helplessness and the behaviours associated with it have become accepted within educational explanations. Some pupils display learned helplessness in terms of giving up when faced with a situation they perceive to be difficult because they believe any change or progress towards any favourable outcome is beyond their control. Such pupils may feel a global lack of control over their lives and tend to externalise responsibility for important events, including even their successes, to others (Chaplain 2003). From this description it should be clear that imploring such pupils to try harder or make more effort is likely to be futile and is, as Chaplain (2003) suggests, rather like telling someone who is clinically depressed to 'pull themselves together'.

Reflective Exercise 7.1

Self-efficacy, locus of control and attributions: implications for practice.

- Within your classroom how are pupils provided with the opportunity to make decisions that affect what happens to them and influence events in the classroom?
- Are behavioural rewards and consequences presented as resulting from choices the pupil makes rather than arbitrary decisions by the teacher?
- When following up incidents are pupils given the opportunity to give their 'take' on events? (This allows us to gauge whether they 'internalise' or 'externalise' causes).

Learning behaviours linked with relationship with self

In Chapter 5 learning behaviours considered to be linked to relationship with self that impact on relationship with the curriculum were considered. These behaviours largely reflect the emotional component of learning. They involve the pupil developing the interest, commitment and belief that allow them to actively process the curriculum, respond to feedback, monitor their own progress and develop some responsibility for their own learning. In addition there are other learning behaviours that can be considered appropriate to promote when seeking to improve relationship with self in school contexts that have been noted in the literature, including:

Those that relate to the pupil's general disposition:
• has positive self regard;
• is interested;
• is emotionally stable;
• has an appropriate sense of self-efficacy.

Those that relate to curriculum processing:
• willing to engage with the curriculum;
• takes responsibility for own learning;
• shows good self-control;
• willing to try new things and 'take risks';
• can make mistakes and 'move on';
• is self-aware, knows how and when to get help.

Those that relate to working with others:
• is willing to work independently as appropriate;
• is socially aware of what is going on around him/her;
• is willing and able to empathise;
• is willing to ask for help;
• is able to balance self reliance and sociability;
• is willing to behave respectfully towards staff e.g. respects staff and answers them politely; does not interrupt or deliberately disrupt;
• does not annoy or show verbal or physical aggression;
• is selective in the values and habits they pick up from others.

Implications of relationship with self for building a positive relationship with curriculum

It is helpful to consider what it means to have a 'relationship' with oneself. Donaldson (1978) adopted a theoretical framework based on the principle that there is a fundamental human urge to be effective, competent and independent, to understand the world and to act with skill. From infancy it can be seen that individuals follow this urge as they actively explore their environment. This activity is directly influenced by experience of success or failure, which in turn influences levels of interest and the value individuals place on their worth. A relationship with self involves an ongoing need to 'make sense' to oneself and as a consequence activities and experiences are personalised, interpreted and explained in order that some internal equilibrium is achieved. Such a view is useful in that it means that we can understand an individual's behaviour by asking 'how does it make sense to that person?' For example, though it may not make sense to us when a pupil destroys their work, it is likely to be serving a purpose for them. Once we can identify a purpose for the behaviour we can choose an appropriate strategy. The individual's relationship with self has been built up and consolidated over time. The individual's attempts to make 'make sense' may serve to reinforce some dispositions, attitudes and beliefs that impact negatively (or positively) on the their relationship with the curriculum and relationship with others.

Reducing the effects of failure on the relationship

Galloway *et al.* (1996) proposed three pupil responses to failure:

1 Learned helplessness: the pupil becomes unsure about their ability, seeks to avoid challenge, gives up following failure and does not believe they have control over their learning.
2 Self-worth motivation: the pupil believes that they have the ability to do the task but is not prepared to risk self-exposure in the event of failure.
3 Mastery orientation: pupils demonstrate persistence and seek to overcome difficulties when confronted with tasks they find difficult.

From these it can be seen that *failure* has a significant influence on relationship with self. Interestingly failure also has a powerful effect on pupils' relationship with the curriculum. It follows that although teachers may not at times fully understand how individual pupils make sense of their own experience of failure, they do have control and influence over the provision of opportunities for success with the curriculum. This in turn should impact on the pupil's relationship with self. Strategies that seek to promote success for the individual and make constructive use of 'failure' are therefore powerful determinants of both the pupil's relationship with the curriculum and with self. This reflects the interdependent nature of relationship with curriculum and relationship with self.

Fear of failure can be addressed by allowing pupils to see that failure is not an end point. It is a trigger for action and contains information that can be used. It is more of a problem when it is personalised and made public. Consequently, classroom strategies that seek to depersonalise failure through feedback to the whole-group on mistakes that have been made in a particular homework or class task, along with suggestions from the teacher about how work can be improved, can be helpful. Pupils will need to know what is expected of them and have clear expectations about the nature and content of summative external assessments. However, it is important for pupil-motivation that a distinction is made between attainment and achievement when giving feedback so that any 'failure' can be balanced by recognition of progress. Assessment procedures and processes, and the use of rewards and sanctions play an important part in reducing the effect of perceived failure on relationship with self as is noted in other parts of this book.

In building resilience to failure, it is useful to foster a way of thinking in the pupil, through feedback and discussion, that recognises that failure may lead to a range of unpleasant feelings. It is useful to point out that failure and the feelings associated with it are part of human life and learning. These feelings have not been specifically heaped upon the individual because they are inherently a bad and worthless person who is destined and deserving of this experience in greater quantity than others. It follows that when a pupil is unsuccessful at a task, the teacher has to make a judgement about their response. For example:

Option 1
The teacher might say 'Maybe I didn't explain it clearly enough …' in an attempt to take some of the responsibility for the outcome.

Option 2
The teacher might say 'If everything is easy, it means you already knew how to do it, so there's no new learning' (DfES 2004f: 58).

In Option 2 the teacher is attempting to acknowledge that the experiencing of difficulty is a necessary part of learning. It may even be appropriate to draw pupils' attention to the Ofsted perspective that 'Pupils' work that is always marked right is almost certainly too easy' (Ofsted 2003b: 78).

The teacher has an important role in brokering the pupil's relationship with the curriculum, including mediating their experience of difficulty based on knowledge of the individual pupil. It is the balancing of good experiences whilst preparing individuals for any inevitable negative experiences that is the enduring challenge for educational professionals.

Areas of good practice for building resilience include:

- balancing protection from and preparation for failure;
- separating cognitive and emotional learning through depersonalisation so that pupils can tackle the problem through role-play, literature and drama without interference from their own emotional state;
- skill building and practice of necessary curriculum learning in safe settings;
- providing security and structure through visual (because if in an emotional state short-term working memory is affected) planning and consistency in implementation of school rules and regulations;
- allocating some control to pupils by, for example, giving them clear information on what is expected of them and how they can improve, for example through using Assessment for Learning (AfL) and the provision of marking grids containing assessment criteria.

For the teacher it is necessary to be aware of how feedback designed to be beneficial to the learner is likely to be experienced and processed as part of the individual's 'making sense to self' function.

Many of the pupil specific behaviours in Reflective Exercise 7.2 can be addressed within a classroom climate that supports the development of a positive relationship with the curriculum through attention to the social, emotional *and* cognitive aspects of the relationship. Features of such a climate might include:

- involving pupils in some of the decision making within the classroom;
- making sure pupils fully understand the *purpose* of the work and the hoped-for outcomes;
- involving pupils in the identification of criteria that demonstrate success;
- involving them in the evaluation of their learning;
- providing choice as to how activities and tasks are completed and information presented;
- allowing pupils to determine their own questions for enquiry and debate;

- using behaviour management techniques that encourage pupils to make a choice about their behaviour;
- providing opportunities for pupils to determine class and playground rules and routines.

(adapted from DfES 2005c)

Reflective Exercise 7.2

At the start of this section we identified behaviours that have been commonly linked to low self-esteem. From the table below see if you can now identify the purpose of the behaviour from the individual pupil's perspective and then consider implications for strategy choice. Some of the sections have already been completed for you to consider.

Observed behaviours	Explanation from theory	Implication for strategy use
Reluctance to try new things.	Pupil lacks confidence; does not trust new things; feels more in control if they are on familiar ground; fear of failure.	Start lesson with an achievable starter and highlight its status in terms of meeting lesson objectives; reward trying rather than the final answer; encourage planning and identify what the pupil can do within the 'new' task; be careful not to make the entire task 'new' in terms of topic, difficulty and type of response needed.
Easily frustrated from lack of immediate success or understanding.	Current emotional state may result in 'not having the patience' to persist; developmentally the pupil may not be ready for delayed reward/gratification.	Break the task down into steps so that each step builds up towards completion; do not attempt to adjust key variables such as interest, difficulty and success all at once; maybe allow a pupil to work with a peer so that they are supported in task persistence.
Non-compliance to authority.	This may give the pupil some control; they may not know how to comply (e.g. if told to 'get on with work' the pupil may not know what to do); does not predict or plan for consequences; is seeking peer approval; is angry and wants to get back at the teacher/school.	

(continued)

Reflective Exercise 7.2 (continued)

Observed behaviours	Explanation from theory	Implication for strategy use
Withdrawal, depression and unwillingness to communicate.		
Dependency on others to tell them what to do, what is good, what is acceptable.		
Attitudes that are hypercritical, negative, sarcastic and cynical.	May be seeking attention from the teacher or social approval from peers; may not have developed sufficient empathy to realise effect on others; may have developed empathy but is angry and wants to hurt others; may just be a habit developed as part of social interaction; may want to make themselves feel better.	Choice of strategy will depend on what is felt to be the purpose of the behaviour for the individual and on the classroom context in terms of teacher rules about peer chatter. Teacher may need to: reduce peer attention by tackling on a one-to-one basis outside classroom; work on empathy at whole-class level; target anger management; encourage the pupil to reflect on their own thinking (e.g. does hurting others make the pupil feel better?).
Blaming behaviour outside themselves.		
Lying.	Fear of consequences; habit; may believe s/he is mainly telling the truth; has no other strategies in repertoire due to over-use of lying; it has worked in the past, etc.	It can help to outline the consequences by, for example, saying 'if you are using your mobile phone then I'll need to put it in my desk and will return it to you at the end of the lesson' rather than 'Matt, are you using your phone?'; examine serious consequences of lying with the whole class through depersonalised examples from literature and through role-play as well as through consistency of discipline.

This book is concerned with developing learning behaviour in classrooms. In such an environment the individual pupil's relationships with themselves and with the curriculum are going to be influenced by their relationships with others. The classroom requires pupils to both ignore distractions from others and also to be responsive to teachers and work alongside, and at times collaboratively, with peers. The next section takes a closer look at relationship with others.

Relationship with others

> ### Working definition
>
> Being able to take part in learning that involves others, and join in aspects of school life as a member of the school community.
>
> This involves being willing and able to interact socially and academically with others, including the teacher and other adults.

The teacher's relationship with others

Teachers are placed in a vulnerable position within the group setting of the classroom. Any mistakes they make are public and are likely to be remembered by the class. Where the teacher already has an established relationship with the class or has a range of successful previous experiences to draw upon, any mistake can often be easily addressed, being perceived by both teacher and pupils as temporary, atypical and repairable. However, for trainees and NQTs in particular, the relationship with others can be experienced as an unusual one in that, although as a teacher they are in a position of designated authority, they are also acutely aware of the potential of any mistakes to influence pupil perceptions of their competence and authority. With no previous terms of reference within the relationship any mistake may be seen by pupils, and potentially the teacher, as permanent, typical and irreparable. For the teacher this initial relationship with their class may be based on an avoidance of mistakes, perceived as carrying a high-risk and underpinned by an assumption of a lack of empathy from the other party. It is little wonder therefore that a key concern for many teachers at this early stage of their career is losing control of the class.

> ### Reflective Exercise 7.3
>
> Teachers on our courses have noted the following breakdown points in their relationship with their classes:
>
> - when the class is 'out of control';
> - when pupil(s) are blasé and just don't care;
> - when pupil(s) accuse you of being unfair when you were not;
> - when they manipulate the behaviour system;
> - when they simply are not interested in you and ignore you;
> - when they repeatedly do something when you have asked them not to;
> - when they deny doing something when you have seen (or can see) them do it;
> - when they make personal criticism of your teaching or compare you unfavourably with another teacher.
>
> 1 How might a view that *'teaching is all about relationships'* help to analyse what has gone wrong in these instances?
> 2 What do you think are the underpinning issues in relation to your planning and thinking to avoid each of these breakdowns?

Pupil perspectives on the relationship with others

As noted in the earlier chapter on relationship with the curriculum, pupils show a preference for teaching that includes activity and engagement with peers – the teacher on the other hand is often annoyed by the low level chatter that results from this pursuit of social interaction. This difference between teacher and pupil perspectives in relation to the relevance of relationship with others for learning is likely to be increased by the levels of social activity outside the classroom through social networking sites, mobile phones, e-mails and other forms of electronic communication. For some pupils arriving home from school opens up a whole world of communication which is not 'face-to-face' and allows them practice in making relationships in which they have more perceived control. They have time to make their written response, do not have to deal with interruptions, or monitor recipients' non-verbal reactions, and can decide when to switch off communications. In many ways these forms of communication do not involve the same demands as traditional face-to-face interaction or require children and young people to develop the same skills in order to effectively communicate. This is not to argue for a restriction on such activities but to acknowledge that children and young people now have numerous means of successfully communicating with peers and forming relationships that were not open to previous generations. Such increases in opportunities for communication with peers and others also of course increase the chances of experiencing rejection or being bullied and of making comparisons between self and peers.

The potential gap between the relationship with others expected by teachers and that demanded by pupils can lead to the classification of particular social behaviours as behavioural problems. Pupils may, for example, see it as normal and necessary to socialise whilst they are learning whereas teachers may regard too much talking as a behavioural issue.

Learning behaviours and collaborative learning

A pupil's relationship with others cannot be viewed in isolation from the their relationship with self and with the curriculum. There is an interdependence between the three relationships during learning in classroom settings. As Claxton (2002) suggests: 'Good learners balance their relationships with other people, being willing to be interdependent, without becoming either too dependent on others for support or feedback, or too aloof and unwilling to take criticism or to work as part of a team' (Claxton 2002: 43).

Table 7.1 lists those learning behaviours that relate to learning with others. These have been taken from the literature and some are phrased negatively. This is in contrast to the theme of this book in which learning behaviours are positively phrased. We have sought to place these learning behaviours into categories that may help you decide whether they should be primarily addressed through working with others (social), may require additional teaching of skills to individuals (cognitive), or have a strong emotional or dispositional component (emotional). Given the interdependence between these categories it is likely that readers will have differing views as to which column the identified learning behaviours should be placed in. We have also allocated the learning behaviours to the category of either communication or collaboration. In effect the 'social' column requires that the learning behaviours can be applied to a range of settings involving peers and the teacher; the 'cognitive' column looks at the skills that the pupil has or needs to develop; and the 'emotional' column looks at how the pupil might be thinking or feeling. For example, the

Table 7.1 Learning behaviours necessary for collaborative working

	Social	Cognitive	Emotional
Communication	Is an effective communicator; Speaks politely; Uses proper names; Waits turn to speak; Interacts politely with the teacher.	Seeks attention appropriately; Appropriate tone of voice for task; Tone of voice is congruent with body language.	Respects the teacher and is cooperative and compliant, responding positively to instruction; Behaves respectfully towards staff; Shows concern and understanding; Does not talk back to the teacher or aim verbal aggression at the teacher; Does not show physical aggression towards adults or other pupils; Does not physically pick on others; Is not cruel or spiteful to others; Avoids getting into fights with others; Does not strike out in anger, have temper tantrums or aggressive outbursts.
Collaboration	Works efficiently in a group; Has the skills of learning with others; Listens to what others have to say and consequently adds positively to group discussions.	Works efficiently in a group e.g. takes part in discussions; Contributes readily to group tasks; Listens well in groups; Works collaboratively; Only interrupts and seeks attention appropriately; Does not disrupt unnecessarily, or distract or interfere with others.	Respects other pupils and uses appropriate language, e.g. not swearing or calling them names; Treats other pupils as equals and does not dominate them by intimidation or abuse; Respects the views or rights of other pupils and avoids bullying or intimidation; Does not pass notes, talk when others are talking, does not seek unwarranted attention; Is physically peaceable; Respects property.

pupil may have the skill to 'listen to others' but choose not to do so because they need to seek the attention of others at that point in time.

In seeking to examine how relationship with others influences relationship with the curriculum and relationship with self it is useful to consider the following questions:

1 *How best can the child learn as an individual while being taught in the classroom?*
    An appropriate relationship with others in this case may be considered by schools and teachers as one in which the child learns to avoid distractions, other pupils remain controlled and the teacher maintains discipline in order to allow individuals to get on with learning. The purpose of the relationship with the curriculum is mainly evaluated against individual progress in relation to defined curricular objectives. Pupils who persistently have difficulty ignoring distractions from others, or who contribute to those distractions or who fail to relate effectively to their teacher are often considered to have behavioural difficulties.

2 *What does the pupil learn about their relationship with self and relationship with others while they are building a relationship with the curriculum in school-based curriculum contexts?*
    In this case it is accepted that the pupil needs to be placed with others in order to learn and practice the social conventions of behaviour. The pupil also needs to be placed with others as it is through comparisons that the individual establishes their own identity and makes judgements about their own worth. In this case 'others' are a necessary resource.

3 *What can a pupil learn from others that they could not learn as well on their own?*
    In this case others are also a resource but in terms of contributing to a construction of knowledge that the individual could not achieve on their own.

4 *What is it necessary for groups to learn in school contexts that are relevant to groups and to those individuals who make up those groups?*
    This refers to learning as a collective activity and is likely to have a group goal for the organisation or group itself. An example within a school context might be the school football team. Though individuals within the team may be coached, the primary purpose of the coaching is to enhance the individual's contribution to the development needs of the team. Learning is situated, intended to be applied in a particular context – in this case a football match. Whilst there may be some monitoring and evaluation of individual performance, success is ultimately judged against performance of the group.

Reflective Exercise 7.4

In looking at 1–4 above:

• Which purpose or purposes do you tend to prioritise in your classroom?
• How does that impact on your strategies for building relationships with others in your classroom?
• Can you identify some learning behaviours you think it would be necessary to develop in relation to each of the four questions above?

The choice between an approach based on *controlling* peer social interaction and an approach based on *using* peer social interaction is more often based on personal preference and experience than it is on evidence. It also cannot be expected that if a teacher is good at one approach they will necessarily be good at the other. Both require different planning, different objectives, different assessments, different evaluations and different preparation of pupils. Traditionally, when we talk about 'behaviour management' we are usually talking about how to manage the group so that the individual can get on with their learning. However, some researchers have studied how best we can prepare individuals to work in groups and this activity is discussed under the broad umbrella of collaborative learning.

The next section critically reflects on different priorities for collaborative learning that arise from questions 1–4 above. It needs to be noted that although we have used these questions to depict different relationships with others they are not mutually exclusive and so do not appear in classrooms in such a distinct form. We are mindful too of inherent methodological challenges for classroom-based research in this area given Johnson *et al.*'s (2000) view that no other pedagogical practice simultaneously generates such diverse intended and unintended outcomes as collaborative learning.

Critical reflection on different priorities for collaborative learning

Priority 1: Building relationships with others that seek to allow the individual to learn individually in the classroom

Within classroom contexts the kinds of learning behaviour identified in the literature is, not surprisingly, concerned with pupils being able to work together but in an essentially controlled manner. In order for pupils to be perceived to be working effectively in groups they are often expected to work within non-confrontational boundaries in which 'argument' or 'disagreement' with others is not seen as being supportive to academic learning. Table 7.1, for example, contains learning behaviours from the literature considered to be relevant to both communication and collaborative learning. We can see that in these examples the pupil's relationship with others is expected to be one in which emotions and feelings are kept under control in order to minimise discord and disruption.

This contrasts with expectations surrounding pupils' relationship with the curriculum which, as we noted in Chapter 6, is considered to be effective if there is a close interplay between emotional and cognitive aspects of learning. This results in pupils being motivated and involved such that they initiate learning, persist, apply and sustain effort, be creative, and welcome cognitive challenge and dissonance.

Clearly most pupils in schools can, and do, adopt a socially active (e.g. by asking for clarification or help when needed and working collaboratively with peers without 'mucking about') and cognitively active (e.g. thinking and problem solving) approach to learning, while at the same time being controlled and responsive to class rules and disciplinary frameworks. Any mismatch between social and cognitive requirements does not then cause a problem for the pupil and their teachers. However, some pupils may find it more difficult to adapt to the demands for active cognitive processing within a class context based on social peace and compliance and this can lead to behavioural difficulties. Either the pupil does not have the maturity or self-control to switch from noisy but slightly controlled social interaction (low-level chatter) to quiet but internally active learning, or they find it very difficult to achieve active cognitive processing unless they can manipulate and manage the information 'outside their head' through, for example, discussion, hands on activity and ICT. In particular pupils who have low levels of working memory, including many with SEN, struggle to meet the demands of complex tasks that require them to process, maintain, and store information simultaneously. It is suggested that this difficulty may underpin their failures to make 'normal' educational progress (Alloway *et al.* 2005). It follows that those pupils who experience difficulty in retaining and processing information contained in task related or disciplinary instructions may also be wrongly seen at times to be non-compliant.

Schools seek to improve attainment through managing social behaviour in the classroom so that individual pupils can 'get on and learn' and also by providing opportunities for pupils to learn from each other. Schools and their staff will normally reflect a preference towards one or the other approach, as will individual pupils. Closer alignment of teacher and pupil preferences can be achieved through grouping strategies and by adjustments to task requirements and learning objectives.

There is limited evidence that working in a team achieves cognitive outcomes that cannot be matched or exceeded by the most capable group member (Slavin 2004). Slavin writes:

> learning is completely different from 'group' outcomes. It may well be that working in a group under certain circumstances does increase the learning of the individuals in that group more than would working under other arrangements, but a measure of group productivity provides no evidence one way or another on this; only an individual learning measure that cannot be influenced by group member help can indicate which incentive or task structure is best ... learning takes place only between the ears of the learner.

> (Slavin 2004: 275)

The view that the most capable learner in the group can do just as well on their own masks the view that the other members of the group may learn better than they would individually simply by interacting with this 'capable' learner and acquiring strategies and approaches to learning that they did not previously have in their repertoire. Although such individual learning could not be assessed from the group task outcome it still could have taken place 'between the ears of the learner'.

Within schools there is a need to retain a core emphasis on building a positive relationship with the curriculum so that attainment in subject areas can be improved and gaps between high and lower attainment groups can be reduced. However global and national initiatives for social inclusion, alongside a need to prepare young people for teamwork in the workplace and to promote social cohesion and citizenship, indicates that collaborative learning is likely to remain as an area of importance and one for further development within school contexts.

Priority 2: Learning social behaviour from others

Improved social and emotional outcomes such as increased motivation, higher self-esteem, and improved communication are consistently reported as outcomes from collaborative learning. Indeed Kreidler (1984) saw his main educational goal for teaching his primary school class as developing the skills of cooperation through the employment of his six principles: cooperation, caring, responsible decision making and conflict resolution, communication, the appreciation of diversity and the appropriate expression of feelings. He reported that by using these principles children's work and the classroom atmosphere improved drastically (Powell 1993). Such a view on the strength of social learning comes from the work of Bandura who states:

> Learning would be exceedingly laborious, not to mention hazardous, if people had to

rely solely on the effects of their own actions to inform them what to do. Fortunately, most human behavior is learned observationally through modelling: from observing others one forms an idea of how new behaviors are performed, and on later occasions this coded information serves as a guide for action.

(Bandura 1977: 22)

Bandura's Social Learning Theory explains human behaviour in terms of continuous reciprocal interaction between cognitive, behavioural and environmental influences and as such reflects the underpinning principles of the behaviour for learning conceptual framework.

Priority 3: Improving individual academic learning through relationship with others

Damon (1984: 335), reported in Slavin (2004), integrated theoretical perspectives, including Piagetian and Vygotskian, to outline a conceptual foundation for peer-based education, suggesting that:

- Through mutual feedback and debate, peers motivate one another to abandon misconceptions and search for better solutions.
- The experience of peer communication can help a child master social processes such as participation and argumentation, and cognitive processes, such as verification and criticism.
- Collaboration between peers can provide a forum for discovery learning and can encourage creative thinking.
- Peer interaction can introduce children to the process of generating ideas.

(Damon 1984: 335, cited by Slavin 2004: 284)

The use of the word 'can' in Damon's conceptual framework is important. It conveys the potential of peer based education but acknowledges that though research studies have secured the necessary conditions to test out the realisation of these aims, evidence from classroom settings has yet to be secured.

It is likely that peer-based education, not only for improvements in academic learning but also to address concerns about a range of anti-social behaviours, will continue to be on the educational agenda. Parsons *et al.* (2008) reported that schools sought to impact on a number of areas through the use of peer-based strategies. In order of priority these include:

1 improved academic performance/attainment;
2 reduction in bullying;
3 improved attendance;
4 fewer exclusions.

(Parsons *et al.* 2008: 20)

As Parsons *et al.* (2008) acknowledge, findings from such studies are positive and rich in anecdotal and qualitative evidence relating to the 'experience' of both mentor and mentee. However, there is less rigorous data on whether academic attainment, attendance and behaviour had improved as a consequence of peer based interventions.

Priority 4: Learning about groups from groups

Because collaborative learning involves 'team work', a much-valued activity in the work place, there has been interest in work that seeks to harness school and business perspectives to promote more effective learning. In her study on decision making in small groups in primary Science, Maloney (2007) required the group to:

a discuss most or all of the evidence made available;
b test alternative choices and consider both positive and negative issues of the possible outcomes;
c provide claims supported by evidence;
d engage in sustained dialogue by making claims, reviewing evidence and discussing arguments as an iterative process.

(Maloney 2007: 378)

Maloney then used Belbin's (1981) framework for 'useful people to have in teams' to analyse the pupils' roles and responsibilities to see if there was potential from practices within business management to make pupils' learning in groups more effective. Belbin noted that 'what is needed is not well balanced individuals but individuals who balance well with each other' (Belbin 1981: 75). Although a literal interpretation of this comment is not advocated, the sentiment behind it is clear.

Some of the positive and negative roles outlined were chair, discussion manager, information manager, promoter of ideas, distracter, contributor and non-responsive contributor.

Maloney (2007) reported from the research that pupils can be clear about the contribution they make to the team and can be aware of other people's contribution and how this can be coordinated. This has implications for how teachers make decisions about which pupils are placed in what groups depending on the purpose of the task. This resonates with work in multi-agency settings that refers to the 'skill mix' of partners involved.

Having looked at the different perspectives and reasons for building positive relationships with others there are clearly issues for preparing pupils to engage in collaborative activity through the promotion of relevant learning behaviours. These will depend on the purpose for the collaboration, the tasks set and the evaluation criteria used. Grouping of pupils is likely to be different depending on the teacher's perceived need for building relationships with others in the classroom. Given the aspirations for collaborative working in addressing cognitive, social and emotional aspects of learning it is noteworthy that Pollard *et al.* (2000) found that the most common criteria for deciding the composition of groups are ability and behaviour or social relationships.

Summary

Following on from Chapter 6's exploration of relationship with the curriculum, in this chapter we have explored the other two relationships that are central to the behaviour for learning conceptual framework.

Relationship with self is particularly relevant to this book as it helps us to understand how the *individual* pupil interprets and experiences the teaching approaches and management of behaviour that have been designed for the *group* setting of their school.

Relationship with self has historically been discussed in school settings by reference to terms such as self-esteem, resulting in a 'widespread belief that enhancing self-esteem was a panacea of all ills' (Craven and Marsh 2008: 105). Although there remains consensus about the importance of self to school learning and participation there are differing views on its conceptualisation, mechanisms of influence, and impact. The literature is often confusing by its use of differing definitions and terminologies. It refers to both self-esteem and self-concept as key explanatory constructs relevant to the understanding of what we refer to in the behaviour for learning conceptual framework as 'relationship with self'. Of interest to this book is that self-esteem has been shown to share a mutually reinforcing relationship with academic achievement such that prior academic self-esteem influences subsequent achievement, and prior achievement influences subsequent self-esteem. This is useful in that, faced with the task of improving a pupil's learning and behaviour in school, we can either focus on directly improving their relationship with the curriculum or we can focus on improving their relationship with self.

Developments in research into an individual's relationship with self reflect a move away from the acceptance of a unidimensional notion of self-esteem to one that recognises the many facets of self through the use of multidimensional models. The importance of moving away from a unidimensional model is that it challenges the frequent attribution of poor pupil behaviour to global low self-esteem and instead recognises that the pupil may have many facets of self, both positive and negative, that are influencing his/her behaviour. These multidimensional models involve not just academic and non-academic components of self-esteem but also propose further divisions into subject specific academic facets of self (e.g. Mathematics, English) and various non-academic social, emotional and physical components of self. These multidimensional models serve to provide a range of possible explanations for the diverse range of learning behaviours exhibited by individual pupils. This allows us to generate and test the reasons for any seemingly problematic behaviour from the perspective of the individual pupil. From these models we have a framework for understanding why the behaviour makes sense from the pupil's perspective and the purpose it serves for them. For example, it may not make sense to us if a pupil will not persist with a task when we know that they need to get a qualification in order to improve their life chances. We might in this instance seek to keep this pupil on task by saying 'come on, you need to work hard or you will not pass your exams'. The pupil knows that it is desirable in the longer-term to pass their exams. However, they may have experienced academic failure in the past and not believe that any action on their part can change the 'fact' that they are not going to achieve any success with academic learning. The pupil's behaviour makes sense to them and serves the purpose of confirming their academic self-esteem. The same pupil may, however, work hard and persist with a non-academic activity as they may well have a relatively favourable social or physical self-esteem. Strategy choice in this case might include those that challenge the pupil's academic self-esteem by promoting positive learning behaviours that allow increased academic success, and/or getting them to reconsider the evidence that led them to the conclusion that they were never going to succeed in any academic areas. Other strategy choices might seek to use the pupil's relatively good social self-esteem to increase their academic interest and success by increased use of collaborative learning activities. Their physical self esteem and relative success in non-academic areas might be seen as an area where more attention could be given in school and at home and possibly linked to some areas of academic activity. Although increased understanding of relationship with self offers teachers more choice of strategies to improve a pupil's relationship with the curriculum, the nature and complexity surrounding issues and influence of self does not allow predictions about the extent to which an individual's relationship with self can be modified or changed. We do know that early and persistent environmental influences can have long-term effects on an individual's relationship with self that appear resistant to change and impact upon their social, emotional and cognitive development. Given the evidence, albeit correlational, for reciprocal influences between achievement and self-esteem, this chapter supports a view that relationship with self is likely to have the most significant pervasive influence on a pupil's academic attainment, achievement and behaviour. As such the academic and social context of the school and classroom should be one that not only does not compromise or harm this relationship but also seeks to impact positively upon its development. The pupil's relationship with self serves a purpose and as such leads to adaptive behaviour in support of this purpose.

Influences on relationship with self are many and varied and some are likely to have been long term. As such teachers may be limited in the extent to which they can effect change to this relationship. They can, however, through the interdependence of relationship with curriculum, relationship with others and relationship with self, promote appropriate learning behaviours that support the individual to reduce the negative effects of any damaging relationships with self. This enables the pupil to develop increased resilience and control over the pervasive influences of a negative relationship with self.

The school itself and the classroom provide a social context for learning that requires individuals to build relationships with their peers and teachers. Relationships with others is accepted as an integral part of school learning both for the teachers and their pupils. Teachers are typically placed on their own in classrooms to build relationships with individuals in their class whilst pupils are required to learn in groups and relate to one influential but potentially vulnerable adult. The balance of power and dynamics involved ensure that pupil behaviour and teacher competence and confidence in managing this behaviour remains an enduring area of concern for educational policy and practice. This chapter has highlighted the dual aim for relationships with others. On the one hand the pupil is required to ignore distractions and work independently in pursuit of improved attainment. The teacher is required to relate to the group in such a way that individuals can get on with their work and order is maintained. On the other hand, some school learning requires pupils to work in groups not only to allow them access to the ideas and favourable working strategies of peers but also to prepare them to work with others for the world of work and in the interests of social inclusion and cohesion. Grouping strategies in schools that are allegedly designed to promote attainment and secure appropriate behaviour are often undertaken without reference to evidence of their efficacy and appropriateness for individual pupil outcomes and for this reason the chapter identifies some priorities and purposes that that have been identified for collaborative group working. It can be seen from this that collaborative working and the building of social relationships for learning requires direct attention to *purpose* so that planning, preparation and evaluation are linked to that purpose. Planning in particular needs to take account of the fact that some pupils have not yet acquired the learning behaviours that allow them to engage in and benefit from group working. Teachers normally would see group-work as part of their repertoire of teaching approaches and this has potential for offering pupils opportunities to develop learning behaviours that both support improving relationships with others as well as impacting positively on the pupil's relationship with the curriculum. However group-work may offer threats to the pupil's relationship with self and if they seek to preserve this relationship it could compromise their relationship with the curriculum and possibly their relationship with others.

In essence this chapter has sought to highlight that, although the individual's relationship with the curriculum is the priority area for development in schools it is likely that for many pupils their priorities are their relationship with others and the influence of their relationship with self. These relationships have a reciprocal influence on the pupil's relationship with the curriculum. This allows teachers to select the most appropriate strategy from the plethora available based on the extent to which they feel it appropriate and feasible to improve any one of the three relationships through the promotion of the relevant learning behaviours.

Chapter 8

Behaviour policies and learning behaviour

Introduction

As Chapter 2 outlined, a consistent theme within discourse on behaviour in schools is the importance of a whole-school approach. The school's written behaviour policy is the key document in defining the nature of this approach in terms of practices to be adopted by individual staff. This chapter seeks to critically examine school behaviour policies in relation to their capacity to promote learning behaviour and maintain and develop the three relationships that underpin its development.

We acknowledge that individual schools' behaviour policies vary and so this chapter is structured around four core elements set out in government guidance (e.g. DfES 2003a, 2007b) that are likely to be common to most behaviour policies. These are:

- clearly stated expectations of what constitutes acceptable behaviour;
- effective behaviour management strategies;
- processes that recognise, teach, reward and celebrate positive behaviour;
- processes, rules and sanctions to deal with poor conduct.

(DfES 2007b: 13)

We have focused predominantly on these aspects of school behaviour policies as we consider these impinge most directly on teachers' and pupils' experiences in classrooms.

Approaching behaviour policies from a behaviour for learning perspective

In adopting a behaviour for learning perspective in considering school behaviour policies emphasis is placed on clarity about purpose and priorities, awareness of what is implicitly and explicitly promoted, the contribution to the development of learning behaviour and the influence of any practices specified within policy on the three core relationships within the conceptual framework.

Clarity about purpose and priorities

The Elton Report (DES 1989) represented a major shift with regard to the management of behaviour in schools with a move towards whole-school approaches to behaviour and discipline (Hallam and Rogers 2008). The requirement for schools to have a behaviour policy is now firmly established in legislation (e.g. Education Act (1997); School Standards and Framework Act (1998); and Education and Inspections Act (2006)). Undoubtedly, a well formulated, well communicated and consistently followed behaviour policy provides a degree of predictability for both staff and pupils that can contribute to the reduction of many forms of disruptive behaviour.

In unreservedly acknowledging the necessity and utility of behaviour policies, it is also necessary to be realistic about their purpose, priority and what they can hope to achieve. The elements of a behaviour policy that inform day-to-day classroom practice are typically the rules, rewards and sanctions and often some advice on behaviour management strategies. The primary purpose is to promote good behaviour and discourage poor behaviour amongst the majority in order to secure certain standards of behaviour from *groups*, in the form of the school population as a whole and within individual classes. Evaluation of school policy needs to be made against the purpose for which it was designed. The difficulty occurs when policy makers and individual schools attempt to evaluate whole-school policy predominantly in terms of those who fall outside the day-to-day elements of policy. Typically these pupils define themselves through the frequency and intensity of their behaviour (DfE 1994b) and the very fact that this is not ameliorated by the behaviour management techniques usually employed by the school (DfES 2001). Whilst we are not suggesting that these pupils should be seen as exempt from, standing outside of or beyond, the influence of policy, to evaluate behaviour policy against these pupils' behaviour is likely to lead to a frustrating quest for a set of systems that will work for all pupils. The best a school can aim for is a policy that leads to fewer pupils falling outside it, coupled with clear systems of pupil support for those who, within a system designed for groups, inevitably do. Undoubtedly some discipline systems, such as those that either allow minimal scope for professional judgement in responding to pupils as individuals or contain numerous 'obscure, arbitrary or petty rules' (DES 1989) to be enforced are likely to lead to more pupils falling outside day-to-day policy.

From a behaviour for learning perspective it is necessary to accept that a behaviour policy is designed for groups but will be experienced and interpreted by individuals. This means that though the policy may achieve its primary aim of securing the behaviour of groups and could be evaluated as successful against this purpose, individuals may experience it less positively. In aligning behaviour policies more closely with the behaviour for learning conceptual framework, greater emphasis is placed on how individuals might experience and interpret the practices and approaches employed. However, we need to acknowledge, that even when adopting a behaviour for learning approach, decisions about practices and approaches to be encouraged through policy can only be based on a hypothesis about how a 'typical' pupil might experience these. As a basic principle, any practice or approach should not be to the detriment of one of the three relationships. For example, a sanction that contained an element that a pupil may find humiliating or embarrassing would risk impacting on relationship with self. Similarly, using copying out of a reading book as a sanction risks undermining relationship with curriculum as the pupil may come to associate both reading and writing with punishment. As we shall explore in more depth later in this chapter, punishing all pupils for the behaviour of some may be to the detriment of relationship with others if it leads to resentment between peers and towards the teacher. In terms of learning behaviour it would be difficult to claim that every practice or approach actively promotes this. However, attention needs to be given to whether positive learning behaviours are being discouraged or negative learning behaviours promoted by any aspect of policy. For example, if the regime is such that pupils perceive that making a mistake in a curriculum area will be attributed to lack of concentration, poor motivation or lack of effort and result in a reprimand or sanction then we risk undermining risk taking, creativity and the recognition that effective learning involves making errors and learning from these.

What do we promote implicitly?

The behaviour policy, in the language that it uses and the practices and approaches it specifies, contributes to the ethos of the school. However it should be clear from the discussion in Chapter 2 that it is one of a range of contributory factors that also include the quality of leadership, classroom management, the curriculum, pastoral care, buildings and the physical environment, organisation and timetable and relationships with parents (DES 1989).

The implicit messages conveyed by the language within the behaviour policy and the practices it promotes need to be compatible with the type of ethos the school seeks to maintain. For example, if the school considers that its ethos is based on a culture of mutual respect then any practice, including sanctions, used to manage behaviour need to be compatible with this value.

In addition to the issue of compatibility of aspects of the behaviour policy with the ethos the school aspires to maintain, there is the additional consideration of the school ethos specifically in relation to pupil behaviour. The language used within the policy and its day-to-day enactment will convey powerful messages about how behaviour is viewed. The fundamental distinction is between a focus on a 'problem pupil' or 'problem behaviour'. Drawing on the work of Fogell and Long (1997), Reflective Exercise 8.1 provides an opportunity to explore this issue.

It should be clear from Reflective Exercise 8.1 that the atmosphere would be very different for both staff and pupils in a school that adopts a predominantly 'problem pupil' focus compared to one that focuses on the behaviour as the problem rather than the individual. It is also evident that much of the language in the 'problem behaviour' column is that of relationships, using terms such as *collaboration* and *shared aims* and emphasising the importance of active involvement.

A complicating dimension when considering ethos is that practice influences ethos and ethos influences practice in a reciprocal, dynamic relationship. For example, if a school operates a punitive regime based on identifying and punishing wrong-doing and rule-infringement, this creates an ethos where identifying and punishing wrong-doing and rule-infringement is expected. It becomes very difficult for existing staff to break out of this cycle and new members of staff may find it very difficult to resist the ethos. Similarly, for pupils the ethos may be one in which being sanctioned (or 'getting done') is the norm and where minor 'victories' over the system bring esteem among peers. It is equally difficult for existing pupils to break out of this cycle and new pupils may find it very difficult to resist the ethos.

Whilst it is common to talk about the desirability of a positive ethos, it is important to recognise that ethos is something experienced by *individuals*. Therefore what is generally experienced as positive by many may not be for some. For example, a strong academic ethos may positively influence the aspirations of some but be experienced as relentless pressure by others. Though establishing a positive ethos is something schools do in order to benefit *groups*, responses of *individuals* need to be monitored in relation to the development of learning behaviour and the three relationships that underpin this.

Reflective Exercise 8.1

Use the table below to rank your school or a school that you know well against these statements:

Problem pupil	1	2	3	4	5
Reactive Deals with crisis situations; finds culprit when trouble occurs.	1	2	3	4	5
Confrontational Depends on sanctions to control undesired behaviour – emphasis on labelling, reprimand and punishment.	1	2	3	4	5
Fault finding Believes that the pupils are at fault or must change first.	1	2	3	4	5
Individualist Each teacher depends on their own resources.	1	2	3	4	5
Authoritarian Minimal involvement of pupils, parents or staff team in decision making.	1	2	3	4	5
Status focused Concern is with behaviour that challenges staff authority.	1	2	3	4	5

Problem behaviour
Proactive Plans strategies to pre-empt problem behaviour.
Positive Catches spontaneous positive behaviour and rewards it; emphasis on identifying good models of behaviour.
Initiating Involves all staff, pupils, parents to achieve shared aims.
Collaborative Whole-school polices developed.
Democratic All staff, pupils and parents actively involved.
Welfare focused Concern is on relationships between staff and pupils.

Source: From Fogell and Long 1997: 14. Reproduced with permission from the publishers.

What do we promote explicitly?

As indicated at the beginning of this chapter, the suggestion in guidance (DfES 2007a) is that one of the four elements necessary to establish a positive school ethos and promote effective learning is a set of clearly stated expectations of what constitutes *acceptable behaviour*. This requirement echoes the emphasis placed within the behaviour for learning conceptual framework on behaviours that we wish to promote. However, the language of *acceptability* applied to these behaviours introduces a degree of vagueness regarding purpose, priorities and evaluation. For example, are we referring to some kind of universally agreed moral acceptability or acceptability in terms of a level of behaviour necessary for a school to carry out its key functions efficiently and effectively? Ultimately we might conclude we are referring to a mixture. This can cause confusion for both teachers and pupils, particularly if, by their inclusion under the umbrella term *acceptable behaviour*, a behaviour that is mainly routine related appears to be endowed with similar status to a behaviour representing a significant infringement of another's rights. These and other issues are explored through Reflective Exercise 8.2.

Reflective Exercise 8.2

Examine your school behaviour policy. Does it contain clearly stated expectations of what constitutes *acceptable behaviour*? If so, try answering these questions:

1 Prior to consulting your policy for this exercise, did you as the class teacher know what your school policy defined as *acceptable behaviour*?
2 Do members of your class know what these *acceptable behaviours* are?
3 Which of these *acceptable behaviours* are mainly concerned with the management of large groups?
4 Which of these *acceptable behaviours* are predominantly concerned with promoting learning in individuals?
5 Do pupils in your class understand the rationale for these *acceptable behaviours*?
6 How does the school evaluate the efficacy of its policy against the promotion of its written list of *acceptable behaviours*?
7 To what extent does the existence of *acceptable behaviours* within your school's behaviour policy influence your own behaviour management in the classroom?
8 In terms of life-long learning which of these *acceptable behaviours* would be recognised as compatible with those required beyond the school environment? (e.g. the legal system, the pupil's culture, the home).

Reflective Exercise 8.2 begins by raising issues of awareness of *acceptable behaviours*. If the teacher does not know the behaviours that are deemed to be acceptable, then inconsistency in response is a considerable risk. In a secondary school in particular, this can represent a particular problem as pupils encounter several different teachers who may be viewing different behaviours as acceptable. In the case of pupil awareness, this can be viewed as equivalent to knowing the rules of a game. Specifying acceptable behaviours effectively lets the pupil know what is expected of them. Reflecting on pupil awareness may have led you to recognise pupils who clearly do know the acceptable behaviours because they demonstrate them. Your thinking may then have extended to those who you believe know the required behaviours but choose not to demonstrate them and those who may or not be aware of the behaviours but appear unable to demonstrate them. The latter point reflects the important issue that specifying acceptable behaviours at policy level can only ever act to set out what the school feels is required. It does not guarantee that individual pupils within the school will have the *skill* or *will* to demonstrate these behaviours.

In tackling questions 3 and 4 it is likely that you were able to identify a number of *acceptable behaviours* that related to the school's need to manage large groups. You were probably also able to identify some that did seem to have a more overt link with learning. It is also possible that there was some overlap between these categories. Thinking about these issues may have also highlighted explicitly the rationale behind defining a particular behaviour as acceptable. As question 5 explored, an important issue is whether pupils understand this rationale and recognise that there are some behaviours the school seeks to uphold simply because they are necessary for the smooth running of the organisation and some that protect the rights of the individual and would generally be regarded as necessary in a range of settings. This distinction relates to themes explored within question 8 regarding wider relevance. Clearly some behaviours deemed *acceptable* within school would be recognised as compatible with those required by the legal system, the pupil's culture and home environment and many work places. If we are interested in securing the *will* amongst pupils to demonstrate these acceptable behaviours, establishing a shared understanding of the rationale is essential.

In considering how your school evaluates the efficacy of its behaviour policy in promoting *acceptable behaviour* it is likely that you highlighted broad indicators related to groups such as number of exclusions, general impressions of calmness and order, frequency of more significant incidents or number of referrals to senior staff. Of these indicators a general impression of calmness is probably an exception. It is formed by a judgment about the absence of certain behaviours and the presence of some others. For example, we may note that pupils move in an orderly manner between lessons and there is rarely any physical aggression at break times. The other indicators tend to focus exclusively on the absence or infrequency of unacceptable behaviours. For example, we might judge that behaviour in the school is acceptable because exclusions are low.

In reflecting on question 7, you may have considered the existence of clearly stated expectations of what constitutes good behaviour within your school's behaviour policy to be supportive to your own behaviour management in the classroom. This clarity about what is expected may, for example, have provided you with terms of reference that allow you to make decisions regarding behaviours that you need to act upon and the nature of that response. Conversely, reflection on this question may have brought to mind occasions where the clear statement of acceptable behaviours may have restricted your options in terms of a response. An example might be where though the behaviour was unacceptable the circumstances made it understandable. In the case of some policies the issue might be that though the acceptable behaviours are stated they are very broad, such as 'behaves respectfully towards others'. This reflects a general school desire but is not directly supportive to behaviour management in the classroom as there is so much room for individual interpretation, by pupils and teachers, regarding the types of behaviours that are deemed respectful. In such a situation you might conclude that the *acceptable behaviours* are expressed in a form too general to either inform the teaching of these or provide clear guidance on unacceptable behaviours to address.

Realistically it would not be possible to claim that all the *acceptable behaviours* required by a school can be framed as learning behaviours in terms of the criteria set out in Chapter 4. Within Reflective Exercise 8.2 you will have identified certain behaviours that whilst necessary in your school context do not transcend ages and stages of development, are not of life-long relevance to the learner and are more rooted in the needs of the school rather than those of the individual. In thinking about *acceptable behaviours* we can distinguish between:

- those behaviours that transcend curriculum areas, ages and stages of development, are of life-long relevance to the learner and are rooted in the needs of the individual and could be viewed as *learning behaviours*;
- those behaviours that, if not demonstrated, would affect the rights of others or represent a safety issue;
- those behaviours that are only necessary for the smooth running of school.

This is not to suggest that the third bullet point is unimportant or that behaviours that fall solely in this category should not be upheld. Rather, the argument is that whilst we should certainly have, as the guidance (DfES 2007a) suggests, a clear idea of the behaviour we want in schools, notions of *acceptability* and *appropriateness* need to be unpicked to give greater clarity about purpose and priorities.

Effective behaviour management strategies

Readers will be aware from preceding chapters that the suggestion in the guidance (DfES 2007a) that a behaviour policy should set out effective behaviour management strategies raises a number of issues. It would be unrealistic to believe that a set of universally effective behaviour management strategies could be defined that *every* individual pupil would experience, interpret and respond to in the same way. This raises questions about how *effectiveness* is being judged. Typically strategies recommended in a behaviour policy are designed to be relevant to securing *acceptable behaviour* from a considerable range of pupils. Evaluated against this purpose a range of strategies may be considered effective if generally such behaviour is secured. Such judgements of effectiveness do not however *necessarily* need to make any reference to learning for individuals.

In referring to behaviour management strategies we should remember that this term does not just relate to what the teacher does when the pupil is misbehaving. It should also include strategies for acknowledging positive behaviours. We should recognise that individuals will experience and interpret these differently.

From a behaviour for learning perspective, the message we would reiterate is that any behaviour management strategy advocated within policy in order to secure acceptable behaviour of groups should not compromise the three core relationships, undermine the development of positive learning behaviours or encourage negative learning behaviours. Chapter 10 critically examines a range of behaviour management strategies in more depth.

Rules, rewards and sanctions

As outlined in the introduction to this chapter, guidance (DfES 2007a) on behaviour policies refers to the need to define processes which recognise, teach, reward and celebrate positive behaviour and processes, rules and sanctions to deal with poor conduct. The behavioural trinity of rules, rewards and sanctions is rooted firmly in a behaviourist tradition. The underlying assumption is that if pupils are demonstrating the required behaviour, as defined by the rules, and something rewarding happens as a result it will increase the likelihood of them behaving in this way in the future. Similarly if pupils misbehave and something they dislike happens they will be less likely to behave in this way in the future. The origins of the behaviourist approach can be traced back to the work of Skinner, Watson and Pavlov. Skinner's experiments in this field were laboratory based and involved rats and pigeons being trained to carry out simple tasks such as pressing buttons to release food. The behaviour pattern of pressing a button became associated with a reward, in this case food, and hence the desired behaviour pattern was repeated again and again by the rat. Though the behaviourist approach is typically associated with the use of rewards and punishment, Skinner himself did not favour the use of punishment, believing it to be ineffective (Wheldall and Glynn 1989, Pound 2005).

Of course our pupils are not rats. This has a number of important implications when we attempt to utilise behaviourist approaches, including:

*   What as adults we consider to be aversive may not be for the pupil. Some pupils might for example like being out of class and therefore a time-out room that has the intention of reducing a particular behaviour may be reinforcing it.
*   What as adults we consider to be rewarding may not be for the pupil. Being singled out for praise for example may be embarrassing for some children and consequently they may exhibit less of the behaviour that gains praise.
*   Unlike pigeons or rats, the majority of pupils can interact verbally with us. Others can interact through alternative and augmentative communication. This provides plenty of other ways of promoting positive behaviour and developing higher level problem solving skills.
*   Pupils will have a view of the person providing the reward or sanction. A reward or sanction may mean more or less to the individual depending on whether they like or respect this person. Pupils may also have a perception of the rewarder or sanctioner's view of them. Relationships therefore are important.
*   The pupil can reflect upon the experience of being disciplined and render it as 'unfair' in their minds.
*   There may be many other rewarding or punishing factors present besides the ones the teacher is controlling. For example, whilst the teacher may use ignoring as a response to attention seeking behaviour, it may be the attention of peers that is more important to the pupil.
*   For those pupils who *do* respond to the approach there is a need to consider why they do and whether what they are learning from this is helpful. If for example the reason that the pupil behaves is to avoid sanctions or to gain reward we might question whether this is sufficient learning. There is an issue that they may *only* demonstrate these behaviours where these rewards or sanctions are available. In other words, there may be little intrinsic motivation to behave in a particular way and so

the behaviour is unlikely to transfer to occasions and situations when the reward is not available. For example, the pupil may behave in the classroom but not in the playground.

These points raise a number of issues for practice:

- It is necessary to recognise that a set of rewards and sanctions devised for a group will impact differently on individuals.
- Because we are dealing with people rather than rats or pigeons we have other tools at our disposal – such as talking to them!
- Relationships are important. For example, a reward from someone who is liked and respected is likely to be more powerful in influencing behaviour.

A number of studies indicate that behaviourist approaches can be effective in reducing classroom disruption and off task behaviour. Miller (2003) cites the work of Tsoi and Yule (1976) who used extra break time as a reinforcer. They found two types of strategy to be effective: one where the behaviour of a single child formed the basis for reinforcement for the whole class, and one in which changes in the behaviour of the whole class were required. Merrett and Wheldall (1978) also investigated whole-class management using their 'rules, praise, ignore' technique. This also showed improvements in the level of class on task behaviour. Render, Padilla and Krank (1989) reviewed several studies which found that Canter and Canter's (1992) Assertive Discipline approach, which, in the emphasis it places on rewards and sanctions, is essentially behaviourist in nature, decreased the number of discipline problems (Woods 2008). In an EPPI review looking at the effectiveness of interventions for pupils with emotional behavioural difficulties, Evans et al. (2003), concluded that there was some evidence that behavioural approaches to discipline were effective in reducing disruptive behaviour. Within a broader review looking at teaching strategies and approaches for pupils with special educational needs, Davis and Florian (2004) also concluded, after considering several review articles, that behavioural approaches seemed to increase on task behaviour among children with social, emotional and behavioural difficulties or with attention deficit hyperactivity disorder (Woods 2008). We should also acknowledge the role the behaviourist approach played in moving people, institutionalised as a result of being medically diagnosed as ineducable, into education (e.g. Clarke and Clarke 1958).

Behaviourist approaches have been criticised at a number of levels. The success criteria are typically either that the pupil displays the desired behaviour or ceases to display the undesired behaviour. Humanists (e.g. Kohn 2001) are critical of this emphasis on compliance, seeing it as an inappropriate goal for educators (Porter 2007). Kohn argues that both punishments and rewards adversely affect the relationship between the adult and child, making the point that:

> With punishments we come to be seen as enforcers to be avoided; with rewards, as goody-dispensers on legs. In neither case have we established a caring alliance, a connection based on warmth and respect. Like punishments, rewards try to make bad behaviours disappear though manipulation. They are ways of doing things to students instead of working with them.
>
> (Kohn 2001: 36)

In addition to these primarily philosophical arguments, there is also the practical concern expressed by Porter (2007) that behaviourism seems to be ineffective with the core 5–7 per cent of pupils with whom teachers most want it to work. It does not work, Porter (2007) suggests, because reinforcement must be internalised for gains to occur or to be maintained. In other words, it is dependent on pupils *wanting* to cooperate with the system. However, given our earlier comments concerning realism with regard to the purpose of the behaviour policy, the 93–5 per cent success rate implied by Porter's (2007) estimate would support a view that behaviourist approaches have some utility in *managing* behaviour.

It should be remembered that neither rewards nor sanctions can compensate if the pupil is either not developmentally ready or has not yet acquired the underlying skills to demonstrate the required behaviour. Rewards and sanctions are only likely to make an impact in cases where:

- the pupil knows what is expected of them;
- the pupil has the necessary skills to do what is expected of them;
- the pupil is developmentally able to do what is expected of them;
- the pupil is not meeting other more important needs by *not* demonstrating the required behaviour. For example, the pupil may value the sense of belonging they feel when their peers laugh at their disruptive behaviour more than they value any reward on offer or fear any sanction.

With these preliminary thoughts in mind we will consider rewards and sanctions individually and in more depth.

Rewards

A school behaviour policy will typically set out the school-wide systems for rewards. Some systems are based on teachers and others giving a reward that has value in its own right to the individual. Other schools will operate systems where a reward given to an individual or group contributes towards an individual, class or house total that will eventually lead to a higher reward.

Examples of rewards include:

- 'congratulations' and 'good news' postcards home (DfES 2007);
- personalised letters to parents (DfES 2007);
- certificates that recognise positive contributions to the school community (DfES 2007);
- celebration assemblies, involving parents (DfES 2007);
- special privileges (DfES 2007);
- prizes or, in the case of younger children, gold stars (prizes could be purchased from a school reward shop) (DfES 2007);
- positive phone calls home (Dix 2007);
- positive referral (Dix 2007)
  This involves sending the pupils, either during a lesson or at an appropriate time, to see a colleague for further acknowledgement and praise;
- raffle tickets
  These are given to pupils as a reward and a draw is conducted, perhaps at the end of the week, and prizes are awarded. Pupils need to have a basic grasp of probability at

the level of recognising that gaining more tickets increases the chance of winning. The frustrating element for some pupils may be that they have received a lot of raffle tickets but win nothing whereas a pupil who gained just one was drawn as the winner. Older pupils may simply accept that this is an inevitable characteristic of a raffle, but younger pupils may feel that this is unfair.

In addition to these generic reward systems, there are also examples linked to particular packages. Jenny Mosley advocates the use of 'golden time' (Mosley 1996, Mosley and Sonnet 2005). This can be viewed as a strategy in its own right for 'rewarding and celebrating behavioural success' (Mosley and Sonnet 2005: 19). However it is important to acknowledge that Mosley (Mosley 1996, Mosley and Sonnet 2005) has presented it as part of a broader whole-school approach to behaviour.

The use of 'golden time' involves establishing with classes that there is a period of time, usually part of a Friday afternoon, when pupils will be able to engage in an activity of their choice from the range that is offered. Where this is used school-wide it can even be organised with different activities offered in different classes, with the pupils choosing which room to go to. At the start of the week every pupil starts off with the same amount of 'golden time'. If an individual pupil misbehaves they lose some minutes of 'golden time'. Misbehaviour is any behaviour that infringes the 'golden rules'. Although therefore 'golden time' is presented primarily as an approach for rewarding behaviour, the sanctions are inextricably linked. The appeal for many teachers of 'golden time' is that it addresses the concern that some pupils who behave well all the time can get overlooked in reward systems. Using the 'golden time' approach every pupil gets the reward unless they do something that causes the teacher to deduct minutes.

Visual warnings are used before minutes are deducted, based on the principle that the pupil is then able to make a choice about whether to continue with the behaviour that will lead to the loss of minutes. At the end of the week the pupil has to sit and wait for this period of time before being allowed to start their 'golden time' activity. The use of a sand-timer is advocated so that the pupil can see this time passing. The suggestion is also that the waiting pupils should be able to see the others who are engaging in the golden activities. Mosley and Sonnet (2005) state: 'It is essential for the child to have their metaphorical nose pressed against the window of opportunity they chose to kick in! The sound of laughter, the chinking of dice and flourishing of dressing up clothes are all reminders of what they are missing' (Mosley and Sonnet 2005: 45).

Arguably, the implicit message this gives is 'See, if you'd behaved yourself, you could be having fun now'. Rogers (2002) advises against saying this sort of thing verbally when, for example, keeping a pupil behind at break time, and we would suggest that it is also questionable whether we should be taking an action that conveys this implicitly. Mosley and Sonnet, however, defend the system stating:

When they have lost five minutes, or one minute, and are looking at a sand-timer, they will be very clear – if the visual warnings are properly carried out – that they chose that consequence. They are reflecting on their behaviour – they are reflecting on the fact that they have lost a part of their privilege – and that this was their choice. So, I believe that sanctions uphold the self-esteem of children because they give them safe boundaries and show them that adults care enough about them to put the consequences into action.

(Mosley and Sonnet 2005: 116)

Ultimately, whether the pupil experiences loss of 'golden time' in the positive manner, Mosley and Sonnet (2005) suggest, depends on the individual pupil's interpretation and attributions. Some may well view it as a just consequence for their actions, others may see this as their teacher trying to hurt or embarrass them. Individual interpretation and experience is always the challenge to whole-school systems.

Rewards need not just be for the individual pupil, they can be for the whole class or groups. It is important to ensure, particularly with individual reward schemes, that motivation to achieve the reward does not lead to a level of competition between pupils that undermines the desirable learning behaviours of cooperation and collaboration. Individual rewards that contribute to a class reward can help to overcome this issue and readers may wish to consider this option.

A well-known class reward system involves the class collecting marbles in a jar, which was popularised through Canter and Canter's (1992) Assertive Discipline programme. When the teacher, or other adult, spots an individual or group demonstrating positive behaviour they award a marble which is placed in a jar. When a certain level is reached, the class receives a treat such as watching a DVD. We are sceptical about the operation of this system when the class' marble-linked reward always seems to coincide with the end of term; for such a system to be credible pupils need to have a sense that the reward can be gained either more or less quickly and that this is influenced by their behaviour, not by the calendar.

If we are using class rewards it should be framed in such a way that a strong emphasis is on the positive effects of working together rather than on highlighting those individuals who hinder progress towards the goal. There should also be a balance between rewards for individuals, for groups and for the whole class. If, for example, marbles are only ever given for the whole or the vast majority of the class behaving well then, on the occasions when the teacher does not consider that a marble is deserved, it can send a message to individuals that their decision to behave in the required manner is neither recognised nor rewarded. Whole-class rewards used in this way may begin to share some of the disadvantages of whole-class sanctions which are described later.

We would suggest that marbles, like any reward given for a *specific* piece of behaviour, should not be taken away. Our argument is that any reward given is for the piece of positive behaviour that has occurred and any subsequent misbehaviour does not change that fact. To remove the reward effectively sends the message that the earlier positive behaviour counted for nothing. An exception is where the reward is in the form of ongoing higher levels of independence or responsibility and is contingent on the behaviour continuing. An example might be a pupil who, after a history of absconding from school, has sustained a period without incident and is now allowed to take the register to the school office accompanied by a peer. If this pupil leaves the premises whilst on this errand it would be reasonable to withdraw this level of responsibility. The purpose here is not to remove responsibility as a sanction but to protect the pupil.

Within the reward system when any reward is given it should always be clear to the pupil what it is for. The accompanying verbal or written comment is the opportunity to exert a mediating influence on what is learned. The fundamental principle underpinning the use of rewards is that reinforcing the desired behaviour will lead to it occurring more often. If we just give rewards without making it clear what they are for we are not capitalising on this, and are at best only creating a 'feel good' factor for the pupil. The use of positive feedback is discussed in the next chapter.

Sanctions

A sanction can be considered as a formal action taken by the school in response to misbehaviour that has not been ameliorated by a range of strategies. Government guidance suggests that the purpose of sanctions is to:

- impress on the perpetrator that what he or she has done is unacceptable;
- deter the pupil from repeating that behaviour;
- signal to other pupils that the behaviour is unacceptable and deter them from doing it.

(DfES 2007b: 31–2)

Learning does not feature highly within this agenda, but this does not mean learning does not take place. The individual pupil's interpretation will determine the resulting learning and this may not reflect any of these purposes. The three stated purposes do not have strong connotations of learning from your mistakes or learning better ways of behaving or relating to others, except in the sense possibly of learning not to commit the same offence again because something unpleasant will befall you *if* caught.

Sanctions, in the traditional form of responding to misbehaviour by doing something to the pupil that we believe they will dislike, offer little potential to promote positive learning behaviours. They also carry an inherent risk of impacting negatively on the three relationships that underpin the development of learning behaviour. Particular problems associated with this type of sanction include:

- They form an inappropriate model for human relationships (Kyriacou 1991).
- They may foster anxiety among some pupils. Typically those pupils who are most worried by sanctions are those who would respond to skilful use of other strategies – such as talking to them about their behaviour.
- The pupils who most frequently encounter the sanctions are likely to be those with little regard for authority or the values of the school and are therefore the least likely to respond by better behaviour in the future (Kyriacou 1991). Behavioural change in these pupils is more likely to be achieved through cognitive-behavioural interventions that tackle underlying beliefs, attitudes and attributions.
- They run the risk that any remorse the perpetrator may feel is replaced about concern for what will happen to them. Effectively this allows the perpetrator to transform themselves into the victim (Galvin 1999).
- They lead to resentment of the person enforcing the sanction. Resentment is not a good basis for a positive relationship.
- They tend not to motivate pupils to improve and may instead encourage pupils to develop strategies to avoid being caught.
- They focus on the misbehaviour (Kyriacou 1991) rather than alternative ways of behaving in the future.
- They do not promote good behaviour directly but simply serve to suppress misbehaviour (Kyriacou 1991).

Within the context of the behaviour for learning conceptual framework, sanctions need to be seen for what they are: a means by which the school can demonstrate its disapproval that *may* have a deterrent effect on the individual and on others. This is not intended as pejorative comment; pragmatically sanctions are necessary to allow staff to feel supported, for pupils to recognise that there are consequences and to maintain parental confidence. Though sanctions primarily have a role in limiting behaviour (Hook and Vass 2002), by consideration of the nature of the sanction and the manner in which it is applied we can seek opportunities to develop learning behaviour or the three relationships that underpin its development, or at least ensure we do not undermine these.

Some writers (e.g. Hook and Vass 2002, Canter and Canter 1992, Dreikurs *et al.* 1998) and some schools use the term 'consequence' as an alternative to 'sanction' with the intention of conveying the idea that the pupil, through their behaviour, is making a choice and so determining what happens. The term has less punitive connotations than the word 'sanction' and from our behaviour for learning perspective we would endorse the idea that potentially the language of consequences encourages pupils to recognise that through their actions they determine what happens to them, thus contributing to the development of self-efficacy and responsibility. However different writers, like different schools, attach different meanings to the term 'consequences'. Canter and Canter (1992) for example refer to consequences such as being last in line, working away from peers for a period of time in the classroom, staying behind after class, missing free time and having their parents called. To us this does not sound significantly different to the traditional idea of a sanction, particularly in view of Canter and Canter's (1992) suggestion that to be effective a consequence must be an action the pupil does not want or like. Hook and Vass (2002) attach a different meaning to the term 'consequence', drawing parallels with the natural consequences people experience in life as a result of the actions they take. For Hook and Vass (2002) consequences, whether positive or negative, result directly from the choice the pupil makes. They suggest that in constructing consequences it is important to consider five key questions:

1 Are they fair?
2 Are they reasonable, i.e. matched to the event?
3 Are they in the person's best interests in terms of helping them to make more useful choices?
4 Are they related as far as possible to the event so the connection is obvious?
5 Are they largely known or predictable so people can make informed choices?

(Hook and Vass 2002: 47)

Hook and Vass' (2002) use of the term consequences draws on neo-Adlerian theory (Porter 2007), which advocates the use of both natural and logical consequences. A natural consequence is the natural outcome of an individual's actions that occurs without adult intervention, such as getting wet when you stand outside in the rain (Harrison 2004, cited in Porter 2007). Simply letting events take their course poses considerable problems in school contexts as we cannot legitimately allow pupils to put themselves or others in dangerous situations. Porter (2007) also makes the point that pupils deserve protection from other events, which though not physically harmful, may be psychologically harmful. Therefore though, for example, a natural consequence of antisocial behaviour may be rejection by one's peer group, the detrimental effect on the pupil's relationship with self and relationship with others is too high a price to pay in order to teach that there is a consequence for the behaviour (Porter 2007).

Logical consequences attempt to retain the cause-and-effect quality of natural consequences but are defined by the teacher. Unlike Canter and Canter's (1992) concern with the pupil's dislike of the consequence, a logical consequence should be helpful rather than hurtful (Nelsen *et al.* 2000). For example, completing work missed through misbehaviour makes up for the missed learning, apologising privately to a peer helps the aggrieved party to feel better and cleaning graffiti off the wall restores the area to its original condition. Logical consequences typically have a reparative, 'offence-related' quality.

The emphasis on choice and consequences is not without critics. Kohn (2001), criticising the work of writers such as Canter and Canter (1992) and Dreikurs *et al.* (1998), suggests that the choice offered is little more than a pseudo-choice amounting to doing exactly what is expected by the teacher or facing the consequences and argues that the distinctions made between punishment and consequences are little more than semantics.

Arguably, whether we define what we do when pupils infringe the rules as a sanction, punishment or consequence, it is the pupil's experience and interpretation that matters. For example, what the school considers to be a logical consequence designed to develop responsibility may be perceived by the pupil as an arbitrary punishment. With any sanction it is important that we consider carefully what we are promoting and the learning, helpful and unhelpful, that might occur as a result. This is illustrated through Reflective Exercise 8.3 in the next section, which looks at the use of whole-group sanctions.

Whole-group sanctions

Reflective Exercise 8.3

A Year 4 teacher has given her class several warnings because they are being too noisy. She then tells them that they will all have to stay in for 10 minutes at lunch time and sit in silence. When she spots an individual talking she names the pupil and extends the period of detention by one minute.

At lunch time she keeps the class in and makes them sit in silence for a period of 13 minutes.

- Why do you think the teacher used this strategy?
- What do you think the pupils will learn from this strategy?

The practice of punishing whole classes by, for example, keeping all children in at break time because a significant number have misbehaved is, according to the Elton Report (DES 1989), always seen as unfair by pupils and the resulting sense of grievance is likely to be damaging to the school atmosphere. Recommendation 26 from the Elton Report clearly states: 'We recommended that head-teachers and teachers should avoid the punishment of whole classes' (DES 1989: 101).

DfES (2007b) has also stated that schools should 'avoid whole-group sanctions that punish the innocent as well as the guilty' (DfES 2007b: 33).

Typically teachers justify their use of this strategy based on the belief that it capitalises on peer-group pressure. Rogers (2002) suggests that this is in fact a mistaken belief. The practice of then naming individuals who lead to the period of detention being extended seems to be based on the same belief. Kohn (1999) commenting on a similar practice of naming individuals whose behaviour prevents a class from achieving a promised reward suggests that 'It calls forth a particularly noxious sort of peer-pressure' (Kohn 1999: 56).

Ultimately we would have to question, if indeed peer-group pressure was to occur as a result of imposing a whole-class sanction, whether there is any socially acceptable form this is likely to take. Behaviours such as socially isolating 'culprits' or physically coercing them are surely not behaviours that we would want to promote? The use of this strategy is potentially damaging to relationships between pupils, being underpinned by a 'divide and conquer' (Kohn 1999: 56) principle, and also to relationships between the pupils and the teacher because of the inherent unfairness of punishing all pupils for the behaviour of some. We would therefore struggle to justify the approach in terms either of the behaviours it risks promoting or the contribution it is likely to make in the area of relationship with others. There is an argument that a whole-class sanction such as the one described in Reflective Exercise 8.3 might encourage more pupils to be more willing to filter out, rather than joining in with, distractions. The skill and will to ignore distractions can be viewed as a positive learning behaviour in school contexts but we would make two key points:

- As already outlined, the costs associated with achieving this through whole-class punishments may be too high.
- Even if an *individual* chose to take this personal responsibility (a *positive* learning behaviour) and attempted to filter out distractions (a *positive* learning behaviour) this is neither rewarded nor recognised and still leads to the same negative outcome (i.e. staying in) unless sufficient others make similar positive choices. In terms of self-efficacy (see Chapter 7), such a strategy risks sending the unhelpful message that, as an individual, the pupil is able to exert little influence over what happens to them; it is the behaviour of others that determines whether the individual receives the sanction.

Despite the range of literature, in the form of government guidance and the work of independent writers, advising against the practice of whole-group punishments, we are aware that some teachers adopt this practice in situations when it is difficult to identify individual culprits. Cowley (2003) in many ways captures the dilemma for practitioners with regard to this strategy. She is initially forceful and unequivocal in her rejection of this type of sanction, stating: 'When we were discussing sanctions, the students also mentioned that whole-class punishments were extremely unfair, and of course they were right! Why on earth should they all be punished for the misbehaviour of a small minority?' (Cowley 2003: 10).

Logically, in the cold light of day, away from the complexities of classroom, it is very difficult to argue in support of whole-class punishments. It is not, after all, an approach we would be likely to accept without complaint and considerable resentment in any aspect of our own lives. However later in the same text Cowley concedes, 'In some situations, you may find that a whole-class sanction is appropriate, for instance with a class whose behaviour is not particularly bad, but who are very talkative or lively' (Cowley 2003: 67).

Later still, the approach is then positively recommended: 'Impose a whole-class sanction: You need to show your students that peer-pressure to behave in a certain way will be punished' (Cowley 2003: 94).

The irony of the latter suggestion, of course, is that the means by which it is demonstrated that peer-group pressure to behave in a certain way will be punished is to use a strategy that attempts to utilise peer-group pressure to encourage pupils to behave in a certain way.

Unless we have a means of selecting and evaluating a strategy that is based on more than the pragmatics of stopping behaviour, it is all too easy to find ourselves in this situation where we can, like Cowley (2003), recognise a practice as inherently wrong yet at the same time generate a range of caveats to justify why it might be acceptable in practice in certain circumstances.

DO SANCTIONS LEAD TO BETTER BEHAVIOUR?

Findings from the Elton Report (DES 1989) suggest that schools which put too much faith in punishments to deter bad behaviour are likely to be disappointed and that those with more punitive regimes tended to experience worse rather than better standards of behaviour (DES 1989). The key message therefore is that whilst sanctions may be a necessary element of a whole-school policy, expending a lot of time and effort developing additional and ever more elaborate sanctions is unlikely to be productive.

Sanctions have a role in conveying to pupils that there are consequences for actions and providing teachers with a response once a range of strategies have been exhausted. They also create a general sense amongst pupils that the school will take actions to uphold the standards of behaviour it expects and protect the rights of individuals to learn and feel emotionally and physically safe. Sanctions are not however the great modifier of behaviour (Galvin 1999) that some teachers might be inclined to believe they are.

Tariff systems

We have used the term 'tariff systems' to reflect a particular type of behaviour policy that prescribes in quite a rigid way the teacher response to pupil behaviour. Often, these are imported as packages rather than developed by the school itself. A well-known example is Canter and Canter's Assertive Discipline approach. In *Excellence for all Children*, the DfEE (1997b) endorsed the Assertive Discipline approach, suggesting it could help schools to establish settings where pupils were encouraged to behave well and where there were clear guidelines for behaviour (Hallam and Rogers 2008). Assertive discipline is based on establishing clear, unambiguous rules of conduct, together with continuous positive feedback when the rules are followed, and a hierarchy of sanctions for rule-breaking (Fletcher-Campbell and Wilkin 2003).

A more recent approach is one which, unfortunately, shares its name with the title of this book. To attempt to minimise confusion we shall refer to this as BfL. The BfL approach sets out four levels of consequence (abbreviated to C):

C1 verbal warning;
C2 second verbal warning;
C3 detention for one hour, usually the next day;
C4 isolation from peers in the school's isolation unit for one, two or three days; or exclusion.

(Elkin 2004: 6)

Under this system, if a pupil is rude, shouts out or behaves inappropriately in class, they could be issued with a C1 by the teacher. If the pupil persists, the teacher might then issue a C2. The verbal warnings are not centrally recorded but the advice is that the teacher makes a note of them by, for example, writing them on the board during the course of the lesson based on the rationale that pupils can see exactly where they are. The approach keeps dialogue to a minimum. If a pupil misbehaves, the teacher would simply say, for example, 'Kelly – C1.' Teachers are trained to be decisive and clear, but calm and not angry, in communicating a warning (Elkin 2004).

Systems such as this and Assertive Discipline upon which it appears to be based raise a number of issues when considered from *our* behaviour for learning perspective. They can become used in quite a mechanistic manner, based on an almost formulaic principle of 'if the pupil does X, then the teacher does Y', that discourages teachers from using professional judgement about the best approach with a particular pupil at a particular time. Watkins and Wagner (2000) go as far as to suggest that through Assertive Discipline teachers are invited to be come automata rather than professionals or even humans. This can lead to some pupils being escalated rapidly though to exclusion as class teachers rigidly adhere to the predefined sequence of consequences without recognising when an alternative approach might be more appropriate.

Rigid tariff systems do not encourage discussion or problem solving on the part of the teacher or the pupil. Though such approaches often refer to the notion of choice and responsibility, critics suggest that realistically the only choice offered by a package like Assertive Discipline is 'behave or else!' (Curwin and Mendler 1989, Porter 2007). Effectively responsible behaviour is defined as little more than doing what you are told, with 'good choices' being those that the teacher approves of (Porter 2007). Porter (2007) argues that within communication theory, the right to be assertive is mutual: one person's right to assert his or her needs guarantees the other's equal right to the same. It is this reciprocity, Porter continues, that distinguishes assertiveness from aggression. In this sense, the title Assertive Discipline, is something of a misnomer as the approach does not adhere to this principle, but is based entirely on what the teacher will do to the pupil with very little opportunity for the pupil to assert their view. Indeed, attempting to assert their view should, if the system is followed, result in another consequence.

These types of approaches minimise dialogue between teachers and pupils when misbehaviour occurs. This can be beneficial in schools where teachers regularly get involved in long, drawn-out disciplinary interactions (Watkins and Wagner 2000) but ultimately is not based upon relationships. This seems evident in approaches such as 'Kelly, that's a C1' or 'Kyle, that's a warning.' These have the feel of cold transactions rather than proper human interactions necessary for the development of relationships.

Teaching behaviour

It is now expected that a school's behaviour policy is not only 'designed to promote good behaviour and deter bad behaviour' (DfES 2007b: 12), but also covers the 'systems in place to teach appropriate behaviour' (DfES 2007b: 62). The social and emotional aspects of learning (SEAL) materials produced by the Primary and Secondary National Strategies (DfES 2005c, 2007a) are presented within the guidance as a key resource for teaching social, emotional and behavioural skills. The introduction of SEAL materials was based on a view that it could no longer be assumed that such skills would be 'caught' simply by pupils being in an orderly environment maintained by rules, rewards and sanctions and being in the presence of adults and other pupils who acted as role models. Though many pupils evidently did, and would no doubt successfully continue, to 'catch' these skills the concern for those that did not was sufficient to trigger a national strategy for all.

The SEAL programme fits well with many of the priorities within the behaviour for learning approach. We would endorse SEAL's explicit recognition that there are social and emotional components to learning and the emphasis on developing in pupils the behaviours that are necessary for learning in group settings. SEAL has served to extend the discourse on behaviour beyond a traditional predominant concern with the management and reduction of unwanted behaviour.

Implementation of SEAL

As we outlined in Chapter 2, there are distinct differences in how SEAL has been presented to primary and secondary schools. Through the Primary National Strategy, primary schools were provided with a box of materials supporting the themes shown in Table 8.1.

Table 8.1 Primary SEAL themes

Theme number and time of year	Theme title	Key social and emotional aspects of learning addressed
1. September/October	New beginnings	• **Empathy** • Self-awareness • Motivation • Social skills
2. November/December	Getting on and falling out	• **Managing feelings** • Empathy • Social skills
3. One to two weeks in the autumn term (to coincide with national anti-bullying week in November)	Say no to bullying	• **Empathy** • Self-awareness • Social skills
4. January/February	Going for goals!	• **Motivation** • Self-awareness
5. February/March	Good to be me	• **Managing feelings** • Self-awareness • Empathy
6. March/April	Relationships	• **Self-awareness** • **Managing feelings** • Empathy
7. June/July	Changes	• **Motivation** • **Social skills** • Managing feelings

© Crown copyright [2005] Department for Education and Skills (DfES 2005c: 19).

Note: The bold text indicated the main social and/or emotional aspect of learning targeted through the theme.

The production and provision of these materials conveyed a high expectation that primary schools would engage in *direct* teaching of the social and emotional aspects of learning across the age range.

At secondary level the approach has been rather different. Like its primary counterpart, the supporting guidance booklet (DfES 2007a) emphasised the whole-school approach to promoting the social and emotional aspects of learning and stressed the links with existing curriculum areas such as PSHE and Citizenship. However, unlike Primary SEAL, learning materials have initially only been produced for one year group (Year 7). Schools are encouraged to consider how these can be extended into Years 8 and 9 (DfES 2007a) and advised to adapt and develop the curriculum 'to ensure that it promotes social and emotional skills in a systematic, coherent and comprehensive way that matches the needs of all pupils' (DfES 2007a: 26).

Positively we might interpret this as government respect for the professionalism of secondary schools, entrusting them to develop and implement SEAL. However, an alternative interpretation may be that secondary schools, by virtue of their size, a rigid subject-based curriculum taught by subject specialists, and the focus on public examinations, would pose many challenges if an attempt was made to launch a primary-style SEAL resource. Even with the version of Secondary SEAL that has been launched there are decisions for secondary schools about where it is most appropriately located. The guidance (DfES 2007a) suggests social and emotional skills could be specifically taught through:

- integrating social and emotional skills into PSHE, citizenship and tutor time;
- integrating social and emotional skills across mainstream subjects;
- holding 'theme weeks' that focus on social and emotional skills;
- special interventions to teach social and emotional skills more intensively for those with additional needs in this area.

(DfES 2007a: 41)

Though the official encouragement is given to all subject teachers 'to identify how their subject may contribute to developing social and emotional skills and incorporate the SEAL learning outcomes into their planning and teaching' (DfES 2007a: 41), the reality may be that SEAL is mainly located in PSHE, Citizenship and tutor time. This may affect the status of SEAL in pupils' eyes, though this will be largely dependent on the value already attached to PSHE, Citizenship and tutor time by staff and pupils.

Primary schools may not have faced such dilemmas if they have adopted SEAL in the intended manner. Whilst clearly not as simple as using straight from the box, the materials could be introduced into practice relatively quickly. Many teachers, as professionals, are likely to have already identified where the provided materials can usefully be supplemented and extended.

As with most nationally given guidance there are layers of interpretation that influence how this is experienced by pupils. At school-level decisions taken regarding the method of implementation and delivery are a key factor. One area for consideration is how much of the SEAL curriculum is to be delivered through discrete SEAL lessons, and how much through a cross-curricular approach. Whilst the guidance attempts to be non-prescriptive, suggesting that 'some schools may choose to develop children's social, emotional and behavioural skills primarily through core and foundation subjects' (DfES 2005c:11), the structure and nature of the primary materials encourages some discrete SEAL lessons. If elements of SEAL are to be taught through discrete lessons, it raises a school policy issue with regard to who leads these. If the SEAL curriculum is delivered by the class teacher it would appear to offer a number of advantages:

- SEAL is given status because it is delivered by the same person who delivers high status subjects such as literacy, numeracy and science.
- It is delivered in the context of the existing pastoral relationship many primary school pupils have with their teacher.
- It is easier for themes covered within discrete SEAL lessons to be followed up across the curriculum if the person delivering SEAL is also responsible for delivery of the rest of the curriculum.
- The title 'social and emotional aspects of learning' conveys a message that *all* learning has social and emotional aspects. Delivery of SEAL by anybody other than the class teacher would seem to contradict this and may imply that the social and emotional elements are an 'add on' rather than integrated.

Some schools have used teaching assistants to deliver discrete class SEAL lessons or scheduled such lessons to coincide with the class teacher's planning, preparation and assessment (PPA) time so that SEAL is taught by a cover-teacher. Whilst there are ways (e.g. good communication between the cover-teacher or TA with the class teacher) of minimising the potential disadvantages of these approaches, we would contend that it is difficult to fully realise the benefits outlined above.

In addition to these day-to-day practical issues of implementation, there is also the wider question of whether the direct teaching of social and emotional skills is appropriate at all. This a subject for debate and we would draw readers' attention to the discussion of this issue in Chapter 2.

Summary

From a behaviour for learning perspective we accept that a whole-school behaviour policy is an important document. However it can only realistically specify practices and approaches based on a prediction of how these will be experienced, interpreted and responded to by a 'typical' pupil. In identifying such practices and approaches schools need to have regard for:

- the effect on the three relationships within the behaviour for learning conceptual framework;
- the effect on the development of learning behaviour.

It is important to be open to the possibility that some practices advocated through policy are counterproductive when evaluated against these criteria, despite apparent effectiveness in maintaining good order and discipline.

Chapter 9

Promoting learning behaviours in your classroom

Context and conditions

Introduction

For the majority of pupils for the majority of the time the teacher will be seeking to maintain and develop their relationship with the curriculum and the range of learning behaviours associated with this. It will not be necessary to specifically target relationship with self or relationship with others, only to have regard for these. Rather, in seeking to foster a positive relationship with the curriculum, the teacher will:

- seek to recognise any opportunities to strengthen relationship with self and/ or relationship with others in order to support the pupil's relationship with the curriculum;
- keep a watchful eye on any practices and approaches employed to develop relationship with the curriculum to identify any risks they may pose to relationship with self and/ or relationship with others.

Such a remit encompasses all aspects of learning and teaching and clearly full coverage of such a broad topic is beyond the scope of this book. There are numerous texts and National Strategy documents that will support the reader in engaging with these wider issues. Our priority is to equip readers with a way of thinking, via the conceptual framework, that enables them to relate any activity undertaken as part of learning and teaching to the development of learning behaviour and the promotion of the underlying relationships. This chapter therefore seeks to explore a number of generic issues that are relevant to consider across curriculum subjects and age ranges.

The central importance of the teacher–pupil relationship

Though, as indicated in Chapters 6 and 7, the pupil brings something to each of the three behaviour for learning relationships, it is the teacher who plays a significant role in brokering these relationships in the classroom. The teacher–pupil relationship is therefore of major significance in promoting learning behaviour.

Sources of authority

The teacher–pupil relationship involves complex issues of power. Typically the teacher is 'outnumbered' by their pupils and in secondary schools in particular pupils may be physically stronger than their teachers. This is not therefore a simple power relationship involving being able to *make* pupils do something. The Elton Report (DES 1989), commenting on the teacher's sources of authority, identified three areas:

- *Status (or 'traditional authority')*
  This is the authority all teachers have from their status in society. In other words, the authority of the person is accepted because of the regard within which their role is held in society.

- *Personality and skills*
  This is the authority 'earned' based on a combination of the teacher's interpersonal skills and pupils' perceptions of the competence with which the teacher carries out their role.

- *Authority conferred by law*
  The final source of authority is that conveyed by law.

Tattum (1982) cited by Robertson (1996) points out: 'Respect for the teacher qua teacher can no longer be assumed as a social fact. No longer is the office held in awe and teachers who draw heavily upon unquestioned authority as an endowed right leave themselves open to mimicry and ridicule' (Robertson 1996: 57, citing Tattum 1982).

Whilst debates about the status of teachers in the eyes of society in general may have some sociological interest, the message for the class teacher is that an automatically conferred status due to role referred to in the Elton Report (DES 1989) cannot be relied upon.

Authority conveyed by the law has been the subject of recent attention. The security of reliance on the *in loco parentis* principle was questioned by the Elton Report, not least because much of the case law that supported the principle pre-dated the introduction of compulsory education. Acknowledging the Elton Report's concerns, which were not acted upon by the government of the day, the white paper *Higher Standards, Better Schools for All* expressed a commitment to introduce 'a clear and unambiguous legal right for teachers to discipline pupils, backed by an expectation that every school has a clear set of rules and sanctions' (DfES 2005d: 85).

The DfES (2007b) document *School Discipline and Pupil Behaviour Policies: Guidance for Schools* covers the statutory power to discipline introduced in the Education and Inspections Act 2006, as well as a range of other guidance that aims to help schools understand their overall legal powers and duties as regards establishing a school behaviour policy and disciplining pupils. It also provides more specific advice on certain key sanctions such as use of detentions and the confiscation of pupils' property.

A strengthening of the law to reinforce teachers' legal rights can be seen as an attempt to strengthen what the Elton Report (DES 1989) termed authority conferred by law. Whilst there might be a deterrent effect on some, it seems likely only to provide teachers with a defence by which to justify their actions in response to misbehaviour rather than a proactive tool to secure improved behaviour in the classroom. In other words, when the pupil misbehaves and the teacher can apply a sanction such as a detention there is a defence against objections to this from the parent or the pupil concerned. However, whether the teacher's legal power to discipline would cause many pupils, particularly those who are the cause of greatest concern, to stop and reflect on the behaviour they were about to engage in any more than they would prior to a strengthening of the law, is questionable. It is in the middle category, *personality and skills*, that there is most scope for influence. This highlights the importance of relationships.

Building relationships with pupils: teacher behaviour and attitudes

Haim Ginott commented in his 1971 book *Teacher and Child*:

> As a teacher I have come to the frightening conclusion that I am the decisive element in the classroom. It is my personal approach that creates the climate. It is my daily mood that makes the weather. As a teacher I possess tremendous power to make a child's life miserable or joyous. I can be a tool of torture or an instrument of inspiration. I can humiliate or humour, hurt or heal. In all situations it is my response that decides whether a crisis will be escalated or de-escalated, and a child humanized or dehumanized.
>
> (Ginott 1971: 13)

Ginott emphasised the critical role of communication in discipline, especially how teachers talk to and with their pupils (Charles 2002). The quote illustrates the weight of responsibility on teachers but it is also empowering in identifying their influence. This is influence that used well can be extremely powerful.

McGuiness (1993) highlights the qualities of helpful and harmful teachers (Table 9.1). A more recent list (Table 9.2) from Year 8 pupils reflecting similar themes, drawn from Hay McBer research (DfEE 2000), is included in KS3 Behaviour and Attendance materials (DfES 2004g).

Table 9.1 Characteristics of 'helpful' and 'harmful' teachers (McGuiness 1993)

Helpful teachers	Harmful teachers
Are warm, accepting	Bully
Inspire, enthuse	Are sarcastic, put you down
Care, talk to you	Humiliate
Encourage, are patient	Make you feel guilty
Listen to you	Are insensitive
Respect your ideas	Demean you
Give you time	Make you feel in the way
Really love their subject	Seem bored by their subject
Like questions	Seem defensive
Make you feel good	Are bossy
Smile, have a sense of humour	Push, hit, shout
Are themselves, real	Pretend all the time

A key feature of both lists is that interpersonal skills dominate rather than issues of pedagogy and the other technicalities of teaching. This highlights the significance of relationships in learning; when asked to think about what makes a good teacher, respondents typically highlight interpersonal skills first. What we can learn from this is the

Table 9.2 Characteristics of a good teacher, as identified by Year 8 pupils (DfEE 2000)

A good teacher

Is kind	Likes teaching their subject	Makes you feel clever
Is generous	Takes time to explain things	Treats people equally
Listens to you	Helps you when you're stuck	Stands up for you
Encourages you	Tells you how you're doing	Makes allowances
Has faith in you	Allows you to have your say	Tells the truth
Keeps confidences	Doesn't give up on you	Is forgiving
Likes teaching children	Cares for your opinion	

need to actively work to develop relationships. However, balance is important and a useful guiding principle for relationships with pupils is to be friendly but not their friend. This is an important distinction, especially for young teachers just starting teaching in secondary schools who may only be seven or eight years older than members of a Year 11 class. We can distinguish between four different types of teacher relationships with pupils outlined in Reflective Exercise 9.1.

Reflective Exercise 9.1

Relationship	Teacher characteristics	Not at all like me				A lot like me
Friend	Colludes with pupils' expectations rather than setting own.	1	2	3	4	5
	Behaves in a way s/he believes will appeal to pupils.	1	2	3	4	5
	Has no control over the learning behaviours promoted. Without this leadership many learning behaviours that develop may be negative, such as task avoidance.	1	2	3	4	5
	Knows pupils as individuals but climate leads to a lack of boundaries in what personal information pupils share with the teacher and how they share it.	1	2	3	4	5
	Openly shares own personal information.	1	2	3	4	5
	Adopts pupil terminology and style of language when correcting misbehaviour.	1	2	3	4	5
	Has to use higher level sanctions before pupils take notice.	1	2	3	4	5

Reflective Exercise 9.1 (continued)

Relationship	Teacher characteristics	Not at all like me				A lot like me
	Reacts to pupils' responses and attempts to please.	1	2	3	4	5
	Experiences pupil misbehaviour as personal hurt.	1	2	3	4	5
Friendly	States expectations, both academic and behavioural.	1	2	3	4	5
	Models appropriate behaviour (e.g. is polite).	1	2	3	4	5
	Knows pupils as individuals and is clear about his/her pastoral role.	1	2	3	4	5
	Plans lessons that make use of and gently extend pupils' learning behaviours.	1	2	3	4	5
	Only shares personal information s/he is comfortable to share and that is appropriate to a teacher–pupil relationship.	1	2	3	4	5
	Positively corrects misbehaviour.	1	2	3	4	5
	Respects pupils' feelings when correcting work or behaviour.	1	2	3	4	5
	Uses respectful language.	1	2	3	4	5
	Knows when to adopt a flexible approach rather than rigorously pursuing consistency.	1	2	3	4	5
	Uses a staged response when correcting behaviour starting with the least intrusive strategy (see Chapter 10).	1	2	3	4	5
	Decides when to adapt teaching and own behaviour based on pupils' responses.	1	2	3	4	5
	Misbehaviour is seen as something that needs to be dealt with calmly and efficiently in order to cause least disruption to teaching and learning and maintain positive relationships.	1	2	3	4	5
Distant	Assumes pupils know expectations, both behavioural and academic.	1	2	3	4	5
	Doesn't know pupils as individuals.	1	2	3	4	5
	Plans 'safely', based on learning behaviours pupils already have.	1	2	3	4	5

(continued)

Relationship	Teacher characteristics	Not at all like me				A lot like me
	Rigidly adheres to the concept of consistency.	1	2	3	4	5
	Very mechanistic in responses to behaviour, if the pupil does *X* then I do *Y*.	1	2	3	4	5
	Highly task oriented and unwilling to deviate from plans.	1	2	3	4	5
	Doesn't view pastoral issues as part of his/her remit.	1	2	3	4	5
	The notion that pupils' feelings may be affected by his/her style of correction of work or behaviour does not feature in his/her thinking.	1	2	3	4	5
	Misbehaviour is seen as an irritation that gets in the way of plans and is a threat to completion of the task.	1	2	3	4	5
Aggressive	Assumes pupils know expectations, both behavioural and academic, but that many wilfully disregard these.	1	2	3	4	5
	Knows the 'trouble makers'.	1	2	3	4	5
	Responds aggressively to pupils.	1	2	3	4	5
	Confrontational.	1	2	3	4	5
	Regularly makes 'examples' of pupils.	1	2	3	4	5
	Disproportionate responses to minor misbehaviour.	1	2	3	4	5
	Uses personal 'put downs' and sarcasm.	1	2	3	4	5
	Little regard for pupils' feelings when correcting work or behaviour.	1	2	3	4	5
	Misbehaviour is seen as a personal challenge and a threat to status.	1	2	3	4	5
	Judges success in terms of compliance behaviours rather than learning behaviour.	1	2	3	4	5
	Fear and coercion are seen as legitimate methods of achieving good order and discipline.	1	2	3	4	5

The four categories within Reflective Exercise 9.1 are of course stereotypes and do not reflect the fact that teachers can exhibit a mixture of these characteristics and that there can be some variation depending on, for example, pressures on the teacher at a given time. When reviewing your scores you ideally want the higher ratings to fall within the 'friendly' section and your lower ratings to fall in the other three sections.

The characteristics of the teacher in each of these categories will affect the development of learning behaviour. The behaviour of the aggressive teacher may lead to pupil compliance and may even lead colleagues to view this individual as a 'good' behaviour manager if evaluated against this criterion. However, the methods of gaining compliance may stifle risk taking in learning as pupils do just to enough to avoid drawing attention to themselves. Their learning is only at the level of behaving appropriately to avoid being shouted at or sanctioned. As such behaviour can become highly context dependent, with pupils behaving in this class for fear of the adult response but not internalising any notions of how human beings should behave towards one another. Instead, they are presented with a model of a person in a position of authority, who may be bigger and stronger, having the right to coerce those who are in the position of subordinates and who may be smaller and weaker.

The 'distant' teacher denies the importance of the social and emotional aspects of learning. Teaching becomes problematic for this teacher when pupils do not already have the necessary learning behaviours to tackle the type of learning that is required as this is not part of the teacher's planning which instead focuses primarily on content. This teacher is likely to place their faith entirely in systems and pupils who do not respond to standard strategies may quickly be categorised as 'SEBD' or 'SEN'. Typically, the teacher will plan well within the capabilities of pupils' learning behaviour and so lessons may be unadventurous and perceived by many of the class as boring.

The teacher who attempts to be a 'friend' to the class relinquishes his/her social leadership role and effectively hands the agenda to the pupils. The risk is that this teacher may for a time be popular with the class but the pupils may then feel betrayed as soon as an attempt is made to set any boundaries or correct behaviour. The learning behaviours that develop in this class tend to develop in a rather *ad hoc* manner and in some cases may be negative such as task avoidance.

The 'friendly' teacher effectively takes account of and balances the social, emotional and cognitive components of learning. The teacher does not shy away from a leadership role but recognises that the purpose of this is to promote learning behaviour not simply to achieve compliance.

Lesson management: core teacher skills

How the teacher manages the lesson sets the parameters in which learning behaviours and relationships develop. Kounin (1970) studied the practice of a range of teachers, initially with the expectation of finding out more about the nature and effect of what he termed 'desists'. Kounin used the term desist 'to designate a teacher's doing something to stop a misbehavior' (Kounin 1970: 2). He also used the term 'ripple effect' to describe 'the effect of this desist event upon other members of the class' (Kounin 1970: 2). His focus therefore was on a particular element of behaviour management. Examining the videotapes of classroom practice, Kounin drew the conclusion:

An analysis of the desist events observed in the videotaped classrooms showed that the qualities of desists bore no relationship to children's reaction. The finding of no relationship between the teachers' desist techniques and the behaviour of children held for the immediate reaction of children to specific desists, as well as for the overall amount of deviancy and deviancy-contagion present in a classroom.

(Kounin 1970: 143)

Kounin's findings support the view expressed in this book that whilst behaviour management techniques are necessary they are not, by themselves, sufficient in securing better classroom behaviour.

In the light of these findings Kounin reappraised his initial premise and shifted the focus from disciplinary techniques to questions about classroom management in general (Kounin 1970). Kounin identified a set of key teacher behaviours, including:

- withitness
- overlapping
- smoothness
- momentum
- group alerting.

Withitness

Kounin used the term 'withitness' to describe the teacher's ability to be aware, and convey to the class that they are aware of what is going on in all parts of the classroom. In behaviour for learning terms withitness represents the teacher's active awareness and monitoring of the multiple relationships that exist within the classroom.

Overlapping

The multiple events that occur in a classroom do not occur in a step-by-step fashion; lots of things happen at the same time. Teachers learn to monitor, or at least appear to monitor, simultaneous events and some pupils learn to avoid this monitoring (Watkins 2006). Kounin described 'overlapping' as the ability to attend to two or more events simultaneously. This ability directly contributes to the teacher's degree of withitness.

Smoothness

Kounin (1970) defined 'smoothness' as 'the absence of dangles, flip-flops, and thrusts' (p. 74). He used these somewhat unusual terms to describe certain teacher behaviours that could impact on smoothness. A common time when these behaviours can occur is when the teacher is managing the transition between lessons or parts of lesson.

- 'Dangles': Kounin defined a 'dangle' in terms of a teacher starting an activity or instruction and then turning attention to something else before resuming.
- 'Flip-flops': Kounin defined a 'flip-flop' in terms of the teacher appearing to terminate one activity, starting another, and then, for no apparent reason, returning to the first (Froyen 1993).
- 'Thrusts': Kounin defined 'thrusts' in terms of a teacher suddenly 'bursting in' on pupils'

activities with an order, statement, or question, with little attempt to gauge the readiness of the group to receive the message.

Momentum

Kounin used the term 'momentum' to describe the teacher's ability to keep lessons and the activities within them moving forward at an appropriate pace. Kounin uses the contrasting concept of 'slowdowns' to illustrate the meaning of momentum. One of the 'slowdowns' that is worthy of closer examination is 'overdwelling' (Table 9.3).

An important point to note in relation to overdwelling is that it is the *unnecessary* emphasis that is problematic. There may be times when, for example, a Year 1 teacher needs to remind the class about how s/he expects them to sit or the correct way to hold a pencil. Being aware of the potential detrimental effects of overdwelling on momentum allows the teacher to use professional judgement to decide whether to focus on these sub-parts of the main task or not.

Kounin identified fragmentation as a particular form of 'slow down' produced by a teacher's breaking down of an activity into sub-parts when the activity could have been performed in a single unit. Fragmentation can take a number of forms. A teacher might require individual members of a group to do something singly and separately that the whole group could be doing as a unit at one time. Such an approach inevitably leads to some pupils having to wait for extended periods of time. An example would be calling pupils to come and collect a piece of equipment one by one. Another form of fragmentation is when a teacher breaks a meaningful piece of behaviour into smaller components and focuses on these separate sub-parts when the behaviour could have been performed as a single, uninterrupted sequence. The problem is compounded when the sequence is so obvious that some pupils move ahead of the instructions and are left waiting while others catch up.

Table 9.3 Four main types of overdwelling (Kounin 1970)

Type of overdwelling	Description
Behaviour overdwelling	Spending longer than necessary on addressing behaviour, e.g. lecturing the child at length about the misdemeanour.
Actone overdwelling	Over-focusing on a sub-part of a task to the degree that it distracted from the task itself, e.g. over-focusing on how to hold the pencil, how to sit, how and where to stand, which way to face, etc.
Prop overdwelling	Over-emphasising the equipment used in the lesson and losing focus on the activity, e.g. taking too long explaining what equipment is necessary, or how to use it, or slow methods of providing it for pupils.
Task overdwelling	Over-elaboration of explanations and directions beyond what would be required for most children to understand how to get on with the task, e.g. explaining a task and then giving unnecessary examples or adding unnecessary verbal guidance to a group already working.

Group alerting

There will be occasions, which Kounin categorised as 'recitation', when the teacher is addressing the class and requires individual pupils to ask or answer questions or feedback on an activity they have undertaken. A challenge in some classes is to maintain the attentiveness and involvement of others whilst another pupil is speaking. 'Group alerting' refers to the degree to which the teacher attempts to involve *non-reciting* children in the 'recitation' task, maintain their attention and keep them 'on their toes' or *alerted* (Kounin 1970). Questioning technique is therefore particularly relevant in a consideration of more effective group alerting. There needs to be a high expectation among pupils that they could be asked to contribute. The traditional approach of inviting pupils to put up their hands and then choosing someone, often the first with their hand up, to answer is problematic. Pupils are effectively choosing whether to be involved or not. If they choose not to put their hand up then there is minimal risk of being asked.

Evaluating the significance of Kounin's work

The significance of Kounin's work is that it involved comparison of videotaped behaviour of teachers who were regarded as having few discipline problems with teachers who had frequent problems (Kyriacou 1991). Therefore Kounin was not attempting to promote a packaged method of managing behaviour but to understand what it was these two types of teachers did that could explain the differences. The fact that he discovered that the action which teachers took in response to a discipline problem had no consistent relationship with their managerial success in the classroom (Watkins and Wagner 2000) has important implications for the focus of efforts to secure more positive patterns of behaviour in classrooms. The findings challenge the assumption that the answer to the problem of unwanted behaviour is to find more strategies for dealing with it. As Charles (2002) points out in his commentary on Kounin's work, teachers still needed to know what to do when, despite demonstrating the qualities highlighted in the research, problematic behaviour occurred. Whilst this is a valid point, it is important to recognise that this was not Kounin's priority; his emphasis was on developing a better understanding of what happens in classrooms. The enduring significance of Kounin's work is that it provides guidance on behaviours teachers need to develop in themselves in order to manage and promote learning in group settings. In behaviour for learning terms these represent important teacher behaviours in maintaining multiple relationships within the classroom. Our observations in classrooms and discussions with trainees, initial teacher education tutors and practicing teachers would suggest that though over thirty years old, Kounin's categorisations are helpful in identifying what it is that effective teachers do that secures better behaviour.

Planning for predictable occurrences

Watkins (2006) suggests that classroom events are unpredictable and to a large extent this is true. With approximately thirty individuals in a classroom it is impossible to predict with any certainty how each will respond to a given situation. However, within the overall unpredictability there are some predictable occurrences that we can plan for. Examples of predictable events include:

- pupils who arrive late;
- pupils who do not have the right equipment;
- uniform infringements;
- pupils who bring 'banned' items into lessons;
- pupils who have missed important prior learning (e.g. absence through illness);
- problematic behaviours related to the subject being taught;
- pupils who call out;
- pupils who complain about seating plans;
- pupils who refuse to comply with instructions or argue back.

Some of these relate to the individual's behaviour (e.g. arguing back). Chapter 10 provides some guidance on forms of teacher language that may be useful in addressing these issues. Other predictable occurrences on the list are organisational issues (e.g. forgetting equipment) that can lead to delays and loss of lesson pace and impact on behaviour. It is also important to recognise problematic behaviours that relate to the subject being taught. Examples include lessons such as Science, ICT, Music or PE where equipment is available that pupils may either use when they shouldn't or use inappropriately. Modern Foreign Language teachers may also need to give consideration to the point at which they switch from the language being taught to English to address behaviour. The key point about predictable behaviours is that we can be fairly sure we will encounter them at some point and we can therefore plan preventative approaches and responses. In behaviour for learning terms, the teacher, in identifying predictable occurrences, is attempting to avoid events that could put the three relationships (with self, with others, with the curriculum) under unnecessary stress. If we take, for example, a Year 8 pupil who arrives late to a lesson there is potential for difficulty with regard to each of the three relationships:

- relationship with self: 'I'll feel embarrassed walking in after everybody else has started';
- relationship with others: 'What should I say to the teacher? What will my teacher say to me? Will my teacher be cross? How should I act in front of my peers? Can I balance looking nonchalant in front of my peers whilst appearing sufficiently contrite for my teacher?';
- relationship with the curriculum: 'Now I've missed the start I might not know what to do'.

Of course, not all pupils who arrive late will experience this. The point we are making is that some might and this can be planned for by identifying the predictable occurrence and developing some strategies. Table 9.4 provides some examples.

In addition to these types of predictable behaviour-related occurrences there are a number of predictable occurrences in learning that may impact on behaviour. An inevitable occurrence for example is that pupils will, from time to time, encounter a problem with their work and find it difficult to continue. This is a classroom management issue as the teacher needs to be able to share attention between perhaps 30 pupils and at times it can feel like an impossible task to give attention to those who need it at the time they need it. Long queues at the teacher's desk lead to significant loss of learning time. They can lead to problematic behaviour if the teacher's view is obscured or low-level behaviour occurs in the queue or between those in the queue and those sitting down. Whilst moving around the class and going to those indicating that are stuck offers a better alternative it potentially places the teacher in a reactive position and, unless they are able to deal with

Table 9.4 Planning for predictable occurrences

Example of predictable occurrences	Possible strategies
Forgetting equipment	• Have equipment available to loan. If it is functional, but basic, there is less incentive to keep it. • Have systems for monitoring the loan and return of equipment. • Accept you will have some losses of loaned equipment. • Be aware of development issues – how much responsibility can pupils be expected to take? • Support pupils in improving personal organisation by providing checklists. • Enlist parental support if possible and appropriate. • Implement programmes to teach personal organisation skills.
Calling out	• Ensure class rules positively specify the required method of asking for help or making a contribution to discussion. • If expectations apply in a particular lesson that are different to the standard class rules make this explicit verbally and if necessary with visual back up (e.g. a symbol). • Rehearse in advance a range of positive corrections that you will use if pupils call out, including the use of non-verbal cues such as 'blocking' gestures whilst taking answers from pupils who have put their hands up (see Chapter 11).
Touching or generally fiddling with subject specific equipment when they should be listening to the teacher's introduction	• Consider whether equipment needs to be out on desks at this stage. • Consider whether the amount of equipment available can be reduced to bare essentials and the rest given out or collected by pupils when they need it. • Make expectations and time scales clear, letting the class know that you will be talking for a specified period of time and then they will have the opportunity to use the equipment. • Rehearse in advance a range of positive corrections that you will use if pupils touch or fiddle with equipment, including non-verbal cues such as 'looks' and tactical pauses. • With younger classes consider a 'good listening' posture such as hands in laps or arms folded. We would recommend teaching 'natural' listening postures such as these that might be used in adult life rather than unnatural positions such as 'finger on lips' or 'hands on heads'. It is important to remember teaching a listening position does not ensure good listening is taking place, only that equipment is less likely to be touched.
Arriving late to lessons	• At the start of the academic year establish an expectation that pupils who arrive late to lessons briefly apologise for this and go straight to their seat. • Follow up on the reasons for lateness later if necessary. • Ensure accessible seating is available for latecomers, preferably in groups that can absorb the new arrival with minimal fuss. • Have time filling activities available to occupy those whose lateness causes them to miss instructions necessary to start the planned task. Once others are working independently you can then go to the latecomer and explain the task to them.

individual difficulties quite quickly, leaves other pupils waiting passively for assistance. There is a need therefore to develop in pupils strategies to use rather than waiting for adult intervention. When pupils are stuck it is an opportunity to develop resourcefulness and encourage them to take responsibility for finding a solution rather than dependency on adult intervention. This development can be supported by the teacher establishing an explicit, stepped process that they expect pupils to work through when they are stuck before asking for adult help. This should be displayed and if appropriate visually supported by cartoons or photographs.

Using the language of learning behaviour

An important way in which we can promote learning behaviour is by explicitly focusing upon it in the lesson. This simply involves the teacher looking for opportunities where they can comment on the learning behaviours that either pupils have already demonstrated or those that will need to be employed in tackling a task. In many ways this does not involve teachers in adopting a new practice. It would not be unusual, for example, for a teacher to say 'I'd like you to work together to find as many different circuits as you can that will light the bulb'. However, often the 'working together' element remains just a necessary part of the instruction. Other learning behaviours such as 'resourcefulness' (i.e. the pupils need to find *different* ways, not just one right answer) and 'resilience' (i.e. some ways will not work and pupils will need to accept this and continue trying to find ways that do) remain at an implicit level. Approached from a behaviour for learning perspective the teacher might:

*   Place more emphasis on the learning behaviours in the introduction to the activity. For example, the teacher might say something like, 'For this activity you are going need to collaborate. Can anybody tell me what *collaborate* means?' or 'For this activity, you're going to need to be resourceful. You'll need to come up with lots of different ways to light the bulb. Not all of the ways you think of will work, but that's OK because even when things don't go right we can learn from it.'
*   Acknowledge the learning behaviours while monitoring pupils' involvement in the activity. For example, by saying something like 'I can see you're taking time to listen to everyone's suggestions' to pick up on a specific aspect of collaboration. Alternatively, targeting resilience, the teacher might say 'It can be frustrating when things don't work out first time, but you stuck at it. How did those first unsuccessful attempts help you to find the circuits that did work?'
*   Draw attention to the learning behaviours used in the plenary. Typically the plenary will focus on eliciting from pupils what have they learned about circuits. This, of course, remains an important element but in addition the teacher might ask 'What do you think helped your group to collaborate successfully?'

Many readers will recognise that there is a relationship between the ideas presented here and increased emphasis on encouraging pupils to think not just about *what* they are learning but also about *how* they are learning. All readers are likely to be aware of the inclusion of a section on thinking skills within the National Curriculum (DfEE/QCA 1999a,1999b). Some readers may also have encountered the work of Wallace (2000, 2001) or Claxton (2002). Both authors offer approaches intended to develop pupils' capacity to think strategically about the skills they use when learning.

Identify the learning behaviours required within the lesson

As the DfES (2004d, 2004e) highlighted, it is possible to think, when planning, about the different phases of the lesson and the learning behaviours that are required. Using this approach potential pressure points can be identified where it is clear that pupils' existing learning behaviours will need to be extended. For example, if the teacher has planned part of the lesson to involve group discussion this will demand certain learning behaviours related to turn taking, listening to others, sharing resources, compromising if someone holds a different view and so on. Providing pupils have developed the necessary learning behaviours such an activity does not present a significant problem. Where it is judged that collectively within the group these learning behaviours are not sufficiently developed the teacher is then able to take a decision. The conclusion may be that the activity represents the next stage of development of these learning behaviours and is appropriate. Alternatively the judgement might be that the activity needs to be undertaken but with support, by, for example, introducing more structure. A third decision might be that the learning objective for the lesson could be achieved through a different activity. This line of thinking in relation to the class as a group can also be applied to individuals when planning lessons.

Managing feedback

The Assessment Reform Group (2002) advises that teachers should be aware of the impact that comments, marks and grades can have on pupils' confidence and enthusiasm and should be as constructive as possible in the feedback that they give. Their advice is that comments that focus on the task rather than the person are more constructive for both learning and motivation. We would endorse this; as we shall discuss later, the more feedback relates to an evaluation of the person the greater the potential for problems, even when that evaluation is positive. However we would add that comments should also focus on the learning behaviours exhibited by the individual.

It is common in texts on behaviour management for the message to be given that we must praise pupils. DfES (2004e) even attempt to define a ratio for this, suggesting eight positive comments for every negative comment. Whilst we recognise that the intent is to reinforce the message that teachers should attempt to create a positive ethos that would be easily eroded by the dominance of negative comments, defining a ratio does neglect the point that factors such as whether the opinion of the praiser is valued by the praisee will have an impact. From a behaviour for learning perspective, that seeks to maintain strong links between learning and behaviour, we do not make distinction between *praise* and other forms of teacher feedback. If a pupil has completed a learning task suitable to their level of ability the teacher is likely to have few qualms about providing some positive feedback, together with some constructive, developmental comments if there are errors. Positive feedback in relation to behaviour should be little different.

Unlike praise, positive feedback places less emphasis on the *evaluative* element (e.g. 'good', 'well done', 'brilliant', 'fantastic', etc.) and more on the *descriptive* element. For example, we might say to a group of pupils: 'This group's worked well together. I liked the way you took turns using the equipment. That's good cooperation.'

We can analyse each component:

- 'This group's worked well together.'

This includes some evaluation through use of the word 'well' and serves to cue the group into the fact that the positive comment is directed at all of them.

- 'I liked the way you took turns using the equipment.'
  This is a specific statement describing the behaviour and is the key element in the message.
- 'That's good cooperation.'
  In this case the teacher takes the opportunity to relate the specific behaviour (turn-taking) to a broader learning behaviour.

It will not always be possible to capture all these elements, but wherever possible there should be a descriptive element present. For example, a secondary teacher might say to a Year 9 pupil who frequently forgets their planner but has brought it on this occasion, 'Glad to see you've remembered your planner. Well done.'

Again, we can analyse each component:

- 'Glad to see you've remembered your planner.'
  This contains a brief evaluative comment ('glad') but the major focus is on description. The learning behaviour is not explicitly acknowledged, but the particular piece of behaviour identified ('remembering your planner') recognises links to *responsibility* and *independence*.
- 'Well done.'
  This is an evaluative comment, but the assumption here is that the teacher is just passing pleasant comment, accompanied by a smile. It would be less appropriate if the teacher delivered this in a highly effusive manner as both teacher and pupil know that bringing a planner is a basic expectation.

The important feature of the descriptive element is that it is factual. In a sense, even the accompanying evaluative component of 'I liked the way you …'in the first example is also factual as it is a statement of the teacher's opinion, which can still exist as true even if the pupil has a different view. In contrast more full blown evaluative praise is easier for the pupil to reject on the grounds that:

- It does not fit with their image of themselves either as a learner or as a person. For example, a pupil with low self-esteem might find it difficult to accept a judgement such as 'Well done, what an artist you are!' as it does not fit with how they view themselves. The pupil may attempt to resolve any dissonance between their own view and the positive evaluative comment by attributing externally (e.g. the teacher is just saying it but doesn't really mean it) or by taking some action (e.g. destroying their work or misbehaving) that attracts peer and adult reactions more consistent with their own view of themselves.
  A descriptive comment such as 'I like your choice of colours and the way you've blended the reds and oranges together for the sunset' might be easier to accept. It is couched in terms that make it explicit that this is the teacher's opinion and it may not necessarily be the same as the pupil's. The descriptive comment can still exist as true even if the pupil dislikes their piece of work or subsequently destroys it.
- Many evaluative terms such as 'fantastic', 'great' and 'well done' are cultural and generational. Children and young people may have a different vocabulary for expressing

approval. However this should not lead us to assume that 'borrowing' their language of approval will address this issue. Older pupils in particular may resent it simply because the language is *theirs*. It is also often difficult for the adult to use credibly.

• They do not believe the praise. They may think the teacher is just praising them because it is their job. They may even construe it as simply an attempt to manipulate and modify their behaviour. Age and stage of development are factors of course, but when teachers engage in gushing praise over, for example, remembering to bring a pen or a ruler it is understandable that some pupils may be a little cynical.

The third point (above) raises the issues that positive feedback and any rewards should provide feedback on performance and provide some encouragement. The feedback or rewards given should not feel manipulative or controlling or encourage the individual to depend solely on someone else's approval (Kohn 1999). The aspiration for any reward, including positive feedback, is the development of intrinsic motivation. Ultimately our use of positive feedback is part of a learning process that allows pupils to develop their own aspirations, set themselves standards and goals, and make honest appraisals of their performance in relation to these. This is not achieved if we adopt approaches that foster and sustain dependence on adult evaluations and decisions about what is 'good' or 'bad', rather than helping them to form their own judgements (Kohn 1999).

Depersonalising positive feedback

For some pupils even descriptive praise may be difficult to accept. In such case teachers may find it beneficial to depersonalise praise. The teacher might, for example, say 'I'm pleased with how everyone collaborated on this activity today'. In this situation the teacher is recognising the learning behaviour ('collaboration') explicitly but is leaving the individual pupil to recognise that they, through the use of the word 'everyone', are included in this comment. Essentially, the teacher is recognising what the pupil is bringing to the situation in terms of their relationship with self and making a judgement about a strategy that allows reinforcement of the learning.

Public or private positive feedback

Some pupils prefer public acknowledgement while others prefer low key and one-to-one feedback. If we are adhering to the principle that a major purpose of providing positive feedback is to encourage more of this behaviour in the future then it makes sense to attempt to deliver any positive comment in the form that the pupil prefers. To return to a familiar theme, it is a question of evaluating the efficacy of strategy based on how the individual experiences this. If the individual finds coming to the front to hold up their good piece of work embarrassing or an ordeal then their interpretation may be that this is not positively reinforcing at all and to produce adequate work is the safer option to avoid this in future.

   With all of these thoughts in mind, consider how you would respond to each of the brief scenarios in Reflective Exercise 9.2.

Reflective Exercise 9.2

In each of these short scenarios there could be justification for providing some positive feedback. Consider:

1 What, if anything, would you say or do?
2 What were the factors you took into account in making your judgement?
3 What learning behaviour(s) were you attempting to promote or reinforce?

- You notice that a group of six Year 4 pupils, supported by a teaching assistant, are engaged in the lesson. They always get on quietly and behave well (based on DfES 2004g).
- Kyle, Year R, has been at primary school for four weeks. He has often been resistant to written activities during teacher directed learning time. You notice today that he has chosen to do a writing activity during child initiated learning time for the first time.
- Stacey and Naomi, both Year 7, hardly ever volunteer to give answers, they are quiet, always complete work to a good standard and rarely ask for help. Today is no different (based on DfES 2004g).
- Sunil is a shy Year 1 pupil. You notice him contributing verbally to a group activity (based on DfES 2004g).
- Staff believe Krishtina, Year 9, seeks attention through confrontation. Today you see her standing calmly in the lunch queue (based on DfES 2004g).
- Chris, Year 5, frequently calls out in lessons. You have had to give him a couple of reminders so far this lesson to put his hand up. During the independent working phase of the lesson you notice that he has put his hand up and is waiting.
- This morning you had to ask the deputy head to collect Robbie from your lesson because he was being so disruptive. This afternoon Robbie has settled well to his work.
- Despite his protestations of innocence, you have given Emir, Year 8, a lunchtime detention for flicking a pen top across the room. At the start of break Ryan comes to you and admits that he flicked it and feels that Emir shouldn't take the blame. (As well as considering how you would respond to Ryan, what are you going to say to Emir?)

Mediating the interpretation and experience of feedback

If a teacher says to a pupil 'I know you are having difficulty with this. Don't worry – I'm going to help you' (DfES 2004f: 58), a number of interpretations are possible. The pupil might simply conclude, 'I've made some mistakes. The teacher understands that it's causing me some problems and is going to go through it with me.' However they may make less positive interpretations such as 'difficulty is just another word for failure' or 'why am I being told not to worry? Does this mean there is something I should be worrying about?' Even the notion of 'help' may carry connotations of neediness and dependency.

As an alternative we might reframe this line in a manner that conveys that learning is sometimes challenging and involves making mistakes. Alternatives include:

- 'It's making you think because you are learning something you didn't know before and I am here to help.'
- 'When you find something challenging, it is an opportunity to learn something new.'
- 'Now you'll learn something that you didn't know before. Then it won't be hard the next time you meet it.'
- 'This is how we learn. If everything is easy, it means you already knew how to do it, so there's no new learning.'

(DfES 2004f: 58)

Though these statements target the maintenance of a positive relationship with the curriculum, they are also framed in such a way that the pupil's relationship with self is not compromised. The implicit message is, 'It's not you that is at fault, this is what learning is sometimes like.' However, having said that, if this is what learning is *always* like for an individual it requires considerable resilience to remain engaged. We should also recognise that, however appropriate, positive and well-intentioned the comments, the pupil will experience and interpret them as an individual. For example, the pupil who regularly hears 'If everything is easy, it means you already knew how to do it, so there's no new learning' may well glance around and make some negative appraisals about self from the fact that the teacher is seemingly not needing to have this interaction with most other pupils.

For some pupils we need to go further in attempts to protect the three relationships and adopt a form of language that focuses any sense of blame away from the pupil. Examples include:

- 'What do we need to remember here?' (DfES 2004h, 2004i)
  This has a less negative connotation than 'What have you forgotten?' and puts the emphasis on something positive the pupil can do (i.e. remember) rather than a failing (i.e. forgetting).
- 'Lots of people get mixed up on this bit.' (DfES 2004i)
  This depersonalises the error and encourages the pupil to recognise that others also make mistakes. We should be aware that this may not be effective with all pupils as they may only be concerned that *they* are experiencing this difficulty currently – whether anybody else has may be of little consequence or comfort. Think of anything that you have failed at, such as a driving test or an interview for a job you really wanted. Would it have helped if someone had told you at the time that it happens to lots of people?
- 'I'm sorry, I should have made it clearer.' (DfES 2004h, 2004i)
- 'Which part didn't I explain well enough?' (DfEs 2004h, 2004i)
- 'Maybe I didn't make that clear enough.'
  These last three examples are effectively saying 'It's not you, it's me.' The teacher is tactically taking the blame for the difficulty the pupil is experiencing in order to avoid damage to an already fragile relationship with the curriculum and relationship with self.
- 'OK, so you haven't quite mastered it yet.' (DfES 2004h, 2004i)
  The use of 'yet' demonstrates an expectation that the pupil is capable of mastery. The statement also recognises that there are necessary stages in learning on the way to mastery.
- 'Up to now this bit has proved a little tricky.' (DfES 2004h, 2004i)

This is a deliberate attempt to diminish the significance of the difficulty. The teacher is attempting to limit the possibility of the pupil seeing this as a global failing. The use of the word 'bit' conveys that this piece of learning is only one element; by implication there are other 'bits' that the pupil may be able to do. The assessment that this activity is 'a little tricky' conveys that the difficulty is not insurmountable. Coupling this with 'up to now' encourages optimism that this difficulty will not always be present.

Positive feedback and behaviour for learning: a summary

Well-timed, targeted and formulated positive feedback can be very important in terms of its potential to reinforce a learning behaviour and positively affect the three behaviour for learning relationships. As the preceding examples have shown, feedback can be phrased to explicitly or implicitly reinforce a learning behaviour. By positively commenting on pupil performance the teacher can also seek to develop each of the three relationships. For example, if a pupil has a poor relationship with a particular curriculum area then the teacher could combine the setting of a task where there are regular opportunities for success with a heightened level of positive feedback. Likewise, a teacher may seek to build their relationship with the pupil by making a point of recognising and remarking positively on the pupil's efforts. For example, the teacher may not view a Year 9 pupil remembering to bring a planner to a lesson as praiseworthy in itself but may recognise that to pleasantly acknowledge this behaviour is an implicit way of saying to the pupil 'I *do* notice when you get things right too; this relationship isn't about me giving you a hard time when you get things wrong.' Positive feedback also has the potential to contribute to the development of a positive relationship with self. However we make this point with some caution. As we considered in Chapter 7, feedback from a variety of sources is important in developing a positive relationship with self. Many pupils probably like and benefit from some positive comment on their efforts. This should not lead us to assume that apparent difficulties in the area of relationship with self can be resolved by providing *more* positive comments. As we have considered in discussion of more descriptive approaches to positive feedback, pupils who present as experiencing difficulties with relationship with self may reject positive comment. In such cases the use of positive feedback needs to be handled carefully and would necessitate close monitoring of the pupil's response to judge how this is being experienced and interpreted.

The use of extrinsic rewards

Clarke (2001) has argued that external rewards such as stickers, smiley faces, team points, gold cards and various other schemes encourage children to strive for reward rather than achievement. She also claims that a negative by-product is that pupils focus on ego-involved attributions and comparisons with peers. In this second observation, Clarke (2001) is highlighting a potentially detrimental effect on the pupil's relationship with others. Pupils are effectively encouraged to develop a relationship with others that is based on competition rather than collaboration.

Kohn (1999) has also produced compelling arguments against the use of extrinsic rewards, suggesting that individuals' interest in what they are doing typically declines when they are rewarded for it. Kohn (1999) reports for example, work carried out by Lepper *et al.* (1973). In this American study 51 pre-school children were given the chance to draw with Magic

Markers. Some of them were told that if they drew pictures they would receive a special personalised certificate, decorated with a red ribbon and a gold star. Between a week and two weeks later the children were observed again. Those who had been told in advance that they would receive a certificate seemed to be less interested in drawing with the Magic Markers than the other children were. Not only that, they were less interested in using the Magic Markers than they themselves had been before the reward was offered. Kohn (1999) also makes the point that, 'If you have been promised a reward, you come to see the task as something that stands between you and it' (Kohn 1999: 65).

If Kohn is correct, then the potential for damage to the individual's relationship with the curriculum is clear: individuals are discouraged from taking risks, thinking creatively and challenging themselves. Instead the focus may be on doing what is sufficient to secure the reward. Arguably, whether the use of rewards has this effect or not is likely to be determined by how they are used. If a teacher regularly says directly to a pupil, 'If you do this page of questions you will get a sticker', then the risk is likely to be increased that the pupil will focus on the reward and see the task as an obstacle in the way of this rather than something intrinsically valuable.

The arguments presented by Kohn (1999) and Clark (2001) serve to illustrate that we need to continually monitor the effect of our strategies on the pupil in terms of the learning behaviour encouraged and the effect on the three behaviour for learning relationships.

Extrinsic motivators such as stickers and house points can make a useful contribution in positively reinforcing learning behaviours and can also be used to maintain and develop the three behaviour for learning relationships. However as a class-wide strategy they need to be used to spontaneously reinforce positive learning behaviours exhibited, rather than in the context of 'if you do X then you will get Y'. This is not to dismiss the utility of a more structured behaviourist approach of this sort in changing the presenting behaviour of individuals by explicitly linking the demonstration of required behaviour to a particular reward. Rather we recognise that at a class level this type of approach is neither desirable nor necessary.

Extrinsic rewards should always, if at all possible, be accompanied by feedback that lets the pupil know what the reward is for. The long-term purpose should be to develop in the pupil learning behaviours that are sustainable without reliance on external reward. The emphasis is on moving the pupil on, eventually, to the point where the reward is no more than an appreciative gesture that says to the pupil 'you're doing OK and I've noticed'.

Managing the physical environment to promote learning behaviour

The seating arrangements within the classroom convey a powerful message about the type of learning that will take place and the learning behaviours that the teacher wants to promote. The arrangement in Figure 9.1 suggests that much of the learning will be teacher-led with the teacher imparting knowledge in quite a didactic way from the front that learners are expected to absorb. For the teacher the question is whether this arrangement, though good for teacher control, promotes learning behaviour. It does not preclude it but the teacher will need to give particular consideration to the promotion of learning behaviours like collaboration and cooperation and the opportunities to develop pupils' relationship with others as these are not naturally encouraged by the seating arrangement. In supporting pupils in whom the teacher wants to promote the learning behaviour of

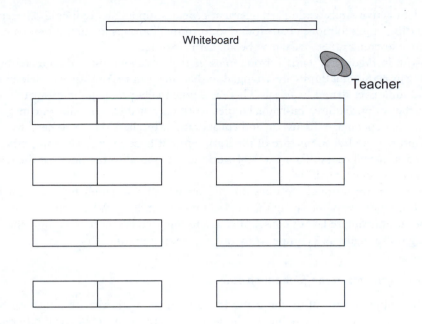

Figure 9.1 Seating in rows.

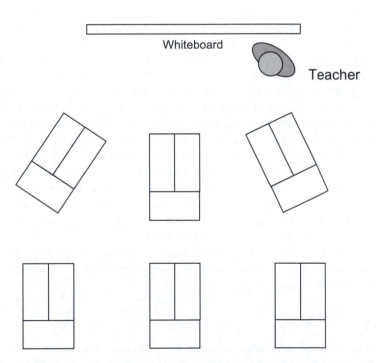

Figure 9.2 Seating in groups.

'independent activity' this seating arrangement provides support by reducing distractions. Simply getting pupils to move chairs round to form small groups in certain lessons where collaborative learning is necessary may be all that is required.

The layout in Figure 9.2 sends a strong message that collaboration and cooperation are desired in this classroom. Pupils are arranged so that they can make easy eye contact with others and look over shared materials. There is a potentially problematic mismatch if the nature of the lesson requires individual, quiet working but desks are laid out in groups like this, which encourage discussion and collaboration. Teachers therefore need to either move furniture to reflect the nature of the learning or at least be very clear in setting out their expectations when a different way of working is required to the one that the seating layout appears to encourage.

Positioning of furniture alone does not dictate whether learning behaviour will be developed and there is no one layout that is ideal for its promotion. What is important is that the teacher uses furniture layout consciously as a resource to promote learning behaviour, capitalising on strengths and compensating for the limitations of each design.

Seating arrangements in the foundation stage

Due to the unique nature of teaching and learning in the Early Years Foundation Stage (DfES 2007c), seating arrangements in the classroom are likely to be very different to those found in Key Stage 1 and 2 and secondary schools. The Foundation Stage teacher is starting from the priority of establishing a classroom (and outdoor) environment that represents the six areas of learning from the Foundation Stage curriculum – though it is generally accepted that Personal, Social and Emotional Development spans across the other five areas and does not need to be represented by a separate physical area. A significant proportion of learning is child-initiated and involves pupils moving to different areas to take advantage of the learning opportunities that the teacher has set up. The learning behaviours the Foundation Stage teacher aims to promote do not necessitate a seated place for each pupil and indeed this might be counterproductive, discouraging them from experiencing activities located in other areas. Instead with a class of 30 the teacher might, for example, make provision for two groups of pupils to be seated around tables at a time. A 'group' might consist of six pupils. There may also be another group of tables without chairs where craft or construction activities may take place. Thought would also need to be given to the location of these different areas and the atmosphere that it is desirable to achieve within them. For example it would be sensible to locate the reading area (needing calm and quiet) away from the construction or music area where noisier activities may take place. There will be times during the day when the teacher needs to group all of the pupils together and, to achieve this, a large carpeted area in the room is necessary. A teacher's desk is unnecessary, apart from perhaps as a flat storage surface, as the nature of Foundation Stage teaching and learning is such that there would be few, if any occasions, when the teacher should be seated at it.

Summary

This chapter has focused on a range of factors that influence the development of learning behaviour and the promotion of the three relationships within the behaviour for learning conceptual framework. The teacher, as Ginott (1971) noted, is a powerful influence and the first part of the chapter, through a consideration of characteristics and qualities, implicitly invited readers to consider the question 'Who is this *me* that I take into the classroom and present to my pupils?' (McGuiness 1993: 46). In behaviour for learning terms, this consideration deals with what the teacher brings to relationships within the classroom.

Kounin's (1970) work provides a powerful example of the need to maintain a focus on the teacher behaviours that *keep* the classroom running smoothly rather than placing undue faith in what he termed 'desists', but we might term 'behaviour management strategies', as a means of promoting learning behaviour.

This chapter has also given consideration to teacher language in relation to the management of feedback. The teacher's language has a significant role in developing and maintaining the three behaviour for learning relationships in the classroom. Chapter 10 devotes considerable attention to teacher language in relation to positive correction.

Positive correction

Protecting relationships

Introduction

The term 'positive correction' relates to what Kounin (1970) referred to as 'desists'. These are behaviour management techniques used when a pupil behaves in a manner considered by the teacher to be unacceptable in the classroom context. As readers will recall from Chapter 9, Kounin's (1970) research found that desist techniques for dealing with misbehaviour 'are not significant determinants of managerial success in classrooms' (Kounin 1970: 71). The implication is that, whilst teachers need to be competent and confident in the use of a range of strategies to respond to individuals, ultimately becoming better at desist techniques alone, where *better* is interpreted as simply meaning knowing *more* strategies, is unlikely to make a significant impact on how the class behaves as a group.

The strategies outlined in this chapter need therefore to be afforded their proper status. They are not a substitute for a well-planned lesson that sets suitable learning challenges, recognises and responds to pupils' diverse needs, and identifies and seeks to overcome potential barriers to learning and assessment for individuals and groups (DfEE/QCA 1999a, 1999b). However we do not seek to reassure teachers or trainees with the 'pious platitude that provided you have spent enough time preparing your lessons properly, you will never have discipline problems' (Wheldall and Glynn 1989: 2). There are inevitably times in classrooms when pupils will need to be corrected and directed. The Elton Report (DES 1989) was clear in its message that 'Reducing bad behaviour is a realistic aim. Eliminating it completely is not' (DES 1989: 65). What we have presented in this chapter is an example set of strategies that we believe represent better practice in those situations where, despite the approaches like those described in Chapter 9 being in place, it is necessary to correct or direct a pupil's behaviour. Our selection has been made based on the potential of the strategies to be delivered in a manner that protects the three behaviour for learning relationships.

Why positive correction?

The phrase 'positive correction' is used within National Strategy documents (e.g. DfES 2003c, 2004g) to capture the idea that teachers should seek to frame their correction and direction positively when misbehaviour occurs. It had been used prior to this by Rogers in number of his publications.

A positive correction might, for example, be:

'Stacey, facing this way, thanks.'

We could contrast this with what could be termed a negative correction, such as:

'Stacey, stop turning round.'

The message that it is better for teachers to frame corrections in terms of the behaviours they want to see is frequently stated. Such an approach keeps the atmosphere of the classroom more positive than frequent use of statements beginning or containing 'don't', 'no' or 'stop'. If we accept the Elton Report finding that 'schools with a negative atmosphere will suffer more from bad behaviour than those with a positive one' (DES 1989: 89), then there is an obvious rationale to this approach. There is also an argument that by stating the required behaviour, it encourages the pupil to bring an image of this to mind rather than the unwanted behaviour (Hook and Vass 2002). Comedian, actor and broadcaster Russell Brand illustrates this point when recounting a childhood incident:

> But in the sentence, 'Don't stamp on those flowers', the word 'don't' is feeble, impotent and easy to ignore, whereas 'STAMP ON THOSE FLOWERS' has a real linguistic verve; 'stamp on those flowers' could be a slogan, a catchphrase, a banner under which nations could unite. So the moment he shuffled out of view, all old and friendly, I stamped on them flowers.
>
> (Brand 2007: 30–1)

From a behaviour for learning perspective the reason for the use of positive correction relates to its contribution to the three relationships that underpin the development of learning behaviour. Primarily, positive correction minimises the risk of undermining the pupil's relationship with self and their relationship with others, particularly with the adult who is doing the correcting or directing. A poor relationship with a particular teacher at secondary school can also lead to a poor relationship with the curriculum subject they teach, even to the extent of influencing the pupil's choice of GCSE options. This notion of damage to the three relationships is illustrated through the examples in Table 10.1.

Table 10.1 Examples of teacher comments that can negatively impact on the three relationships

Statement	Potential negative impact on
'Johnny, are you completely stupid?'	Relationship with self Relationship with others (i.e. with the teacher)
'I've just about had it up to here with you.'	Relationship with self Relationship with others (i.e. with the teacher)
'If you carry on like that you'll have no friends.'	Relationship with self Relationship with others
'This is the kind of writing I'd expect from a Reception child' (said to a Year 4 pupil).	Relationship with self Relationship with the curriculum

Hopefully these represent extreme examples that are seldom heard in classrooms, but they are nevertheless illustrative of how the language we use can be very powerful in its negative impact on the three relationships.

When thinking about positive correction and a form of language that maintains the three behaviour for learning relationships there are a number of general principles that we can adhere to. These are outlined in Table 10.2.

Table 10.2 General principles for positive correction

General principle	Reasons
Language used is respectful. Keep the focus on the behaviour. Avoid 'put downs' and de-valuing terms.	• Maintaining the pupil's relationship with self by showing that, whatever their behaviour, they are still worthy of being spoken to respectfully.

Avoid strategies aimed at embarrassing in front of peers.	• Maintaining the pupil's relationship with others:
	  – it is difficult to maintain a relationship with someone who speaks to you disrespectfully;
	  – peers may form a negative image of the pupil and be less willing to form and maintain relationships;
	  – peers may use the pupil as a scapegoat;
	  – if the pupil has been embarrassed in front of peers this may adversely affect his/her relationship with them.

Model appropriate behaviour. Encourage reflection, emphasise choice. Any strategy or approach used should contribute to pupil learning more than just not to do it again or not to do it in order to avoid punishment/getting caught.	• The pupil will learn from what you model. If you respond to misbehaviour with verbal aggression, disproportionate anger, sarcasm, etc., you are modelling many of the behaviours that we would not wish our pupils to exhibit. • Your responses to misbehaviour can encourage the use of learning behaviour (e.g. reflection, taking responsibility). • Some approaches that may be effective at stopping behaviour are not necessarily effective at promoting learning behaviours.

Rogers (2002) and Hook and Vass (2002) have comprehensively described the language teachers can use in the management of behaviour, particularly in the area of positive correction, and we would commend these sources to readers. A number of Rogers' (1990, 1997, 2002) techniques have been advocated in KS3 National Strategy Behaviour and Attendance materials (DfES 2003c, 2004g). The risk, however, is that teachers become attracted to techniques and place their faith in the magic of the method. In other words, it would be possible to arm ourselves with a stock of lines acquired from Rogers (2002), Hook and Vass (2002) and National Strategy documents (e.g. DfES 2003c, 2004g) without fully grasping that:

• Though the adoption of these forms of language can contribute to more positive relationships, they are always delivered within the context of an existing relationship, which may be good, bad or indifferent, and this will influence how they are received.
• We need to be able to deliver the line credibly, in a way that fits with our personality and values.

- We need to be able to select and adapt the line for different pupils.
- The pupil will have a reaction to the line and we need to be responsive to this – we cannot expect any interaction to follow a rigid script.
- These lines will not work every time with every pupil, we are simply increasing the likelihood of a more positive outcome because they are respectful and rooted in relationships.

With these cautionary thoughts in mind, we can consider a number of key strategies that the reader may find useful in maintaining relationships at times when these are potentially under pressure.

Key strategies for positive correction

Physical proximity (Hook and Vass 2002)

By moving into the pupil's area of the room, perhaps while continuing to address the class, and just pausing by the pupil momentarily, the teacher can convey the message that the behaviour has been noticed. This strategy is mainly suitable for minor off task behaviour.

Tactical ignoring (Rogers 1990, 1995, 1997, 2002, Rogers and McPherson 2008)

Tactical ignoring involves consciously deciding not to directly address a particular behaviour. This strategy is useful for minor off task behaviour where the teacher is confident that the pupil will re-direct themselves to the task in hand without adult intervention.

Proximity praise

Proximity praise is used in conjunction with tactical ignoring. Again, mainly useful for low level misbehaviour, this involves tactically ignoring the pupil's misbehaviour whilst praising a pupil nearby who is demonstrating the required behaviour. For example, if Kerry in Year 4 is turning round talking the teacher might say to another pupil near to her, 'Naomi, I can see you're sitting up straight ready to listen.' The premise is that Kerry will hear what the required behaviour is and adjust her behaviour accordingly. The technique is made more powerful if, as soon as Kerry demonstrates the required behaviour, the teacher directs some positive feedback to her. Overall, this is probably a strategy that has less utility in a secondary school environment. It is only likely to be effective if it is teacher approval that *matters* to the pupil concerned. As pupils get older it is likely that peer-group approval will matter more.

Depersonalised comment

Rogers (2002) uses the term 'incidental language' to describe a technique involving the teacher making a casual observation with the implied meaning that the pupil or pupils need to address the issue. An example would be the teacher who, walking past a group, comments 'it's a little noisy over here' or 'one or two people are talking a little too loudly.' The strength of this technique is that it depersonalises the correction. However it needs to be used with some thought as some pupils, such as those on the autism spectrum, may apply a literal interpretation and not pick up on the implied need for action.

There are other forms of depersonalised comment. For example, the teacher may say 'I can still hear one or two people talking' or 'I'm just waiting for everybody to be facing this way.' Essentially, the teacher's purpose is that individuals privately recognise that they are required to adjust their behaviour and take responsibility for this. It is important to note that the strengths of depersonalisation are undermined if, for example, a teacher, having noticed a particular pupil has not joined in an activity, says 'next time I expect everyone to join in, even Jessie.' If we have judged depersonalisation to be the correct strategy then it is important that we understand and stick to the principles as adapting in this way changes the strategy into something very different in terms of pupil experience.

Non-verbal signals (Rogers 1997, 2002, Rogers and McPherson 2008)

Readers may already use a range of non-verbal signals or have seen teachers use them. Teachers of younger pupils in particular may place a finger against the lips to convey the need for quiet. The teacher might catch the eye of a pupil who is frequently turning round and make a rotating movement with their hand to indicate the need to face the right way. If a pupil is talking whilst the teacher is addressing the class, then this could be addressed by a brief pause in speech and directing eye contact in the direction of the individual concerned. Even if the pupil is not looking towards the teacher, the momentary gap in what the teacher is saying is usually enough to prompt the pupil to look up and towards teacher. At this point they will, of course, notice that the teacher is looking in their direction. Then, with eye contact made momentarily, the teacher can look away and continue addressing the class.

Non-verbal signals do not just have a role in positive correction. A thumbs-up signal, for example, can be used to convey approval and is likely to be understood as such by most pupils.

Rogers (1997) extends the idea of non-verbal cues to include what he terms 'privately understood signals'. It is possible for the teacher to establish with individuals or the class specific signals that will be used. One example given by Rogers is the 'four on the floor signal'. This involves the teacher holding out one hand palm down with four fingers extended downwards to convey to pupils who rock on their chairs that all four chair legs should be on the floor. This is a far more positive alternative to repeated requests to 'sit properly' or 'stop rocking.'

Simple direction (Rogers 1990, 1997, 2002)

A simple direction, as its name suggests, involves telling the pupil what you require. An example would be 'John, getting on quietly, thanks.' Using the pupil's name helps to alert the pupil that there is an incoming message. This is important as pupils can sometimes find themselves in trouble simply because they have not heard the first part of the instruction and have consequently not done as asked. Rogers (1995) advocates the 'pause … direct' technique, which involves saying the pupil's name, more than once if necessary, pausing and then delivering the message. The example would therefore become 'John … John … getting on quietly, thanks'. Tone of voice is important; the teacher should not signal growing irritation through the way in which they repeat the pupil's name.

Rule reminders (Hook and Vass 2002, Rogers 1990, 1995, 1997, 2002)

Having a clear, positively expressed set of rules opens up a range of positive, correctional language for the teacher. It is possible to say for example, 'John, what's our rule for asking for help?' or, if we do not want to invite a response, 'John, remember our rule for asking for help.'

Use of questions

Hook and Vass (2002) refer to the use of casual questions. Examples include:

* 'How's it going here?'
* 'OK, so you're clear about what you're doing?'
* 'Have I explained that well enough for you?'
* 'Do you know what you need to do next?'

The strength of the examples given here are that they encourage a learning rather than disciplinary focus to the interaction. In terms of strategy selection the teacher needs to bear in mind that by asking a question it invites an answer. Often the priority is to maintain the pace of the lesson and so the teacher would not want to open up dialogue.

Rogers (1990, 1997, 2002) and Rogers and McPherson (2008) describe a more structured use of questions. This is a more complex technique than Hook and Vass' (2002) casual questions as the teacher enters into the dialogue with a particular sequence of questions and responses in mind. Again, this approach would only be used if the teacher wanted to open up dialogue. The 'question and feedback' technique involves the teacher asking an open question such as 'what are you doing?' Even this first question needs careful consideration. Tone of voice will be a major factor in determining how the pupil experiences and interprets this question. The aim is to deliver it as a neutral, quite casual enquiry. It would be possible however to deliver it accusingly or inquisitorially and so caution needs to be exercised.

Readers are probably already able to predict the range of answers to the question, which might include, 'nothing', or, 'my work'. As with all techniques, the teacher's personality is a factor. Effective use of this technique depends on the ability both to ask the initial question in a neutral manner and to react calmly to the pupil response in order to steer the focus back to learning. If as an individual, a teacher feels that they cannot do this, then this technique is not for them. With this caveat in mind, the two examples below illustrate how this technique can be very effective:

Example 1
Teacher: 'What are you doing?'
Pupil: 'Nothing.'
Teacher: 'What should you be doing?'
Pupil: 'My work.'
Teacher: 'OK, so what's the next thing you need to do?'

Example 2
Teacher: 'What are you doing?'
Pupil: 'My work.'
Teacher: 'OK, so what's the next thing you need to do?'

In both examples there is the possibility that the pupil may respond to the teacher's last question by saying that they do not know. In this case the teacher is able to return to a learning focus and explain. If however the pupil gives a response that indicates that they do know what to do then the teacher can simply say something like 'OK, so if you make a start now and I'll come back in a few minutes and see how you're getting on.' Again, the dialogue and the teacher–pupil relationship have returned to a learning focus.

In most cases pupils will recognise the implication within the 'What are you doing?' that the teacher has noticed exactly what they are doing and will reply 'nothing' or 'my work'. However as we have indicated we are not working to a script. Some pupils may reply with a description such as 'I was only talking to Terry', or 'I needed to get something from my bag', or even the very honest, 'I was just messing about.' The teacher is still able to follow this with the question, 'What should you be doing?', and then use the sequence outlined in examples 1 and 2. Alternatively, the teacher might decide partial agreement, outlined below, is the more appropriate strategy to use.

Partial agreement (Rogers 2002, Hook and Vass 2002)

Partial agreement is a powerful technique when pupils attempt to argue back. Imagine that you say to a pupil 'John, the writing needs to be finished by break. If you choose to carry on talking, then you will need to stay in and complete it.' This is a quite reasonable reminder of the consequence if the behaviour continues. However, as we have indicated, whilst we can use a good practice strategy to increase the likelihood of a positive outcome, we cannot guarantee the pupil response. John might respond with 'I wasn't the only one talking, why don't you tell them?' Partial agreement involves framing a response that acknowledges the concern expressed but re-states the original message. For example, the teacher might say something like 'Maybe you weren't the only one, but at the moment I need you to get on quietly. I'm keeping an eye on the others.'

For secondary colleagues in particular there is the potential for conflict with pupils brought about by the inconsistent enforcement of school rules. For example, when directed to follow a seating plan a pupil might say 'Mr Smith, lets us sit where we like.' Typically this will not be delivered by the pupil as a casual observation of inconsistency in school, but accompanied by body language and tone of voice that challenges the teacher to justify their use of a seating plan. Partial agreement can be used here as a way of avoiding either attempting to justify use of the seating plan, publicly criticising a colleague for not following school policy or reacting with an aggressive response like, 'I don't care what happens in Mr Smith's class, in my class you sit where I tell you.' Using partial agreement, the teacher could instead say something like, 'Maybe he does … (small pause to allow the pupil to recognise that the teacher is not going to argue or confront), in our class we have seating plan, so I'd like you to sit there.' Depending on the pupil and the situation it might be appropriate to offer, 'if you are unhappy with where you are sitting then we can talk about it at the end of the lesson.'

Hook and Vass (2002) argue that it is better to frame partial agreement statements as 'Maybe … and …', rather than the more natural, 'Maybe … but ….' Their premise is that if the teacher says, 'Maybe you weren't the only ones talking but …', it immediately conveys a message that disagreement, discord or criticism is going to follow and thus invalidates the agreement in the first part of the sentence. It may also cause the pupil to turn their attention to defence against anticipated criticism rather than hearing what is actually said. We believe

Hook and Vass' (2002) point is valid, but we would suggest the use of 'and' as opposed to 'but' may help rather than make the critical difference between a successful and unsuccessful interaction. If teachers do use 'but', the key point we would take from Hook and Vass' observation is that it should not be emphasised within the sentence. The key parts that the pupil must hear are the partial agreement and the statement of the required behaviour.

Some general principles for strategy use

'Take up' time (Hook and Vass 2002, Rogers 1997, 2002, Rogers and McPherson 2008)

When directing or correcting a pupil it is important to allow 'take up' or thinking time. In a secondary school a teacher might say, 'Put your mobile away, thanks.' This brief interaction has significance in terms of the pupil–teacher relationship and the pupil's relationship with their peers. The pupil, in putting the phone away, is effectively showing to the teacher and to their peers that they are accepting the teacher's authority over them. For some pupils this may represent a loss of face. To remain standing over the pupil awaiting compliance can exacerbate this feeling as the pupil needs to comply under the teacher's gaze and inevitably with other pupils watching to see what will happen. Allowing take up time avoids this. It involves the teacher issuing the direction and then moving away to talk to another pupil or attend to something else. It gives the pupil the opportunity to process the request, which is important for some, and then to take the decision whether to comply or not, out of the spotlight of teacher and peer attention.

As well as the benefits for the pupil in terms of allowing them to save face by not having to comply so publicly, take up time is also beneficial for the teacher. When the teacher moves away they, of course, remain vigilant with regard to whether the pupil has complied with the direction or not. If the pupil has complied, then the teacher can decide when to go back and engage in a positive interaction about the task or behaviour to show that the relationship is still intact. If the pupil has not complied, then, having moved away from the interaction, the teacher is in a far better position to take a considered decision about the next action necessary than if they were standing over the pupil awaiting compliance.

Tactical ignoring of secondary behaviours (Hook and Vass 2002, Rogers 1990, 1995, 2002, Rogers and McPherson 2008)

Secondary behaviours are behaviours that the pupil exhibits in response to teacher correction. Typically these are behaviours with an irritating or provocative quality. They convey a degree of minor resistance, implying 'I'm doing it, but grudgingly.' For example, a pupil told to put a toy away in their tray might comply but slide the tray under their desk in an unnecessarily noisy manner. A common form of secondary behaviour is a 'tut' or a mumbled comment.

The default position is to ignore secondary behaviours and keep the focus on the primary behaviour. The primary behaviour is the behaviour that the teacher originally set out to address. Some pupils may be consciously or subconsciously using secondary behaviours as a way to deflect attention from the primary behaviour. By attending to the secondary behaviour the teacher is effectively both succumbing to this agenda and reinforcing the diversionary use of secondary behaviour as a successful strategy. Other pupils may be using it as a face saving strategy to show either the teacher or their peers that although they are complying they are offering some resistance. Some readers may be wondering whether we should be concerned with allowing pupils to save face. If we are concerned with the pupil's relationship with self and relationship with others then we should. Demanding total capitulation is not good for either of these relationships. If the secondary behaviour is of concern then it is usually better to call the pupil aside at the end of the lesson 'for a quick word' and address the issue privately and calmly.

We have said that the *default* position is to ignore the secondary behaviour to capture the sense that there will be times when professional judgement, based on knowledge of the pupil and the context, determines a different response. The most obvious example is if the secondary behaviour is of a level that means that it assumes the status of a primary behaviour and has to be dealt with. There are other occasions however. For example, if a young child appeared to be trying out a phrase learned from a television programme or an adult or older sibling without realising it was an inappropriate response to adult direction, then the teacher might choose to act on it straight away.

The key point is that the teacher should not simply be *reacting* to secondary behaviours. When unsure, the default position is to ignore, keep the focus on the primary behaviour, and follow up the secondary behaviour later if it is a cause of concern.

Use of 'thanks' (Rogers 2002, Hook and Vass 2002)

Readers will have noticed that in giving examples of how a strategy might be used we have incorporated the word 'thanks'. The use of 'thanks' after a request instead of the more usual 'please', conveys a stronger sense of expectation whilst still maintaining a polite tone. It helps the teacher to appear confident in two important ways. First, that when they ask for something to happen they have no doubt that it will because they are confident in themselves and their authority. Second, that when they ask for something to happen they have no doubt that it will because they are confident in the pupil's desire and ability to do the right thing. There may be some schools where the word 'thanks' is considered to be too informal as a form of language to be used by teachers or where there is an insistence that pupils say 'thank you' rather than use this abbreviation. In such cases, there is the option to use 'thank you' instead but teachers would need to be aware that this potentially loses some of the relaxed, friendly quality because of the formality of the term.

Relaxed vigilance (Rogers 2002)

Relaxed vigilance is similar in many ways to Kounin's (1970) concept of withitness and is a more positive alternative to notions of 'zero tolerance'. The use of the word *relaxed* is important in reflecting that this is not about obsessively fault finding or identifying wrong-doing. Instead, 'relaxed vigilance' conveys the sense that the teacher is aware of what is going on within the classroom and is prepared to act on behaviour that infringes the class rules. In behaviour for learning terms, relaxed vigilance involves the teacher monitoring group relationships.

The least to most intrusive approach (Rogers 1997)

The previous section identified a range of techniques that can be used to address misbehaviour. These need to be used within the context of a least to most intrusive framework as shown in Figure 10.1.

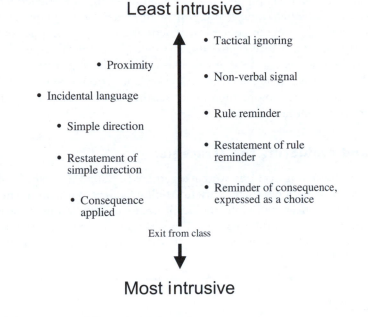

Figure *10.1* Least to most intrusive approach.

Figure 10.1 is not meant to be prescriptive – it is, for example, debatable whether 'tactical ignoring' is less intrusive than 'proximity'. Rather, the example is intended to convey the idea that the teacher should always start with the *lowest* level of intervention that they can that causes least disruption to teaching and learning and settles the behaviour. Neill and Caswell (1993) found that a lot of classroom behaviour fell into the category they defined as 'closed challenge'. This was behaviour that was relatively low-level, typically occurred between a pair of pupils and involved no attempt to draw others into the interaction, as it was not intended to entertain the class or annoy the teacher (McPhillimy 1996). Neill and Caswell (1993) suggest that such incidents rarely evolve into disruption that carries a higher risk to the teacher's authority. Their video evidence showed that the majority of such incidents died away by themselves without the teacher intervening or even necessarily being aware. If the pupil did notice the teacher was aware of them this was usually sufficient to call them back to work (McPhillimy 1996). This supports the view that using the least intrusive strategy is the most appropriate approach.

Neill and Caswell (1993) also refer to 'open challenges'. These are more concerning as they are intended to involve other pupils or to annoy the teacher. Unlike a 'closed challenge', pupils engaged in 'open challenge' may show a high level of 'control checks', glancing frequently at the teacher to check whether they are being observed or otherwise trying to conceal their actions from the teacher in order to avoid detection. The assumption within Neill and Caswell's categorisation is that pupils have developed the necessary social, emotional and behavioural skills to behave in the manner required by the teacher. This is not always the case, even with secondary-aged pupils, and we should be wary of ascribing motive to *all* pupils who appear to demonstrate an 'open challenge'. Realistically, however, there will be some pupils whose behaviour does fall into the category of 'open challenge' and is underpinned by a conscious intent to disrupt and challenge the teacher. McPhillimy (1996) suggests that if the behaviour is not dealt with effectively, the pupil may become less concerned with attempting to conceal their actions and engage in open attempts to disrupt. The least to most intrusive approach is still appropriate for this type of behaviour, but teachers should be aware that an approach like 'tactical ignoring' may reinforce to the pupil that the behaviour has gone undetected. Low key corrections using simple directions and rule reminders may be a more appropriate starting point within the least to most intrusive hierarchy in such situations.

Selecting and evaluating the strategies

Essentially in the preceding sections we have gathered a range of positive correction strategies that we consider represent a useful toolkit and fit with the principle that any strategy used to manage behaviour should promote, or at least not undermine, the development of positive learning behaviours and should not compromise any of the behaviour for learning relationships. Scenario 10.1 demonstrates how a combination of the strategies described could be used.

Scenario 10.1

Situation		*Commentary*
Jason is texting on a mobile phone during the lesson and is spotted by the teacher.		**Relaxed vigilance/withitness** – the teacher notices the unwanted behaviour.
Teacher:	*Teacher says nothing but calmly walks round to Jason's area of the room while still speaking to the class.* *Jason continues texting.*	The teacher starts with a **non-verbal** technique as this is the least intrusive strategy. Jason either does not notice or is unconcerned that he might have been noticed.
Teacher:	'Jason.' *As Jason looks up, the teacher makes a non-verbal gesture pointing at own ear and then downwards to indicate the phone should be put away. Jason puts the phone down on his desk.*	The teacher cues the pupil in by name and then uses a **privately understood signal**. The teacher accepts this partial compliance.
	After a few minutes Jason picks up his phone.	**Relaxed vigilance/withitness** – the teacher notices the unwanted behaviour.

Scenario 10.1 (continued)

Situation		Commentary
Teacher:	'Jason, put the phone away, thanks.' *Teacher moves away and talks to another pupil about the task. The teacher looks over and sees Jason still has the phone in his hand.*	The teacher makes use of a **simple direction**, followed by **take up time** to give Jason the chance to comply.
Teacher:	'Jason, you either put the phone away in your bag or put it on my desk.'	The teacher offers a **choice** (with one option that the pupil is likely to find preferable).
Jason:	'OK, OK, I was just checking it was turned off.'	
Teacher:	'Maybe you were, but now I need you to put it away and get started on the writing.'	The teacher uses **'partial agreement'** rather than entering into an argument.
Ending 1A		
Jason:	'Tut' *(audibly). Slides chair back with unnecessary noise and puts the phone in his bag. The teacher makes no comment on this.*	The teacher chooses to **ignore the secondary behaviour**.
Ending 1B		
Jason:	'Why don't you just get out of my face? I don't want to do the stupid writing and you can't make me.'	The teacher, recognising a rapidly escalating situation, sends another pupil with a red card to the 'on call' member of the Senior Leadership Team.

The teacher is careful to avoid inflaming the situation and uses respectful language throughout. Though this ends up being a protracted interaction the teacher attempts to use the least intrusive strategy possible to address the behaviour each time and bides their time between individual interactions. In ending 1A the pupil complies and puts the phone away. In ending 1B, despite the teacher's best efforts, the situation erupts. This alternative ending is provided to illustrate the important point that we cannot predict every pupil's response. In making a strategy selection we are effectively making a prediction about how the pupil will respond. Knowledge of the pupil will clearly help in making a more accurate prediction. The strategies suggested in this chapter are those that we consider on *more* occasions stand a *greater* chance with *more* pupils of leading to outcomes of the type described in ending 1A. The same cannot be said of strategies employed in Scenario 10.2. Whilst strategies in Scenario 10.2 may be successful in stopping behaviour on many occasions, when they do not succeed the failure is likely to be public and spectacular. The strategies in Scenario 10.2 are high risk strategies and, as we explore next, also contribute little to the development of learning behaviour.

The strategies used in Scenario 10.1 promote learning behaviour, or at least do not contradict the principles of the behaviour for learning approach by impacting negatively on relationship with self, others or the curriculum. This remains true whether the interaction results in ending 1A or ending 1B and provides the criteria by which to judge the effectiveness and the *appropriateness* of the strategy. Judging effectiveness simply by whether the behaviour stops places the teacher in a reactive position where they are trying and discarding strategies based on the response of the pupil which may be influenced by all manner of complex interacting factors.

Scenario 10.2

Situation	*Commentary*
Jason is texting on a mobile phone during the lesson and is spotted by the teacher.	**Relaxed vigilance/withitness** – the teacher notices the unwanted behaviour.
Teacher: (Loudly) 'Jason!... What on earth do think you're doing?! Bring that here now.' *Jason gets up and takes the phone to the teacher at the front of the class.*	The teacher uses a **highly intrusive** approach that, by its volume, is arguably more disruptive to the class as a whole than the behaviour it seeks to stop.
Teacher: 'You obviously don't know what the school rule is about mobiles so you'd better stay in at lunch time and copy out the school's Code of Conduct. And you won't be seeing this again until the end of the day (*puts the phone in desk drawer*). Now sit down... you've wasted enough of everyone's time already.'	The teacher uses this as an opportunity to demonstrate that they are in a position of authority and will not tolerate any challenge to this.

Ending 2A

Jason goes back to his seat, the class is completely silent.	

Ending 2B

Jason: 'You give that back! If anything happens to my phone my dad's going to be up here. D'you hear me!?'	
Teacher: 'How dare you talk to me like that!? Get out!?' *Jason storms out, slamming the door.*	

In Scenario 10.1, the teacher's use of respectful language throughout recognises the need to avoid damaging either the relationship with the pupil or the pupil's relationship with self. The interaction seeks to re-focus Jason on learning, which currently the mobile phone is distracting him from. In contrast, strategies in Scenario 10.2 are focused on quelling a perceived challenge to authority and taking opportunities to demonstrate that any challenge of this sort will be dealt with in a similar manner. The strategies in Scenario 10.1 place the responsibility on Jason through choices and time to consider his actions. Moreover the teacher models appropriate behaviours for dealing with a situation that is currently not as they would wish it to be. The teacher in Scenario 10.2 however models that if someone is in a position of power through the authority conveyed by their role, and possibly also through other factors such as their physical size, strength, command of language or greater intellect, it is acceptable to use coercive means or disrespectful language to secure their desired outcome. In terms of self-regulation the teacher in Scenario 10.1 keeps the events in proportion and manages themselves well, recognising that though the behaviour needs to be addressed it does not warrant the disproportionate anger and aggression demonstrated by the teacher in Scenario 10.2. Again, this is a modelling issue. The teacher in Scenario 10.1 models effective management of their own frustration and irritation through the use of assertive language, calmness and persistence.

A final point to note is that in the case of ending 1B from Scenario 10.1 the teacher–pupil relationship may be strained but is readily recoverable. The same cannot be said of ending 2B from Scenario 10.2 where considerable effort is likely to be necessary to repair and rebuild the relationship.

Analysing individual interactions

Taking the behaviour for learning conceptual framework further, it is also possible to scrutinise individual statements to consider their likely contribution to the promotion of learning behaviour and their potential effect. Consider the following scenario.

Scenario 10.3

A pupil in the Reception class, Terry, is making a tower out of plastic building blocks. He has been working on this for some time and then it collapses. The teacher hears Terry swear and makes the judgement that this is out of frustration. Teacher A responds with a focus on the promotion of learning behaviour whereas teacher B responds with a focus on the challenge to authority:

Teacher A: 'Terry (*said calmly, with a pause to get attention*), we don't use language like that in our class. You know our rule … now what's the difficulty?'

Teacher B: 'How dare you use that language in my class! Go and sit on the naughty chair!'

If the intention is to remark upon the unacceptability of swearing then either response achieves this outcome. If the outcome is to remark on the unacceptability of swearing *and* promote learning behaviour teacher A's response is more likely to achieve this. Teacher A uses the pupil's name. This not only cues Terry into the fact that the teacher wants him to listen but also demonstrates that he is worthy of being spoken to with respect. A person's name is a central element of their identity and therefore an important element of relationship with self. The image we may have of the stereotypical, often male, often secondary school teacher beginning corrections and reprimands to male pupils as 'You, boy …' is the antithesis of this. Teacher A's pause after the pupil's name cues him in and avoids this becoming a 'thrust' (Kounin 1970). The intention is not to surprise the pupil, but to prime him to hear an important message. The statement 'We don't use language like that in our class' does not seek to moralise. The phrasing allows for dual expectations to exist in the pupil's life. Such swearing may be viewed as acceptable in the pupil's home, but the teacher does not seek to pass judgement on this and just conveys clearly that a particular set of expectations apply in the classroom environment. Unlike teacher B, who refers to 'my class', teacher A's use of *our* class' emphasises participation and collaboration. The reference to the rules by teacher A emphasises the relationship with others, demonstrating that when living and working alongside others, in almost any context, there is a set of rules that apply. Teacher B misses this learning opportunity and moves straight to a sanction which is a period of time out on the 'naughty chair'. The use of the term 'naughty chair' conveys a label in the sense that presumably anybody who sits on it is naughty. The problems of labelling and self-fulfilling prophecy have been well documented. There is potential for a negative impact on the pupil's relationship with self if the pupil continually receives the message that they are naughty. Though it has become something of a mantra within the field of behaviour management, it is worth restating that we should label the behaviour, not the child. The other criticism in behaviour for learning terms is that a title of 'thinking chair' would convey a better sense of the behaviours we want the child to engage in whilst there, such as reflecting on their own behaviour. Teacher A finishes the interaction with a focus on learning by asking 'What's the difficulty?' and takes the opportunity to promote resourcefulness and resilience by conveying the message that it is recognised a difficulty has occurred and that this is something to be tackled.

The suggestion is not that a teacher should seek to break down every interaction they have with pupils in this way. After all, as Watkins (2006) suggests, the teacher may be involved in a thousand or more interactions in a day. Rather teachers should reflect generally on the sorts of language they use within their interactions. Neither is the suggestion that, in this case, Terry will be psychologically damaged by teacher B's handling of the situation or that teacher A's handling will have developed his learning behaviour dramatically. It is of course the cumulative effect that we are concerned with. If Terry's experience is *frequently* of teacher B-type responses that focus on the challenge to authority, label and move rapidly to sanctions, this may have negative effects. If however, Terry's experience is *frequently* of teacher A-type responses that focus on the promotion of learning behaviour and have regard for the three relationships, then this is likely to have more positive effects.

Summary

This chapter has dealt with the very practical concern of what to do when a pupil misbehaves. As we indicated at the beginning of the chapter it is almost inevitable that this will happen. We have provided teachers and trainees with a basic toolkit of strategies for positive correction for dealing with such situations. The strength of the approaches encouraged within this chapter lies in their focus on relationships. They provide a form of language that the teacher can use that is respectful and reduces risk both to the teacher–pupil relationship and the three behaviour for learning relationships.

We are sure readers will already have ideas about which of these strategies are immediately applicable to their contexts, which have some utility if adapted and those that are likely to be of limited use. Readers will also want to expand the toolkit by accessing a variety of sources. Though we would warn against the indiscriminate pursuit of behaviour management strategies in the mistaken belief that the universally effective set exists, to professionally consider the utility of any new approaches and engage with literature on the subject is something we would encourage. As we indicated in Chapter 3, the behaviour for learning conceptual framework should support teachers in this activity.

Chapter 11

Dealing with more challenging behaviour

Introduction

This chapter invites the reader to consider what we might term more challenging behaviour and how this can be managed in a way that retains a focus on promoting learning behaviour and does not compromise or undermine the three behaviour for learning relationships.

From our experience working with schools, there seem to be two distinct categories of challenging behaviour that concern teachers. The first is behaviour exhibited with a high degree of frequency by certain individuals. In other words the problem is not the seriousness of the behaviour but the fact that the pupil does it a lot. The second is higher-level behaviour, such as physical and verbal aggression, usually underpinned by anger. The chapter considers both forms of challenging behaviour.

High-frequency behaviour

This section of the chapter is concerned with individuals who exhibit certain behaviours frequently. The behaviours are not especially serious or unusual; the problematic dimension is the fact that the pupil exhibits them often and may not respond to the teacher's prompts and corrections. This type of behaviour falls into two distinct areas. There is behaviour that is repeated within the same teaching session and behaviour that occurs on a regular basis across teaching sessions. In the first category we would include the pupil who, despite the use of a number of strategies, moving from least to most intrusive, continues to exhibit the same or other similarly problematic behaviours. In the second category we would include the pupil who in most sessions is likely to exhibit the same or similar problematic behaviour but generally moderates their behaviour when corrected. In both cases it is important to respond consistently and make use of school systems at the time when the behaviour occurs. To reiterate a point made earlier in the book, we should seek to employ strategies before sanctions. That is we should employ a range of strategies, moving from least to most intrusive, to attempt to moderate the behaviour. If the pupil moderates their behaviour in response to one of the least to most intrusive strategies employed or when a sanction is issued the immediate problem is resolved. However, as we have previously noted, this does not necessarily mean any learning has or is likely to take place. It is important to recognise that the use of least to most intrusive strategies is not a formulaic exercise; we should always be monitoring carefully the pupil's responses and gauging our next step accordingly. This should inform us when to pursue a particular line, perhaps by being more insistent with a re-statement of a rule or reminding of the consequence of continuation of this behaviour, moving in closer for a quiet word or physically and metaphorically taking a step back.

Using the sorts of least to most intrusive strategies described in Chapter 10 will help to ensure that behaviour is managed in a way that does not compromise the three relationships that underpin the development of learning behaviour. What happens at the most intrusive level varies between schools and it is important for the teacher to be aware of and confident in the systems that are in place. Knowing the stage available next, including how to access support from a colleague, can give the teacher greater confidence in using the less intrusive strategies.

Typically it is not the sort of sequence of events described previously that cause the teacher greatest concern. In simple terms, if the pupil responds to one of the least to most intrusive strategies or to a sanction that is imposed, the teacher no longer has a behaviour problem at that moment. The greater concern is when despite using a sequence of least to most intrusive strategies and imposing a sanction, the pupil continues with behaviour that impacts significantly on the learning of others. Many schools have systems in place for this sort of situation that involve summoning assistance from a (usually) senior colleague. It is important for teachers to know the system that operates in their school and expectations regarding its use. The latter point is important. Most schools for example would not expect assistance to be summoned for refusal to work unless this took the form of a behaviour that had a significant negative impact on other pupils' learning. Passive non-compliance of this sort can usually be dealt with later. Individual teachers have a responsibility not to over use such a system, senior leaders have a responsibility to ensure that when requested such support is quick and effective, secure in the knowledge that it is a genuine need.

Colleague support in exiting a pupil

In thinking about colleague support when exiting a pupil there are few guidelines we can consider:

*   The supporting member of staff should be given a brief, quiet, factual account of the situation. The referrer should not use this as an opportunity to express their own frustrations or publicly list all the pupil's misdemeanours in front of the class. Typically this should be a quiet conversation just inside the classroom door where at least one of the adults has sight of the pupil concerned and the rest of the class.
*   The referrer should avoid comments to the colleague providing support such as 'I'm not prepared to teach this pupil', 'he needs to be excluded', or 'I will not have him back in my class.' They are emotive and the reality is that the referrer does not have the power to make these decisions anyway. This fact will of course be abundantly obvious to the class and the pupil when they are not excluded and later return. Such comments also place the supporter in a difficult position because of course they cannot agree to any of these points on the spur of the moment and they only serve to make relationships more difficult with the pupil when they do return.
*   The supporter should not question the referrer or start to suggest other strategies that should have been tried. If there are issues about how the referrer handled the situation prior to referral or advice that can be offered on additional strategies these should be discussed in a supportive environment later.
*   As a general rule, the supporter should not engage the pupil in conversation within the classroom and should use a brief, respectful directive statement such as, 'I need you to come with me now' and turn expectantly, conveying confidence that the pupil will follow. Placing one hand on the edge or handle of the open door whilst extending the other arm outwards as you might do in an 'after you' type gesture can add to this air of

confidence. An exception to this principle of minimal dialogue is when the supporter's professional judgement is that this is an escalating situation and allowing the pupil to talk would be beneficial in diffusing a potentially more serious situation.

- The referrer needs to be given feedback later on what happened to the pupil when they were removed from class. If this feedback is not forthcoming the referrer should take the initiative in requesting this.
- Consideration needs to be given to how relationships are repaired between the referrer and the pupil. This is especially important in a secondary school where several days may elapse before the timetable brings the pupil and teacher together again. The central focus of any meeting with the pupil prior to the next lesson should focus on what the pupil can do differently next time rather than over dwelling on events that led to their exit from the class last time.

The out-of- or after-class discussion

Pupils will sometimes need to be spoken to out of class. Teachers meeting one to one with a pupil need to be aware of the risk of malicious allegations. The generic advice would be to make sure colleagues are aware of the meeting and that you can be easily observed, keeping a door open if necessary. However readers would be well advised to check with their school's policy for further guidance on this issue. Frequently such meetings will be at break time but may also take the form of brief conversations just outside the classroom door. The latter approach raises issues in relation to the supervision of the rest of the class so again readers should be clear on their school policy and expectations of the senior leadership team with regard to this.

The brief out-of-class discussion

We need to recognise the limitations of the brief out-of-class discussion. If the teacher is briefly seeing a pupil just outside the classroom during a lesson it clearly limits the scope of the conversation. Despite the briefness, the teacher's language needs to remain positive and respectful throughout so as not to impact negatively either on their relationship with the pupil or the pupil's relationship with self. Typically there is opportunity for little more than a conversation that:

- summarises events that have led to this point, e.g. 'John, I've reminded you several times about the need to work quietly without disturbing the rest of the group';
- states the likely consequences of continuation of this behaviour, e.g. 'If you continue then you will need to stay in at break time and complete your work';
- states or offers any options available to the pupil that may help, e.g. 'Would it help if you moved seats and sat at the spare desk by the window?';
- ends positively, e.g. 'OK, let's go back into class and I'll come and see how you're getting on in a few minutes.'

Protracted conversations about what the pupil did and why they did it are neither possible nor desirable. They leave the class unsupervised, unless another adult is present who is capable of taking on this duty, and run the risk of arousing strong emotions or opening up issues that the teacher then has insufficient time to deal with. If this kind of conversation is necessary it is better that it is deferred until quality time can be devoted to it.

When returning to class from a conversation such as this, the teacher needs to be realistic in their expectations of the pupil's behaviour. For the pupil their relationship with others may be a key factor at this point and they may exhibit some secondary behaviours (see Chapter 10) to save face. It is important to recognise that it is difficult to return to the classroom with potentially 29 other pupils watching. Teachers should accept therefore that the pupil may grin at friends when passing, slump heavily into their seat or exhibit some other form of low-level but potentially irritating behaviour. As we indicated in Chapter 10, the default position regarding secondary behaviours is to ignore them. Following the pupil into class allows the teacher to see their behaviour and lets them know that their behaviours can be seen and helps to curb some of the more overt secondary behaviours that the pupil may be tempted to exhibit if following the teacher.

Used sparingly, the brief out-of-class conversation can be effective. It is a way of removing the pupil from the immediate environment and making a personal link. It takes the pupil away from an audience that may, either through comments, looks or just their presence, be reinforcing the behaviour.

Follow-up discussions

Unlike the brief out-of-class discussion, the follow-up discussion takes place at a set time. For example, the teacher might have asked the pupil to see them at break or lunch time. In thinking about this meeting there are a few guidelines we can consider.

- Distinguish between those who 'can't behave' and those who 'won't behave'. Before speaking to the pupil, consider their level of understanding of the behaviour. Age and level of development will inform this assessment. Your approach to a pupil who, due to age or stage of development, does not understand why a behaviour is unacceptable or problematic, will need to be different to the approach used when you are confident the pupil knows how to behave and is developmentally able to demonstrate the behaviour required. This issue is explored in Reflective Exercise 11.1.

Reflective Exercise 11.1

John, aged four, has taken another pupil's set of colouring pencils and is observed by a member of staff putting them in his own bag. You have had a number of reports from parents of their children's belongings going missing and unsubstantiated claims from other pupils that John has taken them.

Kerry, aged 13, has taken another pupil's calculator and is observed by a member of staff putting it in her own bag. You have had number of complaints from pupils about possessions going missing and a number of them have suggested that Kerry could be the culprit.

- In both cases what would be the purpose of your interaction with the pupil?
- How would the interaction be different?

(continued)

> *Reflective Exercise 11.1 (continued)*
>
> Note: For the purpose of this exercise we have made the assumption that developmentally Kerry is functioning broadly in line with her chronological age. Individual knowledge of the pupil would determine whether this was a reasonable assumption.

- Allow sufficient time. It is important to allow sufficient time, free from interruptions, to talk with the pupils.
- Label the behaviour not the pupil. A key principle when managing behaviour is to label the behaviour, not the pupil. This relates to the pupil's relationship with self, as the purpose is to avoid the behaviour becoming part of the pupil's identity. Therefore the teacher would talk of the action as being unkind or disruptive rather than the pupil. This is a useful rule to adhere to but needs to be expanded a little. Sometimes even when we label the behaviour there is a strong connotation of what that makes the individual. Examples might include 'What you did was bullying' or 'That is stealing.' Though such phrases are labelling the behaviour and as such are considerably better than 'You're a bully' or 'You're a thief', the terminology is still emotive. Instead describe what the pupil actually did. In the case of a younger pupil suspected of bullying the teacher might begin:

  > 'I understand that you have been calling Sam names during break time. I know this is not the first time you have done this to Sam. When someone keeps making life unpleasant for the same person I take it very seriously ...'

  If the teacher feels it is appropriate to use the label then it can be used in an explanatory, educative way, such as, 'I understand that you have been calling Sam names during break time. I know this not the first time you have done this to Sam. When someone keeps making life unpleasant for the same person it is called bullying. I take that sort of behaviour very seriously'.

  This confronts the pupil with the reality of what they have done in a manner that reflects back to them how others view the behaviour or collection of behaviours exhibited currently. The pupil is therefore encouraged to reflect on whether how they currently present is how they want to present, thereby showing them that choice is available and change possible.

- Recognise underlying feelings. If the teacher asks to see a pupil after a lesson or asks to see them for a moment outside the class, this carries a connotation that something is going to happen which is not going to be an entirely comfortable experience. There may be feelings of anxiety coupled with annoyance and irritation (Hook and Vass 2002), particularly if seeing the teacher involves loss of the pupil's time. Older pupils may refer to the practice as 'getting done', as in the phrase 'You're going to get done', meaning that a reprimand or sanction is likely (Hook and Vass 2002). The fact that after-class follow-up discussions have this status should be reassuring to teachers when using deferred consequences, as it means that dealing with a situation later rather than confronting directly in class is not seen by other pupils as a weakness or a sign that pupils are 'getting away with it'. The other, more important message, however is that we need to recognise that we are dealing with a pupil who may already be feeling anxious, aggrieved or inconvenienced (Hook and Vass 2002). To adopt a heavy-handed approach by attempting to dominate through our body language, tone of voice or use of disparaging or belittling language, is therefore both unnecessary – as pupils already perceive the event as significant – and unhelpful – as it may be the trigger that causes an unnecessary escalation.

• Be aware that any heightened emotional state will adversely affect the ability to take in and cognitively process information and instruction. For this reason communications need to be clear, short and consistent.

• Thank the pupil for staying behind or returning. Hook and Vass (2002) suggest thanking the pupil for staying behind, which may at first seem strange given that it is the teacher's decision that they have stayed behind, and the reason for this decision has been the pupil's misbehaviour. The strength of this approach is two-fold. Firstly, it is a defusing strategy. It is harder to be angry with someone who has just thanked you. Secondly, it is a point of success from which to start. The pupil has already chosen to be cooperative by coming to speak with the teacher. Hook and Vass (2002) sum up the rationale behind thanking the pupil succinctly: 'You are in effect, making a positive emotional deposit into the emotional account you have with the student before you make the inevitable withdrawal by discussing more difficult issues' (Hook and Vass 2002: 78).

Beyond managing behaviour

The fact that the pupil is frequently progressing though the range of least to most intrusive strategies and receiving sanctions or perhaps on occasions needs to be collected from class by a colleague is data that should be interpreted as an indicator of a need for other interventions. As we have seen in Chapter 8, sanctions often do little to *change* behaviour. A pupil who is regularly reaching the sanctions level is effectively providing the proof of this point. Therefore, though the class teacher may still need to continue managing behaviour through consistent application of school policy, it should be recognised that it will be other interventions that change behaviour. In future planning we would want the teacher in their planning to use their knowledge of the event to consider the learning behaviours they need to develop in this pupil as well as make an appraisal of whether any of the management strategies used risk undermining relationship with self, relationship with the curriculum or relationship with others.

Behaviour as an expression of anger

When a pupil does not respond to directions and is non-compliant the temptation may be to dismiss the behaviour as attention-seeking, fun-seeking, pushing the boundaries or simply rooted in a desire to give the teacher a hard time. Though with some pupils such an assessment may be accurate, we need to be alert to the possibility that this behaviour is an indicator of physiological or psychological arousal. Monitoring and responsiveness on the part of the teacher is the key to avoiding escalation. Much of the more extreme behaviour teachers experience is due to pupils' anger and in most cases it is possible to spot the signs of this arousal before a major incident develops. This relies on the teacher not only spotting the signs but responding appropriately.

The assault cycle

The assault cycle (Figure 11.1) is useful in helping us to understand events when a pupil or adult becomes angry. Breakwell (1997) presented the assault cycle as a way of understanding the process that occurs during a typical episode of physically aggressive behaviour. This understanding helps us to identify our priorities at each stage. The model has been presented in a more generic form as the anger mountain (Long and Fogell 1999, Long 1999), relating the process to other incidents in addition to those that involve physical aggression. Therefore, whilst originally presented as a way of understanding the process when an assault or other physical aggression is likely, the assault cycle is also relevant when considering events such as verbal aggression, panic attacks or any loss of control such as a pupil storming out of the room or off site. Within this chapter it is this broader perspective that is applied to the assault cycle.

The assault cycle links to the instinctive survival response of fight or flight. The fight or flight response has its origins long ago in human history, when our ancestors were faced with dangerous, but not especially complex threats such as the approach of a sabre-toothed tiger or a member of another tribe. It is important therefore that we recognise the fight or flight response as both primitive and instinctive. It involves physiological changes as the body alters its priorities from long-term survival to emergency short-term survival.

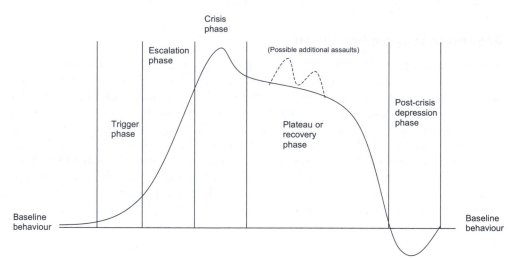

Figure 11.1 The assault cycle (Breakwell 1997: 43).
Reproduced with permission of Blackwell Publishing Ltd.

Trigger phase

People have a normal baseline set of behaviours, and for almost everybody this normal behaviour is non-aggressive most of the time (Breakwell 1997). In the trigger phase something occurs that is *perceived* as a threat. It does not matter whether the teacher, another person or peers would perceive this as a threat, the important factor is that the individual concerned views it as such. The threat may be to physical or emotional well-being. Anger therefore is caused by the reaction to an event, not the event itself. During the trigger phase the fight or flight response is just beginning, the body has not yet become fully aroused physiologically (Faupel *et al.* 1998).

The priority during this phase is removing or distracting the individual from the trigger, or removing the trigger itself. At this stage it is also often possible to appeal to reason, suggest alternatives, remind of any 'calm down' techniques already taught (now is not the time to teach them!) and, if considered helpful, remind of the consequences of reacting to the trigger. The latter option should be used with caution. It is important to express it in terms and in a tone of voice that conveys that you are focused on the best interests of the individual concerned, not issuing a threat. For example, you might say, 'John, I can see you're angry. If you damage the chair you know you're likely to end up in detention. Leave it now, we can sort this out.'

Escalation phase

During the escalation phase the body is preparing itself physiologically for the fight or flight response. The release of hormones such as adrenaline, cause blood pressure to increase and breathing to become more rapid as the body prepares itself for the muscular effort involved in making a fight or flight response (Faupel *et al.* 1998). The person may start to pace up and down and the speed and volume of their speech may increase (Breakwell 1997). There may also be more subtle physical movements signifying increased agitation such as drumming fingers on the table. As the escalation phase moves towards crisis the individual becomes increasingly unlikely to make rational judgements. The priorities at this stage are similar to those at trigger phase; we are still trying to remove or distract the individual from the trigger, or remove the trigger itself if still present. Appealing to reason at this stage is likely to be less useful but it is still relevant to offer clear alternatives and remind of any 'calm down' techniques that the pupil has *already* been taught or has used successfully before. It is also important to remember that the teacher's own presence may be acting as an ongoing trigger at this point. This is a real possibility if the incident started as a result of an interaction between the teacher and the pupil. In such cases it may be better that a colleague takes over the management of the situation.

Crisis phase

During the crisis phase the individual will be unable to think clearly, make rational judgements or respond to requests and instructions. They may however pick up on tone of voice or body language so it is important that the teacher does not signal additional threat by invading personal space, moving quickly or becoming highly animated or raising their voice. It is of little use and potentially aggravating to the situation to threaten with sanctions or the displeasure of senior staff who may need to be summoned.

The priority for the teacher at this stage is keeping the individual, others and themselves safe. Clearing the audience is important as it keeps them safe and also removes additional stimulus for the individual who is in crisis. To do this sometimes requires removing the whole class. Many teachers we speak to are very anxious about this prospect. This is understandable as continually removing the class has a detrimental effect on teaching and learning. However at the point of crisis, if the judgement is that removal of the rest of the class would reduce either the level of arousal or the danger, then it is a procedure that needs to be followed. The place for debate and deliberation is after the event when alternative approaches can be considered, in particular identifying where there is scope for earlier intervention before the crisis point is reached.

If it is safe to do so, remove any objects nearby that may endanger the individual, could be thrown or may lead to the individual being in more trouble if broken.

Plateau or recovery phase

For the teacher involved in managing the incident, it can feel like the hard work is complete once the crisis begins to subside. In practice we need to give careful consideration to the final two phases of the assault cycle. The first of these is the 'recovery phase'. At this point the anger begins to subside but the individual is at heightened level of susceptibility to triggers. Events that are quite minor in nature and which normally the individual would not react to may be sufficient to re-ignite the anger during this phase. It is not the time to start analysing the incident with the pupil or demanding explanations (Breakwell 1997). Breakwell (1997) suggests that this phase could last 30–90 minutes, whilst Faupel *et al.* (1998) suggest leaving at least 45 minutes but ideally an hour before discussing a major incident with a young person. There will be differences between individuals and also age and the severity of the incident are likely to be factors, but the key message is that time needs to be allowed for the physiological and psychological arousal to subside. The implication therefore is that we need to have the facility for the pupil to calm down away from obvious triggers, including inquisitive passers by who may ask questions.

Post-crisis depression phase

The 'post-crisis' phase is one of resting and recovering from the high state of arousal that the body has just experienced. The ability to think clearly and to listen begins to return at this stage. The pupil may become tearful, remorseful, guilty, ashamed, distraught or despairing. The pupil is quite vulnerable at this stage and so it is important that the teacher or adult managing this part of the process supports them in distinguishing between guilty feelings about themselves and remorse about the behaviour. Guilt directed at oneself may reduce self-esteem and impact negatively on the pupil's relationship with self. In contrast, remorse about the behaviour could lead to effective responses such as apologising and making amends which may help to rebuild relationships with others, or lead to the generation of alternatives to this behaviour in the future (Faupel *et al.* 1998).

Non-confrontational approaches: looking at our behaviour

As the assault cycle illustrates, when an individual is moving towards and into the crisis phase their thinking becomes less rational. This means their responses are also less predictable. Therefore there is no recipe of strategies that will guarantee a positive outcome; all we can realistically do is ensure that we use good practice approaches that increase the chances of a positive outcome.

Positioning

If you need to get closer to the pupil, which in most cases will be more helpful than attempting to talk to them from a distance, then it is important to consider how you approach. It is helpful to imagine a line extending directly out in front of the pupil and ensure that you keep to one side of this (Figure 11.2). This is less threatening than walking directly at someone. This is especially true if you are physically bigger than them.

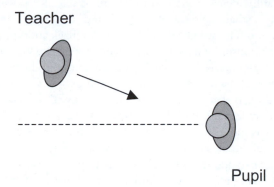

Figure 11.2 Approaching a pupil.

When talking to the pupil stick to the same principle of staying off the imaginary line (Figure 11.3). Standing square on to the pupil would be far more confrontational and also means no 'flight' response is available to the pupil to the front and so risks increasing the possibility of a 'fight' response.

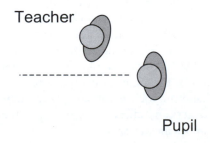

Figure 11.3 Talking to a pupil.

Proximity is also an issue to consider. It is considered that a distance of 15–46 cm is the intimate zone into which people only allow those who are emotionally close such as lovers, parents, spouses, our children, close friends, relatives and pets (Pease and Pease 2004). We need to ensure we stay out of this zone as it is provocative and entering it is likely to be perceived as a threat. Outside the intimate zone is the personal zone which extends from 46 cm to 1.22 m. We tend to stand this distance from others at social functions and friendly gatherings (Pease and Pease 2004). When talking to the pupil we need, as a rough guide, to be standing at the outer end of this range or just into the social zone, which extends from 1.22 to 3.6 m (Pease and Pease 2004). The social zone tends to be the distance we stand from people we do not know very well such as a new colleague, trades people doing repairs in our homes and so on. Braithwaite (2001) offers a rule of thumb guide suggesting that the average space requirement is about two arm lengths if standing and perhaps one-and-a-half arm lengths if sitting.

Positioning is also important in keeping the adult safer. Having established that it is desirable to keep off the imaginary line extending out in from in front of the pupil we can look more closely at the stance the adult adopts. The sideways position depicted in Figure 11.3 allows the adult a clearer view of the pupil so that it is possible to notice any arm, hand or leg movement that could signal an attack and so increases the chance of being able to take avoiding action. The weight should be on the back foot but without actually leaning back. This is the opposite of an aggressive stance when the weight would often be on the front foot (Braithwaite 2001). It is a stable position and so if the pupil moves forward it is easier to take a step back to maintain a safe distance or step to one side to allow the pupil to pass if the decision is that it is better to allow a 'flight' response. This stance also means that if the pupil does lash out with hands or feet and avoiding action is not possible then at least any contact is more likely to be made with the harder parts of the teacher's body, rather than more vulnerable areas to the front of the body.

So far we have assumed a standing position, but if the pupil is seated on a chair or another piece of furniture or on the floor it is often helpful to come down to their level by crouching, or sitting alongside. Sitting down whilst the pupil is standing is a de-escalating gesture giving a clear signal of non-aggression and a sign of negotiation (Braithwaite 2001). Most fights involve the protagonists standing up, at least initially, but rarely sitting down. The gesture of sitting down therefore conveys a powerful message that this incident is not going to go in this direction. However if you feel insecure or sense that a physical assault is imminent it is unwise to use this strategy as it limits escape options and makes you more vulnerable.

Rapid or big arm and hand movements may well be perceived as threatening gestures. Pointing or wagging the index finger at the individual is also provocative and in close proximity is likely to encroach too far into the pupil's personal space. Hands should ideally be in view, open, with palms visible and held in a relaxed position by the sides. They can also be used either singly or together in a gentle palms down motion to accompany a 'Let's calm down' message (Long 1999). Posture should show an appropriate level of interest, involvement and appreciation of the significance the source of upset has to the pupil. Braithwaite (2001) suggest hands in pockets can convey disinterest and a thumb stuck in a belt loop or the top of a pocket can indicate arrogance or intransigence. Arms folded or hands on hips may convey similar messages.

Facial expressions

Generally smiling should be avoided as this may be misinterpreted as a smirk (Braithwaite 2001) or an indication that the situation, which is a cause of obvious distress to the individual, is not being taken seriously. This is not as easy as it sounds as smiling or laughing are often ways used by people as a means of alleviating discomfort when they are in a situation that feels uncomfortable. Many readers will no doubt have noticed this phenomenon when speaking to certain pupils who grin or giggle when being spoken to about their misbehaviour.

Eye contact

Eye contact should be established if possible but without staring as this may be perceived as a challenge (Braithwaite 2001). We should not demand eye contact (e.g. 'Look at me when I'm talking to you') as it is likely to escalate matters (Long and Fogell 1999). The best advice is to try to keep eye contact natural. In normal conversations we rarely look at each other for more than one or two seconds at a time, and the listener tends to look more than the speaker (Long 1999). In a confrontation the aggressor may stare, retaining eye contact for an unusually long period. We need to avoid matching this as this would be conveying an aggressive signal back.

Verbal communication

The tone of voice we adopt needs to be calm but firm (Long and Fogell 1999). Remaining unnaturally calm or assuming what we might term almost a clichéd calm tone is not likely to help matters.

We should listen more than talk. Usually if the pupil is talking, even if this is a rant and/ or contains language that on other occasions we would attempt to limit there is a greater chance that the situation will end without physical aggression. The adult needs to monitor the pace and pitch of their own speech. Increase in the pace of speech or raising the pitch of the voice are associated with emotional arousal and so do not convey calming signals to the pupil. Unless monitored, these changes in speech can inadvertently happen because the adult's state of emotional arousal increases when faced with a difficult situation.

A large percentage of the meaning we communicate is conveyed not by the actual words we say but by tone of voice and body language. Nevertheless we need to pay attention to the words we use.

SOME 'DOS' AND 'DON'TS'

*   Avoid phrases like, 'I know how you feel ...', 'I understand how you feel ...'. These are assumptions as it is unlikely that you do know how they feel. It is far better to name the feeling that the outward display of behaviour conveys to you rather than claiming to know how the individual feels by saying for example, 'I can see that you're angry/ upset/frustrated ...' A degree of judgement applies as to whether to use the term 'upset' as for some older pupils the fact that they have lost control and perhaps are starting to cry may be a source of embarrassment. To reinforce this with the word 'upset' may therefore be unhelpful and 'angry' may be the better generic phrase. However this is not an exact science and there is a counter argument that 'upset' conveys sympathy which is a good way of building a caring relationship (Long 1999).

    If applicable you can also name the source of the anger, for example, 'I can see that you are upset because you think I was unfair ...'
*   Avoid phrases like 'Don't be silly ...', 'It's not worth getting upset/angry over it ...', 'Come on, it can't be that bad ...' and 'There's no need to get upset about it ...' Whatever has triggered the incident *is* of significance to the individual and isn't silly and so clearly at some level for them it was worth getting upset/angry over. We need therefore to use phrases that reflect this such as, 'It sounds really awful ...', 'That must have been really difficult for you ...', 'I can see that this has made you angry ...' or 'I can see this is really important to you ...'
*   Use phrases like 'I hear what you're saying ...', 'I can see where you're coming from ...' in moderation. They can be useful but they have become somewhat clichéd to the point where they can appear as simply a form of jargon with little personal engagement. It would be far better to use phrases such 'It sounds awful ...' or 'Yes, I see' (Braithwaite 2001).

- Avoid prohibitions such as 'can't …', 'mustn't …' and 'shouldn't …' Readers will be familiar from Chapter 10 with idea of framing their language positively. The same principle applies with more difficult incidents. Negative words only add to the negative state of aggression being expressed (Braithwaite 2001). Phrases such as 'I can help you if you can stop shouting …', 'We can work this out if you come and sit down …', that suggest possibilities of what can be done are generally better than prohibitions.

- Avoid phrases like 'Come on, let's see a smile …', 'Cheer up' and 'Pull yourself together.' The individual is showing strong emotions and as the assault cycle tells us it will take a while to recover. To assume the individual can switch emotions is trivialising, patronising and ultimately unrealistic.

- Avoid phrases such as 'Well, this isn't going to achieve anything ….' and 'You won't get anywhere like that …' The implication of these phrases is that there is rationality behind the behaviour. However the incident is a loss of control on the part of the individual so they are unlikely to be able to contemplate the pros and cons of this behaviour as an attempt to achieve anything.

- Avoid phrases such as 'I don't know what your parents are going to think …' or 'I don't know what (the Head) will say when s/he hears about this …' At the point of crisis an individual is unlikely to think rationally about the consequences of their actions. We would also have to question whether adding to the situation any feelings of fear, guilt or embarrassment that such a comment might engender would be at all helpful.

- Check your understanding using a phrase such as, 'Let me see if I've got this right, you're angry because …', or inviting more information by asking 'I'm not sure I understand, could you tell me a little more?' (Long 1999). These phrases are preferable to 'So what you're saying is …', which would convey more of a sense that the pupil's form of expression was inadequate or that the adult is able to say it better. Checking for understanding serves to slow the pace down which is a useful de-escalation technique and also shows that we are not just listening but are also keen to fully understand (Long 1999).

- Use positive affirmations such as 'Yes', 'right' and non-specific utterances (e.g. 'uh-uh', 'aha' and 'ehm') to demonstrate that you are listening and to encourage the speaker to continue. Combine this with body language such as the use of occasional nods and appropriate subtle changes in expression to show surprise, disbelief, concern and so on.

- Offer diversions. This might be in the form for example of giving the pupil the option of going to splash some cold water on their face, getting a drink or going for a walk around the playground. The purpose is to give them a way out of the immediate situation and provide time to calm down. With pupils who often exhibit angry behaviour it is possible for the teacher to have available a range of strategies such as running errands to another class that can be used at the initial sign of a problem developing.

- Use 'sorry' sparingly but effectively. You can be sorry even if you are not at fault in phrases such as 'David, I'm sorry this has happened' (Braithwaite 2001), or 'I'm sorry you're feeling like this.' If there is an element of fault on your part you can also acknowledge this by for example saying 'I'm sorry I shouted at you.' It is also possible to use a token concession (Long 1999) such as 'Yes, I admit I could have handled it better', as a strategy for diffusing current negativity within the relationship. Braithwaite (2001) advises that overuse of 'sorry' can cause it to lose its impact and risks misinterpretation as a manipulative tool.

Understanding more about anger

Anger is an emotional reaction to something that is perceived as a threat. Therefore, it is more accurate to view anger as an emotion that influences behaviour rather than a behaviour in itself. The display of anger and the surface emotionality associated with it will often cover up very different eliciting emotional states (Bowers 2005). Different people will display their anger in different ways, and different events will trigger different levels of anger in different people. This variability means predictably is difficult, so we need to become proficient at reading the signs. The variability can be explained by looking at anger in terms of the following:

Thinking

It is how the individual views an event that leads to the feeling. This is why several people can experience a similar event yet react to it in very different ways. There is an interpretive element. For example, a pupil who is given a detention by his teacher after a sequence of rule reminders and warnings might interpret this as 'It's fair enough, I could have chosen to knuckle down to the task when asked', or 'My teacher keeps picking on me, why can't she just get off my back?' This relates to considerations in Chapter 7 of locus of control and attributions.

Feeling

The interpretation leads to the feeling. The pupil who interprets the receipt of a detention as a result of their own actions may feel regret either at the level of recognising that their behaviour infringed the rules of the classroom, or that they were foolish not to heed the warnings or simply that they got caught. Whatever the reason for regret, it is likely to result in reasonably accepting behaviour. If however the interpretation is 'My teacher keeps picking on me, why can't she leave me alone', then this is likely to lead to feelings of anger in response to perceived injustice.

Behaviour

The behaviour is what results from the feeling. The form in which anger is expressed will be influenced by a range of factors, including inhibitions formed by prior learning in school, within the family and within the wider community. If for example, the individual has been instilled with a moral code which says physical aggression is wrong, the trigger and the subsequent feeling of anger experienced would need to be far greater to lead to this behaviour.

Different types of anger

Faupel *et al.* (1998) define three types of anger:

A response to frustration

This can take many forms. It may be frustration with ourselves because we have not met either our own expectations or the expectations of others who are important to us, it may be because we are prevented from doing something we consider we have a right to do, made to do something we do not think we should have to do, spoken to or treated in a way that we do not like or because we perceive something to be unjust. It is important to recognise the role of the individual's perception; therefore, for example, a reasonable request from the teacher may not be perceived as such by the pupil, causing frustration and possibly an angry response.

Instrumental

Anger can be used in quite a calculated way to get what we want (Faupel *et al.* 1998). Some children may learn at an early age that creating a fuss in a supermarket causes their parent/carer to give in and buy them the sweets that were originally denied. Developmentally this sort of incident may not cause us undue concern provided there are other occasions when the child is learning that they cannot always get what they want or that sometimes they need to wait. It is more problematic if older children and adults use anger in a manipulative or coercive way to achieve something they want.

A major difficulty with the concept of instrumental anger is our readiness to attribute behaviour to it. Even in the earlier example of the toddler throwing a tantrum to secure the packet of sweets there is a sense in which we are ignoring the frustration and ascribing motive. An alternative perspective is that developmentally this child is egocentrically focused on his/her immediate need which is not being met and is unable to articulate the frustration that this causes. To accept this is not to suggest that the response should be to buy the sweets as this is likely to have a reinforcing quality, but rather that we should avoid casting the child as a calculating individual who is rationally plotting to achieve a goal. Our readiness to judge anger as instrumental relates to the tendencies described in Chapter 7 to overemphasise personality, as opposed to situational attributes, as causes of behaviour (Chaplain 2003). If we extend this to a school setting, we need to be cautious in judging pupils' anger to be instrumental. Such a mindset leads us to a narrow set of responses rooted in the notion of 'not letting them get away with it.'

Pent-up release

Angry behaviour can be the result of pent-up emotions. A number of factors, possibly unrelated, may have contributed to this build up of anger. This release can be cathartic as we feel better for having released the physical and emotional energy that has been built up over time. The release can be triggered by a very small event. An example would be the pupil who comes to school with a high level of pent-up anger due to experiences at home overnight and then releases this in response to a minor positive correction from the teacher.

What do people do with their anger?

Displaced anger

Rather than directing their anger at the cause, the individual displaces this on to another person or object (Faupel *et al.* 1998). The everyday terminology for this is 'taking it out on somebody else'. An example would be the pupil who has been angered by an event at home displacing this on to their class teacher or one of their peers. The displacement occurs when there is some constraint preventing the individual from directing their anger at the source of this feeling. This might be because the individual recognises that it is unsafe or unwise to do so. A child in a physically or emotionally abusive home environment might justifiably feel angry about this but recognise that it would make matters worse to express this anger within this setting.

Practical reasons may also exist. Sometimes we cannot change a situation or series of events that have made us angry or we cannot get to the person who is the source of our anger. We may displace this anger on to someone else who perhaps causes us some minor irritation.

Expression of displaced anger may help the individual feel better temporarily but in the longer term it can be damaging to relationships as partners, friends and colleagues tire of being the subject of this displaced anger. Neither does it resolve the source of the conflict (Faupel *et al.* 1998).

Suppressed anger

Sometimes we may be consciously aware of our anger but choose not to express it (Faupel *et al.* 1998). In the right context this can be seen as a positive skill. We can use it to give us time to think through exactly how we wish to broach a difficult issue and so avoid hurting others' feelings or causing offence by a knee-jerk response. The danger is that strong feelings that are not expressed or resolved in some way may build up and leak out on to unimportant matters or result in an emotional explosion that causes more problems than expressing the anger originally would have done.

Repressed anger

Repressed anger can be thought of as anger which is affecting our behaviour but of which we are unaware (Faupel *et al.* 1998). It occurs as a result of past experiences we 'forget' because perhaps they are too upsetting or difficult to deal with at the time. The term repression is used extensively in the field of psychoanalysis which is based upon uncovering and working with the unconscious mind. To truly understand the causes of angry outbursts that emerge as a result of repressed anger we would have to help the individual bring the unconscious memories and feelings into conscious awareness. This may be beyond the skill-base and professional remit of the teacher.

The link with suppressed anger should be noted as too much suppression can lead to repression. In thinking about schools and classrooms we need to think carefully about the messages we give pupils about the expression of emotions. In this respect, the advent of SEAL materials at primary (DfES 2005c) and secondary (DfES 2007a) level and a concern for pupils' emotional health and well-being enshrined in *Every Child Matters* (DfES 2004a) outcomes and promoted through the National Healthy Schools Standards are positive developments. However pupils are subjected to a wide range of influences. Lawrence provides the example of a child told by a parent: 'There is no need to be upset! Don't cry. Only babies cry!' (Lawrence 2006: 89). If the child is frequently discouraged from expressing strong emotions and consequently tries hard not to cry or pretends not to be upset this may eventually lead to them denying the feeling of distress and relegating it to an unconscious feeling (Lawrence 2006).

Express ineffectively

Ineffective expression of anger may take a number of forms. Often it is anger that is out of rational control and may manifest itself in the form of verbal and/or physical aggression. Damage to relationships is almost inevitable. This may be in terms of the relationship with the individual who has been directly subjected to this anger or in terms of relationships with others who witnessed the display of anger. These witnesses may have experienced feelings of embarrassment or fear at the time which lead to future wariness towards the individual based on an awareness of their unpredictably and knowledge of what they are capable. It is important to remember that the person who has expressed the anger may also have feelings of regret and embarrassment that affect future relationships after their loss of control.

Express effectively

If anger is expressed effectively then it can provide an opportunity for learning and change (Faupel *et al*. 1998). Expressing anger effectively involves focusing on the issue and communicating our concerns and strong emotions without attacking either physically or verbally the other person. Faupel *et al*. (1998) make the distinction between 'problem' anger and 'normal' anger, which is useful in reminding us that everybody gets angry at some time or another and that it is how and where this anger manifests itself that determines whether it is a problem. However, we should remember that distinctions between 'normal' and 'problem' or 'effective' and 'ineffective' anger are subjective assessments made by the observer; for the individual the way the anger is expressed may seem neither problematic nor ineffective.

'But I don't go around hitting people!'

One reaction to this discussion of anger and attempts to understand the feelings that underlie the unacceptable aggressive behaviour that results may be a degree of frustration. We all have to put up with things we do not like and endure set backs and irritations from time to time but we do not tend to lash out verbally or physically. Davies and Frude (2000) provide a useful model that both helps us understand why some people may be more likely to display their anger in the form of violence and aggression and gives us clues to areas where we may be able to intervene proactively.

- *Situation*
  The 'situation' is the triggering event. Davies and Frude (2000) suggest that there are typically three elements that may lead to anger. These are:

  1   irritants – these might be aspects of the physical environment (e.g. loud or repetitive noise, smells, etc.), or the irritating actions of others;
  2   costs – of something, but also loss of status or 'face';
  3   transgression – these involve a person breaking a rule (or doing something 'out of order').

  We can work proactively with pupils to help them identify the things that make them angry and the strategies they could use to deal with the trigger or calming techniques to minimise its effect.

- *Appraisal*
  It is not the situation in itself that produces the emotional responses. To take the example provided by Davies and Frude (2000), it is not someone stepping on my toe that makes me angry but my appraisal of that situation. I may view it as deliberate or as an unfortunate accident. Many situations can, of course, be interpreted in a variety of ways, and the interpretation made by the individual will determine the emotional impact. There are a number of influencing factors on the appraisal an individual makes, including:

  - The way the individual usually views things – do they usually put a negative slant on events?
  - The individual's mood at the time – people who are already angry or pressured tend to view things in a more negative way.
  - What other people are saying about the situation – peers or others significant in the pupil's life may encourage a particular appraisal, by for example suggesting that a particular act was underpinned by malicious intent or that to not interpret it as hostile is a sign of weakness.

  We can work proactively with pupils through a variety of scenarios to help them to recognise the appraisals that they make and look at alternative appraisals that can be made that do not encourage such a strong emotional response.

- *Anger*
  As we covered earlier, anger is an emotional state which can, but does not necessarily in all individuals or on all occasions, lead to aggression. It does however need some form of outlet because, as outlined earlier, whilst suppressing anger can be a useful and necessary strategy, too much suppression can be problematic and lead to repressed anger which seeps out and influences our behaviour in ways we may not even be aware of.

  There are a number of proactive interventions we could use. We could seek to develop the pupil's emotional vocabulary so that they have the language to express their feelings. We could explore with the pupil ways of releasing their anger that are less likely to damage relationships or lead them into trouble. For some pupils cathartic activities such as hitting a punch bag or pillow may be helpful. The pupil could be supported in identifying possible relaxation and calm down activities that may work for them.

- *Inhibition*
  It is conceivable that two individuals may have been exposed to the same situation, made the same appraisal and experienced the same feeling of anger yet only one reacts aggressively or violently. This difference can be explained in terms of the individual's *inhibitions*. Table 11.1 distinguishes between 'internal' and 'external' inhibitions. You may be able to identify some others in each category.

Table 11.1 Internal and external inhibitors (based on Davies and Frude 2000: 21)

Internal inhibitors	External inhibitors
• Strong self-control	• Fear of physical retaliation. E.g. 'He's bigger than me – I could get hurt.'
• The individual is naturally disposed to – or has learned to – manage strong feelings.	• Fear of social consequences. E.g. Disowned by friends.
• Anticipated feelings of guilt. E.g. 'If I hurt this person I'll never be able to forgive myself.'	• Fear of other consequences, E.g School exclusion or police involvement.
• Moral inhibitions. E.g. 'I'm a pacifist – I don't believe in being physically aggressive.'	• Fear of embarrassment. E.g. 'I'll go red, my voice will go all squeaky and I'll just look silly.'
•	•
•	•
•	•

It is important also to recognise that inhibitions may be high toward the actual source of anger. The result may be the displaced anger that we referred to earlier, as the pupil directs their anger at a target where their inhibitions are lower.

There are a number of proactive interventions we can use. Through scenarios, role play, puppets and stories we can encourage pupils to make predictions about the different forms of consequence characters may encounter. We can use the SEAL materials to target self-regulation. We can make sure that school consequences are known to all pupils and we can use the elements of the Citizenship curriculum to explore potential legal consequences.

• *Aggression*

Aggression is the final stage of Davies and Frude's (2000) model. The term 'aggression' covers a wide range of behaviours ranging from the verbal through to the physical. Physical aggression covers a wide range of behaviours from aggressive or intimidating posturing through to pushing, pulling, hair grabbing, biting, punching, kicking and, at the most extreme end, use of weapons.

In a sense, the proactive strategies for the previous stages represent the proactive strategies for this stage. If we work on these we are attempting to reduce the likelihood of the pupil reaching this final stage. Thinking specifically about the 'aggression' stage however we can work with the pupil to ensure they know how to exit the situation when they recognise their anger is building rather than reaching the aggression stage. We can work with the pupil to identify an area that they can go to in order to calm down. It is important that the pupil contributes to choosing this. Simply imposing a location, such as the seats outside the secretary's office, is unlikely to work. Remember that the pupil will typically be accessing this at the point of crisis so it needs to be an area that comes to mind quickly, is easily accessible and does not require them to talk to anyone or seek permission.

We can ensure that a 'flight' response is available rather than intentionally or inadvertently standing in front of doorways. We can make sure that the pupil's seat is in a position that allows a quick exit should they wish to make a 'flight' response.

Summary

The consistent message from government reports (e.g. DES 1989, DfES 2005a) on behaviour in schools is that it is low-level persistent behaviour that concerns teachers most and that most pupils most of the time are well-behaved and work hard. This is a reassuring message and should inform where we put the majority of our efforts. However this does not change the fact that some times, some pupils engage in behaviour that is of a higher level or happens with such frequency that it has a damaging effect on the learning of the class.

This chapter has provided some coverage of strategies relevant to behaviour of a more challenging nature. To re-iterate a message from preceding chapters that is perhaps even more pertinent here due to the nature of behaviours covered; what we are effectively providing is a set of strategies and approaches that increase the probability of a more favourable outcome for both pupil and teacher on more occasions. Teachers cannot realistically anticipate and prepare for the entire range of pupil responses they will experience in the classroom (Powell and Tod 2004) and behaviours driven by anger in particular are especially unpredictable. However, even when pupils engage in behaviour that is of a higher level or happens with such frequency that it has a damaging effect on the learning of the class, we should still aspire to manage this situation in ways that protect and maintain the three relationships that underpin the development of learning behaviour.

Chapter 12

Reframing special educational needs (SEN)

'No matter how strange, behaviour always has a purpose or function.'

(Donnellan and La Vigna 1986)

Introduction

This chapter looks at how the behaviour for learning conceptual framework can be applied to those individual learners who may experience particular difficulty, delay or difference in developing the relationships that underpin their learning in school contexts. These learners are likely to include, but are not necessarily restricted to, those who are described as having special educational needs (SEN). Within this chapter we look at three different types of need: dyslexia, Asperger syndrome and social, emotional and behavioural difficulties (SEBD). We have selected these because they reflect three of the four categories of need taken from the *Code of Practice* (DfES 2001). These are *Cognition and Learning, Communication and Interaction*, and *Behavioural, Emotional and Social Development*.

The behaviour for learning conceptual framework endorses a bio-psycho-social view of individual diversity. The individual is not seen as the 'cause' of their learning difficulties. The individual pupil does however bring a unique combination of skills and dispositions based on biological factors and their own environmental, social and cultural backgrounds. This unique combination of skills and dispositions influence, and are influenced by, the interactions and experiences available in the pupil's school environment. In seeking to identify strategies to address behaviour we need therefore to address this dynamic and changing *interaction* between the individual and their school environment. This leads to the view that schools and teachers need to be *resourceful* in developing environments that are *responsive* to individual diversity. There is also a need to develop in individual pupils the *responsibility* and *resilience* needed in order to increase their chances of becoming beneficiaries of the learning environments in which they are placed.

For this to happen it is necessary to focus on promoting the learning behaviours in individuals that are required for the development and maintenance of positive learning relationships within schools and classrooms. This is irrespective of whether the individual has SEN or any other label. Some teachers may feel that they have insufficient SEN experience and, as with all learning, it is important that we do not start from a stance of what the teacher does not know or cannot do. For this reason the behaviour for learning conceptual framework places its primary focus on teachers' main area of expertise – that is the ability to promote learning in classroom contexts.

Many pupils with designations of SEN do have poorer longer-term outcomes from schooling than those without such designation (e.g. ICAN 2006). While this, to some extent, is not surprising given existing methods for identification and classification, it is a serious issue for the individuals concerned and society in general. As such SEN warrants the attention and concern that continues to be given to it by policy makers, academics and practitioners.

Readers will implicitly know that there are many sound principles, and tried and tested practices within the field of behaviour management that suffice for much of the time and allow the majority of pupils to learn, attain and achieve in the group setting of their classroom and school. However each individual will experience this provision differently and respond accordingly. This applies to all individual pupils whether they have a SEN label or not. In their search for solutions some teachers may still perceive SEN to be an area of practice in which a label or category carries with it a prescription for provision.

In an era of inclusion it is timely to take readers through our thinking in relation to our reframing of SEN within the behaviour for learning conceptual framework. This thinking is summarised in the bullet points below and expanded within this chapter:

* *Key point: Whether pupils with SEN require specialist assessment and teaching should not necessarily be the main focus for concern.*

  Traditional thinking about SEN involves placing children into 'categories' or assigning descriptors or labels based on a judgement about how far their learning and behaviour deviates from a hypothetical norm or average. This can lead to the following line of thinking: 'Daniel is messing about in class and having trouble reading and writing – he seems quite bright, maybe he is dyslexic – perhaps I should get him seen by the SENCO or suggest he gets referred to the educational psychologist. If he is dyslexic then I will need to find out how I should be teaching him.'

  In looking at this line of reasoning it is not without substance. Decisions about provision should be guided by assessment and investigation of individual learning and behavioural difficulties and this will *sometimes* require the involvement of outside agencies. It is also true that there is a body of knowledge and accompanying strategies that has been developed over the years for particular categories of SEN.

* *Key point: Categories of SEN do not contain homogeneous groups of individuals and the utility of a label is necessarily limited.*

  The core problem is that, even though the individual pupil may on testing have a cognitive and attainment profile that is consistent with a particular diagnostic category such as dyslexia, that particular individual will not exactly match the overall learning profile of a hypothetical typical dyslexic individual. Even if the pupil's cognitive profile is considered typical their social and emotional learning behaviours, that reflect their response to their dyslexia, will be different. Therefore what a teacher can predict about an individual pupil's learning and behaviour from a label is necessarily limited.

* *Key point: Social, emotional and cognitive aspects of learning are interdependent. An SEN label based on one area of difficulty may serve to restrict choice of strategies.*

  Another problem with tackling decisions about provision from a perspective that relies on labels and categories is that it limits potential for choices of strategies. If a pupil in their class has a label of SEBD the teacher's first thought might reasonably be to concentrate on the social and emotional aspects of learning. However while one individual with such a label may respond positively to having attention directly focused on their social and emotional problem another individual with the same label may find emphasis on how they are 'feeling' too much for them to handle at that point in time. Such a pupil may benefit more by having the emotional aspects of learning 'detached' from cognitive aspects. Strategies could include those that promote the development of learning behaviours through the pupil's engagement in routine, structured cognitive tasks in non-competitive contexts.

- *Key point: It is important to recognise and harness what the individual pupil brings to the relationship.*

  The use of the term *relationship* and the associated language is deliberate. It emphasises that the pupil is not a passive recipient of provision. It serves to focus attention on the skills and dispositions that the individual pupil with SEN *contributes* to the relationship. Some of these skills and dispositions may be very similar to those of their peer group or they may be distinctive and different.

- *Key point: Evaluation of strategy use is based on the pupil's experience of relationships and progress in learning.*

  In looking at provision for those individual learners who exhibit particular and significant difficulty, delay or difference in developing the learning behaviours required for building positive relationships we are conscious that they may have developed a cluster of learning behaviours that requires the teacher to focus on the *learning relationship* itself rather than any one underlying learning behaviour. The individual may have developed a cluster of these behaviours over a long period of time. It follows therefore that if the teacher successfully eliminates or reduces one specific behaviour (e.g. shouting out in class) the likelihood is that the pupil will simply replace this behaviour with another from their repertoire. A relationship is evaluated over time and observed inconsistencies in responses (e.g. 'bad days') should be balanced with overall progress.

- *Key point: There is an emphasis on what teachers bring to the relationship through their personal qualities and expertise in promoting learning.*

  Provision for SEN involves taking note of individual diversity but acknowledging that all pupils, including those with SEN need a classroom environment that places emphasis on building positive learning relationships. This provision is addressed in Chapters 8, 9 and 10.

- *Key point: The existing knowledge base for SEN, brokered through categories and labels, can provide access to overall principles and/or distinctive strategies that can be used in school settings.*

  For a few pupils, including some with SEN, there will be a need to make some adaptations to existing provision that involves applying existing strategies more explicitly, and with more intensity and/or frequency. Teachers may also need to consider provision that combines these adaptations with some 'different' strategies. It is important to note that such provision should be designed to be complementary and not compensatory.

As can be seen from the above key points, our reframing of SEN within the behaviour for learning conceptual framework affords teachers the following planning decisions when seeking to address behavioural issues in the classroom for pupils with SEN:

- What is the relationship that I need to promote for learning in a group setting?
- Is it better for the individual pupil if I focus directly on the target relationship or seek to develop it via one of the other two relationships?
- Is there a relationship area that I feel more confident/competent to work in initially?
- Which cluster of learning behaviours (or specific significant learning behaviour) do I need to promote in order to have a pervasive, positive effect on the relationship?
- What strategies, interventions and approaches can I use to promote the targeted relationship?
- What knowledge, skills and understanding does the pupil bring to this relationship?
- What knowledge, skills and understanding can I contribute to this relationship?
- Do I need any additional advice, guidance and support from within my school or from multi-agency partners?
- How will I know if I'm being successful in promoting the target relationship?

This planning cycle allows teachers to respond to the behaviour that is causing concern through their knowledge about teaching and learning in their classroom rather than being overly dependant on 'waiting for the SENCO and/or psychologist to come.'

In this chapter we have chosen three categories of SEN to explore using the behaviour for learning conceptual framework. *Cognition and Learning* is explored with specific focus on dyslexia; *Communication and Interaction* is explored with a specific focus on Asperger syndrome; and *Behaviour, Emotional and Social Development* as an overall category. We recognise, of course, that within each of the *Code of Practice* (DfES 2001) categories there are many other forms of need. It is hoped that the examples we have selected will provide illustrations of how thinking about special educational needs can be reframed via the behaviour for learning conceptual framework.

Inclusion and the behaviour for learning conceptual framework

As we highlighted in Chapter 1, pupils who exhibit differences or delay in learning and behaviour when compared to their same-age peer group have been the focus of considerable debate and ongoing policy changes. Since the early 1990s, and in response to global concerns around social and educational exclusion, the policy trend within the UK has been towards increasing inclusive policies and practices within mainstream school settings. However inclusion is not a clearly defined construct within educational contexts and means different things to different people (Ellis *et al.* 2008).

In practical terms it is easy to understand that in order for an individual pupil to be included we have to offer them more than just a *place* in a mainstream school. For an individual to *experience* being included in their classroom or school they need to be able to:

- *Access* (predominantly cognitive): approach, receive, actively process and respond to information and learning opportunities that are available from the curriculum.
- *Participate* (predominantly social): learn with and form positive relationships with others in the classroom.

- *Engage* (predominantly emotional): feel sufficiently emotionally settled and 'OK' with themselves to be able to learn in a group setting.

The behaviour for learning conceptual framework makes reference to inclusion through the terms 'access', 'engagement' and 'participation' as described above (see also Chapter 3). These terms illustrate the processes that underpin learning and support inclusion in group settings. These processes are fostered by the development of three relationships, which provide the focus for assessment, intervention, and positive change.

The behaviour for learning conceptual framework can be applied across contexts. As such it does not locate inclusive education within any one particular type of educational setting but focuses upon the experience and progress of the individual as the measure of inclusion.

Do pupils with SEN require specialist teaching?

Readers will be aware from Chapter 1 that there has been debate about the extent to which pupils who are categorised as SEN require special or different approaches. The DfES commissioned research which considered whether there is, or should be, a specific SEN pedagogy. The resulting report, *Teaching Strategies and Approaches for Pupils with Special Educational Needs* (David and Florian 2004), was clear in its statement that:

> The teaching approaches and strategies identified during this review were not sufficiently differentiated from those which are used to teach all children to justify a distinctive SEN pedagogy. This does not diminish the importance of special education knowledge but highlights it as an essential component of pedagogy ... questions about whether there is a separate special education pedagogy are unhelpful given the current policy context, and that the more important agenda is about how to develop a pedagogy that is inclusive of all learners.
>
> (Davis and Florian 2004: 6)

In spite of this finding, trainees and teachers continue to express concern about their lack of SEN expertise and training. A standards raising agenda alongside an inclusion agenda has prescribed a dual and interrelated challenge for schools through a focus on improving provision for all pupils alongside strengthening SEN expertise. Government guidance has reflected this dual approach through the provision of *Inclusion Development Programme* (IDP) support materials (www.standards.dcsf.gov.uk/sen) that seek to enhance SEN provision alongside materials and guidance to raise standards at whole-school level. Specific SEN support for trainees has been provided by the Training and Development Agency through the Teacher Training Resource Bank (www.sen.ttrb.ac.uk).

Our approach to issues of special educational needs and inclusion allows teachers to select from the full range of available strategies, irrespective of whether these are deemed to be 'special' or 'mainstream'. It is not the designation of the individual or the strategy as either 'special' or 'mainstream' that is important but the appropriateness of provision for the development and maintenance of the three relationships for learning. In seeking to explore SEN within the behaviour for learning conceptual framework we support the view expressed by Norwich and Lewis (2001) that there are common pedagogic principles that provide a classroom context that supports all pupils, including those with SEN, in developing good relationships with the curriculum. The fact that these principles and strategies are applied within the group setting of the classroom can result in insufficient precision and rigour needed for some individual pupils. Norwich and Lewis' (2001) synthesis of existing evidence bases led them to conclude that:

> the notion of the continua of teaching approaches is useful as it makes it possible to distinguish between the 'normal' adaptations in class teaching for most pupils and the greater degree of adaptations required for those with more severe difficulties in learning, those designated as having SEN. These are adaptations to common teaching approaches, what (*sic*) have been called specialised adaptations, or 'high density' teaching.
>
> (Norwich and Lewis 2001: 313)

Such 'high density' teaching within the behaviour for learning conceptual framework involves the manipulation of variables that underpin the development and sustaining of the three core relationships for learning. This might include varying the frequency of intervention, the intensity of intervention, and increasing the monitoring of the individual pupil's response to strategy use.

Cognition and Learning

Pupils who experience delays or differences in their *cognitive* development are likely to experience learning difficulties that directly affect their relationship with the curriculum. Such pupils are classified under the *Code of Practice* (DfES 2001) as falling into the SEN category of *Cognition and Learning*.

As described in Chapter 5, a relationship with the curriculum can be understood in terms of any other relationship even though we are dealing with a non–human component in the form of the curriculum. However the relationship is distinctive in school settings in that it is largely brokered by the teacher and typically has defined intended outcomes and purpose. As such this relationship requires the pupil to develop appropriate dispositions towards the curriculum and display learning behaviours that reflect 'willingness' and 'interest' along with some personal responsibility for maintaining this relationship. The skills needed by the pupil for this relationship are those that enable them to actively process information and monitor the efficacy of their activity in meeting curricular requirements. Hence within our behaviour for learning framework we use the term *relationship with* the curriculum rather than terms such as *access to* or *delivery of* the curriculum.

There is extensive guidance relating to pupils who have SEN (e.g. ATL 2002, TDA 2005, DCSF 2008a) for trainees and teachers. This section does not seek to replace such guidance but to reframe its utility in the context of the behaviour for learning conceptual framework. It is anticipated that this will support teachers in selecting the most appropriate strategies from these and other sources.

Pupils who experience difficulty in cognitive processing

Some individuals will experience significant difference, delay or difficulty with the cognitive demands involved in accessing and processing information required for making and sustaining a relationship with the curriculum. Some pupils have low levels of working memory and struggle to process, maintain, and store information simultaneously (Alloway *et al.* 2005). Such pupils would include those who have an overall developmental delay, those with language difficulties and those who are categorised as having dyslexia. In the next section we will consider what a pupil might experience if they have a difficulty with the interplay between the oral and written language systems that are used in school contexts to develop a relationship with the academic curriculum.

A closer look at dyslexia

Although pupils who experience specific difficulty with the interplay between oral and written language may share a label of 'dyslexia' their pattern of difficulties varies, as does their response. For this reason it has been argued that as a group they are not distinguishable or different from others who exhibit delay and difficulty with written language (Elliot 2005). However, the first tranche of *Inclusion Development Programme* (IDP) support materials (DCSF 2008a www.standards.dcsf.gov.uk/sen), have targeted dyslexia and the government has recently ordered a review of provision in schools for pupils with dyslexia.

The British Psychological Society (BPS 1999) defines dyslexia as evident when accurate and fluent word reading and/or spelling develops very incompletely or with great difficulty. Within the literature on dyslexia there is some consensus that pupils who share this categorisation exhibit:

• a *discrepancy* within their cognitive profile with weaker performance in those areas that necessitate that the sound system of language is represented and processed in the written format;
• a *delay* or *deficit* in the development of phoneme: grapheme correspondence, which in turn reduces the capacity of short-term memory and the efficiency of working memory;
• a *delay* in the development of automatic word identification;
• a *difficulty* in generating written (and sometimes oral) language in the sequence needed for accurate spelling and fluent communication;
• a *difference* in form and function of some areas of the brain.

(Tod 2000: 11)

Pupils with dyslexia are reported to exhibit and experience a wider range of difficulties than those that specifically impact on their progress with literacy. However it is clear from the above descriptors that their specific cognitive processing differences are likely to have a significant impact on their relationship with the curriculum.

Planning for relationship building

Knowledge about difficulties, delays and differences that are thought to characterise dyslexia, can be useful when trying to understand how a pupil might experience some aspects of their relationship with the curriculum.

Individuals with dyslexia might experience a number of feelings in school settings, including:

• *Confusion* and *frustration* from knowing that they can achieve in some areas of school work but struggle in others. They may not understand why this is when peers seem to read and write more quickly, fluently and without so much effort.

- Feelings of *uncertainty*, *anxiety*, and *annoyance* when having to manipulate information that requires changing it speedily from one format to another – usually oral to written. They may not be able to easily retain or make sense of such information – especially if a response is required within a given time frame.
- *Tired* from the effort it takes to cope frequently with written formats of language. It takes effort to copy from the board and most of all when the teacher requires the pupil to simultaneously listen, read and write.
- *Enjoyment* and understanding of books and written information when listening to someone else reading. This may be coupled with *frustration* at not being able to easily read *and* at the same time understand and retain this written information.
- *Cross* that it takes longer for them to read and write than others. It is hard to think what to write, put it in order, hold the words in the head and then break them down and build them up again. Homework can take a long time and yet the teacher may not know this. Work can look scruffy with spelling errors even when effort has been given to the task.
- *Sad* when work is not as good as that of their peers and 'fed up' when it is so hard to achieve success at school, particularly at secondary school.
- *Happy* when with friends talking and discussing but *worried* that a difficulty with written language might be seen as being 'thick' and 'stupid'.
- *Great* when people understand things from your perspective and work with you to improve things.
- *Brilliant* when you get things right or receive good marks.

We have already noted that every individual will have different experiences of their dyslexia resulting in a different balance of positive to negative feelings. The above list only gives a flavour of how dyslexia might affect a pupil's experiences.

Relationship with curriculum and impact on the other two relationships

Pupils with dyslexia and others who experience difficulty with the sound system of written language will have often learned to use oral language in a meaningful social context. Typically they will arrive at school with the ability to comprehend, reason and relate to others through the use of oral language. Much of the work in the classroom requires accessing, processing and reproducing language in a written form. To do this the pupil has to break down this *meaningful* language into what is for them *meaningless* sound components and then reformulate them in the sequence that reflects conventions for written communication, including correct spelling. It follows that the relationship between oral and written language needed for school learning is difficult to develop and sustain and this may lead to the individual pupil developing adaptive behaviours (e.g. task avoidance) that further impair their relationship with the curriculum and could result in them being reclassified as having a behavioural problem. This is illustrated in Scenario 12.1.

Scenario 12.1

Rupert has been assessed as exhibiting some learning difficulties that are considered to be characteristic of dyslexia. He brings to the class literacy task a negative view of himself as a learner of literacy. The class teacher, with Rupert's best interests at heart, allocates him some additional support from a Teaching Assistant (TA). At the end of the lesson Rupert is publicly praised for his effort. This makes him a focus for attention and he feels that his peers are making judgements about his lack of progress in literacy and generally about him 'being thick'. At the start of the next lesson he refuses to work with the TA, 'messes about' and is disciplined accordingly. He is then referred to the school's special educational needs coordinator (SENCO) as having a behaviour problem and this becomes a cause for concern about his progress – thus affirming to himself what he thinks others think about him.

In this example we can see that there is a dynamic interaction between the pupil's relationship with self, relationship with others and relationship with the curriculum. He and others in the classroom, including the adults, are seeking to make sense of their experiences and feelings and behave accordingly. In this case we can see behaviour changes that can occur within a relatively small space of time with all parties involved acting with purpose and 'making sense' of their ongoing experiences and actions.

- *Teacher*
  The teacher initially feels positive towards Rupert and allocates support and praises his efforts. The teacher then disciplines Rupert and feels that he now has a behaviour problem as well as a learning difficulty.
- *Teaching Assistant*
  The teaching assistant (TA) offers support. Rupert progresses well and the TA feels it appropriate to follow school procedures for 'reward'. The TA may then feel negative about Rupert once he refuses to work with him/her.
- *Peers*
  We do not know what Rupert's peers are learning. Some may feel that it is 'not cool' to be rewarded for good work and give some subtle negative feedback to Rupert. Others may think it is fine to be rewarded and in fact are not thinking Rupert is 'thick' – this perception is in Rupert's head. Some may see Rupert getting attention for refusing to work and be pleased by his interruption of the lesson whilst others may be irritated and annoyed with him. They confirm Rupert's own perceptions of his status among his peers through their behaviour towards him.
- *Rupert*
  Rupert feels he is not much good at literacy, then experiences success during the task. He feels embarrassed when praised. He then feels angry that the class procedures have 'made' his peers judge him negatively. He behaves so as to make sense of and confirm that he is no good at his work. His adaptive response is to avoid doing his work and in so doing he develops a revised identity as a 'behavioural problem'.

Rupert's case illustrates that many pupils who exhibit behavioural difficulties in the classroom also have an underlying learning difficulty.

Implications for the classroom

Pupils with dyslexia experience particular difficulty in relating to the curriculum because the input and output to this relationship frequently require different formats. For example, the teacher may be talking to the class with an expectation that the pupils will be making notes. In so doing the pupil has to simultaneously cognitively process and comprehend the oral language *and* translate this oral input into a written output. This demand on cognitive capacity is normally addressed in primary settings through the teacher emphasising the need to focus on sequential rather than simultaneous processing. For example, the teacher might talk to the pupils and then invite questions that serve to secure an understanding of the oral input. The teacher might support this further with mind-maps and writing frames. With these visual representations on hand the pupil then only has to concentrate on generating their own written response. The teacher has adapted their input and response requirements in order to develop and sustain the pupil's relationship with the curriculum. At secondary level learners have typically automated the translation of oral to written language forms. Therefore it is often assumed that they can apply their cognitive capacity to processing language, whatever its format. Clearly for some pupils, including those with dyslexia, this is not the case. Teachers often require pupils to multi-task, expecting them to read, listen, comprehend and write notes. This poses problems for pupils who have not automated the rapid interchange between oral and written language that is required in school contexts. The production of written language for pupils who experience dyslexia typically takes longer and requires more effort. Difficulties with spelling often remain a residual problem. Written work produced by some pupils may therefore provoke a response in teachers that the pupil has not given sufficient interest or time to the task, when in reality the production of work may have involved considerable attention and effort.

Transition from primary to secondary school may, through a change of teaching strategy, highlight the difficulties experienced by some pupils with dyslexia and, for some, lead to the development of social, emotional and behavioural difficulties that were not apparent in the primary setting.

A key point is that although the individual's underlying cognitive difficulty may stay the same, their *experience* of this will be dependent on the context in which they are placed and the strategies they develop both independently and with support.

Knowing more about the processing differences of a pupil with dyslexia does not necessarily allow the teacher to generate and select strategies. It does however allow for the essential prerequisites in forming a relationship with the pupil by understanding what they bring to the relationship. If a teacher understands more about the pupil's processing differences they are less likely to attribute the pupil's response to the curriculum as laziness, challenge or lack of interest. Such understanding engenders attention to the reciprocal components that underpin all relationships.

There are many strategies available for pupils with dyslexia (e.g. the *Inclusion Development Programme* materials (DCSF 2008a), Peer and Reid (2001) and Reid (2005)). The following list is intended to help readers to understand why a particular strategy might be useful in addressing the specific cluster of difficulties that characterise dyslexia and can impact negatively on a pupil's relationship with the curriculum. The list allows for an informed choice to be made from the many strategies that are available in published texts and via online support materials.

Understanding which strategies support relationships with the curriculum

- *Multisensory approaches*
  Typically relationships require communication and active processing of information. Multisensory approaches seek to stimulate all the available senses in order to give the pupil more support and choice in developing ways that best enable them to synthesise learn, retain and manipulate the oral and written components of language.
- *Meaningfulness*
  Effective relationships need to be meaningful if motivation is to be sustained. Pupils with dyslexia have relative strengths in comprehension and reasoning. Relating to the curriculum through written text initially involves breaking down meaningful language into *meaningless* sound components. Those with dyslexia experience specific difficulty with holding 'meaningless' material in their short-term working memory systems. Useful teaching strategies aim to allow individuals to give personal meaning to meaningless materials such as phonic sounds – thus the pupil may make a set of sound cards with, for example the 'i' sound represented by their own picture memory e.g. 'iguana'. Commercial schemes use similar approaches but it is important that pupils with dyslexia supply their own meaning as this supports active processing through personalisation.
- *Memory*
  Relationships with the curriculum require that information is retained in order that it can be processed and used. The most common problem for pupils with dyslexia is overload simply because they have often not automated basic decoding skills and all of these require attentional space. Memory skills are enhanced by *active* processing and any activity that encourages this is useful for all pupils. To support memory, it can be helpful for teachers to ask pupils to re-process information in a different format to the one they have been given (e.g. through mind maps, flow diagrams, presentations, 'discuss and explain to a peer', role-play etc.). In the case of pupils with dyslexia they usually need more practice and overlearning with phonics and additional support with generating their own written language, including spellings.
- *Metacognition*
  It is important that a pupil's relationship with the curriculum is reciprocal and that they play an active role. For this they need to develop self-knowledge about what has to be learned and how they are responding as a learner. The more understanding the pupil has of their own learning and the more they are able to adopt and/or develop the most effective strategies then the more *resilience* they will be able to develop. There are many strategies that encourage the development of metacognition through opening up debate with pupils on the process of learning rather than just the product. Strategies in use include study skills programmes that cover time management, organisation, setting personal targets, self-assessment and monitoring, reading skills such as skimming and scanning, listening skills, self-questioning, planning, revision strategies and so on.
- *Manageability*
  As mentioned previously, if a skill or activity cannot be carried out automatically and

still requires conscious effort then overload and breakdown of the processing system becomes a real threat. In the case of pupils with dyslexia who may not have automated activities involving written language, having to listen to the teacher, copy from the board and/or make notes, and think at the same time is clearly very difficult. Work needs to be pre-structured and planned. More time needs to be given for the production of work – or less written work given. This is not because such pupils are lazy, it simply takes them longer. It should also be remembered that a generic strategy of giving extra time to all pupils with dyslexia may not, in itself, suffice to address the range of individual variability in processing that characterises dyslexia. Pupils might need to make use of visual planners and electronic organisers, and preparation for coursework and exams need to be carefully structured if they are to complete on time. As we have indicated, thinking, reading, writing, spelling and checking is often done sequentially by pupils with dyslexia rather than simultaneously and teachers need to be aware of this if they are to work with the pupil to identify and develop appropriate strategies. As an example, the use of revision guides at the start of the course, rather than at the end, gives the opportunity for pupils to gain an overview of the syllabus and areas to be covered, estimate time frames involved, identify high risk areas in relation to their difficulty and gauge the relative worth of different areas in contributing to the overall grade.

In reducing the cognitive load any strategy that seeks to take information 'out of the mind' and transfer it into more permanent and accessible formats such organisers, lists and electronic formats will support pupils to manage their relationship with the curriculum.

- *Motivation*
Any relationship requires motivation on both sides for it to be initiated and sustained. Obviously a pupil who experiences success at school and in personal relationships is likely to be more motivated and successful, which in turn enhances the likelihood of maintaining or increasing positive self-perceptions (Blatchford 1992, Burns 1982). In contrast relatively negative feelings about self may result in less success and lead to reduced motivation and further impaired performance (Chapman 1998). Pupils with learning difficulties generally have been found to have lower self-perception (Lindsay and Dockrell 2000). Pupils tend to compare themselves with their peers and for those with dyslexia this comparison may lead to disaffection. There is a need to ensure that a required emphasis on skill development does not deprive pupils of balanced opportunities to access and engage with meaningful texts that are commensurate with their level of language and reasoning ability. This would involve parents/carers and teachers reading to their children in order to sustain interest, motivation, enjoyment and confidence in literature. Such an approach has been endorsed by research that has sought to improve teachers' knowledge and experience of children's literature in order to help them increase all pupils' motivation and enthusiasm for reading, and especially of those less successful in literacy (Cremin *et al.* 2008).

Motivation is relative and not absolute and it is necessary to target both the learning settings and the cognitive, social and emotional behaviours of the pupil – or, in the case of the behaviour for learning model, relationship with curriculum, relationship with self and relationship with others.

In looking at the key priorities for developing a positive relationship with the curriculum by using the example of dyslexia, it can be seen that the strategy groups above are entirely appropriate for building positive relationships with the curriculum for *all* pupils, including those with dyslexia. This supports Davis and Florian's finding that 'There is little evidence of the need for distinctive teaching approaches for children with specific learning difficulties although responding to individual differences is crucial' (Davis and Florian 2004: 5). 'Responding to individual differences' is likely to involve personalising these generic strategies through increasing the intensity and/or frequency of their use.

Which relationship should be prioritised?

In looking at the cluster of difficulties, differences and delays that characterise dyslexia, it is likely that in applying the behaviour for learning framework the teacher would prioritise developing the pupil's relationship with the curriculum. In seeking to do this there is a particular need for teachers and parents/carers of children with dyslexia to make sure that the child's relationship with self and relationship with others are not compromised. Schools have traditionally placed high value on written recording as a means both of acquiring and demonstrating acquisition of knowledge, skills and understanding. It is a challenge for schools not to create the impression that written recording is a very important skill because, of course, it is. However, pupils who experience difficulty with written language, including those with dyslexia, are conscripts to an environment in which they are required to spend a considerable proportion of their time doing something that they know they are not very good at. Inevitably such conditions are likely to impact negatively not only on the pupil's relationship with the curriculum but also on their relationship with self.

Providing opportunities for success involves identifying alternatives to written language production both in accessing (being read to, having story tapes, films etc.) and in responding through offering alternative forms of recording. A range of alternatives to written recording are provided in Figure 12.1. These have not been designed specifically for pupils with dyslexia but such pupils may find a number of them beneficial.

Building relationship with self provides a powerful route for supporting curriculum-based strategies and this in turn can be enhanced by working on relationship with others. In the case of dyslexia, using the pupil's relative strengths in the area of relationship with others offers opportunities to improve relationship with self through group work (Burton 2004). Parents/carers have an important role in supporting the development of the three relationships through their involvement in academic work (Goler and Booth 2008) and in building their child's confidence and competence through participation in other extra curricular pursuits.

The next section explores an example of a cluster of learning behaviours that has a pervasive effect upon the development of relationships for learning within group settings.

Communication and Interaction

Introduction

Relationship with others involves the social interactions that are linked to learning with others, such as listening, turn taking, and joining in aspects of school life as a member of the school community. It is concerned with how pupils interact socially and academically with others and is subsumed within the *Code of Practice* (DfES 2001) category of *Communication and Interaction*, described in the following terms:

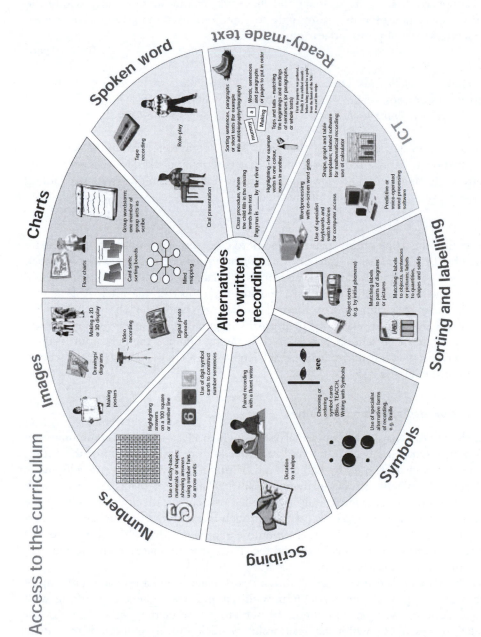

Figure 12.1 Alternatives to written recording (from DfES 2004j: 43).

© Crown copyright [2004] Department for Education and Skills (from DfES 2004j).

The range of difficulties will encompass children and young people with speech and language delay, impairments or disorders, specific learning difficulties, such as dyslexia and dyspraxia, hearing impairment and those who demonstrate features within the autistic spectrum; they may also apply to some children and young people with moderate, severe or profound learning difficulties.

(DfES 2001: 86)

Within the *Code of Practice* (DfES 2001) there is also emphasis placed on the pupil's participation in decision making processes about their own education. Citing the *United Nations Conventions on the Rights of the Child* Articles 12 and 13, the *Code* states:

Children, who are capable of forming views, have a right to receive and make known information, to express an opinion, and to have that opinion taken into account in any matters affecting them. The views of the child should be given due weight according to age, maturity and capability of the child.

(DfES 2001: 27)

It is not within the scope of this chapter or book to consider all examples of need that are subsumed by the *Code of Practice* category *Communication and Interaction*, so we have chosen to take a look at those individuals who experience particular difficulty with relationship with others and who are categorised as having an autism spectrum disorder (ASD). From the overall autism spectrum we have focused on Asperger syndrome. The reason for this choice is twofold. First, it is likely that the majority of pupils with Asperger syndrome will be placed in mainstream schools. Second, we frequently find it is the behaviour of these pupils, rather than their learning difficulty, that becomes the focus of concern for the schools in which they are placed.

A closer look at Asperger syndrome

Individuals with ASD have a developmental disorder which affects social and communication skills. Asperger syndrome is often referred to as the 'high functioning' end of the autism spectrum as it is characterised by higher levels of language and cognitive development. The school environment includes many potentially challenging elements for a pupil with Asperger syndrome. They will typically experience particular difficulties in building the relationships with others needed for learning through interaction with teachers and peers in group settings. People with Asperger syndrome experience difficulties in the areas of social communication, social interaction and social imagination. This is often referred to as the 'triad of impairments' (Wing and Gould 1979).

The behaviour for learning conceptual framework places emphasis on the building of positive relationships with the curriculum, with self and with others. In working with pupils with Asperger syndrome it is therefore useful to give some thought to preparing for these relationships. Ideally within any relationship we seek a 'meeting of minds' so that we can be sensitive to other person's needs, and they to ours. This is not easy as individuals with Asperger syndrome find it difficult to understand what others are thinking and those who do not have Asperger syndrome can only surmise about the 'mind' of pupils with the condition. In thinking about the relationship issues within the classroom both pupils with Asperger syndrome and their teachers and peers who do not have the condition can be seen as being 'outside each others' culture' and unable or struggling to tune into the meanings that are embedded within each others' social world.

The following section does not list 'difficulties' as these are found in abundance in books on autism. Instead it seeks to allow us to think about, through the use of the existing knowledge base, how a person with Asperger syndrome might experience their differences in the classroom. Our use of terms such as 'happy' and 'confused' are intended to allow us some understanding of the nature – positive or negative – of the experience, although we acknowledge that the person with Asperger syndrome may not share our understanding of those terms. We are also using a hypothetical person and it is important to note that although as a group those individuals with Asperger syndrome may share diagnostic indicators each individual will manifest different behaviours and have different experiences in their schools and classroom environments.

Preparing for a relationship with a pupil with Asperger syndrome in the classroom

In this section we look at the experiences a pupil might have in a classroom setting that emanate from the triad of impairments that is characteristic of autism. This should support teachers and peers to prepare to relate to a pupil with Asperger syndrome.

Experiences of social communication

The National Autistic Society website notes: 'If you have Asperger syndrome, understanding conversation is like trying to understand a foreign language' (National Autistic Society (NAS) website: http://www.autism.org.uk/nas/jsp/polopoly.jsp?d=212).

This observation has a number of implications for the experience of individuals, including:

*   Frustration and anxiety about not being able to express feelings or easily relate socially to others.
*   Feeling confused and bewildered by seeing, but not understanding, the rapidly changing gestures and facial expressions of others.
*   Feeling under pressure when having to decide what to talk about and not easily knowing when to start or end a conversation.
*   Feeling able to use complex words and phrases but feeling less confident about what they actually mean.
*   Feeling perplexed when rules of language don't apply and meaning is changed by others when they want to. An example of this is when people say 'pull your socks up' and sometimes they want you to perform that action and sometimes it means 'work harder' or 'get moving' or something else. They don't tell you which one they mean, but other people seem somehow to just know.
*   Feeling lonely when other people are laughing at a joke or a remark that does not seem to be particularly interesting or different from other things they are saying.
*   Feeling scared when others keep making comments that include your name or say words that are called 'swearing' or 'spiteful'.

Experiences of social interaction

Many pupils with Asperger syndrome want to be sociable but have difficulty with initiating and sustaining social relationships. This can lead to the following feelings and experiences for children:

- Wanting to play with others but not knowing what to do. Play seems to be something others like to do and so you have to do it if you want friends. Play keeps changing all the time so it is difficult to learn what others want you to do.
- Wanting to be with others but at the same time getting easily cross with people because they are annoying or because it takes a lot of concentration and effort trying to work out why they are doing what they are doing and how to get them to like you.
- Feeling cross when the teacher asks you a question and you tell them the answer and they are not pleased. The teacher asks you not to answer but lets other people answer first. They say this is 'waiting your turn' and if you do this they are pleased.
- Being cross when others push you away or the teacher tells you off when you get very close to people or touch them when you are just trying to get their attention or be friends.
- Having to do things that are not interesting but other people want you to do them.
- Feeling anxious when the teacher says things like 'how do you think John feels when you push him out of the way?', and you do not know the answer.
- Feeling sad when the person who was your friend on Tuesday is now not your friend and you do not know why.
- Feeling anxious when the teacher says 'Now you can go out to the playground', but does not say if we are coming back.

Experiences of social imagination

People with Asperger syndrome experience differences and difficulties with regard to *social imagination*. This can lead to the following feelings and experiences:

- feeling worried because of being unable to imagine and predict what people are going to do next;
- feeling inadequate by being expected to guess what other people are thinking and feeling; others can make good guesses but you do not know how they do this;
- feeling less anxious when you are allowed to keep repeating movements and following routines so that you can predict what is going to happen;
- feeling anxious when people stop you from doing what they call rituals and repetitions;
- having no idea what 'let's pretend' means and not knowing why other children make tea and cook in the play house when they do not end up with a cup of tea to drink or something to eat.

In addition to the triad of impairments, some individuals with autism may also experience hypersensitivity to auditory, visual and kinesthetic features of their physical environment. This hypersensitivity may manifest itself in a range of behaviours that are seen by the teacher and others to be 'odd' and/or disruptive, particularly given that the teacher often has no idea that the trigger for such behaviour was this hypersensitivity.

In seeking to build a relationship with pupils with Asperger syndrome it is necessary to try to understand what purposes their seemingly 'odd' behaviours are serving. This should result in a change of thinking that accepts that these behaviours, far from being odd, are *adaptive* and can be understood and discussed as such. Furthermore, it is useful to look at the behaviours and feelings that a pupil with Asperger syndrome shares with those with whom they seek to have a relationship and that may be exhibited, albeit less frequently and with less intensity, by most 'neurotypical' (Sinclair 1998) individuals.

Reflective Exercise 12.1

Sainsbury (2001) states:

> Many people with Asperger's syndrome, like me, spontaneously compare themselves to extraterrestrials – one woman on the internet brilliantly describes autism as "Oops-wrong-planet" syndrome – or to humans on an alien planet (as in Temple Grandin's famous self-description as an 'anthropologist on Mars'). Others find a kindred spirit in *Star Trek*'s Mr Spock, perpetually baffled by the illogical behaviour of humans, or his successor in *Star Trek: The Next Generation*, the literal-minded android Data.
>
> (Sainsbury 2001: 19)

Based on this quote from a book written by a person who has Asperger syndrome, consider how you might feel if you had landed on Mars and could not fully understand the language, interpret the inhabitants' social behaviours, and could not predict from your own knowledge and experience how these Martians might behave. You might also not be used to, or indeed comfortable with, the physical features of the environment.

How might you adapt and respond?

- Would you set up some routines to make your world more predictable and give you some sense of control?
- Might you appear to be aloof at times to the Martians?
- Would you try and find things to do that had a purpose for you – even though they are odd to the observing Martians?
- Would you at times 'go crazy' with frustration?
- Might you avoid social contact with Martians at times and find a safe place of your own?
- Would you feel very isolated because you were 'not one of them'?
- Would you get very stressed and worried if the Martians tried to make any close contact with you?
- Would you know when to join in with their activities?
- Could you think of anything to say to them – and if you did, would you feel embarrassed if they did not respond as you had hoped?

What would you like the Martians to do in order to enable you to live and learn on Mars?

Reflective Exercise 12.1 is designed to stimulate thinking about how you might respond if you were in a situation similar to that experienced and encountered by pupils with Asperger syndrome on a daily basis in a school context. It can be seen from this exercise how important it is to consider the notion of the three relationships that underpin the behaviour for learning conceptual framework. While we understand the processes involved in relationships, and their interdependence and notions of reciprocity, it is more difficult for us to understand the experience of school relationships for individual pupils with Asperger syndrome.

If we look at how such developmental differences affect the behaviour of pupils with Asperger syndrome in class, we can see why teachers and schools may classify such pupils as having social, emotional and behavioural difficulties.

Implications for relationship building

It is useful for teachers and others to try and address the question: 'How are relationships with curriculum, self and others being *experienced* by a pupil in my class with Asperger syndrome?' Learning to understand what things mean cannot be accomplished alone, and traditionally in school contexts we use personal relationships to build and develop this meaning. As noted earlier in the book, building relationships involves a 'meeting of minds' and this is an area of particular difficulty for pupils with Asperger syndrome. Many (e.g. Baron-Cohen 1995) refer to such individuals as not having a 'theory of mind' that they can use to understand and respond to the social behaviour of others. However, individuals with Asperger syndrome have strengths in that they are able to pay attention to detail and develop and retain knowledge in particular areas of interest to them.

Relationship with the curriculum

Many pupils with Asperger syndrome in mainstream classrooms can and do exhibit a strong, if narrow, relationship with the curriculum. They may differ from their classmates in that they are much less teacher-led, more persistent and self-directed, and will often choose to pursue their particular curriculum to the exclusion of contact with peers and others. The manner in which areas of interest are pursued was noted by Baron-Cohen (2008) to be a characteristic feature of autism. This he called 'hyper-systematising' and described it as the drive to construct any kind of system – or set of rules – that govern the system so that it is possible to predict how that system will behave.

Examples of hyper-systematising by individuals with Asperger syndrome given by Baron-Cohen include:

- *natural systems*: learning the Latin names of everyday plants and their growing conditions;
- *motion systems*: analysing exactly what specific events occur in a repeating cycle.

Baron-Cohen (2008) has attempted to explain his view that the characteristics of Asperger syndrome include both a lack of 'theory of mind' *and* hyper-systematising by concluding that a two-factor theory – the empathising–systematising (E–S) theory – is required:

1   a theory that explains the observed social and communication difficulty by reference to delays and deficits in empathy – 'mindblindness'.

2   a theory that explains areas of strength by reference to intact or even superior skills in systematising – 'hyper-systematising'.

Building relationships with pupils who experience particular difficulties in these areas requires that teachers and peers seek to understand the reasons behind the behaviour and understand the adaptive nature of this behaviour from the pupil's perspective. The classroom can be a frightening and confusing place for pupils with Asperger syndrome and predictably there is no one definite teaching method.

Strategies for building relationships in school contexts

In applying the behaviour for learning conceptual framework we have started by thinking about what a 'typical hypothetical' pupil with Asperger syndrome might experience in a classroom setting. From this we can be clearer about the core *purpose* behind our choice of possible strategies. These core purposes underpin the many strategies that are available in a variety of guidance and texts (e.g. Plimley and Bowen 2006) for use with pupils with Asperger syndrome in mainstream and other settings. The core purposes are:

1   To address the anxiety and uncertainty experienced from receiving too much stimulation and information. Strategies are chosen to stabilise emotions, and provide a more predictable environment within which the pupil can begin to develop independence.
2   To recognise and build on particular strengths that the pupil brings to the relationship. Such strategies aim to stimulate intellectual and cognitive growth through a broad and age appropriate curriculum that allow for individual interest and talents to flourish and success to be achieved that is of value to the individual. In selecting and implementing strategies, teachers need to take account of any individual modifications necessary for each individual pupil.
3   To promote communication necessary for relationships to develop with self and others. This is likely to involve adaptations to existing strategies and contexts or use of distinctive approaches for inter- and intra-personal communication that take account of the particular social differences that characterise pupils with Asperger syndrome.

Teachers can select from existing strategies those that best meet the purposes outlined above for any particular individual in their class. Some of these (e.g. visual timetables, adjusting of communication style to make implicit instructions explicit, use of ICT to support learning, avoidance of exaggerated praise or positive touch to acknowledge success, working closely with parents/carers and others involved, and acknowledging the need for personal space) can be used at whole-class or small-group level. For some individuals there will be a need to make greater adaptations to teaching. Specialist strategies for pupils with Asperger syndrome consistent with the above generic purposes and useful for building relationships with self and others include:

- *Picture exchange communication system (PECS)*
  PECS uses visual ways to enhance and facilitate communication. It initially aims to promote functional communication (Liddle 2001).
- *Social stories* (Gray 1994a, Smith 2003)

These 'stories' give pupils access to information about social activities and relationships in a clear format so that they can 'follow' this format in real social situations. Working on relationship with others through explicit means such as use of social stories could be a useful way of improving reference points for pupils with Asperger syndrome as they construct and understand their relationship with self.

- *Treatment and education of autistic and related communication handicapped children (TEACCH)* (see Howley and Mesibov 2003)

  TEACCH starts with what the pupil brings to the relationship and capitalises on existing strengths and interests, even if those interests might appear peculiar from others' perspectives. The TEACCH approach pays due regard to the physical environment and to the use of schedules and work systems that promote predictability and independence.

- *Comic-strip conversations* (Gray 1994b)

  Comic-strip conversations are a technique used to solicit a pupil's understanding of a social interaction (Gray 1994b). It has been found to be useful when following up a social incident that requires the pupil to reflect upon and account for their actions. This activity can serve to reduce anxieties for the pupil and provide a shared medium for discussion with the teacher.

We now move on to examining in more detail how we promote learning behaviours in pupils who are referred to as having social emotional and behavioural difficulties.

Social, emotional and behavioural difficulties

Introduction

In considering autism spectrum disorders and dyslexia we started from the perspective that pupils who are categorised in this way shared some characteristics in common with others in the same category. Effectively, to be placed in one of these categories requires the pupils to display a *cluster* of difficulties that potentially negatively impact on their learning in class contexts. Our argument was that the teacher, through being aware of some of these common characteristics, would have some knowledge of what the pupil brought to the relationship. Even if the teacher did not have experience in the area, just this awareness that the pupil may be viewing the world differently (in the case of autism) or processing information differently (in the case of dyslexia) would encourage a more responsive, reciprocal relationship.

As we considered in Chapter 2, SEBD is an exceptionally broad category, stretching from withdrawn behaviour through to severe 'acting out' behaviour, and also includes categories with a biological dimension such as Attention Deficit Hyperactivity Disorder (ADHD). There may be very little that pupils sharing the SEBD label have in common. All we might broadly be able to identify is that they do not relate to others in the manner generally expected, or required, in group settings. Arguably, this is true for those who exhibit withdrawn behaviours as well as those who are disruptive, aggressive or violent. The distinguishing feature of SEBD is that the pupil exhibits social and emotional aspects of behaviour that may be:

- more frequent;
- more intense;
- persistent;

- resistant to the influence of the behaviour management techniques usually employed by the school;
- negative in their effect on peers and teachers.

The *Code of Practice* (DfES 2001) is predicated on a staged approach which assumes levels of need that the school is required to address. This allows schools to plan provision with early identification and intervention as a priority. In the case of pupils with SEBD, their behaviour is particularly susceptible to changes in their school and home environment and as such their need is variable. This raises the question of whether a pupil with SEBD who is behaving well has SEBD. We might also speculate on how long a pupil has to go without incident to no longer be considered to have SEBD. Or could we liken SEBD to an allergy? The individual still has it, but it lies dormant all the time they are not exposed to particular triggering contexts and conditions.

Such considerations demonstrate the challenges posed for schools in determining whether a pupil has SEBD, identifying appropriate strategies and allocating necessary resources.

Using the behaviour for learning conceptual framework

As noted previously in the book, the behaviour for learning conceptual framework is rooted in building relationships for learning. Of all the SEN categories, SEBD is perhaps the one that most reflects the interdependence of the three relationships for learning. The inclusion of the terms 'social' and 'emotional' should definitely not preclude teachers from paying due regard to the pupil's relationship with the curriculum as either a cause for, or a route to, addressing behavioural concerns.

Relationship with the curriculum as the target relationship

Pupils with SEBD cover the full range of ability. However their difficulties are likely to be a barrier to academic learning. Learning difficulties and behaviour difficulties are often characterised by a reciprocal relationship. For some pupils, behaviour difficulties may frustrate access to the curriculum, for example if the presenting behaviour is such that it leads to exclusion from some classroom activities or from the school. For others, a learning difficulty may lead to or exacerbate behavioural and emotional difficulties. For example, a pupil who has difficulty in grasping the basics of literacy or numeracy may withdraw from lessons or try to divert attention away from their learning difficulty by disruptive behaviour. The DCSF (2008b) suggest that difficulties in acquiring basic skills can also lead to low self-esteem and even depression, providing a salient reminder that difficulties with regard to the pupil's relationship with the curriculum may impact on relationship with self. By the time behaviour has reached the stage of being classified as a social, emotional and behavioural difficulty it can be difficult to tell whether a deteriorating relationship with the curriculum preceded and contributed to difficulties in relationship with self and relationship with others or vice versa. The interdependent nature of the relationships also means that even if a poor relationship with the curriculum was the cause, perhaps through an unrecognised learning difficulty, measures to address this may be frustrated by the difficulties that have developed with regard to relationship with self and relationship with others.

Relationship with others as the target relationship

The presenting behaviour will often determine the nature of the pupil's relationship with others. Aggressive behaviour in particular is likely to alienate teachers and peers, especially those it is directed towards. Research has been consistent (e.g. Clough and Lindsay 1991, Croll and Moses 2000, Avramidis *et al.* 2000) in suggesting that teachers view the integration or inclusion of pupils with SEBD in mainstream schools as particularly problematic. This is understandable given that the types of behaviour presented by many pupils with SEBD do not lend themselves to the development of positive reciprocal relationships that underpin learning in group settings. The fact that the teacher may experience the pupil's behaviour as a personal or professional threat is not conducive to the development of a positive relationship. The variability of some pupils' behaviour, often due to emotional factors, can also lead to the teacher feeling 'let down' or even betrayed. Sometimes headway is made in the relationship, often through compromise or considerable effort on the teacher's part, and the pupil then does something that undermines this. In short, the pupil's relationship with others, including that with the teacher, is frequently vulnerable. Because of the teacher's responsibility for the group they will also have to impose sanctions, often knowing that this will not change the pupil's behaviour, which again is not conducive to a good relationship.

Peers' relationships with the pupil are likely to be strongly influenced by the presenting behaviour. Unpredictable behaviour, particularly that which is physically and/or emotionally hurtful to others, is unlikely to lead to durable positive relationships with others.

Within a consideration of relationship with others it is also important to recognise that a significant proportion of pupils experiencing behavioural difficulties also experience communication difficulties (Cross 2004, ICAN 2006). As Cross (2004) debates, though these difficulties occur together we cannot necessarily conclude that the link is causal. However teachers need to be aware of the association between communication disorders and behaviour problems when the pupils involved have difficulty in areas such as constructing language to express themselves, and in understanding the language needed in order for them to respond to the teaching and learning opportunities on offer in group settings.

Relationship with self as the target relationship

The term 'social, emotional and behavioural difficulties' highlights that there is likely to be an emotional component to the presenting difficulty. Because of the understandable angst the behaviour of pupils with SEBD can engender this is sometimes overlooked. Bowers (2005) conducted research looking at the Statements of Special Educational Need of 16 pupils with SEBD. He found plenty of descriptions of behaviour but only limited reference to emotions. Examples of emotions within the pupils' statements including 'low self-esteem', 'low self-confidence', 'anxiety', 'frequent mood swings', and 'anger'. In a similar study Swinson (2008) found that self-esteem was included in 34 out of 35 statements of pupils with SEBD in one Local Authority. Interestingly, and of concern, is that the inclusion of self-esteem within the Statement did not necessarily reflect the needs of the pupil as described by those who had been asked to provide evidence to the authority as part of the statutory assessment procedure. In this instance a need was assumed as belonging to the SEBD category but was not based on any detailed assessment or standardised information. The assumption that low self-esteem is a necessary characteristic of SEBD is not backed by research evidence where both very low and very high self-esteem have been identified in only a proportion of individuals within the category (e.g. Emler 2003, Swinson 2008) Through identifying low self-esteem as effectively a special educational need there is a message to teachers that they should 'enhance it' for those pupils with SEBD. Smith (2002) points out that the enhancement of self-esteem in itself is not a chief aim of education, nor is the provision of therapeutic approaches. We share his view that self-esteem is just one of the outcomes of school experiences. For this reason we prefer to use the term 'relationship with self' to cover the range of terminologies used to explain the emotional aspects of individual learning behaviour and seek to provide school learning experiences that positively influence the development of this relationship.

The behaviour for learning conceptual framework is concerned with how pupils *experience* the learning opportunities on offer in their school context and as such pays due regard to how individuals make sense of their world.

In building relationships with pupils it is paramount that we seek to understand the processes and purposes that underpin this 'making sense' function. As noted throughout the book, behaviour that serves a purpose for the pupil and is thus *adaptive*, can be troublesome to others.

The skill and will behind learning behaviour

As stated earlier in this chapter, in seeking to improve a target relationship we would normally aim to identify and improve the cluster of learning behaviours that will have a pervasive, positive effect on it.

Within Chapter 4 we noted that commonly cited learning behaviours reflect both skills and dispositions ('will'). It is significant that the 2007 guidance document on behaviour policies (DfES 2007b) distinguishes between pupils who do not have the necessary understanding or skills, pupils who can behave but choose not to, and pupils who have the necessary competences but 'are experiencing such stress that they are temporarily unable to make rational choices' (DfES 2007b: 57). Whilst this is an artificial distinction, and the categories themselves are not mutually exclusive, they can act as reminder that for some pupils the issue may be more one of disposition than a lack of skills, or vice versa. This has implications for strategy choice and reflects, in behaviour for learning terms, the important distinction between the 'skill' and 'will' components of behaviour as well as the interdependence of those components.

Strategy selection

There are numerous strategies available for pupils with SEBD and many of these will already be known to readers and their schools. It is also salient to note Ofsted's (2005a) observation that the most effective teaching for pupils with the most difficult behaviour is little different to the most successful teaching for others. Therefore, many of the strategies and approaches outlined in Chapters 8, 9 and 10 will continue to be applicable. As part of a continua of teaching approaches, a few pupils with SEBD will require greater levels of adaptation, involving variations in the frequency and intensity of intervention and subsequent monitoring of pupil response. This may involve additional staffing and support from multi-agency partners. Although there will be an overlap of elements of practice within and between these strategies we have sought to group them according to the core *purpose* against which they will be *evaluated*.

Strategies for pupils with SEBD typically fall into five main categories that reflect their overall purpose and address concerns about both 'will' and 'skill':

- to bring about changes in the school context and conditions;
- to improve the skills of pupils with SEBD;
- to change the observable behaviour;
- to promote thinking about the behaviour;
- to address deep-rooted, entrenched and sometimes subconscious emotional elements of behaviour.

CHANGING CONTEXTS AND CONDITIONS

This group of strategies involves bringing about changes to the contexts and conditions and are often referred to as systemic approaches. In behaviour for learning terms, systemic approaches are evaluated against the extent to which they promote the development of learning relationships and improve the pupil's learning behaviour(s).

Systemic approaches should always be the starting point in preparing to improve any of the three behaviour for learning relationships and aspects of this have been covered in Chapters 8, 9 and 10. Certainly where a significant number of pupils present as SEBD it would be important to identify factors within the environment that serve to maintain or exacerbate behavioural difficulties.

When thinking about an individual pupil (or groups) there are two key questions to ask:

- In what situations does the behaviour occur? *In what settings/contexts, with which others?*
- In what situations does the behaviour NOT occur? *In what settings/contexts, with which others?*

(Watkins and Wagner 2000)

In answering these questions it is important to think about all aspects – including the teacher, the peers who are present, the subject, the type of lesson and the physical environment. This systemic approach represents a systematic form of problem-solving essentially asking, 'under what conditions does the pupil behave best?' The teacher can then seek to replicate these conditions across a range of lessons. In the case of a few pupils, the behaviour is serving such a significant purpose for them that it is for much of the time impervious to contextual changes.

IMPROVE THE SKILLS

In operating strategies that seek to improve skills it is assumed that the problematic behaviour presented by some pupils can be attributed largely to a delay or difference in the skills expected of their age group for learning in group settings. Skill areas linked to SEBD that can usefully be developed or enhanced include:

- language and communication skills;
- essential curriculum skills (e.g. subject knowledge, study and organisational skills);
- social skills;
- conflict resolution skills.

For all of these areas there are either universal programmes (e.g. SEAL, circle time, thinking and study skills) or targeted programmes (e.g. social skills and anger management groups, the *Social Use of Language Programme* (Renaldi 2001)) for groups and individuals. Although such programmes are often structured around the development and rehearsal of *skills*, (e.g. SEAL and circle time), they also necessarily, and often intentionally, impact on how a pupil thinks and feels. As such they may influence both the 'will' and 'skill' components of learning behaviour.

CHANGING THE OBSERVABLE BEHAVIOUR

This approach is rooted within behaviourist theory that, in its essence, sought to minimise reference to the cognitive aspects of human behaviour. It is concerned with bringing about changes in observable behaviour in response to different configurations of 'rewards' and 'punishments'. A standard approach seen in schools is the use of overt and more subtle reward schemes. For pupils with SEBD these may be individualised. For example, in a primary school a pupil might have their own sticker chart. The general principle is that a target behaviour is identified, taught and rehearsed if necessary, and then reinforced by a reward. The apparent simplicity of the behaviourist approach belies the skill required for its effective use.

Schools are usually very aware of the problem behaviour, but the element that is frequently missed is the identification of antecedents and consequences. If the teacher can identify the antecedents, which may be in the form of people, events or environmental factors it is possible to alter these or at least be aware of when a potential trigger situation is developing and intervene early. The use of the term 'consequences' here simply refers to what happens after the behaviour. This might, for example, be that peers laugh, the teacher gives attention or work is avoided. This potentially gives the teacher an indication of what is serving to reinforce the behaviour. It might then be possible to change the consequences in some way to remove the reinforcement. The obvious example is where teacher attention seems to be reinforcing the behaviour. The teacher might make a point of withholding attention when the pupil displays this behaviour but giving attention when the required behaviour is demonstrated. A number of potential limitations associated with a behaviourist approach are identified in Chapter 8. This type of approach may have utility in promoting a specific learning behaviour but it should be recognised that the unwanted behaviour the teacher is attempting to target may be serving an important purpose for the pupil and so may be very resistant to change. This is particularly the case for pupils with SEBD.

CHANGING THE THINKING ASSOCIATED WITH THE BEHAVIOUR

It is often possible and desirable to bring about improvements in the behaviour of pupils with SEBD through systematic use of behaviourist approaches, combined with systemic changes. This sets the scene against which we can progress to develop in individuals the thinking they need in order to develop resilience to the many situational changes they experience in their school, family and community. For some pupils the internal processes and explanations they have developed around their behaviour serve to render them relatively impervious to systemic changes and behaviourist approaches.

Whether we tackle this thinking explicitly or implicitly will depend on the extent to which, from the pupil's viewpoint, the presenting behaviour must be retained. It is necessary to keep in mind that for some pupils with SEBD the behaviour is the solution, irrespective of whether for the teacher, or others, it is a problem. An example might be the pupil who disrupts lessons to avoid work and so protect themselves from the risk of failure.

The collection of strategies designed to address the links between thinking and behaviour generally fall within the category of cognitive behavioural approaches. When approaching behaviour from this perspective a teacher would be concerned with factors such as the pupil's attributional style, their perceived level of self-efficacy and whether they have an internal or external locus of control. Readers will note from Chapter 7 that these are all factors that predominantly relate to relationship with self. If the target relationship is 'self' then cognitive-behavioural approaches offer some scope for intervention. Emler (2003) suggests that those programmes that use a broad cognitive-behavioural approach seem to be particularly successful in bringing about changes in self-esteem.

ADDRESSING DEEP-ROOTED, ENTRENCHED AND SOMETIMES SUBCONSCIOUS EMOTIONAL ELEMENTS OF BEHAVIOUR

In the previous section it can be seen that cognitive-behavioural approaches can be applied at group as well as individual level. However, for some pupils the depth and purpose of their thinking underpinning the behaviour is such that either individual or very small-group interventions of varying intensity are likely to be necessary. For such pupils the presenting behaviours are likely to relate not only to how they are perceiving and interpreting the present but also their past life experiences. This may necessitate tackling not only aspects of behaviour that are in the pupil's conscious awareness, but also those that are influenced by factors that are not within their conscious awareness and as such may seem to be irrational to the observer.

Strategies within this category range from forms of counselling undertaken by trained and supervised staff in school, through to psychodynamic approaches delivered by appropriately qualified staff. Such approaches are often categorised as 'therapeutic'. The appropriateness of the use of this group of strategies in school contexts remains under debate (e.g. Ecclestone and Hayes 2008, Smith 2002). As with all interventions, ethical issues need to be considered and addressed.

Strategy selection where 'will' is the issue

From the strategies above, it should be clear that changing observable behaviours and improving skills are focused towards targeting the skill element of learning behaviours. Cognitive behavioural approaches explicitly seek to bridge the 'skill' and 'will' issues of learning behaviour. Approaches seeking to address the interpretation and sense making function of behaviour are concerned mainly with addressing the 'will' aspect of learning behaviour. Given that the behaviour of many pupils with SEBD is likely to include a 'will' component, it is important to consider it in more detail. Within the behaviour for learning conceptual framework an issue of 'will' would typically suggest relationship with self as the target relationship.

Directly targeting relationship with self

If directly targeting relationship with self, the focus will often be on working with the pupil to identify, share and change the way in which they perceive or interpret events as a means of positively influencing their behaviours. In essence, in using perspectives from attribution theory, the concept of self-efficacy and the construct of locus of control, the teacher is attempting to identify the extent to which the pupil is likely to take responsibility for changing their behaviour. These terms are discussed in more detail in Chapter 7. For the teacher the aim is to critically explore with the pupil the validity of their causal explanations for events with a view to modifying these. The teacher might use proformas (see Ayers *et al.* 2000, for example) on which the pupil gives their own perspective on events. This form of self-reporting potentially provides the teacher with some insight into how the pupil is currently viewing particular situations. In the follow-up to any incident, care would be taken to allow the pupil to state their version of the events. The purpose is to attempt to understand the attributions the pupil makes. For example, if a pupil makes comments like 'He made me do it', or cites some minor provocation such as, 'She was looking at me', it is an indication that the pupil is attributing externally and taking little personal responsibility. Sometimes it is appropriate to talk this through and supportively challenge attributions in relation to the specific incident.

For some pupils concentrating on what they are thinking and how they are feeling simultaneously is problematic due to overload. A depersonalised approach that removes the emotional component may be more effective. Puppets could be used to act out a similar scenario or role play could be used. A young pupil may be quite happy to comment on what they think caused a puppet to behave in a particular way whereas they may be extremely resistant if required to talk about their own behaviour. Stories can also be used. Comic-strip conversations which, as we noted earlier, are often used with pupils with autism, can also be helpful. In a depersonalised way they let the pupil reflect on what they were thinking during the incident and offer their suggestion of what the other pupil or pupils involved in the incident may have been thinking. The pupil might, for example, suggest that the other person in the cartoon has malicious feelings towards them. It may be this 'faulty' appraisal that then drives their behaviour. Rogers (1994) has made use of cartoons to reflect back to the pupil how they present behaviourally, and the reaction of others, in a given situation. The cartoon is used as a focus for discussion that draws out both the feelings of the pupil and the effect on others involved, including the teacher. The premise is that the pupil does not normally have opportunities to see what their own behaviour looks like or the effect it has on others.

When thinking about attributions it is also necessary to be alert to what, on the surface, appear to be internal attributions but place the locus of control outside the individual. For example, a pupil might say, 'It's my temper', as an explanation for a violent incident. The pupil is seemingly locating responsibility internally but in attributing cause to a fixed trait is, in reality, absolving themselves from responsibility for change.

Within this section we have primarily talked about the problems that occur when a pupil always attributes causes externally. It is important to remember that to attribute totally internally is also problematic. There may be some pupils within the broad category of SEBD whose behaviour is driven by feeling that every unfortunate event that befalls them is totally their responsibility.

Targeting self via relationship with others

The teacher may decide that targeting relationship with self via one of the other two behaviour for learning relationships is the better option. It may, for example, be preferable to target relationship with self via relationship with others.

DEVELOPING THE TEACHER–PUPIL RELATIONSHIP

By necessity the teacher has probably had to positively correct the pupil, impose sanctions or ask for them to be exited from the class. Even supportive conversations with the pupil about their behaviour, such as those that might be undertaken to directly target relationship with self, may be experienced as 'going on about it'.

In targeting relationship with others the teacher is deliberately seeking to 'back off' from the behaviour, though of course keeping in mind the cluster of learning behaviours that would be indicative of an improving relationship with self. Many of the strategies designed to improve the teacher–pupil relationship are quite informal in nature. The teacher is essentially attempting to relate to the pupil through a shared interest that is *not* the pupil's problematic behaviour. The teacher might, for example, find out what interests the pupil and make a point of spending some time talking to them about it. For younger pupils, an activity like helping the teacher rearrange furniture or reorganise resources will also provide opportunities for non-behaviour-related conversations. For older pupils, there might be opportunities to help with painting scenery for a school production. Many teachers and other adults who work with pupils with SEBD in specialist settings will attest to the value of trips and extra curricular activities in building relationships. The precise nature of the activity is not the important element. The aim is to form relationships with others that positively impact on relationship with self. Learning more skills, acquiring more confidence, having more good times with others, feeling part of the group and developing an identity that is not prescribed by behavioural problems, all contribute to the pupil's bank of positive experiences against which they make judgements that inform their relationship with self.

As well as being a potential beneficiary of an improving relationship with others, relationship with self can impact negatively at times. Sometimes pupils will begin to build this positive relationship with others and then do something that threatens it. This can be disappointing for the teacher but should not be surprising. Firstly, the new relationship may represent a threat to stability because it is different to the antagonistic relationship with adults that the pupil may be familiar and even comfortable with. The pupil may attempt to resolve this difference in favour of the familiar. Secondly, some pupils have, or perceive they have, been let down by adults in the past. Forming a close relationship runs the risk of being let down again. The pupil can protect themselves from this risk and exercise some control in their life by behaving in a way that wrecks the relationship before it starts to matter to them. Others will test the relationship through their behaviour to see just how serious the adult is about making this work.

BUILDING RELATIONSHIPS WITH PEERS

Even when a pupil begins to see that change is necessary it can be difficult because they have become locked into a role by the expectations of their peer group (McNamara and Moreton 2001). Effective use of pupil grouping and collaborative activities can help to change these expectations.

The teacher might monitor the target pupil's behaviour and identify whether when in the company of certain pupils the difficulties are less. Equally there may be other pupils whose presence frequently exacerbates difficulties. Seating can be adjusted accordingly. This can be accompanied by increased monitoring to pre-empt problems. By recognising the first signs of tension or agitation the teacher can act to distract or divert the pupil before they embark on a familiar pattern of behaviour. The purpose of these approaches is to mediate the pupil's experience of peer relationships so that they are successful. By effectively keeping the pupil away from incidents, the teacher is avoiding situations where existing patterns of problematic behaviour can be reinforced. There is also the benefit that by minimising incidents other members of the class will develop a more positive view of the pupil. S/he will no longer be solely associated with trouble and upset.

Some pupils may be able to cope with paired work even though they present difficulties within a larger group. Setting up a paired activity, perhaps to research a topic within a particular curriculum area, can help both pupils to get to know each other better, encourage them to use communication skills, and allow a relationship to develop (NcNamara and Moreton 2001). The common advice is that the other pupil should be a good role model, but in reality the main priority is that it is somebody the focus pupil has some chance of relating too. It should be remembered that the priority is not the task but to enable the focus pupil to form a relationship with a peer. McNamara and Moreton (2001) note Sullivan's (1953) research that pupils who had a 'best friend' had a higher self-esteem. Coopersmith's work (1967) also showed that the regard of the peer group was important to self-esteem. As readers will be aware from Chapter 7, though we question the readiness of some teachers and others to ascribe all pupils' difficulties to global low self-esteem, a person's judgement about their own worth is an important element of their relationship with self. If we accept Lund's (1988) view that pupils with SEBD tend to have lower self-esteem then, in the light of Sullivan's (1953) and Coopersmith's (1967) findings, there is a rationale for targeting relationship with self via relationship with others.

Some pupils with SEBD respond well to either being tutored by a peer or being a peer-tutor themselves (McNamara and Moreton 2001). The latter approach in particular may be counterintuitive, as the natural teacher tendency may be to restrict responsibility rather than give more, particularly where this may involve influence over younger pupils. Pupils with SEBD may have particular issues with those, like teachers, who are in a position of authority. A well-trained peer-tutor may be able to work more effectively with the pupil because the power element in the relationship is significantly reduced. The peer-tutor can talk in the language the pupil understands, particularly if they, unlike many teachers, share the same cultural and social background (McNamara and Moreton 2001).

The pupil with SEBD may benefit from acting as peer-tutor to younger pupils. Pupils with SEBD can get locked into their role by the expectations of their peers (McNamara and Moreton 2001) and their teacher. Peer-tutoring places the pupil in a completely different context and allows them to try out a new role. Rather than their role as 'disruptive pupil' or 'class clown' they are placed in the role of responsible and more experienced peer. This requires them to draw on communication and social skills that are usually masked by a whole range of adaptive behaviours.

Targeting self via relationship with the curriculum

Relationship with the curriculum can be an effective route to addressing relationship with self. If observations suggest that the behaviour is rooted in task-avoidance to protect the individual from failure then there is certainly a rationale for this approach. Negative self-reference statements, such as 'I can't do it', 'I'm useless at Maths' or 'I'm thick', may cue the teacher into strengthening relationship with the curriculum as a route to strengthening relationship with self. However this is not the only type of pupil who might benefit from targeting an issue related to 'self' via the curriculum. Many pupils with SEBD who exhibit disruptive, acting-out behaviours, have what might be considered an anti-authority, anti-establishment attitude. They may appear to the observer to actively look for situations that bring them into conflict with the system, whether this is through uniform infringements, jewellery, unusual hairstyles or the behaviour they display in the classroom. As soon as the school acts by reprimanding or imposing a sanction this serves to reaffirm the pupil's view of authority. If the teacher is able to build the pupil's relationship with the curriculum then this can help to break the cycle. The pupil's SEBD should not detract the teacher from their particular area of expertise in brokering positive relationships through the curriculum in group settings. This expertise is a resource that can be brought to bear in developing adaptations to provision for pupils with SEBD. The priority is to achieve some shared interest and to secure motivation. This may be achieved through:

- *Content*
  This may involve identifying the pupil's area of interest and structuring learning activities around this or attempting to enthuse the pupil about the curriculum by enabling them to see the relevance.
- *Teaching style*
  This may involve varying how the task is introduced to the pupil and how they are expected to tackle it. Examples include reducing periods of extended listening, incorporating more kinesthetic elements, finding alternatives to written recording, use of ICT and breaking the lesson into smaller learning episodes with mini plenaries in between.
- *Groupings*
  Variations in this area have been touched on within discussion of relationship with others. The teacher can seek to develop shared interest and secure motivation by careful consideration of which peers work with the target pupil.
- *Assessment*
  Using the principles of Assessment for Learning, the teacher can seek to secure motivation by involving the pupil in setting their own targets, monitoring progress and recording achievements.

Some pupils will develop a positive relationship with an extra-curricular activity. This may be the only aspect of the curriculum the pupil has a relationship with. The relationship with the person who runs it may also be the only positive relationship with a member of staff the pupil has. For this reason, we consider that schools that ban pupils from football club or some other extra curricular activity due to behaviour in class may effectively be 'shooting themselves in the foot'. We can, of course, understand the school's rationale. The club matters to the pupil so banning them from this is a negative consequence. Because it matters to the pupil, the belief is that they will behave better to get back this privilege. Improving behaviour therefore becomes a shared agenda for the teacher and pupil. Unfortunately, due to the attributions some pupils make, they are unlikely to share in this logic. To them this action may simply act as further evidence that teachers, the school and possibly the world in general, are unfair, hostile and 'deserve' the behaviour they get.

Evaluating against the target relationship

Readers will recall from Chapter 3 that when using the behaviour for learning conceptual framework in extended form we evaluate based on improvements to the target relationship. This is assessed with reference to all participating members – the pupil, the teacher and peers. The approaches given here involve changing peer and teacher responses in order to develop the pupil's relationship with self. Though they may not have the same reassuring feel as putting in a tangible, structured intervention, they are potentially very powerful in behaviour for learning terms. The teacher is trying all the time to place the pupil in situations where the social, cognitive and emotional experiences of school learning are improved. This prompts a need in the pupil to reappraise their relationship with self in terms of questioning the purpose behind their behaviour, their perceptions regarding the causes of their behaviour, their beliefs about their ability to change their behaviour and their view of self. If the teacher can engineer a gradual improvement in relationship with self they will have contributed to development of the pupil's responsibility and resilience needed to bring about longer-term change.

Looking at some specific strategies for pupils with SEBD

The strategies and approaches outlined in Chapters 8, 9 and 10 are relevant to pupils with SEBD, just as they are to all pupils. The positive correction techniques within Chapter 10 for example are particularly framed in such a way as to reduce the potential for conflict. Reflective Exercise 12.2 covers a range of strategies that could be considered to be more specific to pupils with SEBD. The exercise requires you to draw on Norwich and Lewis' (2001) notion of a continua of teaching approaches ranging from 'normal' adaptations in class teaching for most pupils through to greater levels of adaptation required for those with more severe difficulties in learning.

Reflective Exercise 12.2

Consider each of the strategies in the table below. Indicate whether you consider it to be (i) a strategy that is a 'normal' adaptation that can readily be made to class teaching; (ii) a strategy that could be deemed 'specialist' due either to the requirement for specialist knowledge to implement it and/or the high level of adaptation necessary to incorporate into class teaching.

Description of strategy and behaviour for learning comment		'Normal' adaption	'Specialist' approach
Strategy	Maintain unconditional positive regard during any disciplinary interaction, making it clear that it is the behaviour that is the problem not the pupil.		
Behaviour for learning perspective	This relates to relationship with others in the sense that the teacher is conveying to the pupil that despite the behaviour they still have a positive relationship. This also relates to relationship with self as it conveys to the pupil that they are not a bad or unlikeable person.		
Strategy	Maintain a positive attitude and encourage the pupil to do likewise. Make it clear that you expect an improvement (ATL 2002) and specify what this is in terms of required behaviours.		
Behaviour for learning perspective	Any incidents are a snapshot in time of a relationship that has a past and a future. The latter needs to be perceived as changeable. No grudges are held.		
Strategy	Develop strategies to avoid conflict and confrontation. This involves trying to develop an awareness of anything that triggers unacceptable behaviour, and intervening or distracting the pupil before a problem occurs. A relationship is much harder to repair after a major breakdown. Also, a public loss of control by the pupil is likely to adversely influence their relationship with peers who may subsequently perceive them as 'scary', 'dangerous' or 'weird'.		
Behaviour for learning perspective	This strategy is rooted in preventing harm to the relationship with others and relationship with self.		

Description of strategy and behaviour for learning comment		'Normal' adaption	'Specialist' approach
Strategy	Consider giving additional individual attention and support in order to more closely monitor the pupil response.		
Behaviour for learning perspective	The pupil's responses can provide vital clues about their causal explanations and attributions. Do they, for example, always misattribute or jump to conclusions in ambiguous situations? (E.g. glances or looks from peers are always interpreted as hostile (Ayers *et al.* 2000).		
Strategy	Provide the pupil with opportunities to take on responsibilities and give praise when these are carried out (ATL 2002).		
Behaviour for learning perspective	We can consider 'responsibility' to represent a cluster of learning behaviours. The strategy shows the pupil that they are trusted and valued by another person and gives them an opportunity to strengthen their relationship with others and also with self as it shows they are worthy of this.		
Strategy	Use of rewards that have value and meaning for the pupil, delivered with due regard for the pupil's preference for private or public recognition.		
Behaviour for learning perspective	This strategy seeks to secure motivation to support the development of learning behaviour. As emphasised in this chapter however, behaviour is adaptive and so we may secure one behaviour through a reward system only to find it replaced by another behaviour that serves the same purpose.		
Strategy	If a pupil is too wound up to listen, don't try to reason with them but allow a cooling-off period. When the pupil has calmed down, try to find time to discuss together what has happened and how it can be avoided the next time (ATL 2002).		
Behaviour for learning perspective	This strategy recognises that the level of emotional arousal will be a barrier to cognitive processing necessary to be able to reflect on the incident.		

(continued)

Description of strategy and behaviour for learning comment		'Normal' adaption	'Specialist' approach
Strategy	Consider incorporating a social element into any individualised reward system. For example, if for a primary pupil collecting a certain number of stickers leads to additional time using computer they could choose another pupil to join in this activity with them. Through this strategy other pupils may be less inclined to see the pupil negatively and have a vested interest in supporting the pupil to improve his/her behaviour.		
Behaviour for learning perspective	This strategy recognises that the behaviour of pupils with SEBD can lead to strained relationships with peers, either because the behaviour is irritating, harmful or seems to attract a lot of the teacher's attention. There may also be others who quite like it when the pupil misbehaves. The strategy seeks to change the way peers relate to the pupil.		
Strategy	Plan curriculum activities that incorporate a collaborative element that is initially within the pupil's capability. For example, create situations where the pupil is included in activities first with one other pupil, and then with a small group (ATL 2002).		
Behaviour for learning perspective	This strategy is useful if the concern relates predominantly to underdeveloped skills related to relationship with others. It may also be useful where the issue is more one of 'will', if there are certain individuals the pupil appears more ready and willing to work with, or a small group context has been identified as a contextual factor that positively influences behaviour.		
Strategy	Help the child to develop social skills, i.e. knowing how to join in, how to ask for things, how to express his/her point of view (ATL 2002).		

Description of strategy and behaviour for learning comment		*'Normal' adaption*	*'Specialist' approach*
Behaviour for learning perspective	The main focus is relationship with others and the assumption is that presenting difficulties relate to underdeveloped skills. Relationship with the curriculum may also benefit because the pupil will increasingly be able to take advantage of learning activities that involve others. Relationship with self may also improve as the pupil is likely to experience less social rejection.		
Strategy	Teach and rehearse useful strategies that the pupil can use to either deal with or extricate themselves from social situations that they currently find difficult. This could include the sometimes vacuous, but socially useful, language and behaviour of apology. It might also include developing socially acceptable responses to criticism.		
Behaviour for learning perspective	The purpose of this approach is to develop self-regulation and resilience by providing choice and alternatives to current response patterns. As such it targets relationship with self, but benefits are also likely to be accrued in the area of relationship with others as the pupil will be involved in less disputes. Readers will note that the strategy focuses initially on skills (ie making an apology, responding to criticism). This is to show the pupil that a different approach by them can lead to a different response from others.		
Strategy	Provide opportunities to explore the attributional style of others and themselves in a non-threatening, safe setting. This could be through characters in stories, role play or use of puppets.		
Behaviour for learning perspective	The purpose of this strategy is to encourage the pupil to critically question their own current explanations and interpretations for their successes and failures in behaviour and learning. The key focus is relationship with self. However it is likely also to benefit relationship with curriculum and relationship with others.		

(continued)

Reflective Exercise 12.2 (continued)

Description of strategy and behaviour for learning comment		'Normal' adaption	'Specialist' approach
Strategy	Analyse an incident (either real or from literature) in order to identify the key triggers, choice points, the efficacy of the responses and the outcomes for all involved. Write about, discuss or role play alternatives.		
Behaviour for learning perspective	Depending on the nature of the incident selected this could target any of the three relationships.		
Strategy	Provide opportunities for the pupil to identify their existing effective self-regulation strategies and to explore socially acceptable strategies used by peers and others.		
Behaviour for learning perspective	This strategy targets relationship with self. However, the development of greater self-regulation is also likely to benefit relationship with others as the pupil is less likely to come into conflict with and/ or alienate peers and adults through unpredictable behaviour.		
Strategy	Identify a 'safe' place or person that the pupil can go to as an alternative to a behaviour that would impact negatively and significantly on self and/or others.		
Behaviour for learning perspective	This strategy also targets self-regulation and so targets relationship with self. In this case self-regulation involves the pupil relocating themselves either in the classroom or to another identified area in the school. It would be hoped that the pupil could be supported to progress to using mental self-regulation strategies in situ rather than physical relocation. The use of a 'safe' person attempts to capitalise on an existing positive relationship with an adult. The use of the 'safe' adult or place should be monitored, as for some pupils it may serve to reinforce the behaviour and others may use it as an avoidance strategy. However, even if the teacher's view is that this is the case, the strategy should not be withdrawn spontaneously at the point the pupil is attempting to access their 'safe' person or area. This is discussed further in relation to the next strategy.		

Description of strategy and behaviour for learning comment		'Normal' adaption	'Specialist' approach
Strategy	Implement agreed (with the teacher) non-verbal systems for conveying emotional state and action. (E.g. green card – 'I'm OK'; amber – 'I need support'; red – 'I'm going to my safe place').		
Behaviour for learning perspective	This strategy is typically used to support the pupil in accessing their 'safe' place, particularly when this is out of class. This is not an approach that would be used with many pupils and represents a significant compromise as we would not normally let pupils leave classrooms without permission. It targets self-regulation. The pupil's use of the cards should be monitored. Even if it is felt the pupil is manipulating the system as an avoidance strategy this should not be challenged at the point they present the red card. This could be the one time the pupil *really* needs to use it. Also by unilaterally and spontaneously removing an agreed approach it may undermine the pupil's trust in adults. Instead the suspected manipulation should be addressed through a planned meeting involving the pupil, the teacher and anybody else involved in operating the system.		
Strategy	Identifying with the individual pupil a particular role (e.g. leader, participant, reporter) within a collaborative group work activity that seeks to address their particular behavioural and/or learning difficulty. Some may need a script to support them in the role.		
Behaviour for learning perspective	This strategy is based on providing a structure to support and develop the pupil's relationship with others. Effectively, by allocating a role it sets some limits on the learning behaviours that the pupil is required to draw upon when working in a group.		
Strategy	Working with the pupil one-to-one or in a small group to identify the difference between designating a choice as 'good' because of its impact on the individual pupil (e.g. immediate sense of fun and excitement) and 'good' in relation to the effect on others.		

(continued)

Reflective Exercise 12.2 (continued)			
Description of strategy and behaviour for learning comment		*'Normal' adaption*	*'Specialist' approach*
Behaviour for learning perspective	The strategy tackles cognitively what is predominantly an issue of empathy through making explicit to the pupil that they may not experience whatever choices they make about their behaviour in the same way as their peers.		
Strategy	Adopting a restorative approach to incidents, focusing on the key questions of 'What happened?' 'Who has been affected and how?', 'How can we put right the harm?' and 'What have you learned so as to make different choices next time?' (Hopkins 2004).		
Behaviour for learning perspective	There is a focus on relationship with others through the emphasis on the effect on the other person. However, it also targets relationship with self by emphasising personal responsibility.		

Summary

In this chapter we have examined in more depth individual pupils who are often categorised as having special educational needs (SEN) due to their differences and delays in development that result in them experiencing difficulties in school-based contexts. The preferred policy trajectory for such pupils is one of inclusion that seeks to enable them to access, engage and participate in school-based learning. This is intended to secure outcomes that improve their chances of being socially included in, and making a contribution to, their communities and society. Within such a policy trajectory our preferred approach is not to identify difficulties and differences in such individuals that serve to distance them from a hypothetical average or 'normal' learner, but to consider them along with all pupils as individuals who seek to make social, emotional and cognitive relationships within the group setting of the classroom. Within such a context, and within the behaviour for learning conceptual framework, we call these relationships respectively: relationship with others, relationship with self and relationship with the curriculum.

Within school settings we suggest that provision for all pupils should pay due regard to the need to prepare for such relationships through the school and their teachers using existing pupil information, previous experience, and existing evidence bases. For most pupils this preparation will lie within the area of good inclusive practice that is in place for all pupils and which is based on what all individuals expect and need from a relationship. This includes an understanding of notions of interdependence, reciprocity and involvement that have been discussed throughout this book. Some groups of pupils may need some additional attention to factors that influence the quality of one or more of the three relationships. This may be necessary in order for them to experience enhanced involvement in these learning relationships and increase the opportunities for their distinctive responses to be understood and valued. For a few individuals there may be a need for a significant change to the variables that impact on the building and maintenance of relationships. This may involve, for example, an emphasis on closer adult monitoring, and for those involved with the individual to make significant changes or adjustments to their style of communicating and responding such that a 'meeting of minds and methods' needed for the relationship is developed.

Individuals whose experience of school-based relationships may be very different from that of their peers are at risk of being excluded from the social and cultural milieu of their classroom and community. Schooling can provide the social context to develop responsiveness, responsibility and resilience through the development of the school-based relationships described within the behaviour for learning conceptual framework. Resilience is defined by Alvord and Grados (2005) as the skills, attributes and abilities that enable the individual to adapt to hardship, difficulties and challenges. This involves the targeted development of learning behaviours that sustain these individual characteristics for, and from a focus on relationship-building.

Within this framework there is emphasis on 'different' relationships rather than 'deficient' relationships. The language of relationships should not serve to place one member in a disadvantaged position. We need to identify what the pupil brings to the relationship and what we need to do to adjust our own behaviour and the contexts and conditions of the classroom and school to allow relationships to flourish. Relationships are reciprocal and dynamic. This interdependence ensures that each individual experiences the relationship differently irrespective of the extent of their individual differences.

This chapter has sought to provide information that allows teachers to prepare for relationship building with individuals who may experience particular differences in their relationship with self, others and the curriculum. The extent to which adjustments have to be made to the variables that impact on relationship building and maintenance within classroom contexts thus lie on a continuum of provision.

Some people may choose to refer to these adaptations to the variables that impact on relationships within the classroom as 'specialist teaching'. They may also choose to refer to those whose experience of relationships in classroom contexts is very different from others as SEN.

Within the behaviour for learning conceptual framework these adjustments are clearly stated and monitored by the impact they have on the individual's experience of, and response to, the relationships involved. Of importance is the development of learning behaviours within individuals that underpin positive relationships within the classroom and the maintenance of a balance between the cognitive, social and emotional aspects of learning that are involved.

Chapter 13

Transitions

Introduction

Pupils make educational transitions as they start school, as they progress through school, and as they move between schools. These transitions require pupils to acclimatise to new surroundings, to adapt to new ways of working, to make sense of new rules and routines, and to interact with unfamiliar adults and peers (Sanders *et al.* 2005). Transitions therefore make intense demands on the three behaviour for learning relationships. It is important that we retain a focus on each of these relationships, but relationship with self assumes particular significance in relation to transitions. It is this relationship above all others that determines the pupil's ability to respond to the challenges of transition. It is this ability that may influence the ways in which the pupil progresses and develops (Sanders *et al.* 2005). It has been suggested pupils' experiences of transition in the early years may be particularly influential:

> Each of these experiences is likely to affect children and their capacity to adjust and to learn. Such is the significance of early transitions for young children that it is essential that parents, educators, policy makers and politicians pay close attention to young children's experiences in order to provide well for them.
>
> (Fabian and Dunlop 2002: 1)

Within this chapter we have concentrated on four transition points:

- Foundation Stage to Key Stage 1
- Key Stage 1 to Key Stage 2
- Key Stage 2 to Key Stage 3
- Key Stage 3 to Key Stage 4

We have used the term 'transitions' within this chapter rather than making the distinction that is sometimes made between a 'transfer' as a move between two settings (e.g. from primary school to secondary school) and a 'transition' as a move within a setting, such as between year groups or from Key Stage 1 to Key Stage 2. We feel the term 'transition' better conveys the idea that what occurs is a process that starts before the change and finishes afterwards, rather than being a single event. Importantly, it is also a process that will occur whether the school intervenes in any mediating role or not. This chapter is concerned with how schools can mediate the experience of transition in a manner that has regard for and maintains the three relationships that underpin the development of learning behaviour.

All transition points mark a progression, a 'moving on' not just in education, but though life, and it is entirely appropriate that within the new setting there are some differences and new experiences and challenges. Referring to the transition from primary to secondary school, Galton *et al.* (2003) talked of the importance of *discontinuities* as well as continuities, challenging the dominant assumption that it is the *continuities* that need to be strengthened.

Change and difference are not inherently bad and are important elements of transition. The challenge for schools is to manage the process of change in a way that recognises that there is a need to attend to each pupil's relationship with self, relationship with the curriculum, and relationships with others. Planning to support transition, at any age, involves thinking about three key elements shown in Figure 13.1.

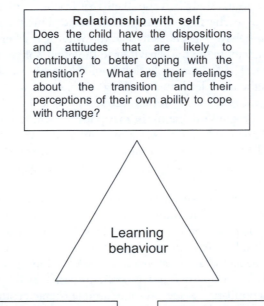

Relationship with self
Does the child have the dispositions and attitudes that are likely to contribute to better coping with the transition? What are their feelings about the transition and their perceptions of their own ability to cope with change?

Learning behaviour

Relationship with others
What skills does the child currently have and what additional skills will be necessary to form new relationships with staff and peers and deal with increased expectations of abilities to learn and socialise in group settings?

Relationship with the curriculum
What skills does the child currently have and what additional skills will be necessary to deal with differences in the curriculum, teaching methods and increased expectations of personal organisation of learning?

Figure 13.1 The three relationships at transition.

Continuity and progression in learning behaviour

Pupils start school and change schools according to age rather than developmental readiness. There is a practical logic to this as it would be difficult to predict class sizes, the physical space required to accommodate pupils and the number of required personnel if any other system was operated that allowed variable numbers to transfer. However, the choice of ages for the key transitions of starting primary school and transferring to secondary school are only based on historical assumptions about the right times for transfer for the majority of pupils developmentally.

The result of age–related transition is that there is a broad set of skills that it is assumed pupils will have developed by each transition point. A major threat to successful transition is the adoption of age–related expectations of the learning behaviours that pupils bring with them. The issue of what teachers expect from pupils at particular ages has been explored by Bate and Moss (1997). An important finding was that in each Key Stage the teacher expected certain behaviours to have been taught the previous year, with secondary school teachers expecting the vast majority of behaviours to have been taught prior to the point at which they received the pupil. This research was revealing at a number of levels. It suggested that teachers were not adopting a developmental approach to the acquisition of these behavioural skills and instead connected them almost entirely with chronological age. In addition, the higher up the age-range the pupil moved the less the teachers saw it as their role to teach behavioural skills. It is also likely that teachers' attributions reflect these beliefs. Secondary school teachers may be more likely to attribute the misbehaviour to the pupil knowing how to behave but choosing not to, whereas teachers of younger pupils may be more likely to attribute the misbehaviour to the pupil not yet having acquired the necessary skills to behave. The former attribution inevitably leads to a system of behavioural consequences whereas the latter leads to a teaching response.

'Continuity' and 'progression' are terms frequently used in relation to transition (e.g. DfES 2004k). By 'progression' we mean that pupils' learning builds sequentially on what has been learned previously and shows an upward gradient in demand as they move from year to year (DfES 2004k). By 'continuity' we mean there are planned links and similarities to ensure that there are no unnecessary jumps and gaps in pupils' learning or repetition (DfES 2004k).

It is doubtful whether policy-makers, schools or teachers view continuity and progression in the same way in relation to behaviour. In relation to learning, there is a strong sense of needing to look at what the pupil can already do and gradually increase that demand, ensuring that there no sudden jumps in the expectations of them. We rarely adopt the same approach in relation to behavioural, emotional and social development. The transition from the Early Years Foundation Stage to Year 1 is a case in point. As the next section of this chapter illustrates, the Foundation Stage has some unique characteristics and is quite overt in both its focus on the development of learning behaviour and the pupil's relationship with the curriculum (e.g. *Problem Solving, Reasoning and Numeracy, Communication, Language* and *Literacy*, and *Knowledge and Understanding of the World*); relationship with self (e.g. *dispositions and attitudes* and *self-confidence and self-esteem*); and relationship with others (e.g. *making relationships, behaviour and self-control* and *sense of community*). The Foundation Stage is based on six areas of learning and development that are considered equally important and inter-connected. It focuses on developing learning behaviours through and within these areas. There is also explicit recognition that pupils develop and learn at different rates. Pupils, having experienced the Foundation Stage curriculum, then move on to the National Curriculum which is underpinned by a very different subject-based structure that places a higher value on subject-specific knowledge, skills and understanding. This neglects the obvious fact that the learning behaviours that are rightfully such a dominant focus within Foundation Stage teaching also need to be built on and developed as the pupil moves through their school career. The tendency is to allow this to happen in a relatively *ad hoc* manner, with only limited references in the National Curriculum to the promoting of skills across the curriculum and thinking skills. The behaviour for learning conceptual framework seeks to encourage a more overt focus upon these skills at all Key Stages.

Though Bate and Moss (1997) used an examination of the behaviours expected at certain ages to highlight a potential source of difficulty, an honest appraisal of the *learning* behaviours we expect at certain Key Stages is a valuable activity to undertake. This involves thinking carefully about the sorts of skills and dispositions necessary within the new learning environment, whether an early years setting or a secondary school, that the pupil is about to join. As we have already indicated however, transition is a process that begins before the change, and so there is also a need for the pupil's current setting to consider the learning behaviours required by the receiving environment. It is not unusual to talk about continuity and progression with regard to the curriculum, and we are simply suggesting that the same consideration can be applied to the development of learning behaviour.

The Early Years Foundation Stage: an apprenticeship to the National Curriculum?

The Early Years Foundation Stage can be viewed as an apprenticeship that introduces the skills involved in learning in group settings. Even the regulations regarding staff ratios suggest this. At age two there must be at least one member of staff for every four children, by age three and over this has risen to one member of staff for every 13 children, and for children aged four and over in a Reception class it can be one teacher for 30 pupils. There is a sense in which the pupil is moving from forming a 1–1 reciprocal relationship with a parent or primary care giver at about 18–24 months (Berk 2003) to an expectation that they will function effectively socially, emotionally and academically within a class of 30 by 48 months. Many schools, of course, recognise that there is a need to provide additional adult support in their Reception classes that reduces this ratio significantly. For many pupils, however, this merely postpones the inevitable experience of moving from high levels of adult support to a 1 to 30 ratio.

Many pupils cope with the Foundation Stage environment very well. Part of the reason may be the characteristics that it *does not* share with subsequent phases of education. These differences are highlighted in Table 13.1.

Without the restrictions of items in the second column of Table 13.1 it may be that Foundation Stage pupils (and their teachers) are more able to focus on developing their relationships with others. This is no small challenge. Accepted good practice is to *not* set limits on the number of pupils allowed on a particular activity, and consequently pupils need to be able to share equipment, negotiate and settle disagreements, all with the minimum of adult intervention. Some larger schools operate paired Foundation Stage classes with two teachers and two or more teaching assistants and allow free-flow of pupils both between the two classrooms and to the outdoor learning environment. Potentially a pupil experiencing this arrangement has to interact and form relationships with up to 59 other children. This is in contrast to subsequent stages of their school career when they may only have to interact and form relationships with the pupils sitting either side of them for much of the day.

It is not just socially where Reception-aged pupils are challenged. Once taught where equipment is, what it is used for, how to use it and how to put it away, pupils are expected to be able to access it independently. They need to learn how to make a choice between activities. This may be supported to a degree by, for example, each pupil, after teacher-led group discussion, putting a peg on their chosen starting activity. The peg is a means of focusing the pupil's thoughts at the start of the session; beyond this they would make the choice of when to move on from the activity and which activity to do next.

Table 13.1 Difference between the Foundation Stage and the rest of compulsory schooling

Foundation Stage	Increasingly as the child progresses through the remainder of compulsory schooling
A significant amount of the pupil's time is spent engaged in child-initiated learning.	Most learning is teacher-initiated and -directed.
Though there is a routine and structure to the day, time spent on many activities within this is not prescribed.	A timetable defines when activities are undertaken.
There is minimal restriction on movement between activities, including those in the outdoor learning environment.	Movement is restricted.
Assessment is continuous (DfES 2007c), formative and based on looking, listening and noting, whilst the pupil is engaged in child-initiated learning. A far smaller proportion is through teacher-directed tasks.	Assessment is an 'event' occurring at certain times, ranging from daily marking of work to national testing at set times.
The pupil moves between five[1] areas of learning reflected in the classroom and outdoor learning environment.	The pupil may sit at a desk for the duration of a lesson.
Teacher-directed tasks are frequently supported by an adult in a small group activity.	Mainly pupils with SEN or those experiencing other barriers to learning receive this level of adult support.
There is the opportunity in the majority of schools for the parent/carer to talk to the teacher or a teaching assistant on a daily basis, allowing the teacher to know of any factors that may affect the pupil's learning and emotional well-being during the day.	Contact reduces as the pupil moves through the age-range.
Personal, Social and Emotional Development has equal weighting to the other five areas of learning.	*Personal, Social and Health Education* is covered by non-statutory guidance. The SEAL curriculum does not have the same status as a National Curriculum subject.
The curriculum is thematic.	The curriculum is increasingly subject-based.
Emphasis is placed on a range of skills.	Emphasis is increasingly placed on listening and written recording.

Note: The Foundation Stage has six areas of learning but in terms of classroom organisation 'personal, social and emotional development' is reflected across the other five.

The Early Years Foundation Stage is therefore both a demanding and comprehensive apprenticeship for National Curriculum learning. It is also potentially a frustrating one: having served this apprenticeship, these skills are never likely to be visited so explicitly again in most pupils' school careers. The main exception is some pupils with special educational needs who may experience specific programmes targeting some of these skills. Not only might these skills not be visited so explicitly again, in some cases they may not even be used. Sanders *et al.* (2005) found that skills of independent learning, acquired during the Foundation Stage, were not always being capitalised upon in Year 1.

Strengthening the Reception to Year 1 transition

Though the Foundation Stage to Key Stage 1 transition takes place within the same school, in terms of the extent of change in curriculum and pedagogy experienced, it is on a par with the Key Stage 2 to Key Stage 3 transitions. There are a number of ways we can ease the transition:

- Year 1 teachers should use the Foundation Stage profile as a means of formative assessment. If pupils have completed the Early Learning Goals then they should be working on the National Curriculum. However there will potentially be a significant number of pupils, certainly during the first term, who should be provided with the opportunity to continue following the Early Learning Goals.
- The Year 1 teacher should *gradually* extend the length of time spent in whole-class teaching and teacher-directed tasks. There should still be time available for child-initiated learning.
- Retaining some of the physical aspects/arrangements of the Foundation Stage in Year 1 can help with transition. For example, it may be possible to have a library, role-play, art and writing area and access to the outdoor learning environment.
- Recognise that though the required staffing ratio at Foundation Stage is one to 30, in reality this will not have been the experience of many pupils. They will have been used to being supported in the majority of teacher-directed tasks by an adult. Year 1 needs to retain a similar ratio or at least be aware that pupils have been used to working with this level of support and may find certain tasks daunting.
- Recognise that there will be some pupils who are particularly vulnerable at this transition. These include those with SEN, pupils for whom English is an additional language, summer born pupils and those who have not spent a full year in the reception class (i.e. 'late' transfers from a pre-school provider).
- If pupils have been used to coming into the Reception classroom with their parents, it is beneficial to maintain this routine at the start of Year 1 rather than moving straight to lining up in the playground or whatever other routine is operated in the rest of the school.
- Ensure pupils are explicitly taught the routines for hanging up bags and coats, storing lunchboxes and going to the toilet. As far as possible, try to keep these the same or similar to arrangements in Foundation Stage, at least initially.
- If lunchtime and break times are different to those experienced in the Reception class consider what support will be necessary. In some schools, for example, Reception pupils will have had separate lunchtimes to the rest of the school or may have had their break times in the outdoor learning environment rather than on the main playground.
- Continue to use similar rules and routines for things like asking for help or using equipment. Retain familiar features from the Reception classroom such as visual timetables.
- Where staffing and finances allow it, consider the possible advantages of a teaching assistant from the Reception class moving up with the pupils for the first term of Year 1 or even the whole year. In some schools it may be possible for the Reception teacher to move up to Year 1 with their class and the Year 1 teacher to move down to take the new Reception class. As well as continuity for the pupils in terms of their relationship with the teacher, it also aids curricular continuity and progression.

- Provide opportunities to visit the Year 1 classroom for 'taster' visits. However, think carefully about *what* the pupils will 'taste'. The main purpose is to build confidence by establishing some familiarity with the new teacher and the new environment, therefore it is advisable to organise activities that are not significantly different from those that pupils will be familiar with from the Foundation Stage. To place the pupils in the context of, for example, a structured Literacy Hour or daily Mathematics lesson is likely to dent confidence by stressing the enormity of the change.
- In the last term of the Foundation Stage the Reception teacher can seek to gradually extend the time the pupils spend on particular teacher-directed activities. However we would stress that this should be based on pupils' readiness and part of the natural progression through the Reception class that sees pupils increasingly able to sustain attention for longer on an activity. It should not be driven by the organisational imperative of preparing pupils to sit for extended periods by Year 1.

Reflective Exercise 13.1

To what extent do you think a Reception teacher should seek to make the Summer term of Year R more like Year 1 by introducing elements of the Year 1 curriculum (e.g. the Literacy Hour and daily Mathematics lesson) and increasing the amount of teacher-directed activity?

Unlike other transitions that we cover later, we have not emphasised the preparatory work that can be done by the Foundation Stage teacher. There is a good reason for this: the Early Years Foundation Stage *is* the preparation for Year 1. Our view is that the priority is making the start of Year 1 more like the Foundation Stage. This view is supported by a number of recommendations from a research report by Sanders *et al.* (2005) pointing to the need to give attention to changes in Year 1. They recommended that:

- School managers should allocate resources to enable children in Year 1 to experience some play-based activities that give access to opportunities such as sand and water, role-play, construction and outdoor learning.
- Policy-makers should provide advice to teachers on how to continue elements of the Foundation Stage curriculum and pedagogical approach into Year 1.
- The amount of time children in Year 1 spend sitting still and listening to the teacher should be reduced. Year 1 teachers should be encouraged to increase opportunities for active, independent learning and learning through play.
- Guidance is needed to help reduce the emphasis given to children recording their work in writing at the beginning of Year 1.

(Sanders *et al.* 2005: v–vi)

Sanders *et al.* (2005) found that staff and parents/carers in their study were largely content with the quality of pupils' experiences of the Foundation Stage. The study also found that the pupils were largely content. The main difficulties were associated with the introduction of a more formal, subject-based and teacher-directed approach, with less time for child-initiated activities, choice and play in Year 1.

The transition from Key Stage 1 to Key Stage 2

The transition from Key Stage 1 to Key Stage 2 is likely to be less of an issue in primary schools where the pupil remains in the same school even though they are moving a Key Stage. Nevertheless it is important not to underestimate that 'becoming a junior' will still be a daunting prospect in some pupil's minds even though they are not changing school. The following strategies will help to support the transition:

- Visits to the Year 3 class.
- Visits from the Year 3 teacher to the Year 2 class.
- Ensuring the pupil knows the names of the class teacher and TAs who work in the receiving class.
- Circle time sessions exploring what pupils are looking forward to or worrying about. This can be depersonalised by using puppets and stories. Many pupils will find it easier to articulate the worries the puppet may have about the transfer than to talk about their own concerns.
- Practice through role-play, puppets and stories, skills such as asking for help and introducing yourself to someone you do not know. Many pupils will feel more comfortable advising a puppet on strategies because it depersonalises the situation.
- Ensure transferring pupils know practical arrangements, such as the location of the toilets and their class' cloakroom, where to store lunchboxes and any changes to the procedures for entry to the school, such as a different place to line up or a different door to use. Make sure pupils know these arrangements *before* the summer holiday and are reminded on the first day in September. Such practical details can assume major significance for many young pupils.

The Key Stage 1 to Key Stage 2 transition takes on greater significance where it is from an infant to junior school. In this situation the pupil will be leaving familiar surroundings, familiar staff and on some occasions leaving friendship groups if the infant school feeds several junior schools. Because junior schools do not have infants on site, sometimes the ethos can feel very different to the pupil. Many of the strategies given for transition within the same school are applicable. In addition the following strategies are advisable for transitions to a separate junior school:

- Arrange visits to the receiving school.
- Arrange visits by junior school staff, including the Head teacher, to the infant school.
- With any visits by junior staff to the infant school or infant children to the junior the emphasis should always be on the elements that will be the same and the elements that will be exciting and different. Going through a long list of rules or telling pupils that they have to be a lot more grown up or that they will have to work a lot harder is unhelpful.
- Identify a 'buddy' at the receiving school.
- Plan farewell activities that celebrate past school experiences. This needs to be handled carefully so that it is upbeat, balancing 'what I will miss' and memories with plenty of 'what I am looking forward to'.

Dips in pupil performance have been noted (Ofsted 1999) in Year 3. A variety of reasons have been suggested for this. In a small-scale study Doddington *et al.* (1999) found that some teachers attributed the dip to the side-effects of the Key Stage 1 tests in Year 2, including the intensive teaching of certain limited areas of the curriculum. One effect of this 'hot-housing' may be a certain amount of inflated achievement and artificially heightened expectation. After the summer break pupils then drop back to their 'natural' levels of achievement. Other teachers highlighted social reasons for the dip, suggesting that it reflected a phase of social curiosity and a preoccupation with friendships that could divert interest from classroom learning (Doddington *et al.* 1999). In behaviour for learning terms this reflects relationship with others taking priority for the pupil over relationship with the curriculum.

Doddington *et al.* (2001) pointed to a wider range of factors that could explain the Year 3 dip, including:

- different and heightened expectations, especially in relation to working more independently;
- increased curricular demands leading to feelings of pressure;
- new and unfamiliar ways of working;
- a fall-off in parental involvement;
- the organisation of staffing which may sometimes result in 'weaker' or less experienced teachers being given the Year 3 groups;
- the limited nature of Year 2/Year 3 'liaison' in the majority of schools, which could lead to problems of under-performance being overlooked as children are given time to adjust to their new setting.

(Doddington *et al.* 2001, cited in Galton *et al.* 2003)

The transition from Key Stage 2 to Key Stage 3

For many pupils the Key Stage 2 to Key Stage 3 transition will represent their first change of school since the age of four. The exceptions are those who have attended separate infant and junior schools. Even these pupils will have last changed school at a very different stage in their lives developmentally. The transition to secondary school not only represents a major change for the pupil in the nature of their educational environment, it also coincides with a major change in physical, mental and emotional terms as they move into adolescence.

The pupil moving from primary to secondary education encounters change in a number of different areas. Table 13.2 identifies a number of these.

In addition to these more overt differences there may be more subtle differences such as teachers' heightened expectations of pupils' capacities to collaborate in group-work, to sustain attention on particular tasks and to generally cope with life. When planning activities to support pupils in coping with the changes, the behaviour for learning conceptual framework helps us to keep in mind a clear purpose. This is illustrated by Table 13.3, which demonstrates how even activities undertaken for the purely practical purpose of familiarity with a new environment also link to the three behaviour for learning relationships.

A noticeable feature in Table 13.3 is the frequency with which the link is with relationship with self. Even where the primary purpose is linked to one of the other two relationships, a secondary benefit is frequently in the area of relationship with self due to increased confidence brought about by the experience. This highlights the importance of this particular relationship.

Table 13.2 Differences between primary and secondary school (Ellis 2006: 332)

Primary school	Secondary school
Environment	
Typically smaller.	Typically larger.
Few specialist areas (e.g. ICT suite, hall for PE).	Numerous specialist areas (e.g. gym, dance studio, labs, art room, etc.).
Staff	
Typically one class teacher who teaches the majority of subjects.	Several subject teachers, as well as form tutor.
Limited number of adult roles.	Different adult roles and new terminology (e.g. 'Form Tutor', 'Head of Year', 'Head of Department', 'Assistant Head').
Most staff, including Head, are likely to know students by name.	Staff not involved directly with the student are unlikely by to know them by name.
Personal organisation	
Equipment needed for most lessons is provided and kept in the room.	Students are expected to bring their own equipment and to remember which day they need to bring it. They are also expected to carry it around with them all day.
Timetable shows sequence of day; failure to understand or use it is of little consequence.	Timetable shows sequence and location. Student needs to use it to know where s/he should be, which lesson it is and what equipment is required.
Other pupils	
Year 6 are the oldest.	Year 7 are the youngest in the school.
All students in the school are children.	Population extends from children to young adults.
Many students in other year groups known, at least by sight.	Few students in other year groups known.
Pupil movement	
Lessons take place mainly in one room.	Students move to different rooms for different lessons.
Students usually move as a group to a different location accompanied by an adult.	Students move around the site independently, taking responsibility for arriving at the right time in the right place.
School is often in close walking distance, many pupils taken to school by an adult.	Students often have further to travel to get to school. Often they will need to travel to school independently, using public transport.
Curriculum	
Subject-based but divisions less evident, some subjects incorporated within topic work.	Subject-based, emphasised by movement to different rooms and teaching by different teachers.
Homework set by one teacher, often on an occasional, informal basis.	Homework set by different teachers on a regular, more formal basis.

First published in *The Senco Handbook*, Optimus Education.

Table 13.3 Activities to support primary to secondary transition

Category	Activity	Behaviour for learning relationship (bold type indicates main purpose)
Skills	Learning how to introduce yourself to an unknown pupil or member of staff.	**Relationship with others** Relationship with self
	Learning how to ask for help if lost or unsure of timetable.	**Relationship with self** Relationship with others
	Teaching pupils how to read timetable.	**Relationship with self**
	Target study skills, improve personal organisation.	**Relationship with the curriculum** Relationship with self
Familiarity	'Taster' days where students visit new environment and guided tours.	**Relationship with self** Relationship with others
	Providing in advance welcome packs and opportunities to meet key personnel, Q&A session with current Year 7, etc.	**Relationship with self** Relationship with others
	Providing a map of the new school and teaching pupils how to use it.	**Relationship with self**
Curriculum and pedagogy	Teachers from current and future settings identify differences and similarities in learning and teaching styles.	**Relationship with the curriculum**
	Teacher passes on information regarding curriculum coverage and pupil achievement.	**Relationship with the curriculum**
	Introduce a more subject-based curriculum part way through Year 6.	**Relationship with the curriculum** Relationship with self
	Use subject specialists for some subjects in Year 6.	**Relationship with the curriculum** Relationship with self
	Reducing the number of teachers Year 7 pupils encounter, even if this means some lessons are not taught by subject specialist.	**Relationship with others** Relationship with self
Pastoral	Buddy/mentoring schemes.	**Relationship with others** Relationship with self
	Visits by Year 7 pupils to talk to the transferring Year 6 pupils. This is often most beneficial when it is Year 7 pupils who attended the primary school they visit.	**Relationship with self** Relationship with others
	Year 7 pupils start back in September a few days before the other year groups return.	**Relationship with self** Relationship with others
	Vertical tutor groups made up of pupils from Years 7–11.	**Relationship with others** Relationship with self

Is the pupil's relationship with self the most important relationship in transitions?

In terms of the behaviour for learning conceptual framework it is the relationship with self that is under most threat during transitions and the one that we should strive to protect and maintain. The major transitions (e.g. primary to secondary school), involve moving pupils between settings that will lead them to encounter new forms of curriculum and pedagogy and new peers and adults. The element that stays with the pupil throughout the change is the relationship with self. It is the quality of this relationship with self that will play a key role in determining the relationship the pupil forms with others and with the curriculum in the new environment.

With any transition there is a strong emotional component. Cossavella and Hobbs (2002) outline a number of stages involved in transition. Their work is primarily related to the transition to secondary schools, though the stages may be relevant to any transition point. Table 13.4 draws on and extends their framework.

With a list such as Table 13.4 it is important to recognise that not all pupils will respond to change in the same way. There are a number of influencing factors, including:

* Existing relationships with adults and peers. This will affect how attached the pupil is to the current setting. Quite simply, it may be easier to leave people and places that you do not have a strong attachment to.
* Previous positive experience of a transition. This may help the pupil to recognise that even if the change appears daunting they have coped before. We should remember that younger pupils have fewer experiences of transition to draw upon.
* Sufficient social skills and communication skills to enable them to interact effectively with peers and adults in order to form relationships and to deal with any problems.
* An optimistic disposition that views set-backs and adversity as temporary and changeable.
* In the case of a child starting pre-school, prior experience of time away from their parent/carer will be important.
* Sufficient self-efficacy to allow them to recognise that their actions can determine the nature of their experience. In other words, recognising that they are active participants in change rather than passive recipients.
* Sufficient self-awareness to recognise their own feelings associated with transition.
* The way in which the impending change is talked about by others who are significant in the pupil's life, including teachers, parents, siblings, other relatives and peers.

Some of these points can be considered to be resilience factors in relation to transition and emphasise the need not just to think in terms of support as the transition becomes imminent, but to think how throughout the pupil's time in a setting they are being equipped with the skills and dispositions to deal with change and difficulty. We would suggest that, for example, the final term of Year 6 is far too late to introduce a self-esteem programme as part of a six-session cross-phase project. Last-ditch rescue bids for self-esteem such as this will rarely be successful. It would be more beneficial at this late stage to focus on specific skills, such as rehearsing how to introduce yourself to someone you have not met before or how to ask for help when you are lost, learning how to read a timetable and learning about some of the different terminology used in a secondary school. Such activities may at least develop some confidence.

The other important consideration with regard to the sequence of stages outlined in Table 13.4, is that not all pupils will start on this sequence at the same time. Age and development will be factors in determining how far ahead the pupil looks, but equally there are some pupils who, as part of their personality, do tend to just focus on the here-and-now rather than getting anxious about future events.

Table 13.4 Stages involved in transition

Stage and description	Children might feel	Outward signs that pupils may exhibit:
Numbness		
The first phase is largely characterised by a degree of shock. It is the first recognition that the transition has started.	Overwhelmed. Unsure of what is happening. 'I don't know what to do.' Confused.	Expression of initial realisation – 'I can't believe it's my last year …' Recognition of timescales – 'This time next year I'll be …' or for a young child 'How many "sleeps" until …?'
Minimisation/denial		
This stage is characterised by attempts to minimise the change by trivialising it and in some cases displays of bravado.	'It's nothing.' 'Everything can't change.' 'I'll carry on as if nothing is happening.'	Dismissive of the significance of the change. Reluctance to engage in activities related to the transition or to take these seriously. Dismisses discussion of the change by peers or teachers as 'going on about it'. Feigning enthusiasm for the change – 'Secondary school's going to be so great.'
Anxiety		
At this stage the realities of the change begin to become apparent. The pupil becomes more aware of the realities involved. This leads to many 'What if…?' questions.	'What's going to happen?' 'Everything is going to be different.' 'How can I cope?' 'I'm not going to fit in.' 'Who will I know?'	Concern with detail – 'What if I miss the bus?' 'How will I find my way around?' Concern with diminishing timescale – counting down the days. Expressions of self-doubt – 'I'll never be able to …' Sharing and believing myths about the unpleasant experiences they will face (Maines and Robinson 1988).
Sadness		
At this stage there is acceptance that the change is going to happen. In some cases this may be after the change in the form of realisation that change has happened and there is no going back.	'I'm going to miss this place.' 'I'm going to miss these people (peers and staff).' 'I'm OK today, I wasn't yesterday.' 'Am I going to make any friends?'	'Clinginess', particularly in younger children. Expression of sadness – 'I'll miss this school … and promise to return to visit.' Changeable moods. Changes in social groupings, including the end of some long-term friendships, as pupils align themselves with others moving to the same school.

Table 13.4 (continued)

Stage and description	Children might feel	Outward signs that pupils may exhibit:
Detachment		
At this point the pupil is beginning to let go. The difficulty is that the behaviour that sometimes occurs is difficult for staff in the current setting as it can feel like rejection after what has often been a long relationship.	'There's nothing for me here.' 'There's no point in making the effort.' 'I don't fit in here any more.' 'I've outgrown this school.'	Engaging in behaviour that alienates them from peers or teachers; damaging relationships so that the separation brought about by the change is less painful. Denigrating current environment – 'I didn't like this school much anyway …' Generally appearing less motivated – conveying a recognition that they are in the last throes of this phase of their education. Becoming withdrawn, not joining in activities that previously would have appealed.
Reorganisation		
At this stage there is acceptance and, in many cases, some optimism. The change has transformed from being a threat to an opportunity, albeit one that still includes some challenging aspects.	'Some things will be the same, but many things will be different. These different things may not be so bad.' 'I'm going to learn new things and meet new friends.' 'It's time for a change.'	Talking more openly and positively about the new environment – 'In my new school …' Concerns and queries are expressed as rational requests for a specific piece of guidance.
Adaptation		
At this stage the pupil begins to see themselves as a member of the new school.	'This isn't so bad, I can cope.' 'I'm in Mrs X's class.' 'It feels like I've been here ages.' 'I can find my way around.' 'I'm not alone here – others are new too.'	Clear friendship groups develop. Friendships begin to extend beyond those who transferred from the same primary school. Pupil joins in some voluntary activities (e.g. clubs). Pupil personalises (not always within accepted boundaries) uniform and equipment. Pupil may begin to push boundaries with staff. There may be conflict with other pupils as groupings and 'pecking orders' emerge.

Source: based on Cossavella and Hobbs 2002 and Hopson *et al.* 1992.

For some pupils their first day in Year 6 will herald the start of the numbness stage as they recognise that they will never again be starting a new class in this school. For others it might be after the school Christmas party as they recognise this joyful experience shared with friends, will not be repeated again. For others it might be when their parents are officially notified of the school they will attend. The key point is that there is no fixed time – the calendar is no guide as to the stage the pupil will be at.

Whilst we have highlighted the importance of relationship with self it is necessary to remember that all three behaviour for learning relationships are linked and exert influence on one another.

Are we pathologising transition?

Transition involves change and this may cause a level of anxiety for all pupils. This is entirely natural and it is important that schools do not, in their well-intentioned attempts to support pupils, pathologise transition and the feelings associated with it. The ideas in Table 13.4 are useful in thinking about how pupils may experience transition and it provides some hypotheses about why pupils may present particular behaviours. However, it should not lead us to believe that all pupils will have problems. We should, for example, be open to the possibility that when, as described in Reflective Exercise 13.2, a pupil talks enthusiastically about aspects of the new school, this is because this is exactly how they feel about it. It is not necessarily a symptom of denial or minimisation.

Reflective Exercise 13.2

Think about some of the Year 6 behaviours you have observed. Which of the phases in Table 13.4 do they relate to? Examples of common behaviours include:

- clinginess and reverting to younger behaviours;
- behaving in an uncharacteristic 'too big for their boots' manner;
- refusing to engage with the change process;
- withdrawal;
- not bothering with work;
- being fascinated by rumours and myths about the new school;
- talking enthusiastically about aspects of the new school.

(based on DfES 2005g: 12)

Ecclestone and Hayes (2008) cite critically an article by Tew and Parks (2007) that encourages schools to manage and ease the confused and ambivalent feelings associated with transition by 'eliciting and sharing feelings, encouraging "closure" of relationships that will be ending through activities such as exploring scenario cards, drawing storyboards, doing role-plays and asking children to write responses from agony aunts or problem pages' (Ecclestone and Hayes 2008: 35).

Such a list includes some useful strategies for supporting transition, including a number that are similar to those suggested in this chapter. However, caution needs to be exercised when planning transition work as transition should not be constructed as a problem. This can be the result if schools place too much emphasis on activities to explore worries and concerns. Balance, of course, is important; we need to create an environment where pupils know that it is acceptable to talk about their natural and understandable worries and feelings about transition without, as we suggested earlier, pathologising transitions. Such an approach can be beneficial in allowing pupils to recognise they are not alone in experiencing concerns about change and can positively influence their relationship with self.

The risk, if we get the balance wrong, is that pupils who are not worried come to believe they should be, effectively reconstructing themselves as vulnerable. The additional challenge is that though pupils go through transition as part of a group, they experience it as individuals. Some will therefore need different forms of support. A useful way of thinking about this is to apply the waves model, familiar to many teachers from National Strategy documents (e.g. DfES 2002, 2005b) to transitions (Figure 13.2).

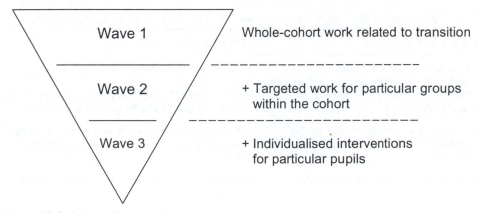

Figure 13.2 A 'waves' approach to transition.
Source: Ellis 2006.

This model recognises that all pupils will benefit from some work to support them as they approach the change of school. Some groups within the class will need additional work and some individuals may need some focused individualised work.

Relationship with the curriculum

By the time most pupils arrive at secondary school they will have views of specific curriculum areas and their abilities within these. This can be considered as part of their relationship with the curriculum. As we have indicated, the transition brings its own anxieties for many pupils which can make their relationship with self vulnerable. A poor relationship with a particular curriculum area, especially Mathematics or English, which the pupil will know are highly valued, can impact on this already vulnerable relationship with self unless carefully handled. Consider the Scenario 13.1.

Scenario 13.1

Jodie has learned by her experiences at primary school that numeracy is difficult. She has regularly been in 'catch up' groups during Key Stage 2 which, though bringing some improvements in attainment, have reinforced to her the idea that Maths is neither an enjoyable subject nor one that she is good at.

At the relationship with the curriculum level the secondary Mathematics teacher is already starting with a pupil who has a fragile relationship with the curriculum. Table 13.5 demonstrates how the Maths teacher at secondary school could either help or hinder this situation.

With the type of approach outlined in Column A it is not only Jodie's relationship with the curriculum that is supported and hopefully enhanced but also her relationship with herself and her relationship with others, in the form of the teacher. With the approach in Column B, the risk is that what was originally a relationship with the curriculum issue transforms into a relationship with self issue.

Table 13.5 Approaches that could help or hinder the relationship with the curriculum

Column A: What would help	Column B: What would hinder
• Start with familiar concepts, or new concepts that can be quickly understood, to build a sense of confidence and competence.	• Start with unfamiliar, complex concepts. • Stress that Mathematics gets a lot harder now the pupils are at secondary school.
• Make clear the procedure for asking for help and also that asking for help is welcomed.	• Make comments like 'If you were listening properly then you would know what to do.'
• Re-explain new concepts patiently.	• Generally sound irritated at having to re-explain.
• Use traffic light systems with the whole class for pupils to communicate their level of understanding: green means that the pupil is confident to get on independently, amber means that the pupil is not completely sure but can make a start, and red means help is needed to get started.	• Make 'not understanding' a public event e.g. 'Anyone who doesn't understand put your hand up now.'
• Make it clear to the whole class that learning involves making mistakes.	• Emphasise the importance of getting it right, e.g. 'Hands up who got them all right … one wrong … two wrong …'
• Mark work constructively.	• Use plenty of red ink.
• Give the pupil the benefit of the doubt – assume that errors are due to conceptual understanding, not behaviour.	• Make comments that assume mistakes are linked to behavioural failings e.g. 'Concentrate harder next time', or 'You need to pay more attention.'
• If you need to see the pupils, frame the request in a friendly manner that informs the pupil of the learning-related purpose of the meeting, e.g. 'Come and see me and I'll go over these with you to check you're OK with them.'	• Simply write 'See me.' The pupil may worry that they are in trouble for not listening or not trying.
• Make it clear how additional help with homework can be sought, through for example attendance at homework club.	• Over-emphasise the consequences for failing to hand in homework.

A complicating factor however is that Jodie's existing relationship with self may determine the effect of the teacher who adopts the approach in Column B, as illustrated in Figures 13.3 and 13.4.

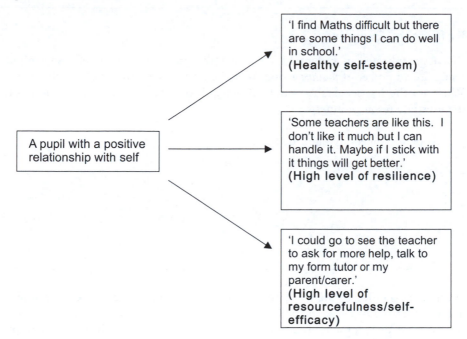

Figure 13.3 Possible interpretation by a pupil with a positive relationship with self.

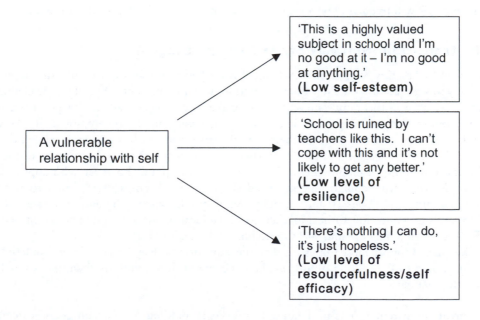

Figure 13.4 Possible interpretation by a pupil with a vulnerable relationship with self.

This illustrates once again the importance of the relationship with self. If we can maintain this through any transition the pupil is more likely to be able to cope with difficulties in their relationships with others and their relationship with the curriculum.

Reflective Exercise 13.3

We have indicated in Figure 13.3 that if Jodie was more resourceful she might recognise a number of *positive* actions to address her relationship with Mathematics. What are the less acceptable actions that pupils may take in such a situation that demonstrate resourcefulness?

* Copying somebody else's answers.

*

*

*

There are two points to draw out from the reflective exercise. First, as we highlighted in Chapter 4, a feature of a learning behaviour – in this case *resourcefulness* – is that it does not always meet the needs of schools or policy-makers and is not always the same as compliant behaviour. Resourcefulness might, for example, take the form of internal truancy or causing sufficient disruption to be sent out of the class in order to avoid the task. Second, behaviour is adaptive. It will frequently be a response to a situation and fulfil a need for the pupil.

The transition from Key Stage 3 to Key Stage 4

The move from Key Stage 3 to Key Stage 4 is a significant transition within the pupil's journey towards adulthood. The choosing of subjects at 14 represents the first real academic and career choices that pupils are required to make. The choices made at this point begin to map out longer-term opportunities, such as further study and future employment. Many pupils will approach this stage of their school career with enthusiasm and excitement, positively identifying subject options that will lead them on a path toward a future in further education, training or employment. There will be some pupils however who approach the transition with trepidation, concerned about factors such as their ability to cope with the demands of Years 10 and 11 and possibly also the impending end of the security of compulsory education. Others may already see education as something that has little to offer and so view Years 10 and 11 as something to be endured.

The main support most pupils need at the transition to Key Stage 4 is of a practical nature related to the making of informed choices about future options. Examples of such activities include:

* involving parents/carers in the options process by holding open evenings and careers conventions to provide a forum for questions and concerns;

- producing written material in easily accessible formats to assist with discussions at home that cover Key Stage 4 courses, careers and coursework;
- arranging interviews where plans for future study, or job interests are discussed in relation to options available now;
- ensuring form-tutors and other key staff take an active role in talking through any worries or complications with the pupil before final decisions are made;
- providing taster sessions in subjects;
- providing group-talks on career-related topics as part of the school's careers education and guidance programme.

Perhaps more significant in behaviour for learning terms however is the extent to which through Key Stage 3 the three relationships have been maintained. Statistics (DCSF 2008c) on school exclusion show that rates rise through Years 7, 8 and 9 before reaching a peak in Year 9. In earlier research Parsons (1999b) placed the peak at Year 10. Ofsted (2005a) reported that in secondary schools behaviour worsens during Key Stage 3. In 2002/03 the percentage of lessons in which behaviour was unsatisfactory rose from less than 5 per cent in Year 7 to over 8 per cent in Years 8 and 9. Barber (1994) analysed a database of 30 000 secondary pupils compiled by Keele University and concluded that, while 60 per cent or so of pupils in early secondary schooling were making reasonable progress, the rest split into three groups:

- 20–30 per cent who were bored – *the disappointed*;
- 10–15 per cent who were beginning to truant regularly and behave badly – *the disaffected*;
- 2–5 per cent who had given up school altogether – *the disappeared*.

The picture that emerges is of Key Stage 3 as a phase in schooling where there are 'casualties'. The vulnerability can begin with Year 8 as it often has none of the unique features that characterise either Year 7 or Year 9. Early Year 7 is a new and exciting experience for the majority of pupils. They are treated differently than in primary school and given more opportunities to take greater responsibility for their own learning (DfES 2004k). They may also be afforded more independence by both school and their parents than they have had before. By the start of Year 8 the excitement of starting secondary school has diminished for some pupils and their relationship with the curriculum begins to suffer as they see Year 8 as 'just more of the same' (DfES 2004k: 2). This point is illustrated by two comments about Year 8 reported by Galton *et al.* (2003), from earlier work by Rudduck *et al.* (1996, 1998):

> You think, 'Oh god! I've got this today!' and so on. It gets really boring and you don't feel excited any more coming to school.
>
> (Rudduck *et al.* 1996)

> Year 7 you have just moved from a different school and in Year 8 you have already been there and you have nothing important to think about.
>
> (Rudduck *et al.* 1998, cited in Galton *et al.* 2003: 93)

For many pupils Year 9 remedies this temporary lapse through its end of Key Stage status. It is the time when they begin to think about Key Stage 4 and the specific opportunities available to them through their subject choices and how these will impact on future life decisions (DfES 2004k). This can provide a 'pick-me-up' towards the end of Year 9 (Doddington *et al.* 1999) that rekindles the relationship with the curriculum and schooling generally.

For other pupils who experience the deterioration in their relationship with the curriculum it is not a temporary lapse. Typically, these are pupils for whom this does not remain a relationship with the curriculum issue but begins to impinge on their relationship with self and relationship with others. If these pupils misbehave as an avoidance strategy or to relieve the perceived 'sameness' of the Year 8 curriculum, they may find their relationship with others is increasingly based on the behaviour they exhibit.

A number of pupils' responses in Galton *et al.*'s (2003) work illustrate the problem when this occurs:

> I think trouble with me were when I come to school I messed about from day one so people got me as a mess-abouter from day one so like if I didn't mess about, 'Oh, you're boring'. You know what I mean? (Year 11 girl).
>
> (Galton *et al.* 2003: 86)

> If you fall into a bad group of friends then … I know one group; their kind of mission is not to do well, to mess around, to get told off … One of them is extremely clever and always does well but … It's part of her group to act like that (Year 10 girl).
>
> (Galton *et al.* 2003: 87)

> You mess around … you get a reputation for yourself as a trouble-causer and you can't lose it – it's like there (Year 11 boy).
>
> (Galton *et al.* 2003: 86)

> Me personally I've brought a reputation upon myself. I'm known to be the class clown and that and it's got me in a lot of trouble. And so I've decided to change and it's just really hard to, like show the teachers that cos … and when, like, I went on report, and I got, like, A1, A1, best, top marks. But there's been some lessons where it's slipped and they're (saying) like, 'Oh, he's still the same.' I can understand how they feel about that (Year 10 boy).
>
> (Galton *et al.* 2003: 86)

The first three quotes illustrate how by Years 10 and 11 the pupil's relationship with their peers is based on the behaviour they exhibit. The fourth quote is notable in demonstrating that, from this pupil's perspective, his relationship with his teachers is also determined by past behaviour.

Typically the individual pupil will not be the only one exhibiting these behaviours and group norms may develop which further complicate the relationship with others. Galton *et al.* (2003) reported pupils finding it difficult to escape the norms of their anti-work peer-group.

Implicit in each quote is also the impact on the individual's relationship with self. The notion of a 'reputation' involves a relationship with others in the sense that it is what others think of us, but there is also a relationship with self dimension if it becomes part of what we think of ourselves. The fourth quote is interesting because the pupil seems to be able to view his reputation as something separate to him. He recognises that he is capable of behaving in manner that is different to his reputation. It would be reasonable to assume from this that his relationship with self is sound; he recognises his reputation is not *him*. We could speculate that because of the nature of this pupil's relationship with self, change

Table 13.6 Maintaining a positive relationship with the curriculum

Effective schools ...	Examples of how this can be achieved
regularly evaluate progress;	Develop whole-school policies on assessment that take account of transition. Ensure that all teaching staff are familiar with the prior attainment of their pupils and use this information in planning. Have systems for tracking pupils' progress in all subjects and ensure that outcomes of assessment are used to inform planning. Use diagnostic assessment at the start of new work.
make each year special;	Plan induction programmes for each new year. Make explicit, in schemes of work and to the pupils themselves, what is special about learning in each year.
recognise the increasing maturity of pupils;	Have reward systems that reflect increasing maturity. Provide opportunities for pupils to take additional responsibilities. Provide opportunities for pupils to benefit from more privileges as they get older. Ensure that schemes of work demonstrate higher learning demands and higher expectations, building on the Frameworks where appropriate.
ensure progression and continuity;	Ensure that the curriculum on offer across all subjects provides appropriate challenge, continuity and lack of repetition. Incorporate progression and continuity into schemes of work, using the Key Stage 3 Frameworks where applicable. Encourage all subject teachers to build a distinctive flavour into the schemes of work for each of the three years of Key Stage 3. Organise pupil groupings to allow pupils to move between groups without jeopardising their learning.
have systems that recognise and correct disaffection early;	Regularly monitor pupils' behaviour and attendance and ensure that the information collected and collated by pastoral staff is used to inform teaching. Provide structures for effective communication between teachers and pastoral staff. Monitor outcomes of any remedial actions.
have effective intervention plans;	Have systems for identifying pupils' needs that build on prior knowledge from Key Stage 2. Ensure that intervention is coordinated across the school and embedded in the school's planning cycle. Use a range of intervention activities to meet the profiled learning needs of individuals and groups of pupils. Use academic tutors or mentors for specific learning issues.
support pupils in their learning as well as their behaviour;	Involve pastoral staff in regular reviews of academic progress. Identify patterns of progress across the school and use any outcomes to plan interventions.
provide opportunities for a fresh start.	Allow pupils to reflect on past success and use the opportunity to plan for new learning. Recognise that whereas learning has to be carried forward, pupils can be helped to make a fresh start in relation to behaviour.

may be more achievable. For many pupils however, their relationship with others becomes part of their image and impinges on their relationship with self. In Galton *et al.*'s (2003) study they reported pupils wanting to change from 'dosser' or 'shirker' to 'worker' but not knowing how to. The labelling terminology used by these pupils reflects that the behaviour has become a part of their identity.

The message therefore is that Key Stage 3 'casualties' need to be minimised as anti-work identities, once established, are difficult to change. It is likely to be more productive to intervene in the early stages than to try to change pupils' identities as learners at Year 10 (Galton *et al.* 2003). Table 13.6 sets out a range of strategies suggested by DfES (2004k) that contribute to the maintenance of a positive relationship with the curriculum and schooling.

Summary

Though work to support transition needs to focus on the social, emotional and cognitive aspects, it is the nature of the individual pupil's relationship with self that is likely to be the key determinant in how successfully they make the transition. A priority for transition planning therefore is ensuring that the individual pupil's relationship with self is protected. As we identified in Chapter 7, relationship with self develops over time and consequently we need to recognise that, due to the relationship with self they bring to the transition, some pupils are more vulnerable than others at these times.

As pupils progress through school the generic learning behaviours, such as 'collaboration', 'responsibility' and 'motivation' that were identified in Powell and Tod's (2004) EPPI review, remain as constant priorities for development. However, there is a whole range of what we referred to in Chapter 4 as 'sub' learning behaviours that are required at different points in the pupil's school career. It is beneficial to consider explicitly what the expectations of learning behaviour are at each phase of education and give thought to how these can be developed.

Concluding thoughts
Over to you ...

In any school context there will be an inheritance from its past, a concern surrounding the activity and accountability of the present, and hopes and plans for the future. For most teachers and trainees their time and attention will be taken up with coping with the demands of the present and for this reason we chose to locate our relatively new conceptual framework within the policy developments of history and existing school policies and practices. Hopefully this will allow teachers and trainees to appreciate that pupil behaviour has been an enduring area of concern for schools and that their school, as part of its remit, will have sought to develop contexts and conditions to address these concerns. For some teachers and trainees this may beg the question as to why 'new' initiatives are so frequently being imposed when schools could simply proceed in a systematic manner and continually develop, evaluate and improve their existing practice. We might speculate on the reasons:

- Is it that political imperatives prescribe a need to find quick fix solutions to public concerns?
- Is it that such initiatives are necessary to fuel ongoing professional development through either inspiring teachers to make such initiatives work, or alternatively leading them to vigorously defend their existing practices and criticise the new?
- Could it be that in spite of all the evidence to the contrary there is still a hope that someone out there does have *the* solution to behaviour problems and that there will be a time when teachers can be assured that they will be able to walk into a class and get on with teaching their subject?

There is of course some substance to all these reasons. Schools could improve the extent to which they systematically evaluate their existing policies and practices for behaviour and build on these evaluations to improve their efficacy. The need for systematic and ongoing evaluation of policy and practices against their purpose for individuals is a key theme within this book. We endorse this in an era where there has been an over-emphasis on the implementation of rapid and frequent change at the cost of directing teachers' time and skills towards professional matters of continuity, consolidation and systematic evaluation. It is also true that new initiatives can serve to revive and refresh our approaches to practice, provided they are feasible and underpinned by an evidence base. In considering whether there is a 'solution' to behaviour problems or whether teachers can expect to be able to teach their subject without fear of dissent or disruption, this book is open in acknowledging that this is unrealistic.

There are individuals and theories that have guided thinking and provided principles for practices for behaviour management in schools. Some of these have been touched on in this book and can be identified by readers as being evident in the policies and practices of their schools. Such principles and practices if applied rigorously and with due recognition to their original theoretical underpinnings have proven to be effective for many pupils. These principles are often evident within re-branded or 'new' initiatives for behaviour management. This book endorses the use of such tried and tested approaches and deliberately recognises that there is a plethora of strategies and guidance in a variety of formats that can be used to resource the behaviour for learning conceptual framework. All of these approaches have some inherent strengths but none of them has provided the panacea for the range of behavioural concerns. This is not a criticism but a reflection of reality: no one approach can expect to address the situational and dynamic variations in individual behaviour. To reiterate the Elton Report: 'Reducing bad behaviour is a realistic aim. Eliminating it completely is not' (DES 1989: 65).

Any strategy or approach to tackle behaviour that is recommended to schools and their teachers is designed for what we might term the 'hypothetical individual'. In other words, any strategy or approach schools and their teachers are encouraged to use proactively or reactively for individuals can only ever be formulated based on how it is anticipated a typical individual will respond. Some approaches have attempted to address this by offering adaptations for atypical individuals. For example Mosley refers to 'children beyond' (Mosley 1996, Mosley and Sonnet 2005), Canter and Canter (1992) refer to individualised behaviour plans, Rogers (1994) offers 'behaviour recovery', and SEAL delivery (DfES 2005c, 2005a) is based on a waves model, recognising that some pupils require an individualised response. Such adaptations focus on what we might consider to be typical *atypical* pupils. They are still therefore aimed at hypothetical individuals. It follows that approaches and strategies for behaviour designed to be effective for *hypothetical* groups of pupils and individuals will not be effective for every *real* group and individual that teachers encounter. This book is rooted within the knowledge that there will inevitably be variations and diversity within individual responses to any strategy or approach, which is why it offers a conceptual framework rather than following the well trodden path of providing strategies and putative solutions.

The conceptual framework within this book seeks mainly to allow teachers to 'make sense' of what they know already and the context in which they are working. Teachers know that their profession is concerned with promoting learning and that this involves developing certain behaviours. While there may be a hope that behaviour can be controlled so that learning can take place, in reality achieving compliance does not necessarily ensure that academic learning will ensue. Teachers also know that the classroom group is potentially a valuable resource rather than a barrier to individual learning. They know that learning and behaviour are intrinsically linked, which is a perspective strongly supported by the behaviour for learning conceptual framework. It is anticipated that the development and use of the framework will lead to an increasing synthesis of teaching and behaviour management policies and approaches in schools and a significant shift in the priorities and purpose of behaviour management.

Most teachers will endorse a view that teaching is about relationships. However they may have yet to explore the implications for practice of the enactment of the language of relationships and the dynamic interactions and interdependence of these relationships. This book accepts that this emphasis on relationships builds on familiar language and concepts but has tackled the less familiar working relationships of the classroom in an exploratory manner that befits the early stage of development of the behaviour for learning conceptual framework. Readers have much to offer the ongoing development of this framework through trying it out in practice and critically reflecting upon their experiences of its use. In offering a framework we expect that a reframing of existing practices and thinking needs to take place and we have attempted to do this in relation to the contested area of special educational needs. Again there is a need to explore and develop this idea further. The conceptual framework is compatible with emergent concerns about the social and emotional aspects of learning through recognition of the interdependence of the relationships contained within the framework namely, relationship with curriculum, relationship with self and relationship with others. It supports a view that pupil learning cannot realistically be compartmentalised because it is not *experienced* by the pupil in this way. For this reason this book places emphasis on the pursuit of practice that seeks to achieve a balance between the relationships and does not risk compromising one or more of the relationships at the expense of another.

Our intention is not that the legacy from this book will be a proposed solution to behaviour problems. Rather it seeks to leave teachers with a framework that allows them to make sense of and harness the plethora of information and guidance that surrounds the area of behaviour management in schools. It is relevant to all teachers, across all phases and for all pupils and is intended to have enduring utility in the face of certain change to both schools and to the cultural and social experiences of their teachers and pupils. This book offers an emergent framework for practice but its use and development lies firmly in the hands of others.

References

Aaron, P.G. and Joshi, R.M. (1992) *Reading Problems: Consultation and Remediation.* New York: Guilford Press.

Aird, R. (2001) *The Education and Care of Children with Severe, Profound and Multiple Learning Difficulties.* London: David Fulton.

Alexander, R., Rose, J. and Woodhead, C. (1992) *Curriculum Organisation and Classroom Practice in Primary School.* London: DES.

Allen, M. and Ainley, P. (2007) *Education Make You Fick, Innit?* London: Tufnell Press.

Alloway, T.P., Gathercole, S.E., Adams, A-M. and Willis, C. (2005) 'Working memory abilities in children with special educational needs.' *Educational and Child Psychology.* British Psychological Society Leicester. **22**(4): 56–67.

Alvord, M. and Grados, J. (2005) Enhancing resilience in children: a proactive approach. *Professional Psychology: Research and Practice* **(36)**: 238–245.

Angus, L. (1993) 'The sociology of school effectiveness.' *British Journal of Sociology of Education.* **14**(3): 333–345.

Argyle, M. (1967) *The Psychology of Interpersonal Behaviour.* London: Penguin.

Armstrong, D. (2005) 'Reinventing "inclusion": New Labour and the cultural politics of special education.' *Oxford Review of Education.* **31**(1): 135–151.

Aronson, E. and Mills, J. (1959) 'The effects of severity of initiation on liking for group.' *Journal of Abnormal and Social Psychology.* **66**: 177–181.

Assessment Reform Group. (1999) *Assessment for Learning: Beyond the Black Box.* Cambridge: University of Cambridge, Faculty of Education. Available online at: http://www.qca.org.uk/libraryAssets/media/beyond_black_box2.pdf) [accessed 17 July 2008].

ATL (2002) *Achievement for All: Working with Children with Special Educational Needs in Mainstream Schools and Colleges.* London: Association of Teachers and Lecturers.

Attfield, R., Blamires, M., Gray, P. and Moore, J. (2004) *Support Services and Mainstream Schools.* London: David Fulton.

Ayers, H., Clarke, D. and Murray, A. (2000) *Perspectives on Behaviour.* 2nd ed. London: David Fulton.

Bandura, A. (1977) *Social Learning Theory.* Englewood Cliffs, New Jersey: Prentice Hall.

Bandura, A. (1986) *Social Foundations of Thought and Action: A Social Cognitive Theory.* Englewood Cliffs, New Jersey: Prentice-Hall.

Barber, M. (1994) *Young People and their Attitudes to School.* England: University of Keele.

Barnes, C. (1992) *Disabled People in Britain and Discrimination: A Case for Anti-discrimination Legislation.* London: Hurst & Co. Publishers.

Baron-Cohen, S. (1995) *Mindblindness: an Essay on Autism and Theory of Mind.* London: MIT Press.

Baron-Cohen, S. (2008) 'Theories of the autistic mind.' *The Psychologist.* **21**(2): 112–116.

Bate, C. and Moss, J. (1997) 'Towards a behaviour curriculum.' *Educational Psychology in Practice.* **13**(3): 176–180.

Beaty, E., Gibbs, G. and Morgan, A. (1997) 'Learning orientations and study contracts.' In Entwistle, N.J., Hounsell, D.J. and Marten, F., eds (1997) *The Experience of Learning*. 2nd ed. Edinburgh: Scottish Academic Press. 72–88. (Now only available at: http://www.tla.ed.ac.uk/resources/EoL.html).

Belbin, M. (1981) *Management Teams*. Oxford: Butterworth Heinemann.

Berk, L. (2003) *Child Development*. Boston, MA: Allyn and Bacon.

Black, L. (2006) 'Young children's perspectives on whole class discussions.' Paper presented at: *British Educational Research Association Annual Conference*, University of Warwick, 6–9 September.

Blamires, M. (1999) 'Universal design for learning: re-establishing differentiation as part of the inclusion agenda?' *Support for Learning* **14**(4): 158–163.

Blandford, S. (1998) *Managing Discipline in Schools*. London: Routledge.

Blatchford, P. (1992) 'Academic self-assessment at 7 and 11 years: its accuracy and association with ethnic groups and sex.' *British Journal of Educational Psychology.* (62): 35–44.

Booth, T. and Ainscow, M. (2002) *The Index for Inclusion*. Bristol: CSIE.

Bowers, T. (2005) 'The forgotten "E" in EBD.' In Clough, P., Garner, P., Pardeck, J. and Yuen, F. (2005) *Handbook of Emotional and Behavioural Difficulties.* London: Sage.

BPS. (1999) *Dyslexia, Literacy and Psychological Assessment*. Leicester: British Psychological Society.

Braithwaite, R. (2001) *Managing Aggression*. London: Routledge.

Brand, R. (2007) *My Booky Wook*. London: Hodder and Stoughton.

Breakwell, G. (1997) *Coping with Aggressive Behaviour*. Leicester: British Psychological Society.

Burns, R. (1982) *Self Concept Development and Education*. London: Holt, Rinehart and Winston.

Burton, S. (2004) 'Self esteem groups for secondary pupils with dyslexia.' *Educational Psychology in Practice* **20**(1): 55–74.

CACE (1967) *Children and their Primary Schools: The Plowden Report*. London: HMSO.

Canter, L. and Canter, M. (1992) *Assertive Discipline: Positive Behavior Management for Today's Classroom*. Santa Monica, CA: Canter and Associates, Inc.

Carr, M. and Claxton, G. (2002) 'Tracking the development of learning dispositions.' *Assessment in Education* **9**(1): 9–37.

Chaplain, R. (2003) *Teaching Without Disruption in the Primary School*. London: RoutledgeFalmer.

Chapman, J.W. (1998) 'Learning disabled children's self concepts.' *Review of Educational Research* (58): 347–371.

Charles, C. (2002) *Building Classroom Discipline*. 7th ed. Boston, MA: Allyn and Bacon.

Chitty, C. (1990) 'Central control of the school curriculum.' In Moon, B., ed. (1990) *New Curriculum – National Curriculum*. London: Open University Press.

Clandini, D.J. and Connelly, F.M. (1995) *Teachers' 'Professional Knowledge'*. NY: Teachers College Press.

Clarke, A. and Clarke, A., eds (1958) *Mental Deficiency: The Changing Outlook*. 1st ed. London: Methuen.

Claxton, G. (1999) *Wise Up: The Challenge of Lifelong Learning*. London: Bloomsbury.

Claxton, G. (2002) *Building Learning Power*. Bristol: TLO.

Claxton, G. (2006) 'Expanding the capacity to learn: a new end for education?' Opening Keynote Address, British Educational Research Association Annual Conference, 6 September 2006, Warwick University. Available online at: http://www.guyclaxton.com/documents/New/BERA%20Keynote%20Final.pdf [accessed 15 July 2008].

Coopersmith, S. (1967) *The Antecedents of Self-Esteem*. San Francisco: W H Freeman.

Cornwall, J. (2004) 'Therapeutic approaches to education: working with individuals.' In Haworth, E., ed. (2004) *Supporting Staff Working with Pupils with SEBD: A Handbook*. Lichfield: QED publications.

Cornwall, J. and Walter, C. (2006) *Therapeutic Education: Working with Troubled and Troublesome Young People*. London: Routledge.

Corrie, L. (2002) *Investigating Troublesome Classroom Behaviour*. London: RoutledgeFalmer.

Cossavella, A. and Hobbs, C. (2002) *Farewell and Welcome*. Bristol: Lucky Duck.

Cowley, S. (2003) *Getting the Buggers to Behave 2*. London: Continuum.

Craig, C. (2007) *The Potential Dangers of a Systematic, Explicit Approach to Teaching Social and Emotional Skills (SEAL): An Overview and Summary of the Arguments*. Glasgow: Centre for Confidence and Well-Being.

Available online at: http://www.centreforconfidence.co.uk/docs/SEALsummary.pdf [accessed 28 July 2008].

Craven, R. and Marsh, H. (2008) 'The centrality of the self-concept construct for psychological wellbeing and unlocking human potential: implications for child and educational psychologists.' *Educational and Child Psychology* **25**(2): 104–118.

Cremin, T., Mottram, T., Collins, M., Powell, S. and Leicester, S. (2008) *Building Communities of Readers*. Available online at: http://www.ukla.org/site/research_projects_in_progress/teachers_as_readers_building_communities_of_readers/ [accessed 2nd February 2009].

Cross, M. (1997) 'Challenging behaviour or challenged comprehension.' *RCSLT Bulletin*. (545): 1–12.

Cross, M. (2004) *Children with Emotional and Behavioural Difficulties and Communication Problems*. London: Jessica Kingsley.

Curwin, R. and Mendler, A. (1989) 'We repeat, let the buyer beware: a response to Canter.' *Educational Leadership* **46**(6): 68–71.

Damon, W. (1984) 'Peer education: the untapped potential.' *Journal of Applied Developmental Psychology*. (5): 331–343.

Darling-Hammond, L. (2001) 'Standards setting in teaching: changes in licensing, certification and assessment.' In Richardson V., ed. (2001) *Handbook of Research on Teaching*. 4th ed. Washington DC: American Educational Research Association.

Davies, W. and Frude, N. (2000) *Preventing Face-To-Face Violence*. 4th ed. Leicester: Association of Psychological Therapies.

Davis, P. and Florian, L. (2004) *Teaching Strategies and Approaches for Pupils with Special Educational Needs: A Scoping Study*. Nottingham: DfES.

Day, D. and Libertini, G. (1992) 'Profiles of children's learning behaviour.' *Journal of Research in Childhood Education*. (6): 100–112.

DCSF (2007) *The Use of Force to Control or Restrain Pupils*. Nottingham: DCSF.

DCSF (2008a) *Initial Teacher Training Inclusion Development Programme Primary/Secondary: Dyslexia and Speech, Language and Communication Needs*. Available online at: http://www.standards.dfes.gov.uk/primary/publications/inclusion/sen_idp_teachtrain_0025708.pdf [accessed 6 September 2008].

DCSF (2008b) *The Education of Children and Young People with Behavioural, Emotional and Social Difficulties as a Special Educational Need*. Available online at: http://www.teachernet.gov.uk/_doc/12604/ACFD633.doc [accessed 6 September 2008].

DCSF (2008c) *Permanent and Fixed Period Exclusions from Schools and Exclusion Appeals in England, 2006/07*. Available online at: http://www.dcsf.gov.uk/rsgateway/DB/SFR/s000793/SFR_14Revised.pdf [accessed 22 February 2009].

Demaine, J. (1999) *Education, Policy and Contemporary Politics*. London: Macmillan.

Dent, H.C. (1942) *A New Order in English Education*. London: University of London Press.

Department for Education and Training (2005) *Research into Learning: Implications for Teaching*. Melbourne: Department of Education and Training. Available online at: http://www.eduweb.vic.gov.au/edulibrary/public/publ/research/publ/Research_Learning_Implications_Teaching-rpt.doc [accessed 7 August 2008].

DES (1980) *A Framework for the School Curriculum*. London: HMSO.

DES (1981) *The School Curriculum*. London: DES.

DES (1989) *Discipline in Schools*. (The Elton Report). London: HMSO.

DfE (1992) *The Initial Training of Secondary School Teachers: New Criteria for Course*. (Circular 9/92). London: DfE.

DfE (1993) *The Initial Training of Primary School Teachers: New Criteria for Course*. (Circular 14/93). London: DfE.

DfE (1994a) *Code of Practice on the Identification and Assessment of Special Educational Needs*. London: DfE.

DfE (1994b) *Pupil Behaviour and Discipline*. (Circular 8/94). London: DfE.

DfE (1994c) *The Education of Children with Emotional and Behavioural Difficulties*. (Circular 9/94). London: DfE.

DfEE (1997a) *Excellence in Schools*. London: DfEE.

DfEE (1997b) *Excellence for All Children*. London: DfEE.

DfEE (1998a) *The National Literacy Strategy: Framework for Teaching*. London: DfEE.

DfEE (1998b) *The Use of Force to Control or Restrain Pupils*. (Circular 10/98). London: DfEE.

DfEE (1999a) *Social Inclusion: Pupil Support*. London: DfEE.

DfEE (1999b) *The National Numeracy Strategy: Framework for Teaching Mathematics from Reception to Year 6*. London: DfEE.

DfEE (2000) *Research into Teacher Effectiveness*. (Hay McBer research). London: DfEE.

DfEE/QCA (1999a) *National Curriculum: Handbook for Primary Teachers in England*. London: DfEE/QCA.

DfEE/QCA (1999b) *National Curriculum: Handbook for Secondary Teachers in England*. London: DfEE/QCA.

DfEE/QCA (2000) *Curriculum Guidance for the Foundation Stage*. London: DfEE/QCA.

DfES (2001) *Special Educational Needs Code of Practice*. Nottingham: DfES.

DfES (2002) *Including All Children in the Literacy Hour and Daily Mathematics Lesson*. Nottingham: DfES.

DfES (2003a) *Excellence and Enjoyment: A Strategy for Primary Schools*. Nottingham: DfES.

DfES (2003b) *Every Child Matters: Summary*. Nottingham: DfES.

DfES (2003c) *Key Stage 3 National Strategy Behaviour and Attendance Training Materials: Core Day 1*. Nottingham: DfES.

DfES (2003d) *Key Stage 3 National Strategy: Behaviour and Attendance Key Messages for Local Authority Inspectors*. Nottingham: DfES.

DfES (2003e) *Advice on Whole School Behaviour and Attendance Policy*. Nottingham: DfES.

DfES (2004a) *Every Child Matters: Change for Children*. Nottingham: DfES.

DfES (2004b) *A National Conversation about Personalised Learning*. Nottingham: DfES.

DfES (2004c) *Key Stage 3 National Strategy: Developing Emotional Health and Well Being – A Whole-school Approach to Improving Behaviour and Attendance*. Nottingham: DfES.

DfES (2004d) *Effective Lessons and Behaviour for Learning*. Nottingham: DfES.

DfES (2004e) *Behaviour in the Classroom: A Course for Newly Qualified Teachers: Course Notes*. Nottingham: DfES.

DfES (2004f) *Planning and Assessment for Learning: Assessment for Learning*. Nottingham: DfES.

DfES (2004g) *Key Stage 3 National Strategy Behaviour and Attendance Core Day 2: Developing Effective Practice Across the School*. Nottingham: DfES.

DfES (2004h) *Unit 18 Improving the Climate for Learning*. Nottingham: DfES.

DfES (2004i) *Creating a Learning Culture: Conditions for Learning*. Nottingham: DfES.

DfES (2004j) *Learning and Teaching for Children with Special Educational Needs in the Primary School*. Nottingham: DfES.

DfES (2004k) *Transition and Progression within Key Stage 3*. Nottingham: DfES.

DfES (2005a) *Learning Behaviour: The Report of the Practitioners' Group on School Behaviour and Discipline*. (The Steer Report). Nottingham: DfES.

DfES (2005b) *Leading on Inclusion*. Nottingham: DfES.

DfES (2005c) *Excellence and Enjoyment: Social and Emotional Aspects of Learning: Guidance*. Nottingham: DfES.

DfES (2005d) *Higher Standards, Better Schools for All*. Nottingham: DfES.

DfES (2005e) *14–19 Education and Skills*. London: TSO.

DfES (2005f) *Transition at Key Stage 2 – 3: Supporting Positive Behaviour and Regular Attendance*. Nottingham: DfES.

DfES (2007a) *Social and Emotional Aspects of Learning (SEAL): Guidance Booklet*. Nottingham: DfES.

DfES (2007b) *School Discipline and Pupil Behaviour Policies*. Nottingham: DfES.

DfES (2007c) *Practice Guidance for the Early Years Foundation Stage*. Nottingham: DfES.

Dix, P. (2007) *Taking Care of Behaviour*. Harlow: Longman.

Dockrell, J. and Lindsay, G. (2007) 'Identifying the educational and social needs of children with specific speech and language difficulties on entry to secondary school.' *Educational and Child Psychology* **24**(4): 101–15.

Doddington, C., Flutter, J., Bearne, E. and Demetriou, H. (2001) *Sustaining Pupils' Progress at Year 3: Research Report*. Cambridge: University of Cambridge Faculty of Education.

Doddington, C., Flutter, J. and Rudduck, J. (1999) 'Exploring and explaining "dips" in motivation and performance in primary and secondary schooling.' *Research in Education*. (61): 29–38.

DoH/DfES (2004) *Promoting Emotional Health and Wellbeing through the National Healthy School Standard*.

Donaldson, M. (1978) *Children's Minds*. London: Fontana.

Dreikurs, R., Grunwald, B. and Pepper, F. (1998) *Maintaining Sanity in the Classroom*. London: Accelerated Development.

Drucker, P.F. (1999) *Leadership Challenges for the 21st Century*. Oxford: Butterworth Heinemann.

Duckworth, A.L. and Seligman, M.E.P. (2006) 'Self-discipline gives girls the edge: gender in self-discipline, grades, and achievement scores.' *Journal of Educational Psychology American Psychological Association* **98**(1): 198–208.

Dunne, M., Humphreys, S., Sebba, J., Dyson, A., Gallannaugh, F. and Muijs, D. (2007) *Effective Teaching and Learning for Pupils in Low Attaining Groups*. Research Brief DCSF – RB011.

Ecclestone, K. and Hayes, D. (2008) *The Dangerous Rise of Therapeutic Education*. London: Routledge.

Education and Skills Committee (2006) *Special Educational Needs: Third Report of Session 2005–6 House of Commons* 2006, London.

Elkin, S. (2004) *Top-performing School Starts by Managing Behaviour*. London: Specialist Schools Trust.

Elliott, J. (2005) 'Dyslexia myths and the feel-bad factor.' *Times Educational Supplement*. Friday 2 September 2005.

Ellis, S. (2006) 'Managing transitions.' In Soan S., ed. (2006) *The SENCO Handbook*. London: Optimus.

Ellis, S., Tod, J. and Graham-Matheson, L. (2008) *Special Educational Needs and Inclusion: Reflection and Renewal*. Birmingham: NASUWT. Available online at: www.teachersunion.org.uk

Emler, N. (2002) *Self-Esteem: The Costs and Causes of Low Self Worth*. York: Joseph Rowntree Foundation.

Entwistle, N.J. and Peterson, E.R. (2004) 'Conceptions of learning and knowledge in higher education: relationships with study behaviour and influence of learning environments.' *International Journal of Educational Research* **41**(6): 407–428.

Evans, J., Harden, A., Thomas, J. and Benefield, P. (2003) *Support for Pupils with Emotional and Behavioural Difficulties (EBD) in Mainstream Primary Classrooms: A Systematic Review of the Effectiveness of Interventions*. London: Institute of Education.

Faber, A. and Mazlish, E. (2001) *How to Talk so Kids Will Listen and Listen so Kids Will Talk*. London: Piccadilly Press.

Fabian, H. and Dunlop, A. (2002) *Transitions in the Early Years*. London: RoutledgeFalmer.

Farmer, M., Robertson, B., Kenny, C. and Siitarinen, J. (2007) 'Language and the development of self understanding in children with communication difficulties.' *Educational and Child Psychology* **24**(4): 116–129.

Faupel, A., Herrick, E. and Sharp, P. (1998) *Anger Management: A Practical Guide*. London: David Fulton.

Finch, J. (1984) *Education as Social Policy*. London: Longman.

Fletcher-Campbell, F. and Wilkin, A. (2003) *Review of the Research Literature on Educational Interventions for Pupils with Emotional and Behavioural Difficulties*. National Foundation for Educational Research (NFER). Available online at: http://www.audit-commission.gov.uk/Products/NATIONAL-REPORT/D3265D20-FD7D-11d6-B211-0060085F8572/ebdreviewFeb03.pdf [accessed 21 February 2009].

Florian, L. and Rouse, M. (2001) 'Inclusive practice in English secondary schools.' In Nind *et al.*, (2005) *Curriculum and Pedagogy in Inclusive Education*. London: RoutledgeFalmer.

Floud, J., Halsey, A. and Martin, F. (1956) *Social Class and Educational Opportunity*. London: Heinemann.

Fogell, J. and Long, R. (1997) *Emotional and Behavioural Difficulties*. Tamworth: NASEN.

Froyen, L.A. (1993) *Classroom Management: The Reflective Teacher-Leader*. New York: Macmillan Publishing Company.

Galloway, D., Leo, E.L., Rogers, C. and Armstrong, D. (1996) 'Maladaptive motivational style: the role of domain specific task demand in English and Mathematics.' *British Journal of Educational Psychology*. (66): 197–207.

Galton, M., Gray, J. and Rudduck, J. (2003) *Transfer and Transitions in the Middle Years of Schooling (7–14): Continuities and Discontinuities in Learning*. Nottingham: DfES.

Galvin, P. (1999) *Behaviour and Discipline in Schools 2*. London: David Fulton.

Gardner, H. (1983) *Frames of the Mind: The Theory of Multiple Intelligences*. New York: Basic Books.

Giallo, R. and Little, E. (2003) 'Classroom behaviour problems: the relationship between preparedness, classroom experiences and self-efficacy in graduate and student teachers.' *Australian Journal of Educational and Developmental Psychology*. (3): 21–34.

Gibson, S. and Blandford, S. (2005) *Managing Special Educational Needs*. London: David Fulton.

Gibson, S. and Dembo, M. (1984) 'Teacher efficacy: a construct validation.' *Journal of Educational Psychology*. (76): 569–582.

Gillborn, D. and Youdell, D. (2000) *Rationing Education: Policy, Practice, Reform and Equity*. Buckingham: Open University Press.

Gillie, O. (1976) 'Crucial data was faked by eminent psychologist.' *Sunday Times* (London). 24 October 1976.

Ginott, H. (1971) *Teacher and Child*. New York: Macmillan.

Godfrey, R., Tod, J. and Soan, S. (2007) *Explorations of Interagency Working in Speech, Language and Communication in England*. Paper presented at ECER, Ghent, Belgium, 2007.

Goleman, D. (1995) *Emotional Intelligence: Why it can Matter More than IQ*. London: Bloomsbury.

Goleman, D. (1998) *Working with Emotional Intelligence*. New York: Bantam Books.

Goler, B. and Booth, J. (2008) 'Paired reading proves its worth.' *SENCO Update*. London: Optimus. (July/August): 8.

Gould, S. (1996) *The Mismeasure of Man*. London: Norton.

Gray, C. (1994a) *The New Social Story Book*. Arlington, Texas: Future Horizons.

Gray, C. (1994b) *Comic Strip Conversations*. Arlington, Texas: Future Horizons.

Hacker, R.J. and Rowe, M.J. (1997) 'The impact of National Curriculum development on teaching and learning behaviours.' *International Journal of Science Education*. **19**(9): 997–1004.

Hadow Report (1926) *The Education of the Adolescent*. London: HMSO.

Haggarty, L. (2002) 'What does research tell us about how to prepare teachers?' Paper presented to the ESCalate PGCE Conference, Univeristy of Nottingham, 9 July 2002.

Hallam, S. and Rogers, L. (2008) *Improving Behaviour and Attendance at School*. Maidenhead: Open University Press.

Halsey, A.H. and Sylva, K. (1987) 'Plowden: history and prospect.' *Oxford Review of Education*. **13**(1): 3–11.

Hammersley, M. (2001) 'On "systematic" reviews of research literatures: a narrative response to Evans and Benefield.' *British Educational Research Journal*. **27**(5): 543–554.

Harlen, W. and Deakin-Crick, R. (2002) 'A systematic review of the impact of summative assessment and tests on students' motivation for learning.' In *Research Evidence in Education Library*. London: EPPI-Centre, Social Science Research Unit, Institute of Education, University of London.

Harris, A., Reynolds, D. and Bennett, N. (2004) *School Effectiveness and School Improvement: Alternative Perspectives*. London: Continuum.

Hayles, N.K. (1991) *Chaos and Order: Complex Dynamics in Literature and Science*. Chicago: University of Chicago Press.

Head, G. (2007) *Better Learning, Better Behaviour*. Edinburgh: Dunedin Academic Press.

Hearnshaw, L. (1979) *Cyril Burt: Psychologist*. London: Hodder and Stoughton.

Higgins, S., Baumfield, V. and Hall, E. (2007) 'Learning skills and the development of learning capabilities.' Report. In *Research Evidence in Education Library*. London: EPPI-Centre, Social Science Research Unit, Institute of Education, University of London.

HMI (1981) *Aspects of the School Curriculum*. London: HMSO.

Hollander, B. (1916) *Abnormal Children (Nervous, Mischievous, Precocious and Backward)*. London: Kegan Paul, Trench, Trubner & Co. Ltd.

Hook, P. and Vass, A. (2000) *Confident Classroom Leadership*. London: David Fulton.

Hook, P. and Vass, A. (2002) *Teaching with Influence*. London: David Fulton.

Hopkins, B. (2004) *Just School*. London: Jessica Kingsley.

Hopkins, D. (2001) *School Improvement for Real*. London: RoutledgeFalmer.

Hopson, B., Scally, M. and Stafford, K. (1992) *Transitions: The Challenge of Change*. Didcot: Mercury Books Ltd.

House of Commons Children, Schools and Families Committee (2008). *Testing and Assessment Third Report of Session 2007–08*. **Vol 1**. London: TSO.

ICAN (2006) *The Cost to the Nation of Poor Communication*. ICAN Talk Series – Issue 2. London: ICAN.

Johnson, D. and Johnson, R. (1987) *Learning Together and Alone: Cooperative, Competitive and Individualistic Learning*. Englewood Cliffs, NJ: Prentice-Hall.

Johnson, D.W., Johnson, R. and Stanne, M.B. (2000) *Cooperative Learning Methods: A Meta-analysis*. Available online at: http://www.co-operation.org/pages/cl-methods.html

Jones, K. (2003) *Education in Britain: 1944 to the Present*. Cambridge: Polity Press.

Jones, J. and Chesson, R. (2000) 'Falling through the screen.' *Royal College of Speech and Language Therapists Bulletin* (576): 8–9.

Kamin, L.J. (1974) *The Science and Politics of IQ*. Potomac, MD: Lawrence Erlbaum Associates.

Katz, L.G. (1988) 'What should young children be doing?' *American Educator* Summer: 29–45.

Katz, L.G. (1993) *Dispositions: Definitions and Implications for Early Childhood Practices*. Perspectives from ERIC/ECCE: a monograph series. (Urbana, IL, ERIC Clearinghouse on ECCE).

Kellett, M. (2004) 'Special educational needs and inclusion in education.' In Matheson D., ed. (2004) *An Introduction to the Study of Education*. London: David Fulton.

Kelly, A.V. (2004) *The Curriculum*. 5th ed. London: Sage.

Kirk, G. and Broadhead, P. (2007) *Every Child Matters and Teacher Education: A UCET Position Paper*. London: UCET.

Kohn, A. (1999) *Punished By Rewards*. New York: Houghton Mifflin.

Kohn, A. (2001) *Beyond Discipline*. Upper Saddle River, NJ: Prentice Hall.

Kounin, J. (1970) *Discipline and Group Management in Classrooms*. London: Holt, Rinehart and Winston, Inc.

Kreidler, W. (1984) *Creative Conflict Resolution: More Than 200 Activities for Keeping Peace in the Classroom*. Glenview, Illinois: Scott Foresman.

Kyriacou, C. (1991) *Essential Teaching Skills*. Oxford: Basil Blackwell.

Kyriacou, C. and Goulding, M. (2006) A Systematic Review of Strategies to Raise Pupils' Motivational Efforts in Key Stage 4 Mathematics. Technical report. In: *Research Evidence in Education Library*. London: EPPI-Centre, Social Science Research Unit, Institute of Education, University of London.

Kyriacou, C. and Issitt, J. (2008) 'What characterises effective teacher-initiated teacher–pupil dialogue to promote conceptual understanding in mathematics lessons in England in Key Stages 2 and 3: a systematic review.' Technical report. In: *Research Evidence in Education Library*. London: EPPI-Centre, Social Science Research Unit. Institute of Education, University of London.

LaVigna, G.W. and Donnellan, A.M. (1986) *Alternatives to Punishment: Solving Behaviour Problems with Non-Aversive Strategies*. New York: Irvington Publishers, Inc.

Lawrence, D. (2006) *Enhancing Self-Esteem in the Classroom*. 3rd ed. London: Paul Chapman Publishing.

Lawton, D. (1989) *Education, Culture and the National Curriculum*. London: Hodder and Stoughton.

Lepper, M., Greene, D. and Nisbett, R. (1973) 'Undermining children's intrinsic interest with extrinsic reward: a test of the "overjustification" hypothesis.' *Journal of Personality and Social Psychology*. (28): 129–137.

Liddle, K. (2001) 'Implementing the picture exchange communication system (PECS).' *International Journal of Language and Communication Disorders*. **36** (Suppl.): 391–395.

Lindsay, G. and Dockrell, J. (2000) 'The behaviour and self esteem of children with specific speech and language difficulties.' *British Journal of Educational Psychology* **70**(4): 583–601.

Lingard, B., Ladwig, J. and Luke, A. (1998) 'School effects in postmodern conditions.' In Slee, R., Tomlinson, S. and Weiner, G., eds (1998) *School Effectiveness for Whom?* London: Falmer.

Lloyd, S.R. and Berthelot, C. (1992) *Self-Empowerment: How to Get What You Want from Life*. London: Kogan Page.

Long, R. (1999) *Challenging Confrontation: Information and Techniques for School Staff*. Tamworth: NASEN.

Long, R and Fogell, J. (1999) *Supporting Pupils with Emotional Difficulties*. London: David Fulton.

Maloney, J. (2007) 'Children's roles and use of evidence in science: an analysis of decision making in small groups.' *British Educational Research Journal*. **33**(3) 3 June 2007: 371–402.

Mason, M. (2005) *Incurably Human*. 2nd ed. London: Inclusive Solutions.

McGuiness, J. (1993) *Teachers, Pupils and Behaviour: A Managerial Approach*. London: Cassell.

McNally, J., l'anson, J., Whewell, C. and Wilson, G. (2005) '"They think that swearing is okay": first lessons in behaviour management.' *Journal of Education for Teaching*. **31**(3): 169–185.

McNamara, S. and Moreton, G. (2001) *Changing Behaviour: Teaching Children with Emotional and Behavioural Difficulties in Primary and Secondary Classrooms*. London: David Fulton.

McPhillimy, B. (1996) *Controlling Your Class: Teacher's Guide to Managing Classroom Behaviour*. Chichester: Wiley.

Meighan, R. (1981) *A Sociology of Education*. London: Holt, Reinhart and Winston.

Merrett, F. and Wheldall, K (1978) 'Playing the game: a behavioural approach to classroom management.' *Educational Review*. (30): 41–50.

Mesibov, G. and Howley, M. (2003) *Accessing the Curriculum for Pupils with Autistic Spectrum Disorders: Using the TEACCH Programme to Help Inclusion*. London: David Fulton.

Miller, A. (2003) *Teachers, Parents and Classroom Behaviour*. Maidenhead: Open University Press.

Miller, J. (1993) *The Passion of Michel Foucault*. London: Harper Collins.

Mittler, P. (2000) *Working Towards Inclusive Education*. London: David Fulton.

Morley, L. and Rassool, N. (1999) *School Effectiveness: Fracturing the Discourse*. London: Falmer.

Mortimore, P., Sammons, P., Stoll, L., Lewis, D. and Ecob, R. (1988) *School Matters*. Wells: Open Books.

Mosley, J. (1996) *Quality Circle Time in the Primary Classroom*. Wisbech: LDA.

Mosley, J. and Sonnet, H. (2005) *Better Behaviour Through Golden Time*. Wisbech: LDA.

Muncy, J. and McGinty, J. (1998) 'Target setting and special schools', *British Journal of Special Education* **25**(4): 173–78(6).

Muschamp, Y., Jamieson, I. and Lauder, H. (1999) 'Education, education, education.' In Powell, M., ed. (1999) *New Labour, New Welfare State?* Bristol: Policy Press.

Neill, S. and Caswell, C. (1993) *Body Language for Competent Teachers*. London: Routledge.

Nelsen, J., Lott, L. and Glenn, H. (2000) *Positive Discipline in the Classroom*. 3rd ed. Roseville, CA: Prima Publishing.

Newby, M. (2005) 'A curriculum for 2020.' *Journal of Education for Teaching*. **31**(4): 297–300.

Norwich, B. (1994) 'Predicting girls' learning behaviour in secondary school mathematics lessons from motivational and learning environment factors.' *Educational Psychology*. **14**: 291–306.

Norwich, B. and Lewis, A. (2001) 'Mapping a pedagogy for Special Educational Needs.' *British Educational Research Journal*. **27**(3): 313–329.

Norwich, B. and Rovoli, I. (1993) 'Affective factors and learning behaviour in secondary school mathematics and English lessons for average and low attainers.' *British Journal of Educational Psychology*. **63**: 308–321.

NUT (2003) *Education, the Law and You*. London: NUT. Available online at: http://www.teachers.org.uk/resources/pdf/law-and-you.pdf [accessed 3 February 2008].

O'Brien, T. and Guiney, D. (2001) *Differentiation in Teaching and Learning*. London: Continuum.

Ofsted (1999) *Standards and Quality in Education 1997/98 (The Annual Report of Her Majesty's Chief Inspector of Schools)*. London: HMSO.

Ofsted (2000) *Evaluating Educational Inclusion: Guidance for Inspectors and Schools* (HMI 235). London: Ofsted.

Ofsted (2003a) *The Key Stage 3 Strategy: Evaluation of the Second Year*. London: Ofsted.

Ofsted (2003b) *Handbook for Inspecting Secondary Schools*. London: Ofsted.

Ofsted (2004a) *Special Educational Needs and Disability: Towards Inclusive Schools*. London: Ofsted.

Ofsted (2004b) *Transition from the Reception Year to Year 1: An Evaluation by HMI.* London: Ofsted.

Ofsted (2005a) *Managing Challenging Behaviour.* London: Ofsted.

Ofsted (2005b) *A 21st Century Curriculum for 14–19 Year Olds.* London: Ofsted.

Olsen, J. and Cooper, P. (2001) *Dealing with Disruptive Students in the Classroom.* London: Kogan Page.

Parsons, C. (1999a) 'Social inclusion and school improvement.' *Support for Learning.* **14**(4): 179–183.

Parsons, C. (1999b) *Education, Exclusion and Citizenship.* London: Routledge.

Parsons, C., Maras, P., Knowles, C., Bradshaw, V., Hollingworth, K. and Monteiro, H. (2008) *Formalised Peer Mentoring Pilot Evaluation.* Nottingham: DCSF.

Pearson, G. (1983) *Hooligan: A History of Respectable Fears.* London: Macmillan.

Pease, A. and Pease, B. (2004) *The Definitive Book of Body Language.* London: Orion Books.

Peer L. and Reid G., eds (2001) *Dyslexia: Successful Inclusion in the Secondary School.* London: David Fulton Publishers.

Perkins, D. (1995) *Outsmarting I.Q.: The Emerging Science of Learnable Intelligence.* New York: The Free Press.

Perkins, D.N., Jay, E. and Tishman, S. (1993) 'Beyond abilities: a dispositional theory of thinking.' *Merrill-Parker Quarterly.* **39**(1): 1–21.

Petrides, K.V., Furnham, A. and Frederickson, N. (2004) 'Emotional Intelligence.' *The Psychologist* **17**(10): 574–577.

Phillips, R. (2001) 'Education, the state and the politics of reform: the historical context, 1976–2001.' In Furlong, J. and Phillips, R., eds (2001) *Education, Reform and The State: Twenty-Five Years Of Politics, Policy And Practice.* London: RoutledgeFalmer.

Pirrie, A. Head, G. and Brna, P. (2005) *Mainstreaming Pupils with Special Educational Needs: An Evaluation.* SEED: Edinburgh.

Plimley, L. and Bowen, M. (2006) *Supporting Pupils with Autistic Spectrum Disorders: A Guide for School Support Staff.* London: Paul Chapman Publishing.

Pollard, A., Triggs, P., Broadfoot, P., McNess, E. and Osborn, M. (2000) *What Pupils Say: Changing Policy and Practice in Primary Education.* London: Continuum.

Porter, L. (2007) *Behaviour in Schools.* Maidenhead: Open University Press.

Poulou, M. and Norwich, B. (2002) 'Cognitive, emotional and behavioural responses to students with emotional and behavioural difficulties: a model of decision-making.' *British Educational Research Journal* **28**(1): 111–138.

Pound, L. (2005) *How Children Learn.* London: Step Forward Publishing.

Powell, R., McIntyre, E. and Rightmyer, E. (2006) 'Johnny won't read, and Susie won't either: reading instruction and student resistance.' *Journal of Early Childhood Literacy.* **6**(1): 5–31.

Powell, S. (1993) 'The power of positive peer influence: leadership training for today's teens.' *Special Services in the Schools.* **8**(1): 119–136.

Powell, S. and Tod, J. (2004) 'A systematic review of how theories explain learning behaviour in school contexts'. In: *Research Evidence in Education Library.* London: EPPI-Centre, Social Science Research Unit, Institute of Education, University of London.

QCA (2001) *Supporting School Improvement: Emotional and Behavioural Development.* Sudbury: QCA.

Radford, M. (2006) 'Researching classrooms: complexity and chaos.' *British Educational Research Journal.* **32**(2) April 2006: 177–190.

Reid, G. (2005) *Dyslexia.* London: Continuum.

Render, G., Padilla, J. and Krank, H. (1989) 'Assertive discipline: a critical review and analysis.' *Teachers College Record* 90: 607–30.

Rinaldi, W. (2001) *Social Use of Language Programme – Revised.* Windsor: NFER-Nelson.

Robertson, J. (1996) *Effective Classroom Control.* 3rd ed. London: Hodder and Stoughton.

Rogers, B. (1990) *You Know the Fair Rule.* London: Pitman Publishing.

Rogers, B. (1994) *Behaviour Recovery.* Harlow: Longam.

Rogers, B. (1995) *Behaviour Management.* Gosford, Australia: Scholastic.

Rogers, B. (1997) *The Language of Discipline.* 2nd ed. Plymouth: Northcote House.

Tod, J. (2000) *Individual Education Plans: Dyslexia*. London: David Fulton.

Tomlinson, S. (1982) *A Sociology of Special Education*. London: Routledge & Kegan Paul.

Tomlinson, S. (2005) *Education in a Post-Welfare Society*. 2nd ed. Maidenhead: Open University Press.

Treasury Office (2003) *Every Child Matters*. London: TSO.

Tsoi, M. and Yule, W. (1976) 'The effects of group reinforcement in classroom behaviour modification.' *Educational Studies*. (2): 129–140.

Turner, J. and Paris, S.G. (1995) 'How literacy tasks influence children's motivation for literacy.' *The Reading Teacher*. **48**(8): 662–673.

UNESCO (1994) *World Conference on Special Needs Education: Access and Quality*. (The 'Salamanca Statement'). Paris: UNESCO.

Union of the Physically Impaired Against Segregation (UPIAS) (1976) *Fundamental Principles of Disability*. London: UPIAS.

Walker, H., Colvin, G. and Ramsey, E. (1995) *Antisocial Behaviour in Schools: Strategies and Best Practices*. London: Brooks/Cole.

Wallace, B. (2000) *Teaching the Very Able Child: Developing a Policy and Adopting Strategies for Provision*. London: David Fulton.

Wallace, B. (2001) *Teaching Thinking Skills across the Primary Curriculum*. London: David Fulton Publishers.

Warnock, M. (1978) *Special Educational Need: Report of the Committee of Inquiry into the Education of Handicapped Children and Young People*. (The Warnock Report). London: HMSO.

Watkins, C. (2006) *Managing Classroom Behaviour*. London: ATL.

Watkins, C. and Wagner, P. (2000) *Improving School Behaviour*. London: Paul Chapman Publishing.

Weare, K. (2004) *Developing the Emotionally Literate School*. London: Paul Chapman Publishing.

Weare, K. and Gray, G. (2003) *What Works in Developing Children's Emotional and Social Competence and Wellbeing?* Nottingham: DfES.

Weiner, B. (2000) 'Interpersonal and intrapersonal theories of motivation from an attributional perspective.' *Educational Psychology Review*. **22**(1): 1–14.

West, A., Hailes, J. and Sammons, P. (1997) 'Children's attitudes to the National Curriculum at Key Stage 1.' *British Educational Research Journal*. **23**(5): 597–613.

Wheldall, K. and Glynn, T. (1989) *Effective Classroom Teaching*. Oxford: Basil Blackwell.

Wheldall, K. and Merrett, F. (1990) *Positive Teaching in the Primary School*. London: Paul Chapman.

White, R. and Mitchell, I. (1994) 'Metacognition and the quality of learning.' *Studies in Science Education*. **23**(1): 21–37.

Wilby, P. (2008) 'Ain't misbehaving.' Interview with Sir Alan Steer. *Guardian Education*. Tuesday 23 September 2008.

Wing, L. and Gould, J. (1979) Severe impairments of social interaction and associated abnormalities in children: epidemiology and classification. Journal of Autism and Developmental Disorders **(9)**: 11–19.

Wood, D. (1988) *How Children Think and Learn*. Oxford: Blackwell Press.

Woods, R. (2008) 'When rewards and sanctions fail: a case study of a primary school rule-breaker.' *International Journal of Qualitative Studies in Education*. **21**(2): 181–196.

Yeomans, J. and Arnold, C. (2006) *Teaching, Learning and Psychology*. London: David Fulton.

Rogers, B. (2002) *Classroom Behaviour*. London: Paul Chapman Publishing.

Rogers, B. and MacPherson, E. (2008) *Behaviour Management with Young Children*. London: Sage.

Rotter, J. (1954) *Social Learning and Clinical Psychology*. Englewood Cliffs, NJ: Prentice Hall.

Rouse, M. and McLaughlin, M. (2007) 'Changing perspectives of special education in the evolving c(of educational reform.' In Florian, L. (2007) *The Sage Handbook of Special Education*. London: Sag

Rudduck, J., Chaplain. R. and Wallace, G. (1996) *School Improvement: What Can Pupils Tell Us?* Lc David Fulton.

Rudduck, J., Wilson, E. and Flutter, J. (1998) *Sustaining Pupils' Commitment to Learning: The Challe Year 8.* (A report for Lincolnshire LEA). Cambridge: Homerton Research Unit.

Rustique-Forrester, E. (2000) 'Exploring the policy influence of England's National Curriculum on s exclusion: a dilemma of entitlement and unintended exclusion.' In Cullingford, C. and Oliver, *The National Curriculum and its Effects*. London: Ashgate.

Rutter, M., Maughan, B., Mortimore, P. and Ouston, J. (1979) *Fifteen Thousand Hours: Secondary Scho(Their Effects on Children*. London: Open Books.

Sainsbury, C. (2004) *Martian in the Playground: Understanding the Schoolchild with Asperger's Syndrome*. B Lucky Duck Publishing.

Salovey, P. and Mayer, J. (1990) 'Emotional Intelligence.' *Imagination, Cognition and Personality.* 185–211.

Sanders, D., White, G., Burge, B., Sharp, C., Eames, A., McEune, R. and Grayson, H. (2005) *A Study Transition from the Foundation Stage to Key Stage 1*. Nottingham: DfES.

Seligman, M. (1975) *Helplessness: On Depression, Development, And Death*. New York: W.H. Freeman.

Sheehy, K. (2004) 'Approaches to Autism.' In Berryman, M., Glynn, T., Richmond, R. and Wearmou eds *Understanding Pupil Behaviour in Schools*. London: David Fulton.

Sinclair, J. (1998) 'About autism: a note about language and abbreviations used on this site.' Available (at: http://web.syr.edu/~jisincla/language.htm [accessed 11 August 2008].

Skinner, B. (1976) *About Behaviorism*. New York: Vintage Books.

Slavin, R.E. (2004) 'When and why does cooperative learning increase achievement?' In Edwards, *A* Daniels, H., eds (2004) *Reader in Psychology of Education*. London: RoutledgeFalmer. 271–293.

Smith, C. (2003) *Writing and Developing Social Stories: Practical Interventions in Autism*. Bicester: Speech Publishing.

Smith, C., Dakers, J., Dow, W., Head, G., Sutherland, M. and Irwin, R. (2005) 'A systematic review of pupils, aged 11–16, believe impacts on their motivation to learn in the classroom'. In *Research Ev in Education Library*. London: EPPI-Centre, Social Science Research Unit, Institute of Educa University of London.

Smith, R. (2002) 'Self-esteem: the kindly apocalypse.' *Journal of Philosophy of Education*. **36**(1): 87–10

Swinson, J. (2008) 'The self-esteem of pupils in schools for pupils with social, emotional and behavi difficulties: myth and reality.' *British Journal of Special Education*. **35**(3): 165 –172.

Tattum, D. (1982) *Disruptive Pupils in Schools and Units*. Chichester: Wiley.

TDA (2005) *Special Educational Needs in Mainstream Schools: A Guide for the Beginning Teacher*. Lor TDA.

TDA (2007) *Professional Standards for Teachers*. London: TDA.

TDA LLUK (2007) *Training and Development Guidance for Teachers of Diplomas*. London: TDA LLUK

TTA (2002) *Qualifying to Teach Professional Standards for Qualified Teacher Status and Requirements for I Teacher Training*. London: TTA.

Thomas, G. (2005) 'What do we mean by "EBD"?' In Clough, P., Garner, G., Pardeck, J. and Yuen, F. (2 *Handbook of Emotional and Behavioural Difficulties*. London: Sage.

Thomas, G. and Loxley, A. (2007) *Deconstructing Special Education and Constructing Inclusion*. 2n(Buckingham: Open University Press.

Thorndike, E. (1920) 'Intelligence and its uses.' *Harpers Magazine*. (140): 233–239.

Thorsborne, M. and Vinegard, D. (2004) *Restorative Practices in Classrooms*. Milton Keynes:. Incer Publishing.

Index

Entries in **bold** denote text in figures, tables, reflective exercises or scenarios.

Warnock Report 19–20
whole-school approach, *see* approaches, whole-school
whole-school elements 31
whole-school level 228

whole-school policies 43–4, 52, 147, 160, 285
withitness 172, 196, 198, 200

zero tolerance 16, 196